Civilizational Discourses in Weapons Control

Ritu Mathur

Civilizational Discourses in Weapons Control

palgrave
macmillan

Ritu Mathur
Department of Political Science & Geography
University of Texas at San Antonio
San Antonio, TX, USA

ISBN 978-3-030-44942-1 ISBN 978-3-030-44943-8 (eBook)
https://doi.org/10.1007/978-3-030-44943-8

Cover illustration: Brain light / Alamy Stock Photo

This Palgrave Macmillan imprint is published by the registered company Springer Nature Switzerland AG.
The registered company address is: Gewerbestrasse 11, 6330 Cham, Switzerland

Foreword

A Middle Eastern country has a secret nuclear weapons program. It acquired the means to develop weapons capability through legal, illegal and illicit means, starting decades ago, beginning with a US Atoms for Peace research reactor. Other means included stealing weapons-grade nuclear fuel from a secure site in Pennsylvania and diverting a shipment of uranium oxide carried by sea. It suborned corporate executives to acquire centrifuge blueprints and relied on the active help of countries such as France and apartheid South Africa to build an unsafeguarded power reactor and reprocessing plant and to test early weapon designs.

This thumbnail sketch is not a description of Iran, Pakistan or North Korea, but perpetual objects of fear and sanctions in the world of nuclear proliferation: it refers to Israel. No international sanctions are applied against Israel, no pressure put on it to change its wayward course. Israel's standing agreement with the US, the world power most set against nuclear proliferation, is simply that it will not be the first to "introduce" nuclear weapons into the region. This carefully crafted language means one thing for Israel and something else for the US, keeping the latter, if not happy, then at least free from too much public embarrassment. The contrasting treatment of Israel and those other "rogue states" is just the most obvious evidence that the international nuclear control regime is not intended necessarily to lead to a safer world, rather it is a technology for not upsetting an unequal one.

Language is key to unpacking the inherent contradictions of nuclear power. Opacity, the term of art that describes Israel's nuclear policy, is a brilliant example of the power of language to shape reality, to materialize the world for worse, not better. Opacity's discordant and contradictory meanings enable Israel to possess nuclear weapons but still not be the first to "introduce" them to the Middle East. The agency of nuclear discourse enables the Middle East to be "nuclear free" in spite of the presence of an Nuclear Weapon State (NWS) in its midst.

We sometimes forget the discourse of nuclear power is built upon an immanent contradiction. Falsely glossed as ambiguity, the ambivalence of nuclear power leaves us with a progression of ever more extreme binaries that structure nuclear discourse: civilian and military uses, political weapons and military weapons, "legal" nuclear weapons states and illegal "rogue" states, Article IV and Article VI, peaceful nuclear explosions and nuclear tests, nuclear fuel and atomic waste—these and other nuclear binaries congeal into a single political truth: good and evil. The keyword here is AND, not the referents on either end of the conjunction. The work of dominant nuclear discourse is to efface the AND by privileging and policing the respective ends of apparent policy binaries. But the conjunction is both material and permanent, and when acknowledged, enables us to think beyond the Manichaean heresy. How do we break with this totalitarian language and imagine "alternative visions of possible futures" as Carol Cohn asked us so long ago?

An essential starting point is a thoroughgoing critique of the international nuclear order, exposing its structural impediments to meaningful change and identifying discursive and institutional practices maintaining the nuclear status quo. While critical scholars from around the world have long been engaged in this struggle, Dr. Ritu Mathur's new book offers a novel and theoretically informed view of the deep structure of nuclearity, read through the lens of civilizational thinking.

Civilization-talk plays a central role in the establishment of nuclear order, always invoking difference as well as universality. The "standard of civilization" has long been a powerful discursive tool for the managers of the modern international system, relegating the darker nations to the margins of international life and dismissing their concerns as always "not quite" enough—symptomatically parochial and incomplete when set against a shifting but always claimed-to-be-universal global standard. As Dr. Mathur shows, race cannot be separated from this cathexis, going back to the *mission civilisatrice* when corrupt trading companies remade themselves as civilizing empires. What never seems to be remembered, although first expressed as early as the end of the eighteenth century, is that the costs of colonial rule are never felt by the colonized alone but indict and engulf the colonizer too. Sleeping Beauty must awake, as Fanon proclaimed. So too it is with nuclear power: a global condition that leaves no one spared when its power is expressed, as it has been, over and over.

Rejection, denial, willful ignorance and unevenness are the real stories of the global nuclear regime as it has evolved from its optimistic and idealist beginnings in the post-Hiroshima era. After the shock of August 1945, it was still possible to imagine the US giving up its miniscule arsenal and the creation of a supranational agency controlling the world's nuclear materials, One World. This vision of renounced sovereignty would last only as long as it took to debate the Baruch Plan in the Security Council. Immediately after, competition and escalation would replace talk of disarmament and sequestering, in the process of establishing new thresholds for international tension and fear. Postcolonial countries, not least Ireland, would seek to moderate our rush toward a descending nuclear spiral, but were stopped far short of allowing a general disarmament to become a sensible and necessary end to mutual hatred and assured destruction. When the Cold War moved to the tropics in the form of the Cuban Missile Crisis, a new system of nuclear governance came into being. It was formed not just through the Nuclear Nonproliferation Treaty (NPT) and other acronyms of nuclear weapons management, but generated an entirely new lexicon that gripped the bodies and focused the minds of "defense intellectuals" on a single overwhelming problem—Who's Next?

How this false question reshaped the meanings and practices of global nuclear control in our historical present is the story of this book. It should be read in order to understand how the technologies of nuclear management reinforce the hierarchies and exclusions of the prevailing global order. This book shows all too clearly that what Dr. Mathur calls the "architecture" of weapons control is a tragic symptom of our times, not a redemptive path out of the disasters we have consciously and unconsciously imposed on ourselves.

Singapore, Singapore — Itty Abraham

Contents

Introduction

This book is a contribution in the contemporary scholarly efforts to decolonize the field of international relations. In an effort to advance such an undertaking, it focuses particularly on civilizational discourses in the field of arms control and disarmament. The need for such an undertaking can be premised on the claim that while problems of modernity, ethnocentrism and universalism are now a central concern within the field of international relations these ideas are scarcely debated or contested within the field of arms control and disarmament. The singular focus on technological innovations and specific policy-oriented agreements in practices of arms control and disarmament appears to stymie the need for such engagements. This book is an invitation to explore such ideas embedded within a historically grounded terrain of weapons control.

In Chap. 1, an exploration of civilizational discourses in weapons control is encouraged by initially drawing on the symbolism of the Doomsday Clock as a remnant of war and a wish image to emphasize the significance of time and temporality in practices of arms control and disarmament. The temporality of the Doomsday clock serves as a helpful moniker to encourage reflexivity on how the problem of time and technology is associated with modern understandings of state and military so central a premise in addressing the problem of weapons. An effort here is made to problematize different conceptualizations of time as an important tool for mapping histories of arms control and disarmament. The Orientalists emphasized linearity of time in their attempt to differentiate modern and archaic civilizations. For analytical purposes this book seeks to make a distinction between civilizational time and postcolonial time. It insists on pursuing a postcolonial disposition toward time to scrutinize civilizational discourses in weapons control.

It is in the context of civilizational time that the intersecting and prolific discourses on racialism, nationalism and humanitarianism are explored further. These discourses constitute a triad and are collectively referred to as civilizational discourses in weapons control. A study of the mobility of these intersecting discourses is facilitated with the help of three particular concepts: stereotyping, sly civility and mimesis in the context of weapons control. The concept of stereotyping alludes to practices of exaggerated fixity about the other, practices of sly civility observe racial etiquette and mimesis is a sensuous knowing to imitate the other in an effort to not necessarily destabilize but to assert the need for a change in status quo. Discourse analysis is the methodological tool deployed for tracing the effects of civilizational discourses in weapons control.

A brief understanding of each of these concepts is articulated at the beginning of the text and further developed and contextualized within each chapter. However, the purpose here is not to write each individual chapter to demonstrate the efficacy of each of these particular concepts with the help of case/country studies. I believe that the field of security studies is surfeit with such undertakings and has the effect of spatializing the effect of practices of stereotyping, sly civility and mimesis. This spatialization diverts attention from the collective impact of these civilizational discourses in constituting the architecture of arms control and disarmament. It is, therefore, an urgent necessity that a genealogy temporalizing practices of arms control and disarmament demonstrate the circulation of these intersecting discourses as an exercise in pedagogical and performative power.

This is facilitated further as Chap. 2 investigates the power of formulaic mantras such as "The West and the Rest" articulated by scholars and practitioners in the field of international relations. It is demonstrated that the invocation of such civilizational mantras is strategic and enjoy currency to help emphasize differences in civilizational encounters. The dangers associated with such strategic invocation of civilizational mantras are underscored by making liminal a racial, colonial and imperialist legacy of violence that is scarcely prefatory in slender narratives of arms control and disarmament. The colonial encounters in Africa and Asia are sketched briefly to make visible differences in approaches to technology and weaponry. An understanding of these differences is imperative to grasp the problematique of universalism associated with discourses emphasizing standards of civilization to regulate and prohibit weapons or clash of civilizations based on the failure of horizontal proliferation of nuclear weapons. The tactical deployment of humanitarian discourses to disarm the natives and sow the seeds of institutionalized practices of arms control and disarmament constitutes an important footnote in this effort at problematizing written histories of arms control and disarmament.

This deliberate and persistent effort to tap into the colonial legacy of arms control and disarmament is continued in Chap. 3. In this chapter much attention is focused on how practices of colonial science are deployed to constitute martial races in the colonies. The tension between the contending forces of colonial science and national science is made visible to bring forth the dilemma of heroic scientists located in the colonies and hybrid scientists navigating the gatekeeping practices of the imperial West. An understanding of this predicament of heroic and hybrid scientists is imperative to gauge the significance of their role in modern state-building empowered with sophisticated weaponry to safeguard sovereignty. This understanding is buttressed with acknowledging differences in nationalism in the colonies vis-à-vis the West. These carefully calibrated differences in nationalism exacerbate the racial tensions associated with waging civilizational wars that reach a climax with the use of nuclear weapons in Hiroshima and Nagasaki.

The subtle but radical shift in discourses deploying stereotypes for more than a century toward practices of sly civility to constitute a constitutional nuclear order exposes the tenuousness of such an arrangement. This vulnerability of the existing nuclear order is deliberated further in Chap. 4. It is helpful to note that the meaning of vulnerability here is not simply in terms of the destructive power of nuclear weaponry but the ethnocentrism that pervades practices of sly civility associated with nuclear testing. It is this racial etiquette that masks vulnerabilities and inequalities by articulating abstract structural assumptions about security in the world order that serve as a premise for negotiating and validating particular arms control agreements such as the Nuclear Nonproliferation Treaty (NPT). Contemporary efforts to question the premise of this constitutional nuclear order or acquire nuclear weapons technology are often met with imposition of punitive measures supplemented with ridicule to dismiss the decorative savages that refuse to conform and comply with existing taboos and norms of weapons control.

In an effort to keep pursuing the dynamic of differences and dynamic of denial in practices of arms control and disarmament, it is helpful to not get stymied by stalemate discourses on nuclear apartheid. It is in this endeavor that Chap. 5 of this book investigates the problem of mimesis and rights in weapons control. Mimetic empowerment for assertion of rights, both sovereign and humanitarian, transforms discourses on weapons control from the stagnant portrayal of victimization at the hands of the aggressor. A study of these practices of mimesis provides insight into the everyday maneuvering within the field of arms control between the developed and developing countries with regard to export control regimes. This mimetic maneuvering is powerful in transforming representations of national scientists into rogue scientists. Mimetic maneuvering encourages practices of hedging and has the potential of remapping our understanding of nuclear proliferation. The diabolical speed of engineering mimetic maneuvers and the strident assertion of rights and exceptionalism generates concerns about the possibility of dismantling the constitutional nuclear order.

In this turbulent passage of time, Chap. 6 explores the possibility of constraining proliferating practices of exceptionalism by insistence on standards of civilization. The exceptionalism claimed by the West through deployment of practices of stereotyping and sly civility is now gravely threatened by the power of mimesis that can empower developing countries to assert their own exceptionalism vis-à-vis the West. The exercise of mimetic maneuvers has the potential of destabilizing linear understandings of time that define progress and development in modernity. The mobilization of mimetic maneuvering and the production of exceptional exceptionalism in practices of weapons control have made it urgent that we consider contemporary revolts to reconstellate security studies and its appendage arms control and disarmament. The urgent necessity of this is emphasized as the Doomsday clock ticks closer to midnight, and the disaster of a nuclear war is sought to be addressed by the illusory canon of universal human rights as a new standard of civilization in weapons control.

This book is an attempt at navigating this messy history of arms control and disarmament. It is hoped that this brief introduction to the chapters in this text will facilitate a timely encounter with those interested in addressing the problem of human suffering. This book is a product of an ongoing quest to provide alternative ways of thinking and writing about the problem of weapons control. This learning was facilitated with the help of teachers both in the East and in the West that patiently took questions from a disgruntled graduate student of International Relations with specialization in security studies. A student that often stared at library bookshelves and saw book covers on the subject of arms control and disarmament gathering dust. A student that read about the horrors of war and the use of weapons to inflict tremendous suffering and was often rendered speechless and perturbed. A student that sought alternative accounts of historical experiences and different approaches to understanding practices of weapons control. The mainstream approaches with their obsession for superpowers, nuclear deterrence, national and international security did not suffice and critical discourses with their promise of emancipation and revolt struggled for meaning. Those feelings of powerlessness and inadequacy have ebbed a little with the pursuit of a career in research.

Some of the ideas and concepts developed in this book were initially sketched out in the form of three academic journal articles. "The West and the Rest: A Civilizational Mantra in Arms Control & Disarmament" was published in the *Contemporary Security Policy.* This paper was nominated for the Bernard Brodie Prize for outstanding research innovation and contribution in 2014. A second paper, "Sly Civility and the Paradox of Equality/Inequality in the Nuclear Order: A Postcolonial Critique," was published in the journal *Critical Studies on Security* (2016). The third paper, "Human Rights as a New Standard of Civilization in Weapons Control?," has recently been published in the journal *Alternatives: Local, Global, Political* (*2018*). I was invited to serve as the Guest Editor of the *Asian Journal of Political Science* and capitalized on this opportunity to provide collective visibility to scholars working in the extremely specialized and marginalized area of *Postcolonial Perspectives on Weapons Control* (2018). It is with the help of these individual and collective interventions that one struggles to reconstellate practices of arms control and disarmament. This book with all its potential and shortcomings is representative of these efforts.

The initial time needed to sow the seeds of this project as the idea was taking shape in my mind was facilitated with the help of the Banting Postdoctoral Fellowship held at McMaster University, Canada. Dr. Marshall Beier and Dr. Porter were of invaluable help to me with their words of encouragement and unstinting support. I would also like to thank our subject librarian DeeAnn Ivey at University of Texas at San Antonio for getting me books and articles that were not easily available. I owe an immense debt of gratitude to Dr. Aaron Karp, Dr. Keith Krause and Dr. Itty Abraham for the generous time they devoted to reading some draft chapters of this manuscript. It was their input that has helped bring more rigor to this project. I would also like to thank Dr. Mary Mathie and my student Emma Strain for helping me get this manuscript ready. I would like to thank all those that sent me emails or spoke to me in person at conferences about how they found my published papers and presentations interesting and helpful.

I would like to especially thank my selfless brother Anand for giving me opportunities and appreciating my desire to learn and explore. My sisters lightened my spirits with their laughter at my trials and tribulations. Anca Pusca was kind enough to invite me to discuss my research, offer me a contract and get this book out. I accept all responsibility for any shortcomings associated with this publication. Thank you.

CHAPTER 1

Time and Weapons Control

Doomsday Clock

How do we think of time in practices of weapons control? What is the significance of time in reimagining and rewriting a postcolonial history of arms control and disarmament? What are the possibilities and limits of a postcolonial intervention in addressing the problem of weapons? It is important to dwell on these questions as it appears as if the violence of Total War has silenced all discourses on temporalizing security and left as a remnant of war only a wish-image in the form of a Doomsday Clock, a wish image that helps calibrate the passage of time within the discipline of arms control and disarmament. The horrifying wish image of a symbolic Doomsday Clock is representative of 'both a mental and physical expression of 'individual and collective desires or (manipulation of those desires)' to avoid a nuclear war.[1] A remnant of Total War, the Doomsday Clock is a wish image circulating in the

> collective consciousness in which the old and the new interpenetrate … in them the collective seeks both to overcome and to transfigure the immaturity of the social product and the inadequacies in the social organization of

[1] Anca Pusca, "Walter Benjamin, a Methodological Contribution," *International Political Sociology* 3, no. 2 (2009): 251.

R. Mathur, *Civilizational Discourses in Weapons Control*,
https://doi.org/10.1007/978-3-030-44943-8_1

> production … what emerges in these images is the resolute effort to distance oneself from all that is antiquated—which includes however the recent past.[2]

The Doomsday Clock is a wish-image in the field of security studies diligently calibrating the growing dangers of nuclear war and seeking to avoid a nuclear holocaust. Since its inception in 1947, the Doomsday Clock has been a 'simple way of demonstrating the danger to Earth and humanity posed by nuclear war.'[3]

The Doomsday Clock as a wish-image occupies a special symbolic place in the collective consciousness of the security studies community.[4] The seeds of this collective consciousness were sowed by nuclear scientists affiliated with the Manhattan Project concerned with the growing disregard for science and the unfolding dynamic of the Cold War and seeking to guide political leadership on the dangers and risks associated with nuclear weapons. Doomsday Clock conveys a 'certain sense of historical time in everyday speech of public life in modern societies.'[5] The movement of this clock is tenaciously reported by journalists and scholars since the end of the Second World War and the transition to a nuclear era. The movement of the hands of the Doomsday Clock is carefully noted by those fearful of a nuclear apocalypse and concerned with risks nuclear weapons pose to 'global civilization.'[6] This wish image 'marks the site of ambivalence' as it seeks to make 'present something that is absent—and temporally deferred: it is the representation of a time that is elsewhere, a repetition.'[7]

[2] Pusca, "Walter," 225, quoting Walter Benjamin, *The Arcades Project*, trans. H. Eiland and K. McLaughlin (Cambridge: Belknap Press of Harvard University Press, 1982).

[3] Amber Jamieson, "Doomsday Clock closer to midnight in wake of Trump presidency," *The Guardian*, January 26, 2017. https://www.theguardian.com/us-news/2017/jan/26/doomsday-clock-closer-to-midnight-in-wakeof-donald-trump-election

[4] The Doomsday Clock was created in 1947 by nuclear scientists affiliated with the Manhattan Project concerned with the growing disregard for science and the unfolding dynamic of the Cold War and seeking to guide political leadership on the dangers and risks associated with nuclear weapons. In the past decade there have been articles reporting not only a growing concern among scientists with regard to the possible threat of use of nuclear weapons but also a growing indifference and denial of science and the need for political leadership to affirm the primacy of science.

[5] Dipesh Chakraborty, *Provincializing Europe: Postcolonial Thought and Historical Difference* (Princeton & Oxford: Princeton University Press, 2000), 87.

[6] Julian Borger, "'Doomsday Clock' ticked forward 30 seconds to 2 minutes to midnight," *The Guardian*, January 25, 2018, https://www.theguardian.com/world/2018/jan25/doomsday-clock-ticked-forward-trump-nuclear-weapons-climate-change

[7] Homi K. Bhabha, *The Location of Culture* (London & New York: Routledge, 1994), 73.

In the last decade there have been several articles reporting not only a growing concern among scientists with regard to the possible threat of use of nuclear weapons but also a growing indifference and denial of science and the need for political leadership to affirm the primacy of science. This awareness is compounded with a growing acknowledgment that 'historians of science and technology, sociologists of science, and political scientists interested in science and security issues rarely discuss each other's work.'[8] This lack of interdisciplinary dialogue and populist discourses have generated concerns with regard to 'casual talk,' 'loose but dangerous rhetoric' and the reluctance to 'embrace science' by statesmen engaged in making important decisions with regard to nuclear weapons.[9] These concerns are compounded with a resurgence of discourses on the dangers of nuclear weapons proliferation and dubious predictions of an impending clash of civilizations between 'The West and the Rest.'[10] Questions are being raised whether we can 'trust' the Doomsday Clock and whether use of 'hypothetical threats' often leads to 'proliferation of nuclear panic' and 'eventually they lose their capacity to make us afraid.'[11] As the Doomsday Clock ticks forward hundred seconds to midnight, it might be pertinent to dwell on the dynamics of temporalizing security with regard to weapons regulation and prohibition.

[8] Gregoire Mallard and Catherine Paradeise, "Global Science and National Sovereignty: A New Terrain for the Historical Sociology of Science," in *Global Science and National Sovereignty: Studies in Historical Sociology of Science*, ed. Gregoire Mallard, Catherine Paradeise and Ashveen Peerbaye (New York & London: Routledge, 2009) 1.

[9] Amber Jamieson, "Doomsday Clock closer to midnight in wake of Trump presidency," *The Guardian*, January 26, 2017. https://www.theguardian.com/us-news/2017/jan/26/doomsday-clock-closer-to-midnight-in-wakeof-donald-trump-election

[10] Samuel Huntington, "Clash of Civilization," *Foreign Affairs* 72, no. 3 (1993):22–49; Samuel P. Huntington, *The Clash of Civilizations and the Remaking of World Order* (New York: Simon & Schuster, 1997); Kishore Mahbubani, "The West and the Rest," *The National Interest*, no. 28 (1992): 3–12

[11] Julian Baggini, "The Doomsday Clock: why there's no point worrying about Armageddon," *The Guardian*, January 26, 2015, https://www.theguardian.com/commentsfree/2015/jan/26/doomsday-clock-no-point-worrying-about-armageddon

Time and Civilization

Siba Grovogui insists, 'Security politics must be construed against the backdrop of a possible apocalypse or the possibility of the end of time as the end of politics.'[12] Andrew Hom describes 'clock time' or 'modern time' 'associated with contemporary clocks and watches' as 'a form of reckoning based on the "continuous indication of equal hours" abstracted from celestial motions.'[13] While 'clock time' is seen as deterministic, a 'slaughter bench' of empirical events, it can be easily subsumed by 'calendar time' which serves as a monument of historical consciousness, providing opportunities for remembrance and recreation 'in which history is made rather than suffered.'[14] It is possible to draw up a calendar tracing the history of the movement of the Doomsday Clock since its inception, but it is questionable whether such a limited exercise can help us 'theorise international political time' in a way that matches up to 'counter-hegemonic aspirations' of critical and postcolonial theorists.[15] In other words, how can we join forces with those that seek 'the (de)fatalization of the "present"'[16]?

In addressing this question, an emphasis on postcolonial scholarship is pertinent considering 'the possibility of theorizing international political time critically without privileging the time of Western modernity' has received sustained attention from postcolonial scholars.[17] These scholars contend, the study of time and temporality (lived experience of time) has been explicitly or implicitly evaded in international relations.[18] It is this evasiveness that is held responsible for much of the research 'being

[12] Siba N. Grovogui, "Time, technology and the imperial eye: Perdition on the road to redemption in international relations theory," in *Time, Temporality and Violence in International Relations*, ed. Anna M. Aganthangelou and Kyle D. Killian (New York: Routledge, 2016), 57.

[13] Andrew R. Hom, "Hegemonic metronome: the ascendancy of Western standard time," *Review of International Studies* 36, no. 4 (2010): 1149.

[14] Kimberly Hutchings, "Happy Anniversary! Time and Critique in International Relations Theory," *Review of International Studies* 33, no. 1 (2007): 80.

[15] Hutchings, "Happy Anniversary," 72.

[16] Anna M. Aganthangelou and Kyle D. Killian, *Time, Temporality and Violence in International Relations* (New York: Routledge, 2016) 12, 16.

[17] Hutchings, "Happy Anniversary," 83.

[18] Aganthangelou and Killian, *Time, Temporality and Violence*, 1–22.

conducted within the frame of western notions of time.'[19] It is argued that the violence of colonialism led to a collapse of the 'indigenous temporal order,' compelling non-Western societies to 'share the temporal structures of the West.'[20] These scholars insist that the 'question of the colonial is a question of time' and that 'interrogations of time from the vantage point of the colonial' point to 'temporal disjunctions accompanying narration, in conflicting or silenced histories.'[21]

In the light of these observations, it is interesting to note how practices of arms control and disarmament are acutely conscious of time, but there is barely any reference to legacies of the colonial and the colonized.[22] This is disturbing, as any possibility of silenced and subjugated histories makes one wary of scholarship that turns the idea of time into a 'mechanism of colonization' distorting our engagement and understanding of practices of arms control and disarmament.[23] These subtle practices of marginalization and colonization can facilitate an 'erasure of other (non-European) conceptions of time and space' with the effect of 'removal of their psychic and intellectual resources from modern consciousness.'[24] An investigation into claims of historical erasure and temporal disjunctions and their effects in practices of arms control and disarmament is pertinent. It is no longer enough to be complacent with slender narratives of arms control and disarmament.

Hom claims, 'Authority over time is a component of post-colonial struggle.'[25] A glimpse of this struggle is gained from subaltern accounts of alternative histories, narratives and schematics in practices of weapons control as a form of resistance. Despite these efforts, it is conceded that it is difficult to find 'a politics that corresponds to its time' as it is at present considered to be engaged in 'configuring a now so plural'[26]—a plural that is often confounded with deliberately divisive rhetoric of an impending

[19] Nishimoto Ikuko, "The Civilization of Time: Japan and the adoption of the western time system," *Time & Society* 6, no. 2/3 (1997): 237.

[20] Ikuko, "The Civilization of Time," 238.

[21] Aganthangelou and Killian, *Time, Temporality and Violence*, 13.

[22] Ritu Mathur, "Postcolonial Perspectives on Weapons Control", *Asian Journal of Political Science* 26, no. 3 (2018): 293–296.

[23] Aganthangelou and Killian, *Time, Temporality and Violence*, 13.

[24] Grovogui, "Time, technology and the imperial eye", 45.

[25] Andrew R. Hom, "Hegemonic metronome: the ascendancy of Western standard time," *Review of International Studies* 36, no. 4 (2010): 1168.

[26] Dipesh Chakraborty, 'Where is the Now?' *Critical Inquiry* 30, no. 2 (2004): 462.

'Clash of Civilizations.' It is in this state of flux, an awareness and understanding of postcolonial time as an intellectual disposition, to question civilizational mantras such as the 'West and the Rest' representative of a 'polarized historicist sensibility' and 'the teleological traditions of past and present' is helpful.[27] A gesture of resistance, a need for a 'heterotemporal orientation' to carefully study the temporal 'effects of institutionalization' of particular practices of arms control and disarmament, can help examine 'political temporalities of violation.'[28] The problem and fear of violation cannot be fully grasped without sufficient engagement with the politics of compliance with institutionalized standards of civilization.

The concept of civilization has been exhaustively debated for centuries, but this book seeks to only trace the temporal effects of civilizational discourses in weapons control. It is interested in the 'temporal movement and passage' of civilizational discourses that 'prevents identities at either end from settling into primordial polarities.'[29] An exploration of this temporal movement might facilitate an engagement with difference 'without an assumed or imposed hierarchy' and might help articulate a 'narrative with a double-edge'[30]—a split narrative that on the one hand refers to the 'accumulative temporality of the pedagogical' and on the other is a 'repetitious recursive strategy of the performative';[31]a disruptive narrative that carefully navigates the terrain of historical and cultural differences signifying the other and draws attention to the 'structure of iteration' that through circulation cultivates historical agency.[32] The structures of iteration are 'not necessarily a faithful sign of historical memory but a strategy of representing authority in terms of the artifice of the archaic.'[33] Similarly the authority of linear, analogical, scientific and historicist narratives often represented as grand narratives 'does not account for the historical traditions of cultural contingency and textual indeterminacy'[34] To write a

[27] Homi K. Bhabha, *The Location of Culture* (London & New York: Routledge, 1994), 220.

[28] Dipesh Chakraborty and Kimberly Hutchings, "What is Orientation in Thinking? On the Question of Time and Timeliness in Cosmopolitical Thought," *Constellations* 18, no. 2 (2011): 201.

[29] Bhabha, *Location of Culture*, 5.

[30] Bhabha, *Location of Culture*, 19.

[31] Bhabha, *Location of Culture*, 209.

[32] Bhabha, *Location of Culture*, 38.

[33] Bhabha, *Location of Culture*, 52.

[34] Bhabha, *Location of Culture*, 248, 249.

disruptive narrative one needs to be cognizant of 'time-lag'[35]—time lag understood briefly as a 'temporal break in representation' or a 'splitting of the discursive present' facilitating a process of articulating new meaning through 'reinscription and negotiation' of intersubjective relations between the West and the Rest.

To reiterate, this book is an attempt to question the juxtaposition of 'The West and the Rest' as a civilizational mantra with a colonial legacy in the field of arms control and disarmament—a legacy that has been reproduced time and again to reinscribe and reinforce hierarchies of power and privilege. It traces these effects by navigating a historical terrain stained by imperial wars and practices of colonial science from the late nineteenth century to the present. It is guided in these pursuits not by a historicist desire to produce a grand narrative but by the counter-hegemonic aspirations of postcolonial scholarship and critical security studies as mentioned above. This scholarship insists, 'temporal reformulations are pivotal to political projects interested in rupturing a present whose inflection is violence and fatalism.'[36] It encourages us to acknowledge the 'parameters of conceptualization and terms of debate over the politics of life change dramatically ... this shift allows greater fidelity to the complexities of lived human experience.'[37]

It is in this effort that this particular chapter encourages one to cultivate an understanding of existing alternative conceptual frameworks of time such as linear time, cyclical time and evolutive time. It offers a distinctive conceptualization of 'civilizational time' and 'postcolonial time' within which practices of arms control and disarmament are carefully embedded. An understanding of these alternative conceptualizations of time is imperative to engage with the social and psychic representations of the Western historicist idea of evolutionary time as 'a progressive, ordered whole' and the Third World 'time-in waiting' anxious about 'world rankings and never "catching up" in its quest for modernization and development.'[38] A historically situated understanding of the differences in practices associated with alternative conceptual frameworks of time might then facilitate questioning a 'polarized historicist sensibility' of civilizational differences

[35] Bhabha, *Location of Culture*, 274.

[36] Aganthangelou and Killian, *Time, Temporality and Violence*, 1.

[37] Aganthangelou and Killian, *Time, Temporality and Violence*, 4.

[38] Itty Abraham, *The Making of the Indian Atomic Bomb- Science, Secrecy and the Postcolonial State* (London & New York: Zed Books, 1998), 19–20.

ensconced in the rhetorical idea of 'The West and the Rest' that pervades and disciplines practices of weapons control.[39]

This polemical polarization of 'The West and the Rest' premised on the impending failure of non-proliferation is explored further by making visible intersecting practices of 'stereotyping,' 'sly civility' and 'mimesis' in the field of arms control and disarmament to question the status quo. A conceptualization of each of these temporal practices of stereotyping, sly civility and mimesis as constituents of civilizational discourses is discussed briefly below and explored further in the text. An understanding of this carefully interwoven conceptual matrix might make it feasible to then suggest a need to be attentive to possibilities and constraints of 'civilizational time' and 'postcolonial time' to help bring about a politics of coevalness in practices of weapons control. It is in this endeavor that the next section engages with existing alternative conceptualizations of time and how they temporalize civilizational differences. These differences articulated in terms of productive discourses address practices of historicism, technological differences and race relations and have a significant bearing on our understanding of civilizational discourses in weapons control.

Standardized Time and Race War

Time after war is a time of upheaval and flux. It produces a sense of disorientation, a restless movement, a disturbance of direction providing an opportunity for scholars to remap the world. Scholars like Mumford, Hom and Landes argue that internalization of a particular time discipline characterizes modern personality and civilization. While different civilizations had their own configurations of time, Landes insists that the mechanical clock was invented in Europe and remained a 'European monopoly for some five hundred years, and that Europe then built a civilization organized around the measurement of time; these were critical factors in the differentiation of the West from the Rest and the definition of modernity.'[40] The ascendancy of Western standard time is traced to an era of the Thirty Years' War in Europe when scholars struggled to provide 'an alternative

[39] Bhabha, *Location of Culture*, 220.
[40] David Landes, "Clocks Revolution in Time," *History Today* 34, no. 1 (1984): 26.

system of assessment' that would 'delimit' virulent ideological competitions and 'preclude their ultimate settlement on the battlefield.'[41]

Hom observes the 'coeval rise of territorial state sovereignty and Western standard time' in Europe.[42] Fabian wants us to remember that 'time is not a mere measure, or vector of culture; it is one of its constituents.'[43] The modern, secular clock time was rationalized and commodified to produce particular modes of social life in which the clock itself became an embodiment of 'high authority' and a 'resource' for conflict and cooperation.[44] It was in the contentious climate of spatio-temporal reordering in Europe that 'political bargains' were struck among sovereigns to exercise a 'controlling presence' on maintaining order, stability and security within a particular legal and ideological framework.[45] It is this orientation of power to maintain 'control over life' that is held responsible for 'the expansive tendencies of modern societies' and 'to a proliferation and intensification of the problem of war between societies.'[46] The use of mechanical clocks is often regarded as an initial 'ticket of entry' that 'unlocked the gates' for the European traders and missionaries into other civilizations.[47] The bargains struck in terms of sovereignty, society, law and ethics continue to provide present-day rationalizations of 'universal' order and security in the international system and are recognized as 'a sign of national achievement or civilization' but 'might alternatively be perceived as the sedimented outcome of historical injustices or differential power relations.'[48]

[41] Andrew R. Hom, "Hegemonic metronome: the ascendancy of Western standard time," *Review of International Studies* 36, no. 4 (2010): 1150–51.

[42] Hom, "Hegemonic metronome," 1151, 1163.

[43] Johannes Fabian, *Time and the Other—How Anthropology Makes its Object* (New York: Columbia University Press, 2014), 50.

[44] Hom, "Hegemonic metronome," 1156, 1163.

[45] Hom, "Hegemonic metronome," 1157–1158.

[46] Julian Reid, "Life Struggles: War, Discipline and Biopolitics in the Thought of Michel Foucault," in *Foucault on Politics, Security and War*, ed. Michael Dillon and Andrew W. Neal (New York: Palgrave Macmillan, 2008), 73–74.

[47] David Landes, "Clocks Revolution in Time," *History Today* 34, no. 1 (1984): 19; David Landes, "Why Europe and the West? Why not China?" *Journal of Economic Perspectives* 20, no. 2 (2006): 11.

[48] Andrew W. Neal, "Goodbye War on Terror? Foucault and Butler on Discourses of Law, War and Exceptionalism," in *Foucault on Politics, Security and War*, ed. Michael Dillon and Andrew W. Neal (New York: Palgrave Macmillan, 2008), 57, 61.

Foucault insists that 'one paradigm does not drive out the other' and that they merely 'displace' one another.[49] How this displacement occurs can be understood if we grasp an understanding of 'politics as war' and 'race war' as historical struggles that are only temporarily 'displaced' but not 'replaced' by ahistorical, impersonal, abstract and temporal rationalizations of society, sovereignty and law achieved in the aftermath of the Thirty Years' War in Europe.[50] He also insists that 'politics as war' is best understood as a 'grid of intelligibility' comprising of a plurality of powerful discourses defying ownership and fixity but that through circulation and strategic polyvalence or metamorphosis radicalizes differences among identity groups.[51] This radicalization of differences can be traced particularly to intersecting discourses on science, race and technology. The antecedents of 'politics as war' discourses can be traced to nineteenth-century transnational race struggles to understand how race war became a 'great schemata' for understanding the 'phenomena of war and relationship of force within political society.'[52]

Scholars engaged in interpreting Foucault's writings on 'politics as war' and 'race war' argue that race war is to be understood as 'a certain kind of struggle, a historically specific struggle waged through circulating narratives' on time, technology and civilization.[53] In such an undertaking, Michael Adas cautions against 'racial reductionism' and insists that 'the impact of racism in the only sense in which it has been a meaningful concept at the level of intellectual discourse—the belief that there are innate, biologically based differences in abilities between rather arbitrarily delineated human groups varied greatly from one time period to another.'[54] Adas argues that race struggles were not grounded only in assertions of hereditary, biological differences but also in cultural attainments and scientific and technological accomplishments. The concept of race was in routine circulation with varied meanings associated with it until the

[49] Mariana Vlverde, "Law versus History—Foucault's Genealogy of Modern Sovereignty," in *Foucault on Politics, Security and War*, Michael Dillon and Andrew W. Neal (New York: Palgrave Macmillan, 2008), 147–148.

[50] Michael Dillon and Andrew W. Neal, ed., *Foucault on Politics, Security and War* (New York: Palgrave Macmillan, 2008), 52–53.

[51] Neal, "Goodbye War," 56.

[52] Vlverde, "Law versus History," 141–142.

[53] Vlverde, "Law versus History," 140–141.

[54] Michael Adas, *Machines as the Measure of Men: Science, Technology, and Ideologies of Western Dominance* (Ithaca & London: Cornell University Press, 1989), 12, 338.

interplay of these varied meanings became more intense in the late nineteenth century when 'theories of racial supremacy and scientific and technological gauges of human worth were widely accepted by European politicians and intellectuals.'[55]

The idea of 'scientific racism' in the nineteenth century endowed the concept of 'race' with color and biological determinism that helped constitute global hierarchies and provide rational justification for the expansion of European empires.[56] It is important to understand that the 'biologism' of the racial theories is 'not a valorization of life as such, still less an application of biology; rather it is a vitalized metaphor of certain sexualized social values: energy, decisiveness, initiative and generally all the virile representations of domination or, conversely, passivity, sensuality, femininity, or again solidarity.'[57] These circulating, repetitive and contingent discourses on 'scientific racism' generated a 'dispositif de securite' deployed time and again to determine 'the ability of African or Asian peoples to use Western tools or firearms.'[58]

This deployment and determination is dependent on the 'rationalizations' and the 'relative novelty of the language' offered by intellectuals as they 'mimic the way in which scientific discursivity articulates "visible facts" to "hidden causes" and thus connect up with a spontaneous process of theorization inherent in the racism of the masses.'[59] Thus, 'racist myths' are 'myths not only by virtue of their pseudo-scientific content' but also 'forms of imaginary transcendence of the gulf separating intellectuality from the masses.'[60] This becomes more evident as 'the logic of neo-racism in the late twentieth century becomes appropriated through the trope of the 'clash of civilizations' to 'legitimate the deployment of "common

[55] Adas, *Machines as the Measure of Men*, 275.

[56] Nicola Short and Helen Kambouri, "Ambiguous universalism: theorising race/nation/class in international relations," *Journal of International Relations and Development* 13, no. 3 (2010): 271.

[57] Etienne Balibar, "Race and Nationalism," in *Race, Nation, Class: Ambiguous Identities*, ed. Etienne Balibar and Immanuel Wallerstein, translation of Etienne Balibar by Chris Turner (London, New York: Verso, 1991), 58.

[58] Adas, *Machines as the Measure of Men*, 290–291; Michael Dillon and Andrew W. Neal, ed., *Foucault on Politics, Security and War* (New York: Palgrave Macmillan, 2008), 15.

[59] Etienne Balibar, "Is there a 'Neo-Racism'?" in *Race, Nation, Class: Ambiguous Identities*, ed. Etienne Balibar and Immanuel Wallerstein, translation of Etienne Balibar by Chris Turner (London, New York: Verso, 1991), 18–20.

[60] Balibar, "Is there a 'Neo-Racism'?", 20.

sense" conceptions of neo-racism in public policy making and discourses' on arms control and disarmament, as discussed in the following chapters.[61]

Scholars such as Etienne Balibar describe neo-racism as a new form of racism practiced in the twentieth century after decolonization, a 'racism without races' or a 'differentialist racism' as articulated by P.A. Taguieff.[62] In this 'neo-racism' the dominant theme is not biological heredity but the 'insurmountability of cultural differences, a racism which, at first sight, does not postulate the superiority of certain groups or peoples in relation to others but "only" the harmfulness of abolishing frontiers, the incompatibility of life-styles and traditions.'[63] The 'suppression of the theme of hierarchy is more apparent than real' and is reconstituted in 'the very type of criteria applied in thinking the difference between cultures' and in 'practical application of the doctrine' of 'cultural racism.'[64]

In the contemporary practices of neo-racism, 'culture can also function like a nature ... locking individuals and groups a priori into a genealogy, into a determination that is immutable and intangible in origin.'[65] The cultural differences are now represented as a 'natural milieu,' and 'abolition of that difference will necessarily give rise to defensive reactions' as the everyday practices of neo-racism 'naturalizes not racial belonging but racist conduct' premised on 'tolerance thresholds' and 'cultural distances.'[66] This practice of neo-racism based on cultural differences is considered to be 'widely developed' in the 'Anglo-Saxon' countries with their emphasis on 'open, competitive, Western attitude' that has significant political consequences in understanding the problem of weapons control.[67] A composite understanding of the political consequences can be grasped further if instead of simply decrying cultural racism as 'hypocrisy' we understand it as 'enduring, widespread and structural.'[68]

This is because of the existing paradox in modernity's quest for 'ideological legitimation of universality' through discourses on 'moral equality and human rights' vis-à-vis everyday practices of racism and sexism that

[61] Short and Kambouri, "Ambiguous universalism," 269, 273.
[62] Balibar, "Is there a 'Neo-Racism'?", 21.
[63] Balibar, "Is there a 'Neo-Racism'?", 21.
[64] Balibar, "Is there a 'Neo-Racism'?", 24–26.
[65] Balibar, "Is there a 'Neo-Racism'?", 22.
[66] Balibar, "Is there a 'Neo-Racism'?" 22.
[67] Balibar, "Is there a 'Neo-Racism'?" 26.
[68] Balibar, "Is there a 'Neo-Racism'?" 30.

are 'intimately and conceptually tied to each other.'[69] These linkages are often ambiguous and contradictory as neo-racism 'functions through ethico-political claims regarding the value of diversity and an aesthetic racial inclusivity.'[70] Its effectiveness 'lies in its ability to regularize differentialist practices through a discourse that accommodates antithetical claims' such as sovereignty and universality.[71] Furthermore, neo-racism 'contains past racisms and transcends them by finding new foundations for social difference and obscuring their most unacceptable elements with an aesthetic of tolerance.'[72] Thus, Balibar observes how, 'in appearance, humanity has been unified by the suppression of imperial hierarchies' but 'it is racism which represents one of the most insistent forms of historical memory of modern societies … which continues to effect the imaginary "fusion" of past and present in which the collective perception of human history unfolds.'[73]

Nationalism and Race

The idea of nationalism is 'if not the sole cause of racism, then at least the determining condition of its production' during 'circumstances in which the nation states, established upon historically contested territories, have striven to control *population* movements, and to the very production of the "people" as a political community.'[74] Short and Kambouri argue that 'if racism is an ever present particularist supplement to nationalism, neo-racism functions analogously through the notion of "civilization," at once providing the grounds for a shared sense of identity while always threatening to disrupt it.'[75] Neo-racism draws upon 'anthropological universals' that refer to 'humanity's genetic inheritance' or 'cultural tradition' to differentiate between 'humanity and animality, the problematic character of which is re-utilized to interpret the conflicts within society and history.'[76] Thus, a '"universal" principle of white superiority was constructed in the

[69] Balibar, "Is there a 'Neo-Racism'?" 29–30, 36.

[70] Short and Kambouri, "Ambiguous universalism," 269.

[71] Short and Kambouri, "Ambiguous universalism," 292.

[72] Short and Kambouri, "Ambiguous universalism," 274.

[73] Etienne Balibar, "Race and Nationalism," 44–45.

[74] Benedict Anderson, *Imagined Communities: Reflections on the Origin and Spread of Nationalism* (London: Verso Books, 2016); Etienne Balibar, "Race and Nationalism," 37, 42.

[75] Short and Kambouri, "Ambiguous universalism," 281.

[76] Balibar, "Race and Nationalism," 56–57.

context of particularist nationalist-imperialist rivalries in the colonial era' as 'the colonial castes of various nationalities (British, French, Dutch, Portuguese etc.) worked together to forge the idea of "White" superiority of civilization as an interest that has to be defended against the savages.'[77]

In articulating this entanglement of racism and nationalism it is helpful to note a time lag between practices of nationalism and racism that gives rise to 'what might be called the pan-ic developments of nationalism (Pan-Slavism, Pan-Germanism, Pan Turanianism, Pan Arabism, Pan-Americanism ...).'[78] This can be attributed to the fact that racism as a 'supplement of nationalism or more precisely a supplement internal to nationalism' is 'always in excess of it, but always indispensable to its constitution and yet always still insufficient to achieve its project, just as nationalism is both indispensable and always insufficient to achieve the formation of the *nation* or the project of a "nationalization" of society.'[79] Thus Balibar observes how 'the European or Euro-American nations, locked in a bitter struggle to divide up the world into colonial empires, recognized that they formed a community and shared an "equality" through that very competition, a community and an equality to which they gave the name "White."'[80] This racist supranationalism tends to idealize 'timeless or transhistorical communities such as the "Indo-European", "the West", "Judaeo-Christian civilization."'[81] The founding of a 'civilization' is the transformation of an imperial mission from 'a mere enterprise of conquest into an enterprise of universal domination.'[82]

An acute awareness of this desire for dominance is grasped through a study of managerial discourses deployed in the field of security studies such as Orientalism and its more prolific and specialized forms of Strategic Orientalism, Military Orientalism and Techno-Orientalism that pervade Western cultural consciousness, a western cultural consciousness that privileges modernity and fears losing 'their perceived "edge" over others.'[83]

[77] Short and Kambouri, "Ambiguous universalism," 276; Balibar, "Race and Nationalism," 43.

[78] Balibar, "Race and Nationalism," 59.

[79] Balibar, "Race and Nationalism," 54.

[80] Balibar, "Race and Nationalism," 62.

[81] Balibar, "Race and Nationalism," 61.

[82] Balibar, "Race and Nationalism," 62.

[83] David S. Roh, Betsy Huang and Greta A. Niu, eds. *Techno-Orientalism: Imagining Asia in Speculative Fiction, History, and Media* (New Brunswick, New Jersey and London: Rutgers University Press, 2015), 3.

Thus practices of Strategic Orientalism are premised on the 'pervasive and axiomatic belief that the West (or occasionally the United States) as a civilization has a special role to play in global security affairs.'[84] Military Orientalism undertakes an investigation of the 'range of assumptions and myths through which Westerners gaze on the military East' in an effort to hopefully confront their own 'fears about themselves, their survival, identity and values through different visions of non-Western warfare.'[85] The dynamic practices of Techno-Orientalism are more focused on representations of the Other in 'hypo-or-hypertechnological terms in cultural productions and political discourse.'[86] The scope of techno-Orientalism is 'expansive and bi-directional,' and racial signifiers deployed in a techno-Orientalist discourse are 'technological and futuristic' in their imagination and are considered to have become a 'part of the West's project of securing dominance as architects of the future.'[87] These discourses carry within them the danger of constituting and reconstituting pedagogical and performative spaces in which racial tropes and stereotypes are inscribed and reinscribed to become 'sites in which racialization is more likely reinforced than challenged' and might be so 'internalized' as to reproduce the 'same dehumanizing model' to meet 'imperial aspirations' repetitively.[88]

An attention to these imperial aspirations is drawn further if one studies inter-war discourses on 'Technics and Civilization.'[89] These discourses demonstrate an acute awareness of civilizational differences to claim that 'other civilizations reached a high degree of technical proficiency without apparently, being profoundly influenced by the methods and aims of technics' and that 'it remained for the peoples of Western Europe to carry the physical sciences and the exact arts to a point no other culture had reached, and to adapt a whole mode of life to the pace and the capacities of the machine.'[90] This differential awareness continues to perpetuate itself and can be exemplified by paying attention to the language deployed in the

[84] Keith Krause and Andrew Latham, "Constructing non-proliferation and arms control: The norms of western practice," *Contemporary Security Policy* 19, no. 1 (1998): 41, 37.

[85] Patrick Porter, *Military Orientalism: Eastern war through western eyes* (New York: Oxford University Press, 2013), 16–21.

[86] David S. Roh, Betsy Huang and Greta A. Niu, *Techno-Orientalism*, 2.

[87] Roh, Huang and Niu, "*Techno-Orientalism*," 2.

[88] Roh, Huang and Niu, "*Techno-Orientalism*," 3, 7.

[89] Lewis Mumford, *Technics and Civilization* (New York: Harcourt, Brace & Company, 1934).

[90] Mumford, *Technics and Civilization*, 4.

contemporary construction of clocks where a selective 'technosocial' metaphor of 'master-slave' is deployed to suggest 'a free master that did no work and a slave that followed the master's orders.'[91] The deployment of this negative technosocial metaphor gained currency and ubiquity in the technical literature in the US, a racially segregated society in the aftermath of the Second World War, to soon become a 'metaphor of choice' in engineering to suggest a 'control relation between two devices.'[92] This control relationship signals the power of the master possessing intelligence and exercising control over the slave to prevent his escape and undermining any efforts to harm the master.

The deliberate choice of this 'ethically suspect' master-slave metaphor has time and again been justified on grounds of 'accuracy,' being 'more intelligible to the ordinary person' and how science occupies a 'culture-free realm.'[93] Despite these claims, one cannot ignore how the 'master-slave' technosocial metaphor persistently signals messages of power vested within this relationship embedded in time. Ron Eglash observes, 'It is almost certain that there was no conscious intention to echo pre-Civil War discourse on runaway slaves, but that still leaves the possibility of a metaphor operating at a subconscious level.'[94] The indiscriminate use of this master-slave metaphor persists despite developments in technology that no longer render a control relationship necessary and the existence of alternative terms such as 'primary' and 'secondary.'[95] The everyday usage of this 'master-slave' metaphor as a technical exercise in engineering is provocative as it can be interpreted as evoking 'a tension between a desire for more autonomous machines and a desire to retain human mastery' of machines.[96] It can also be interpreted as a 'a racist desire to mark technology with white privilege or the Freudian emergence of a sexually charged pathology of dominance.'[97] An awareness of racial tropes being deployed even if only at the subconscious level in contemporary practices of science and engineering is imperative as they signal practices of power, alienation

[91] Ron Eglash, "Broken Metaphor: The Master-Slave Analogy in Technical Literature," *Technology and Culture* 48, no. 2 (2007):361–362.

[92] Eglash, "Broken Metaphor," 361.

[93] Eglash, "Broken Metaphor," 368.

[94] Eglash, "Broken Metaphor," 364.

[95] Eglash, "Broken Metaphor," 366–367.

[96] Eglash, "Broken Metaphor," 367.

[97] Eglash, "Broken Metaphor," 366–367.

and control in a tacit manner that has implications for managerial time in the production and regulation of weapons.

Thus, 'for Foucault the interesting object is not "race", or even the more nominalist notion of "racialisation": the interesting object is a relational, inherently interactive and dynamic one, namely race struggle.'[98] In this struggle, it is an effort to understand how thinkers of race and racism developed 'general purpose terms, such as "the Other."'[99] It is imperative to question the 'logic of race war' to configure how race became a 'principal sorting mechanism' in a relentless quest for political modernity.[100] Thus 'race writing' entails passionate engagement with historically situated knowledge to identify the intense tautological interplay of discourses on racial reductionism and technological determinism as they vary with time and space. In tracing this 'race war' it is imperative to articulate 'demands for justice that arise out of a particular people's history of oppression.'[101] This demand for justice is pertinent as 'scientific and technological achievements' are often touted as 'gauges of racial capacity,' and 'estimates of racial capacity' ascertain that the 'degree of technical and scientific education is made available to different non-Western peoples' as an exercise in 'upward mobility' toward modernity.[102]

Thus time accounts for not only the 'identity of a culture' but also its relationship with others.[103] Adas observes how 'the Europeans who explored, colonized, and sought to Christianize Africa and Asia were setting out from societies dominated by clocks, railway schedules and mechanical rhythms.'[104] The Europeans with their 'new secular and mechanized time sense' were deeply critical of Africans that had 'not only failed to devise astronomic instruments and time-keepers' but 'lacked any sense of time apart from that dictated by nature's rhythms.'[105] While they conceded that 'the ancient Hindus had devised numerous instruments of celestial observation, invented intricate systems of measurement and

[98] Mariana Vlverde, "Law versus History—Foucault's Genealogy of Modern Sovereignty," in *Foucault on Politics, Security and War*, ed. Michael Dillon and Andrew W. Neal (New York: Palgrave Macmillan, 2008), 142.

[99] Vlverde, "Law versus History," 149.

[100] Dillon and Neal, *Foucault on Politics, Security and War*, 8.

[101] Vlverde, "Law versus History," 148.

[102] Adas, *Machines as the Measure of Men*, 275, 318.

[103] Fabian, *Time and the Other*, 50–51.

[104] Adas, *Machines as the Measure of Men*, 243.

[105] Adas, *Machines as the Measure of Men*, 242–244.

enumeration, and worked out remarkably elaborate methods of calculating the flow of history, which they traced eons into the past,' they still found fault and castigated them as 'antiquated and badly flawed.'[106] The existence of alternate time conventions in non-European cultures before and after the development of mechanical clock time in Europe is acknowledged, but there is an insistence that 'the Western version of standardized reckoning achieved a global hegemony.'[107] This view is asserted based on the premise that 'technologies associated with the rise of modern time also facilitated colonial territorial expansion' and 'necessitated a truly globalized time standard.'[108] To quote Hom, 'when colonialism took on a nationalist character, Western European notions of spatial and temporal organization were part of a particular vision of "civilization" that was exported to the colonies.'[109] There was a particular impulse toward 'association of standardization with civilization and legitimacy' that has been quite durable.[110]

Linear Time and Cyclical Time

This European cultural signal of standardization of time associated with civilization is interesting if we consider how time is deployed and 'whether cultures with differing conceptions of time can communicate with each other.'[111] It is in this context that Romila Thapar observes how early Orientalists such as James Mill referred to Indian notions of time and Hindu civilization to the effect that '[r]ude nations seem to derive a peculiar gratification from pretensions to remote antiquity. As a boastful and turgid vanity distinguishes remarkably the oriental nations, they have in most instances carried their claims extravagantly high.'[112] The eighteenth-century Orientalists constituted a classification of time. In this classifica-

[106] Adas, *Machines as the Measure of Men*, 246, 106–107.

[107] Andrew R. Hom, "Hegemonic metronome: the ascendancy of Western standard time," *Review of International Studies* 36, no. 4 (2010): 1150.

[108] Hom, "Hegemonic metronome," 1160.

[109] Hom, "Hegemonic metronome," 1163.

[110] Hom, "Hegemonic metronome," 1151.

[111] Romila Thapar, *Time as a Metaphor of History: Early India* (New Delhi: Oxford University Press, 1996), 8.

[112] James Mill quoted in Romila Thapar, *Time as a Metaphor of History: Early India* (New Delhi: Oxford University Press, 1996), 3, see footnote 1; R. Inden, "Orientalist Construction of India," *Modern Asian Studies* 20, no. 3 (1986): 401–6.

tion, cyclic time and linear time appear to be diametrically opposed to each other. Cyclic time understood to be repetitive, regular, continuous, infinite, and cosmological came to be associated with primitive and archaic societies, a particularly galling indictment given the uncomplimentary definition of 'primitive' in those days.[113] This association of cyclic time with societies deemed to be primitive and archaic 'amounts to a refusal of history, for no event can be particular or unique and all events are liable to be repeated in the next cycle.'[114] Thapar states succinctly, '[A] refusal of history through recourse to cyclic time was identified more frequently with colonial cultures.'[115]

This sense of erasure of history of primitive and archaic societies is further reinforced by an understanding of cyclical time as 'mythical time.'[116] To quote Thapar,

> At the turn of the eighteenth century and shortly thereafter the theory which emerged was that the Indian sense of time was entirely cyclic, was tied into an infinity of recurring cycles, and did not therefore recognize historical change; and in the absence of history there was no differentiation between myth and history.
>
> Two hundred years later the received wisdom on the subject remains largely unchanged, even if the reasons for the continuance of these views differ.[117]

This observation stands true as contemporary accounts of time in the West continue to make stereotypical assumptions that 'many Eastern civilizations have flourished on a loose basis in time: the Hindus have in fact been so indifferent to time that they lack even an authentic chronology of the years.'[118]

These observations are compounded by the constant need to bifurcate and reiterate how 'other societies thought of time as cyclical, returning to earlier stages and starting over again. Linear time can be thought of as progressive or regressive, as moving on to better things or declining from some earlier, happier state. For Europeans in our period, the progressive

[113] Thapar, *Time as a Metaphor of History*, 3–5.
[114] Thapar, *Time as a Metaphor of History*, 5–6.
[115] Thapar, *Time as a Metaphor of History*, 43.
[116] Thapar, *Time as a Metaphor of History*, 6.
[117] Thapar, *Time as a Metaphor of History*, 4–5.
[118] Mumford, *Technics and Civilization*, 16.

view prevailed.'[119] The evolutionary time or linear time increasingly associated with the West is understood 'to have a beginning and an end and emphasized the uniqueness of the particular which made events non-recurring. This was said to liberate history from repetition, deny the reversibility of time, and distinguish history from myth, where myth belonged to a distant time, or even timelessness.'[120] Linear time is associated with the profane and dialectical change and 'the secularization of linear time in Europe incorporated the notion of change in time and the belief that change was progress as defined in the nineteenth century.'[121]

While tracing the history of the 'origins of the Western temporalizing of difference,' Barry Hindess is troubled with 'the unfortunate Western habit of locating others in the past' and this attitude of 'we in the West have already been there. Done that.'[122] Thus compelling those living in non-Western societies to question their place in time. Hindess cautions against a perception that 'there lies an archipelago of deprived temporal gulags which serve as detention centers or rudimentary training camps for contemporaries who have been condemned to the more or less distant past.'[123] On the contrary, he insists that 'the denial of co-evalness is a more general feature of modern Western thought' that can be understood in the form of a 'double move.'[124] To quote Hindess,

> We can observe a double move, involving, *first*, the construction of a generic tribal way of life out of reports from contemporary America and elsewhere and out of descriptions of peoples in the Western past, from the Old Testament, and, *second*, the claim that this tribal way of life is what preceded the emergence of Western civilization.

He suggests that in engaging with the politics of temporalizing difference it is helpful to be aware of 'a broader range of images of the Other' instead of a generic Other.[125] Such a gesture acknowledging plurality has

[119] David Landes, "Why Europe and the West? Why not China?" *Journal of Economic Perspectives* 20, no. 2 (2006): 10.

[120] Thapar, *Time as a Metaphor of History*, 6.

[121] Thapar, *Time as a Metaphor of History*, 5.

[122] Barry Hindess, "Been there, done that..." *Postcolonial Studies* 11, no. 2 (2008): 201–202.

[123] Hindess, "Been there, done that...", 204.

[124] Hindess, "Been there, done that...", 204, 210.

[125] Hindess, "Been there," 204.

to also be cognizant of the Western tendency to consider 'belonging to the past as a bad thing, that is, as a kind of cultural and moral failure,' and also view with suspicion 'those who remained behind the West' as 'less capable of understanding their own pasts.'[126]

Evolutionary Time

Johannes Fabian concurs and suggests that 'historical time for peoples of European descent was represented as a tunnel stretching back to the Garden of Eden—"the tunnel of time." Everything important that ever happened to humans happened in that tunnel. ... Other peoples had their own tunnels—Chinese, Indians, Africans. But little or nothing of importance in human history happened in those tunnels.'[127] It is this 'tunnel of time' and its diffusionist assumptions that have been deployed to justify European colonialism and modernization as 'a result of Europe's internal qualities.'[128] Europe forging ahead of other civilizations is often seen as an 'European miracle' but colonialism for others is interpreted to be 'not spoilation and cultural destruction but, rather, the receipt-by-diffusion of European civilization: modernization.'[129] This patronizing zeal persists to advocate, 'we have all been the beneficiaries, including those civilizations and societies that are now learning and catching up.'[130]

Hom observes how Western standard time was thus in the vanguard of the "great domestication" of the periphery, encouraging the "creation of Modern societies from Indochina to central Africa."[131] The remaking of 'the frontier in the spatial and temporal image of Western Europe' was a form of Western imperialism rooted in a '"will-to-manifest identity"—a particularly Western European identity with specific understandings of space and time.'[132] These epistemic understandings remain as former colonies, in the absence of an explicit criterion for international recognition of

[126] Hindess, "Been there," 211.

[127] Sandra Harding, *Is Science Multicultural? Postcolonialisms, Feminisms, and Epistemologies* (Bloomington & Indianapolis: Indiana University Press, 1998), 23.

[128] J.M. Blaut describes 'the tunnel of time' in *The Colonizer's Model of the World: Geographical Diffusionism and Eurocentric History* (New York: Guilford Press, 1993); J.M. Blaut quoted by Harding, *Is Science Multicultural?*, 23–24.

[129] J.M. Blaut quoted by Harding, *Is Science Multicultural?* 27, 24.

[130] David Landes, "Clocks and the wealth of nations," *Daedalus* 132, no. 2 (2003): 26.

[131] Hom, "Hegemonic metronome," 1164.

[132] Hom, "Hegemonic metronome," 1160, 1165.

the new polities, generally accepted colonial borders as the limits of their new states and also 'adopted without significant opposition the temporal conventions contained in Western standard time.'[133] Third World nationalisms as 'modernizing ideologies par excellence' have contributed to this imaginary.[134] It is this assumption of modernity in Europe and other cultures 'as largely unchanging, timeless, in their social relations' that deserves more careful scrutiny in the succeeding chapters.[135] This is imperative if we 'remember the history of our discipline, it is in the end about the relationship between the West and the Rest.'[136]

But our 'periodization of the present is directly linked to our understanding of the now.'[137] This emphasis on the 'now' exists in tension with the 'not yet.'[138] This not yet, 'waiting room version of history' is further articulated 'through recourse to some version of a stagist theory of history, ranging from simple evolutionary schemas to sophisticated understandings of "uneven development."'[139] These temporal stagist discourses of evolutionism and development can be conceived as particular narrative strategies crafted to help defer the problem of universal disarmament. Fabian argues,

> a firm belief in "natural", i.e., evolutionary time ... promoted a scheme in terms of which not only past cultures but all living societies were irrevocably placed on a temporal slope, a stream of Time—some upstream, others downstream. Civilization, evolution, development, acculturation, modernization (and their cousins, industrialization, urbanization) are all terms whose conceptual content derives, in ways that can be specified, from evolutionary time.[140]

The social evolutionists 'were too full of the conviction that Time "accomplished" or brought about things in the course of evolution ... theirs was a preoccupation with stages leading to civilization, each of them

[133] Hom, "Hegemonic metronome," 1167–1168.

[134] Dipesh Chakraborty, *Provincializing Europe: Postcolonial Thought and Historical Difference* (Princeton & Oxford: Princeton University Press, 2000), 43.

[135] Harding, *Is Science Multicultural?* 23.

[136] Fabian, *Time and the Other*, 28.

[137] Aganthangelou and Killian, *Time, Temporality and Violence in International Relations*, 10.

[138] Chakraborty, *Provincializing Europe*, 8.

[139] Chakraborty, *Provincializing Europe*, 9.

[140] Fabian, *Time and the Other*, 17.

as meaningful as a sentence leading towards the conclusion of a story.'[141] Evolutionism thus needs to be acknowledged as a carefully crafted strategy of cultural governance deployed in an effort to emphasize continuity, 'the similarity between barbaric institutions and those of the European past, or even present,' and often deployed in tandem with a dichotomous discourse on 'barbarous and civilized.'[142]

This is not to discount the possibility that the 'evolutionary sequences and their concomitant political practice of colonialism and imperialism may look incorporative; after all, they create a universal frame of reference able to accommodate all societies,' but to remember that these practices are 'based on the episteme of natural history, they are founded on distancing and separation.'[143] To quote Fabian, 'what makes the savage significant to the evolutionist's Time is that he lives in another time.'[144] This 'temporal distance is objectivity in the minds of many practitioners' instead of 'absentee colonialism.'[145] Furthermore, it is a form of 'conceit that the development of Western Europe (together now with America and a few other places) provides the standard against which the rest of humanity should be measured.'[146] This notable feature of temporalizing difference was an outcome of a significant shift in European historical consciousness that demanded a 'declaration of independence of the present from determination by its past' as a 'necessary condition for the emergence of modern ideas of sovereignty and of citizenship: neither state nor citizen could be autonomous if their conduct was determined by the past.'[147]

Furthermore, 'the possession of time became crucial to the separation of sovereign powers … the possessor of time could determine for its subjects (the flock or the population) the acceptable forms of livable life, conditions of justice, and for the emperor the end of civil order. It is from the vantage point of the civil order that all forms of freedom, liberty, justice, and social peace could be imagined.'[148] Thapar suggests,

[141] Fabian, *Time and the Other—How Anthropology Makes its Object* (New York: Columbia University Press, 2014), 15.

[142] Bhabha, *The Location of Culture*, 185; John Burrow, *Evolution and Society* (New York: Cambridge University Press), 1966.

[143] Fabian, *Time and the Other*, 26.

[144] Fabian, *Time and the Other*, 27.

[145] Fabian, *Time and the Other*, 30, 68–69.

[146] Hindess, "Been there, done that…" *Postcolonial Studies* 11, no. 2 (2008): 206.

[147] Hindess, "Been there," 207.

[148] Grovogui, "Time, technology and the imperial eye," 46.

> The adoption of a short-spanned and more precise time reckoning associated with those in authority was encouraged by the establishing of a state. This time reckoning, even when encompassed by the longer spans of cosmological time, introduces a precision which lends strength to the authority of the state. The need to maintain state records and official documents, not to mention texts legitimizing persons and institutions, tended to make the history of those in authority more evident.[149]

This idea of 'time reckoning' by a sovereign state is supplemented with a new 'positive economy' of time that takes recourse to new disciplinary techniques to intensify use of time, with increased speeds and increased efficiencies especially in the military.[150]

Mumford suggests that the European desire for power via 'conquest of space and time,' 'infected' the 'army' and 'in military arts the cross-bow and the ballista were revived and extended, and on their heels came more powerful weapons for annihilating distance—the cannon and later the musket.'[151] These were considered to be 'restless preludes to the vast efforts and initiatives of the nineteenth century' as 'militarism forced the pace and cleared a straight path to the development of modern large-scale standardized industry.'[152] He further notes how the incessant and growing discipline of time and modernity produces mechanized warfare and standardized production. To quote Mumford,

> the musketeer has been turned into a smart, mechanically responsive infantryman and the musket itself had become more deadly in close fighting by means of the bayonet, and the bayonet in turn had become more efficient by means of drill and mass tactics, and finally, all the arms of the service had been progressively co-ordinated with the most deadly and decisive arms: the artillery.[153]

Foucault documents how modern military organization in Europe cultivated 'meticulously detailed "programmes" according to which the "correct use of the body" would be specified in order to allow for a

[149] Thapar, *Time as a Metaphor of History: Early India* (New Delhi: Oxford University Press, 1996), 33.

[150] Julian Reid, "Life Struggles: War, Discipline and Biopolitics in the Thought of Michel Foucault," in *Foucault on Politics, Security and War*, ed. Michael Dillon and Andrew W. Neal (New York: Palgrave Macmillan, 2008), 70.

[151] Mumford, *Technics and Civilization*, 22.

[152] Mumford, *Technics*, 22, 87.

[153] Mumford, *Technics*, 83.

"correct use of time."'[154] This 'temporal elaboration of the act' generated specific 'military ordinances as to how to fire a weapon' and 'specified distinctions between four different sorts of marching step; the short step, the ordinary step, the double step and the marching step, each differentiated according to duration, extension and comportment.'[155] With these strict regimental exercises and 'the increase in the effectiveness of weapons, came likewise a growing sense of superiority in the soldier himself: his strength, his death-dealing properties had been heightened by technological advance. With a mere pull of the trigger, he could annihilate an enemy: that was a triumph of natural magic' so much so that 'in the act of making himself a master, the solider helps create a race of slaves.'[156] Mumford claims, '[A]n imperviousness to life-values other than those clustered around the soldier's underlying death-wish, is one of the most sinister effects of the military discipline.'[157]

These military techniques of disciplinary power not only encouraged an 'instrumental coding of the body' but also lay the groundwork for an understanding of 'evolutive time' in security studies.[158] This 'evolutive time' or 'new evolutionary accounts of the order of life' brought about an epistemological shift in modern military science. Evolutive time made human life an object of knowledge and power with reference to war, and this has two significant effects.[159] First, it encouraged military sciences to 'conceive of populations themselves as species bodies defined by a common genesis, evolutionary patterns and survival rates.'[160] Second, it nurtured fantasics of a 'society that would function as a machine. Not a mechanical machine, but a machine that functions as a natural body.'[161] It is by taking recourse to evolutive time that the modern state colonizes discourses on race war to construe threats and to 'wage war on enemies that are characterized variously as animal or inhuman.'[162] Siba Grovogui claims,

[154] Reid, "Life Struggles," 69.
[155] Reid, "Life Struggles," 69–70.
[156] Mumford, *Technics*, 85, 95.
[157] Mumford, *Technics*, 95.
[158] Reid, "Life Struggles," 70–71.
[159] Reid, "Life Struggles," 72.
[160] Reid, "Life Struggles," 72.
[161] Reid, "Life Struggles," 72.
[162] Reid, "Life Struggles," 85.

> [T]he possession of time rendered the sovereign responsible for it and gave him (yes, him) the power to allow life, determine life forms, and end life, if necessary for the preservation of the realm. Sovereign violence—that is sacred violence or violence without appeal—emerged as a necessary means by which time was given force and stability.[163]

An evolutionist time further transformed the struggle between 'two competing peoples distinguished on grounds of their differing ways of life' to a 'race war' where competing sovereigns seek to represent 'the one true race, the race that holds power and is entitled to define the norm' and act 'against those who deviate from the norm, against those who pose a threat to the biological heritage.'[164]

The emergence of the modern sovereign states in Europe reinforced this sense of superiority and exercised its influence in matters of security. These powers now distinguished enemies by their racial differentiation from the norm and mobilized populations in defence of racial norms against rival populations.[165] Hom reiterates, '[M]odern time and territorial sovereignty were exported to the colonial frontier during the nineteenth century period of colonial nationalism … and both were part of the effort to remake colonial cultures in the Western European image.'[166] As a result,

> the only matters of interest in the study of non-Western pasts lie: either in the clarification of issues about Western pasts themselves … to resolve issues; *or* in the exploration of differences (of where others have gone wrong or have been particularly fortunate in their deviations from the familiar historical path), and of the complications that result from the interaction of particular pasts with more recent developments.[167]

In effect, 'the Western ego has emerged as the sovereign' and militarization of thought has shaped perceptions of technology.'[168] The 'West determines the requirements of international existence,' and 'language,

[163] Grovogui, "Time, technology and the imperial eye," 46.
[164] Reid, "Life Struggles," 85.
[165] Reid, "Life Struggles," 86.
[166] Hom, "Hegemonic metronome," 1160.
[167] Hindess, "Been there, done that..." 202.
[168] Grovogui, "Time, technology and the imperial eye," 47.

legal institutions, and armament work in this context as technologies of power.'[169]

Grovogui asserts that 'the co-constitution of technology and subjectivity is disguised in the language of cost, efficiency, and progress. Its reality is revealed in decisions on and distinctions … that these weapons belong to combats in different spaces (non-Western), where the terms of morality and ethics functions differently and lives do not accord with the principles of "our time."'[170] He further argues,

> [T]he tone was set at the so-called discovery of the Americas, which ushered in faith in European superiority, followed by ascendancy, and non-European inferiority, followed by subordination … the tone has been adjusted over time but has never repudiated the essential notes: the West must remain the paramount if not the sole proprietor of the will of the international community; the desire of others must be subordinated to Western hegemons; the will of others is substantively and constitutionally inferior to the West; by nature and the order of things, the West in exclusivity may define its interests to encompass things and relations in spaces inhabited by others with no fear of reciprocity. The question was never whether others should surrender their will, blood, and materials to the West; it was always by what amount.[171]

Fabian cautions that one might be tempted to assume that the rejection of evolutionism included its use of time but insists that '[t]his, however, was not the case' as 'the categorical frame of naturalized Time' had become very powerful by the end of the nineteenth century.[172]

It was this understanding of evolutionary, natural and racialized time that facilitated temporal distancing between the West and the Rest. The temporal distance between the West and the Rest premised on a continuous denial of coevalness, designed to maintain a sense of technological and economic superiority, 'expressive of a cosmological myth of frightening magnitude and persistency.'[173] This denial of coevalness fostered by naturalization and distancing is entrenched in vocabulary and encourages deployment of euphemisms such as 'primitive, savage (but also tribal, traditional, Third World)' and displays little interest in thinking, observing or

[169] Grovogui, "Time, technology and the imperial eye," 49.
[170] Grovogui, "Time, technology and the imperial eye," 54–55.
[171] Grovogui, "Time, technology and the imperial eye," 49.
[172] Fabian, *Time and the Other*, 18.
[173] Fabian, *Time and the Other*, 35.

critically studying the 'primitive.'[174] In the denial of coevalness, the emphasis is rather on thinking, observing and studying 'in terms of the primitive. Primitive, being essentially a temporal concept, is a category, not an object, of Western thought.'[175] Furthermore, the naturalization of time 'defines temporal relations as exclusive and expansive … the savage is not yet ready for civilization.'[176] Dipesh Chakraborty notes, '[H]ow we periodize our present is thus connected to the question of how we imagine the political. The reverse must be true as well: that every imagination of the political entails a certain figure of the now.'[177] It is therefore an act of 'imagination and courage to picture what would happen to the West … if its temporal fortress were suddenly invaded by the Time of its Other.'[178]

Civilizational Time

In addressing this question, it is possible to contend that civilizational time constituted via reproductive practices of stereotyping, sly civility and mimesis resists these bold acts of imagination. These practices of civilizational time are discussed briefly here and elaborated upon in the following chapters. Civilizational templates or stereotypes not only simplify complex realities by juxtaposing Cartesian binaries in an equation of negation such as the 'West and the Rest' but are suggestive of a sense of 'fixity' described by Homi K. Bhabha as a 'paradoxical mode of representation: it connotes rigidity and an unchanging order as well as disorder, degeneracy and daemonic repetition.'[179] But stereotyping is not just an act of simplification and therefore,

> a false representation of a given reality. On the contrary, 'stereotype' is a 'simplification because it is an arrested, fixated form of representation, that in denying the play of difference (which the negation through the Other permits), constitutes a problem for the representation of the subject in significations of psychic and social relations.[180]

[174] Fabian, *Time and the Other*, 17–18.
[175] Fabian, *Time and the Other*, 18.
[176] Fabian, *Time and the Other*, 26.
[177] Dipesh Chakraborty, "Where Is the Now?" *Critical Inquiry* 30, no. 2 (2004): 459.
[178] Fabian, *Time and the Other*, 35.
[179] Bhabha, *The Location of Culture*, 95.
[180] Bhabha, *Location of Culture*, 107.

It is 'a static system of "synchronic essentialism", a knowledge of "signifiers of stability" ... continually under threat from diachronic forms of history and narrative, signs of instability.'[181] Stereotype is 'a form of splitting and multiple belief' that requires for 'its successful signification, a continual and repetitive chain of other stereotypes.'[182] Ignoring these signs by observing 'silence' serves as 'the virtual erasure as far as the official representations are concerned of the 'awful gulf' constituted by color lines.[183] In stereotyping Reza Afsahri cautions against the possibility of a nostalgia for 'Orientalism's straightforward positing of the European Self and the Oriental Other.'[184]

Thus, civilizational time represents a politics of continuous negation that is often reproduced in abstract, chronological, evolutionary accounts of arms control and disarmament.[185] This is possible because civilizational time is fetishistic; it continually 'vacillates between what is always "in place", already known, and something that must be anxiously repeated' through a discursive strategy of stereotyping or Orientalism.[186] Thus, civilizational time is to be understood as 'mundane time' indulging in 'grand-scale periodizing,' 'imposing visions' that help maintain 'cocktail talk about primitive mentality.'[187] In civilizational time 'culture is described taxonomically' and therefore there is no appreciation of the 'primitive as producer.'[188] The emphasis on selection and classification renders the 'concept of culture devoid of a theory of creativity or production,' making it difficult to interrogate 'what he thinks and does' and encouraging a catalogue of 'how he thinks and acts.'[189]

A pretentious innocence or 'sly civility' comes into play with the emphasis that a relationship between the West and the other 'is merely taxonomic.'[190] This encourages a taxonomic understanding of time that

[181] Bhabha, *Location of Culture*, 102.

[182] Bhabha, *Location of Culture*, 110.

[183] Michael Taussig, *Mimesis and Alterity: A Particular History of the Senses* (New York & London: Routledge, 1993), 147.

[184] James G. Ferguson, "Of Mimicry and Membership: Africans and the 'New World Society,'" *Cultural Anthropology* 17, no. 4 (2002): 876.

[185] Stuart Croft, *Strategies of Arms Control: A History and Typology* (Manchester: Manchester University Press, 1996).

[186] Bhabha, *Location of Culture*, 95.

[187] Fabian, *Time and the Other*, 223–23.

[188] Fabian, *Time and the Other*, 62–63.

[189] Fabian, *Time and the Other*, 62–63.

[190] Fabian, *Time and the Other*, 63.

easily absorbs historical time.[191] These practices of sly civility categorize time in an effort to 'demarcate the earlier story from the later narrative.'[192] Such 'devices of temporal distancing' provide indications of how the past was perceived.[193] Thus for instance, there is an assumption of 'a greater danger to global order from new nuclear weapons-possessing countries, rather than from the arsenals of the acknowledged nuclear powers, even if this assumption is rarely acknowledged,' and this practice is further reinforced,

> By identifying the first nuclear test as the moment when a threshold has been crossed—the historic moment—analysts have effectively reduced the variety of histories of any nuclear program to the path that led to this particular outcome. The multiple meanings of nuclear power are shrunk into one register—the desire to produce weapons—an analytic shortcoming with both real world and conceptual implications.[194]

The evolutive practices of temporal distancing shrewdly conceal a politics of erasure of temporality as a problem in constituting structural discourses of the West and the Rest. On the contrary there is a diversion of attention toward taxonomy of cultures and the quest for universality. This denial of coevalness is further maintained through varying strategies of circumvention and pre-emption.[195] Taxonomic rewriting and a 'temporal conception of time' serve as a guise to a militarist 'ideology whose ultimate purpose has been to justify the procurement of commodities for our markets' such as uranium from Africa.[196] This taxonomic rewriting of West and the Rest 'is a drawn-out, serious game' and 'behind the mask of the modest, candid, and tentative bricoleur hides a player who is out to win'[197]—win the taxonomic game by 'demonstrating synchronic relations of order beneath the flux and confusion of historical events.'[198] But as Fabian cautions, the outcome of taxonomic games is 'a hierarchy made up

[191] Fabian, *Time and the Other*, 103.
[192] Fabian, *Time and the Other*, 103.
[193] Thapar, *Time as a Metaphor of History*, 37.
[194] Itty Abraham, "The Ambivalence of Nuclear Histories," *Osiris* 21, no. 1 (2006): 51.
[195] Fabian, *Time and the Other*, 37–38.
[196] Fabian, *Time and the Other*, 95.
[197] Fabian, *Time and the Other*, 98–99.
[198] Fabian, *Time and the Other*, 99.

of relationships of order which are sequential and irreversible, hence the seriousness of the taxonomic game.'[199]

To summarize, civilizational time encourages a politics of continuous negation that is often reproduced in abstract, chronological and evolutionary accounts of arms control and disarmament. Civilizational time and its politics of negation make allowances for the constitution of cultural and political identities through a process of alterity. In this process, 'while the phantom figure of the pure Indian becomes the object of desire by the First World, that same Indian tends to be the cause of unease if not the object of erasure in the Third World.'[200] The signs deployed in constituting these identities

> [i]ndicate not only the degree to which that national identity in a Latin American country is bound to First World criteria and First World recognition of palatable and rousing difference, but that carriers of that national identity, which is to say the elites as much as the populace at large, are placed in a basically untenable ambivalence—neither truly Indian nor truly civilized, and forever at the beck and call of the White House.[201]

The two figures of alterity that the White House invokes are the 'noble savage' located within the primitive end of the evolutionary scale, consensual, conforming, collusive and potentially assimilable; and the 'dirty dog' that is inscrutable, dissenting and threatening, and cannot be accommodated and therefore is to be eradicated through violence.[202] These figures of alterity represent limits of tolerance in practices of arms control and disarmament seeking to maintain a particular civilizational order. These figures of alterity generate anxieties that on the one hand 'deflect' attention from the conformists and on the other 'sustain' a perpetual sense of anxiety from the dirty dog.[203] The Western European nationalists applied a socio-cultural pressure to indigenous populations that 'left only one

[199] Fabian, *Time and the Other*, 99.

[200] Michael Taussig, *Mimesis and Alterity: A Particular History of the Senses* (New York & London: Routledge, 1993), 142.

[201] Taussig, *Mimesis and Alterity*, 143.

[202] Shampa Biswas, *Nuclear Desire: Power and the Postcolonial Nuclear Order* (University of Minnesota Press, 2014), 42. Also read Tzetvan Todorov, *The Conquest of America: The Question of the Other* (Oklahoma: University of Oklahoma Press, 1999).

[203] Shampa Biswas, *Nuclear Desire: Power and the Postcolonial Nuclear Order* (University of Minnesota Press, 2014), 46.

rational response: abject imitation as a condition of survival and self-affirmation.'[204]

Taussig suggests that the strategies of mimesis and alterity are deployed toward 'sustaining the realpolitik of these situations.'[205] He argues that there is a deliberate deployment of

> a powerful modern mythology of good savage and bad savage by which the whites of Europe and North America purify themselves through using the good savage to purge the bad one. ... This Janus faced sense of the savage corresponds to the great mythologies of modern progress. The good savage is representative of unsullied origin, a sort of Eden before the Fall when harmony prevailed, while the bad savage is the sign of the permanent wound inflicted by history, the sign of waste, degeneracy, and thwarted narrative.[206]

To grasp these experiences of profound anxiety in civilizational time with its practices of sly civility, mimetic figures of alterity, iteration and reiteration of stereotypes, it is imperative that we 'focus on those moments or processes that are produced in the articulation of cultural difference.'[207]

It is suggested that cultural difference is produced and reproduced through 'a process of signification through which statements of culture or on culture differentiate, discriminate and authorize the production of fields of force, reference, applicability and capacity.'[208] It is also helpful to note how the 'mythology of color' produces a 'hierarchy of alterities within a colonial mosaic of attractions and repulsions.'[209] This mythology of color gets stitched into the 'cultural apparatus of work and bureaucracy' in a remarkable 'feat of racial engineering.'[210] Taussig suggests,

> Racism is seen as a manifestation of what is essential to modern civilization's cultural apparatus, namely continuous mimetic repression—understanding mimesis as both the faculty of imitation and the deployment of that faculty in sensuous knowing, sensuous Othering.[211]

[204] Hom, "Hegemonic metronome," 1164.
[205] Taussig, *Mimesis and Alterity*, 142.
[206] Taussig, *Mimesis and Alterity*, 142.
[207] Bhabha, *The Location of Culture*, 2.
[208] Bhabha, *Location of Culture*, 6.
[209] Taussig, *Mimesis and Alterity*, 144–145.
[210] Taussig, *Mimesis and Alterity*, 145.
[211] Taussig, *Mimesis and Alterity*, 68.

It is in this context of 'sensuous knowing' that in articulating 'objectives of arms control' foundational scholars such as Thomas Schelling, Hedley Bull and Bernard Brodie have articulated ideas on 'tacit restraint.'[212] Brodie has explicitly observed how 'it was once right to make the point that the kind of arms control that may be most important in the long run is that which depends on tacit rather than explicit agreement' and that 'the objectives of arms control are usually not stated, but when they are stated, they are rarely if ever reflectively considered.'[213] This idea of 'sensuous knowing' in practices of weapons control is further reinforced by drawing attention to the significance of the language of 'probability' to argue that the 'probability of war' cannot be addressed adequately through practices of arms control and that 'in a pragmatic approach to arms control the objective of saving money deserves a superior rating to that of saving the world.'[214]

An awareness of such observations made by those writing foundational texts on weapons control as noted above is not to deny the possibility that in the enunciation of cultural differences the 'intersubjective and collective experiences' are negotiated.[215] But it is helpful to acknowledge that during these negotiations there is a possibility of 'power of tradition' being reinscribed through conditions of contingency and contradictories, rendering these 'engagements of cultural difference' often as much 'consensual as conflictual.'[216] To quote Bhabha,

> The subject of the discourse of cultural difference is dialogical or transferential in the style of psychoanalysis. It is constituted through the locus of the Other which suggests both that the object of identification is ambivalent, and more significantly, that the agency of identification is never pure or holistic but always constituted in a process of substitution, displacement or projection.[217]

[212] Robert Ayson, "Arms Control in Asia: yesterday's concept for today's region?" *Australian Journal of International Affairs* 67, no. 1 (2013): 8–9.

[213] Bernard Brodie, "On the Objectives of Arms Control," *International Security* 1, no. 1 (1976): 18.

[214] Brodie, "Objectives of Arms Control," 19.

[215] Bhabha, *The Location of Culture*, 2.

[216] Bhabha, *Location of Culture*, 3.

[217] Bhabha, *Location of Culture*, 233.

Any claims to a particular identity are 'nominative or normative,' capable of 'turning up in-and-as other's difference and turning the right to signify into an act of cultural translation.'[218] There is a denial of reflexivity based on memory that would enable a sharing of 'each other's past in order to be knowingly in each other's present.'[219] Any effort to decry and resist civilizational practices of stereotyping and sly civility based on an evolutive understanding of time through recourse to mimetic assertion of rights and equality carries the possibility of representing a 'sad figure of lack and failure.'[220] Thus, it is only by configuring the 'maneuvers made within the space of the mimetic' that a critical, postcolonial scholar can hope to address the problem of temporal difference and its implications for negotiating weapons control between the West and the Rest.[221] Tracing and configuring these mimetic maneuvers in practices of arms control and disarmament in the following chapters demand a sensuous knowing, a postcolonial sensibility of time or postcolonial time. This is imperative as the resilience and constraints of civilizational discourses in weapons control can often produce 'habits of insensibility' toward suffering.[222]

Postcolonial Time

To address the problem of human suffering, it is therefore helpful to suggest that postcolonial time be understood as a disposition toward time and not as a harbinger of a 'clear cut point of origin.'[223] A disposition that is willing to question whether 'the use of time as a neutral, universal variable ... cloaks a system that carefully preserves spatial distance and separation.'[224] A disposition that is critical of practices of distancing and separation via time, reinforcing the message that 'such societies live in another time' and time was 'a device to define the otherness of those societies.'[225] It encourages a disposition willing to explore the possibility 'once the idea of change is disconnected from the idea of progress or

[218] Bhabha, *Location of Culture*, 335.

[219] Fabian, *Time and the Other*, 92.

[220] Dipesh Chakraborty, *Provincializing Europe: Postcolonial Thought and Historical Difference* (Princeton & Oxford: Princeton University Press, 2000), 40.

[221] Chakraborty, *Provincializing Europe*, 40–41.

[222] Chakraborty, *Provincializing Europe*, 122.

[223] Chakraborty, *Provincializing Europe*, 122.

[224] Aganthangelou and Killian, *Time, Temporality and Violence*, 14.

[225] Thapar, *Time as a Metaphor of History*, 6.

evolution' does it then become 'simply a question of recognizing patterns of adaptation to the "new" and different levels of shock that the "new" brings about'?

It is with these questions and disposition that a postcolonial understanding of time is now acutely conscious of 'the timing of decisions to acquire nuclear power' and willing to complicate 'our usual linear assumptions about the influence of the past on present and future.'[226] A postcolonial understanding of time is willing to engage with the problem of heterotemporality.[227] Thapar contends,

> [T]ime concepts and historical change interact in as much as change can be projected as either repetitive, recurrent or periodic, pointing to a wide stretch of time concepts, ranging from what are viewed as the cyclical to the continuously progressive and directional, suggesting a linear form, with many in-between positions such as a wave or a spiral.[228]

Postcolonial scholars grappling with the problem of change in arms control and disarmament struggle to 'dismantle fictions based on linear narrations' and emphasize a need to 'historicize the present.'[229] But this effort to 'historicize the present' is critical of practices of historicism, as a mode of thinking, articulated in the temporal structure of the statement 'First in the West, and then elsewhere.'[230] These practices of historicism seek to provide 'a frame of a single and secular historical time that envelops other kinds of time.'[231] They produce 'a zero point in history … a tabula rasa' that prevents us from engaging with the problem of 'temporal heterogeneity' and 'reduces the past to a nullity.'[232]

According to postcolonial scholars, this form of historicism has pernicious effects.[233] These effects can be summarized as follows: First, it posits 'historical time as a measure of cultural distance (at least in institutional development) that was assumed to exist between the West and the

[226] Itty Abraham, "'Who's Next?' Nuclear Ambivalence and the Contradictions of Non-Proliferation Policy," *Economic and Political Weekly* 49, no. 43 (2010): 50.

[227] Anca Pusca, "Walter Benjamin, a Methodological Contribution," *International Political Sociology* 3, no. 2 (2009): 239.

[228] Thapar, *Time as a Metaphor of History*, 8.

[229] Aganthangelou and Killian, *Time, Temporality and Violence*, 10.

[230] Chakraborty, *Provincializing Europe*, 6.

[231] Chakraborty, *Provincializing Europe*, 16.

[232] Chakraborty, *Provincializing Europe*, 244.

[233] Chakraborty, *Provincializing Europe*, 7–8, 224–225

non-West.' Second, this denial of coevalness became the ground for legitimating 'the idea of civilization' in the colonies. Time management understood in terms of 'the Victorian fetishes of discipline, routine and order management'' are 'now extolled as critical to the civilization of the country.'[234] Third, it encouraged 'internalist histories of Europe' in which Europe became the site of 'first occurrence' with respect to each and every event of any historical significance.[235] Fourth, it promoted the view that 'to understand anything it has to be seen as a unity and in its historical development.'[236] As a result, this form of historicist consciousness serves a 'recommendation to the colonized to wait' and encourages a 'way of saying "not yet" to somebody else.'[237] Fifth, this 'not yet' is reinforced with practices of anachronism that 'circulate only in a mood of frustration, despair and resentment' that seek to reify the past in terms of the West and the Rest.

A postcolonial critique of contemporary practices of historicism encourages us to problematize 'dominant historical discourses' and question 'calcified nuclear histories.'[238] The urgency of this task is articulated by Itty Abraham in the following words:

> [A] discourse of "control," authored by the overlapping narratives of academic proliferation studies and US antiproliferation policy, has come to dominate our understanding of nuclear histories. This discourse, with its primary purpose of seeking to predict which countries are likely to build nuclear weapons and thereby to threaten the prevailing military-strategic status-quo, has narrowed the gaze of nuclear historians.[239]

Abraham argues against practices of historicism that 'desire to discipline,' exhibit a 'tendency to isolate' and fail to appreciate any 'excesses of meaning' that might 'flow' from 'ideas, rules, procedures and techniques' that might give us 'another history of nuclearism.'[240] There is a further insistence that any endeavor to 'open up nuclear history' be willing to

[234] Chakraborty, *Provincializing Europe*, 7–8, 224–225.
[235] Chakraborty, *Provincializing Europe*, 7–8.
[236] Chakraborty, *Provincializing Europe*, 6.
[237] Chakraborty, *Provincializing Europe*, 8.
[238] Itty Abraham, "The Ambivalence of Nuclear Histories," *Osiris* 21, no. 1 (2006): 50, 56.
[239] Abraham, "Ambivalence of Nuclear Histories," 49.
[240] Abraham, "Ambivalence of Nuclear Histories," 55.

'explore its intimate relationship with the state project of legitimacy in the modern era.'[241]

In acknowledging this struggle for legitimacy and modernity, a critical disposition toward contemporary practices of historicism further encourages us to pause and recollect 'politics as war' discourses based on race not only radicalize differences between different identity groups, they also question 'the purportedly inclusive and universalistic discourses on modern politics' as being 'partisan.'[242] These politics as war discourses based on race serve as a 'direct attack on the institutions and rationalizations of the modern sovereign state, including modern understandings of law.'[243] The 'political legitimacy' of modern 'laws and rights' is not necessarily always based on the strength of one group over another, but on 'pacified universality' which can be denounced if we recognize discourses of law and rights as instruments of ongoing war by other means.[244] To quote Julian Reid, 'political sovereignty invests and takes over the decentering discourses of race struggle and turns it to its own universalizing ends.'[245] To contest these universalizing claims, postcolonial time has to be cognizant of postcolonial science to interrogate 'broad, cultural or civilizational conceptual frameworks limiting certain kinds of knowledge-seeking projects.'[246]

Sandra Harding observes that the West has 'a problem figuring out how to refer to the science and technology tradition of other cultures.'[247] It has tried to address this problem by conceptualizing and contrasting modern science and the 'rational man' (European) by castigating,

> non-European cultures' magic, witchcraft, pre-logical thought, superstitions or pseudosciences; with "folk explanations" or ethnosciences that are embedded in religious, anthropomorphic, and other only local belief systems; with merely technological achievements or merely speculative claims about the natural world; or with "precursors" to true sciences.[248]

[241] Abraham, "Ambivalence of Nuclear Histories," 56.

[242] Andrew W. Neal, "Goodbye War on Terror? Foucault and Butler on Discourses of Law, War and Exceptionalism," in *Foucault on Politics, Security and War*, ed. Michael Dillon and Andrew W. Neal (New York: Palgrave Macmillan, 2008), 53.

[243] Neal, "Goodbye War," 53, 56.

[244] Neal, "Goodbye War," 61.

[245] Reid, "Life Struggles," 85–86.

[246] Harding, *Is Science Multicultural?*, 163.

[247] Harding, *Is Science Multicultural?*, 10.

[248] Harding, *Is Science Multicultural?* 9.

She insists that efforts be made to study how 'the epistemic status of sciences and technologies are always socially negotiated.'[249] This will help cultivate an alternative 'conceptual framework of postcolonial science and technology studies' which is 'organized from the standpoint of other, non-European cultures and the great masses of the world's economically and politically most vulnerable people who live in them.'[250] It will then be possible to 'detect features of different cultures' scientific and technological thought and practices that are not visible from within the familiar western accounts of science.'[251] In other words, the effort here is to present an alternative account of 'past, present, and future possibilities than were visible in the older, eurocentric "Tunnel of time" accounts of European and other scientific and technological traditions.'[252]

Postcolonial science problematizes 'the idea that science and technology were among the gifts that Western imperial powers brought to their colonies.'[253] It is critical of practices of modern science that not only attempts to 'immunize their accounts of nature's order against all cultural elements in their making and continued use that has been responsible for their successes and their failures' but rather seeks to 'neutralize some such cultural elements while fully exploiting others that has been responsible for their successes and their failures.'[254] To advance this critique, postcolonial science pursues a standpoint epistemology to question

> assumptions generated by "ways of life" and apparent in discursive frameworks, conceptual schemes, and epistemes, within which entire dominant groups tend to think about nature and social relations, and to use such frameworks to structure social relations for the rest of us too.[255]

This exercise is to 'produce knowledge that can be for marginalized people and for those who would know what they can know, rather than for the use only of dominant groups in their projects of administering and

[249] Harding, *Is Science Multicultural?*, 53.
[250] Harding, *Is Science Multicultural?*, 8.
[251] Harding, *Is Science Multicultural?*, 8.
[252] Harding, *Is Science Multicultural?*, 37.
[253] Suman Seth, "Putting knowledge in its place: science, colonialism, and the postcolonial," *Postcolonial Studies* 12, no. 4 (2009): 373.
[254] Harding, *Is Science Multicultural?*, 7.
[255] Harding, *Is Science Multicultural?*, 150.

managing marginalized lives.'[256] For this purpose Abraham insists on studying 'contests over western scientific knowledge within contexts of colonial and postcolonial nationalism.'[257]

Sharing the vision of a postcolonial science, Mallard and Paradeise insist on cultivating a 'historical sociology of science' that will be cognizant of tensions between 'the formal requirements of equality' and the 'durable inequalities' that persist between people and states.[258]

This is imperative as the political practices of appropriation of scientific innovations, especially with regard to time and possession of nuclear weapons at the 'national and global level,' can generate and perpetuate inequalities as embodied in the Nuclear Nonproliferation Treaty (NPT).[259] The indefinite extension of the NPT amidst a resurgence of discourses reinvigorating the 'central-modernist dilemma' of European Enlightenment is probed deeper in the succeeding chapters as practices of sly civility encourage such a revival and justify such inequalities.[260] It is not enough to delimit the study of transnational scientific networks and globalization of sciences discourses to stagiest temporal metrics of Cold War and post–Cold War era. There is an urgent need for a more historically contextualized and nuanced problematization of civilizational discourses on weapons control to make visible how the intersecting discourses on racialism, nationalism and humanitarianism have complicated our engagement with the problem of weapons. This will help make visible how 'scientific disciplines and imperializing nation-states understood and thereby re wrote the social fabric in colonized societies.'[261]

It is in this endeavor that this book traces the discursive shifts with reference to heroic scientists, national scientists and rogue scientists engaged in the service of the postcolonial states from the late nineteenth century to

[256] Harding, *Is Science Multicultural?*, 154.

[257] Itty Abraham, "The Contradictory Spaces of Postcolonial Techno-Science," *Economic and Political Weekly* 41, no. 3 (2006): 211.

[258] Gregoire Mallard and Catherine Paradeise, "Global Science and National Sovereignty: A New Terrain for the Historical Sociology of Science," in *Global Science and National Sovereignty: Studies in Historical Sociology of Science*, ed. Gregoire Mallard, Catherine Paradeise and Ashveen Peerbaye (New York & London: Routledge, 2009) 10.

[259] Mallard, Paradeise and Peerbaye, "Global Science and National Sovereignty," 5.

[260] The concept of central-modernist dilemma is borrowed from Itty Abraham, "The Contradictory Spaces of Postcolonial Techno-Science," *Economic and Political Weekly* 41, no. 3 (2006): 213; Ritu Mathur, "Sly Civility in the Nuclear Order and the Paradox of Equality/Inequality in the Nuclear Order," *Critical Studies on Security* 4, no. 1 (2015): 57–72.

[261] Mallard, Paradeise and Peerbaye, "Global Science and National Sovereignty," 9.

the present. Postcolonial science acknowledges that 'scientific and technological ideas have always been the easiest to transport from one culture to another and the quickest to travel through a receiving culture's networks.'[262] Postcolonial science is conscious of the role of 'elites within colonized nations' who, 'while rejecting the notion that science was imported from the West, often shared such sentiments about science's positive and transformative powers, speaking a "language of modernity" that—however uneasily—allied them with imperialist officials.'[263] This nurturing of colonial science and nationalism is to be situated further within an understanding of postcolonial time as it mounts a challenge to civilizational time made more visible in succeeding chapters of this book.

Vulnerability of Time

It is therefore not surprising that 'decolonization movements, however, quickly began to call into question any vision of science, as a positive enterprise that merely accompanied—and did not aid or support—a rapacious colonialism.'[264] A quest for change from anachronistic linear, evolutive and civilizational discourses on time in pursuit of equality and social justice might be facilitated if we remember accelerating technological developments 'reduce spatial and temporal constraints on interactions' and 'suggest vulnerability in Western standard time's reign.'[265] This vulnerability might also stem from a possibility that the 'modern techniques of time measurement' and 'the mechanization of human habits prepared the way for mechanical imitations' in the form of weapons that can challenge primacy of the West over the Rest.[266]

This vulnerability of the 'now' as represented in the calibrated movement of the Doomsday Clock, two minutes to a nuclear holocaust, provides us with two interesting alternatives. One is to take recourse to productive anachronisms that reify differences articulated in civilizational discourses of the West and the Rest forecasting an impending clash of civilizations due to failure to control the horizontal spread of nuclear weapons. The other is to initiate a step in the direction of encouraging an

[262] Harding, *Is Science Multicultural?* 8.
[263] Seth, "Putting knowledge in its place," 373.
[264] Seth, "Putting knowledge in its place," 373.
[265] Hom, "Hegemonic metronome," 1170.
[266] Landes, "Clocks and the wealth of nations," *Deadalus* 132, no. 2 (2003): 26.

understanding of temporal heterogeneity in practices of weapons control. This might be possible by problematizing and making visible particular mimetic maneuvers in an evolutive understanding of civilizational time wielding its productive power via practices of stereotyping, sly civility and mimesis. These civilizational discourses in weapons control have been briefly discussed above and will be embellished further in the text. For the present it is important to heed the dire warning that 'predominantly military forms of civilization have proved self-destructive.'[267]

The Doomsday Clock as a wish image alerts us to the dangerous anachronistic revival of civilizational discourses with all their temporal and spatial implications in the practices of arms control and disarmament that, if not analyzed with care, carries the potential of sweeping us into yet another armed conflict. This chapter, with its brief understanding of myriad representations of time and time as a constituent of civilizational discourses in security studies, is an invitation to pause and dwell on the contemporary acceleration of civilizational discourses, to make visible the recurrence of the productive power of these discourses in the field of security studies. This then sets the stage for exploring contemporary temporal strategies of writing race by reifying civilizational differences between the West and the Rest in practices of arms control and disarmament.

* * *

[267] Mumford, *Technics and Civilization*, 64.

CHAPTER 2

The West and the Rest: A Civilizational Mantra

Introduction

The reiteration and circulation of epistemological violence espoused in the civilizational mantra of 'West and the Rest' in the field of arms control and disarmament for centuries need to be pursued further. In this chapter we deliberate on how contemporary discourses on civilization facilitate the demarcation, regulation, legislation and transformation of temporal hierarchies in arms control and disarmament. How has civilization as a rhetorical resource been deployed in the field of arms control and disarmament? How has arms control and disarmament become associated with a very particular form of institutionalized paranoia encapsulated in the rubric of 'the West and the Rest'? It is a form of 'persecutory paranoia' that must be questioned rigorously with the help of some key insights provided by postcolonial scholars questioning the deployment of hegemonic discourses in security studies.[1]

Thus, in interrogating the potential for identity and alterity or the politics of temporal difference it might be worthwhile to enquire whether the field of international relations has seen a gestalt shift from the juxtaposition of the idea of 'the World and the West' to 'the West and the Rest.'[2] Interestingly this gestalt shift occurred within a time lag of half a century

[1] Arnold Toynbee, *The World and the West* (New York & London: Oxford University Press, 1953); Samuel Huntington, "Clash of Civilization," *Foreign Affairs* 72, no. 3 (1993):22–49.

[2] Toynbee, *The World and the West*; Huntington, "Clash of Civilization," *Foreign Affairs* 72, no. 3 (1993):22–49; Huntington, *The Clash of Civilizations and the Remaking of World Order* (New York: Simon & Schuster, 1997).

R. Mathur, *Civilizational Discourses in Weapons Control*,
https://doi.org/10.1007/978-3-030-44943-8_2

marking the end of the Second World War and then the end of the Cold War, respectively. In the immediate aftermath of the Cold War, characterized as an era of 'turbulence in the world order,' several scholars, such as Francis Fukuyama, Samuel Huntington and others, have championed the idea of the end of history, proclaimed the victory of the West and regurgitated the idea of 'The Clash of Civilizations.'[3] These discourses have become a part of an easy formula for remapping the world order and waging global wars on terror, in populist terms of 'the West and the Rest' espoused by scholars and practitioners working in the field of security studies.

In 1953, Arnold Toynbee, a historian of world politics, published a book *The World and the West*.[4] In this book Toynbee deliberated on the question: 'Why could he not write "The West and the World" instead of writing the "The World and the West"? He might at least have put the West first.' Toynbee argues that he chose the title 'The World and the West' deliberately for two reasons—firstly, because 'the West has never been all of the world that matters'; the second reason he offers is the following:

> In the encounter between the world and the West that has been going on by now for four or five hundred years, the world, not the West, is the party that, up to now, has had the significant experience. It has not been the West that has been hit hard by the world; it is the world that has been hit – and hit hard – by the West; and that is why, in the title of this book, the world has been put first.[5]

He further argues that the rest of the world does 'not draw fine distinctions between different hordes of 'Franks'—which is the world's common name for Westerners in the mass.'[6] He encourages the West 'to slip out of his native skin and look at the encounter between the world and the West

[3] James Rosenau, *Turbulence in World Politics* (Princeton: Princeton University Press, 1990); Francis Fukuyama, *The End of History and the Last Man* (Oxford: Penguin, reissue 2012).

[4] Arnold Toynbee, The World and the West (New York & London: Oxford University Press, 1953).

[5] Toynbee, *The World and the West* (New York & London: Oxford University Press, 1953), 1–2.

[6] Toynbee, *The World and the West*, 3.

through the eyes of the great non-Western majority of mankind.'[7] Toynbee insists that in this encounter one will learn that

> [d]ifferent though the non-Western peoples of the world may be from one another in race, language, civilization, and religion, if any Western inquirer asks them their opinion of the West, he will hear them all giving the same answer: Russians, Muslims, Hindus, Chinese, Japanese, and all the rest. The West, they will tell him, has been the arch aggressor of modern times, and each will have their own experience of Western aggression to bring up against him.'[8]

Toynbee further notes that for Westerners 'it is today still a strange experience to be suffering at the hands of the world what the world has been suffering at Western hands for a number of centuries past.'[9] In Toynbee's deliberations the idea of the West as an aggressor that has inflicted suffering on the rest of the world is articulate, and it is on the premise of the sufferings endured by the rest of the world that he is willing to place the world before the West. Thus after the end of the Second World War, Toynbee is interested in understanding the West from the viewpoint of the world and their experiences and encounters with the West. But in the last decade of the twentieth century, after the end of the Cold War, Samuel Huntington is more interested in asserting, 'How will we know who we are if we don't know who we are against?'[10]

Two Images of the West

Heroic attempts to engage with this identity crisis, experienced at the end of the Cold War, with the absence of an embodied enemy as the alter, have given rise to two contending images of the West.[11] The first image articulated by Huntington portrays the West as a 'powerful but declining entity battling to maintain its strength and influence in a world of multiple and

[7] Toynbee, *The World and the West*, 2.

[8] Toynbee, *The World and the West*, 2.

[9] Toynbee, *The World and the West*, 4.

[10] Samuel Huntington, "Clash of Civilization," *Foreign Affairs* 72, no. 3 (1993): 37, quoted in Jacinta O' Hagan, *Conceptualizing the West in International Relations* (Hampshire & New York: Palgrave, 2002), 160.

[11] O'Hagan, *Conceptualizing the West*, 1.

conflicting civilizations.'[12] The other image painted by Fukuyama argues that the 'West provides a universal model of human progress and development.'[13] These sketchy portraits of the West engrossed in the experiences of 'modern European and American history' are often critiqued for lacking in historical and cultural depth in their 'contemplation of other.'[14] These studies are viewed as attempts to represent the West as a homogenized entity masking internal differences. Furthermore, instead of locating 'the history of the West in a broader world history,' there is an attempt at treating 'world history … as Western history until the current era.'[15] This 'cultural arrogance' is particularly visible when contemporary scholars debate the 'possibility of an African civilization' or argue that African history is only a 'history of Europeans in Africa.'[16]

This parochialism or Eurocentrism in conceptualizing the West is decried by Toynbee and extolled by Spengler. Toynbee argues that this parochialism stems from Western 'cultural chauvinism' rooted in an 'egocentric illusion' of being 'a chosen people,' sharing an 'illusion of progress' while being critical in their view of others as 'unchanging and increasingly left behind by the West.'[17] But Spengler 'excused the tendency to view Western history as world history due to the unique breadth of the West's worldview.'[18] To quote Spengler, 'We men of the Western culture are, with our historical sense, an exception and not the rule. World-history is our world picture and not all mankind's.'[19] There is an emphatic insistence on 'the West is exceptional but not universal' shared to some degree by scholars articulating their ideas of the West.[20] It is the Western cultural hegemony that is held responsible for cultivating a 'false universalism' of shared norms and institutions.[21]

It is often suggested that the West is to be understood as the antithesis of other civilizations. But while a 'central force in world politics,' the

[12] O'Hagan, *Conceptualizing the West*, 1.

[13] O'Hagan, *Conceptualizing the West*, 1.

[14] O'Hagan, *Conceptualizing the West,* 214–215.

[15] O'Hagan, *Conceptualizing the West*, 182, 174.

[16] Samuel Huntington, "Clash of Civilization," 22–49; Ali A. Mazrui, ed., *The Warrior Tradition in Modern Africa* (Leiden: E.J. Brill, 1977), 1.

[17] Toynbee's ideas presented by Jacinta O'Hagan, *Conceptualizing the West*, 101.

[18] O'Hagan, *Conceptualizing the West*, 77.

[19] Spengler cited in O'Hagan, *Conceptualizing the West*, 77; Oswald Spengler, *Decline of the West* (New York: A.A. Knopf, 1928), 12.

[20] O'Hagan, *Conceptualizing the West,* 78.

[21] O'Hagan, *Conceptualizing the West,* 229.

character, composition and agency of the West remain contested.[22] This ambivalence in constituting the West is projected as 'perhaps from this fluidity or plasticity that the idea of the West derives its power and continued currency, allowing it to flow across and coexist with, existing local and regional communities and identities.'[23] This raises the perplexing question of 'how can we understand the co-existence of complex and multiple images of the West without seeking to authorize any of these.'[24] The 'tendency to shy away' from a particular image of the West as a civilization may be embedded in a reluctance to take on board 'how, or if the cultural specificity of the legacy constrains its broader relevance to world politics.'[25]

In any effort to conceptualize the identity of the West there is 'a marked tendency ... to conceive of the West, or argue it conceives of itself, at the apex of a technical and normative hierarchy.'[26] The West is repeatedly cautioned against 'squandering its privileges by foolishly liquidating its monopoly of technical knowledge,' and constant fear is reiterated against the industrialization of other societies. This emphasis on hierarchy generates a concern toward maintaining the status quo and dismal accounts of inter-civilizational encounters. These encounters between the West and the others, according to Spengler, often lead to some cultures being 'snuffed out, 'their creative spirit stifled' and being discarded as the 'scrap material' of history.[27] Toynbee too voices his suspicion of how 'pressure of contact with the West' and 'borrowing of elements of Western culture' contributed toward the breakdown of other civilizations.[28] The contempt for the non-Western civilizations becomes most visible in Spengler's writings when he argues that they can inherit the tools but not the spirit of the West and that their acquisition of science and technology amounted to 'little more than an impressive act of imitation.'[29] In these encounters between the West and the others 'monopoly of technical power and knowledge' is considered to be critical and the solid foundation of West's superior military capacity.

[22] O'Hagan, *Conceptualizing the West,* 9.
[23] O'Hagan, *Conceptualizing the West,* 9.
[24] O'Hagan, *Conceptualizing the West,* 15.
[25] O'Hagan, *Conceptualizing the West,* 14–15.
[26] O'Hagan, *Conceptualizing the West,* 214, 229.
[27] O'Hagan, *Conceptualizing the West,* 64.
[28] O'Hagan, *Conceptualizing the West,* 86–88.
[29] O'Hagan, *Conceptualizing the West,* 80. See reference to Farrenkopf, 1993, p. 399.

Bowden further notes how in the nineteenth-century civilizational discourses in the West, there is an acute emphasis on 'race is everything … civilization depends on it' and an understanding that 'the racial question overshadows all other problems of history' is a key consideration.[30] Toynbee too acknowledges 'race as an important source of differentiation' between the West and the Rest.[31] In contemporary representations of the West it is argued that the 'role of race is least explicit … but it is not absent,' and 'although it is often implicit, racial boundaries contribute both to a sense of the West's identity and to its powerful position in each of these conceptions.'[32] In these civilizational discourses considerations of race appear to exacerbate civilizational differences and it is questionable whether contemporary civilizational discourses with their emphasis on technology can mitigate civilizational differences through standardization.

Contemporary Civilizational Discourses

This problem is significant as scholars argue that 'contemporary neo-racism has found one of its most complete articulations in the work of American IR theorist Samuel Huntington.'[33] The infamous credit for perpetuation of the language of civilizational differences in the last decade of the twentieth century is attributed to Huntington and his book *The Clash of Civilizations and Remaking of the World Order.* In this text, Huntington argues that the 'the idea of civilization was developed by French thinkers as the opposite of the concept of 'barbarism.'[34] The deployment of the term 'civilization' as a 'proxy for race' is a deft sleight of hand by Huntington to reproduce 'common-sense, racialised hierarchies.'[35] In his effort to remap the world order, Huntington encourages us to think that a narrow understanding of civilization focused on 'mechanics, technology, and material factors' has to be supplemented with cultural practices

[30] Brett Bowden, *The Empire of Civilization: The Evolution of an Imperial Idea* (Chicago: University of Chicago Press, 2009), 57–58.

[31] O'Hagan, *Conceptualizing the West,* 219.

[32] O'Hagan, *Conceptualizing the West,* 220.

[33] Short and Kambouri, "Ambiguous universalism," 278.

[34] Huntington, *The Clash of Civilizations and the Remaking of World Order* (New York: Simon & Schuster, 1997), 40.

[35] Short and Kambouri, "Ambiguous universalism," 279.

focused on 'values, norms, institutions.'[36] It is this 'incommensurability of cultures' that is 'essentialized as a "biological" fact in the same way appearance and ancestry functioned in previous racisms.'[37]

While 'Huntington is careful not to fall into the trap of "old fashioned" biologism' and 'in his analysis there is no reference to race as a set of external distinct traits, such as skin color or other physical characteristics,'[38] he does suggest that nineteenth-century Europeans devoted their energies toward 'elaborating the criteria by which non-Western societies might be judged to be sufficiently "civilized" to be accepted as members of the European dominated international system.'[39] Although Huntington acknowledges the elitism associated with these practices, he makes little attempt to cite these scholars or explicate their specific criteria and their application to particular practices such as arms control and disarmament. The demand for these criteria and their application is significant because the 'relevance of the civilizational paradigm' articulated by Huntington is not an ahistorical suggestion, and his rhetorical efforts to cite weapons proliferation as an 'intercivilizational issue' that positions the 'West and the Rest' in confrontation with each other deserve careful consideration.[40] Thus the problem of arms regulation and prohibition is not simply a technical one but also culturally embedded in subtle practices of neo-racism deployed to regulate and prohibit weapons.

In forecasting a future conflict between the 'West vs the rest,' Huntington 'does not conflate the word "civilization" with the superiority of a single culture' but uses 'the term in plural to signify 'his intention to distinguish his theoretical account of contemporary world politics from ideological legitimizations of the West as a single superior civilization.'[41] However, this does not prevent him from describing the non-proliferation efforts of the West as efforts 'to maintain its military superiority through policies of nonproliferation and counter-proliferation with respect to nuclear, biological, chemical weapons and the means to deliver them.' He astutely comments that '[t]he West promotes nonproliferation as reflecting the interests of all nations in international order and stability. Other nations, however, see non-proliferation, as serving the interests of Western

[36] Huntington, *The Clash of Civilizations and the Remaking of World Order*, 41.
[37] Short and Kambouri, "Ambiguous universalism," 278.
[38] Short and Kambouri, "Ambiguous universalism," 278.
[39] Huntington, *The Clash of Civilizations and the Remaking of World Order*, 41.
[40] Huntington, *The Clash of Civilizations and the Remaking of World Order*, 8.
[41] Short and Kambouri, "Ambiguous universalism," 278.

hegemony.' Huntington cites the growing nexus of cooperation between the Islamic-Sinic civilizations 'to develop their military capabilities, particularly weapons of mass destruction and the missiles for delivering them, so as to counter the conventional military superiority of the West.'

Huntington describes these practices of arms regulation and prohibition as 'arms buildup versus hold-down,' in the course of which

> [t]he West's antagonists are attempting to acquire weapons of mass destruction and the West is attempting to prevent them from doing so. It is not a case of buildup versus buildup but rather of buildup versus hold-down. The size and capabilities of the West's nuclear arsenal are not, apart from rhetoric, part of the competition. The outcome of an arms race of buildup depends on the resources, commitment, and technological competence of the two sides. It is not foreordained. The outcome of a race between buildup and hold-down is more predictable. The hold-down efforts of the West may slow the weapons buildup of other societies, but they will not stop it. The economic and social development of non-Western societies, the commercial incentives for all societies Western and non-Western to make money through the sale of weapons, technology, and expertise, and the political motives of core states and regional powers to protect their local hegemonies, all work to subvert Western hold-down efforts.[42]

Huntington cites several examples of difficulties in renewing arms control and disarmament agreements and their violations by weapons technology exchanges among actors belonging to conflicting civilizations.[43] He also identifies the desire to 'protect local hegemonies' and benefit commercially from the 'sale of weapons, technology and expertise' as the motive forces driving the Others to compete with the West. These claims are reinforced with selectively typologized and projected taxonomic responses of how the non-West is engaging in practices of bandwagoning, isolation and balancing vis-à-vis the West.[44]

Huntington is not interested in investigating how civilizational practices reiterated and reinforced can be obstructing progress in the field of arms control and disarmament. There is almost complete silence within the arms control and disarmament community with respect to Huntington's

[42] Huntington, *The Clash of Civilizations and the Remaking of World Order* (New York: Simon & Schuster, 1997), 190–191.

[43] Huntington, *The Clash of Civilizations and the Remaking of World Order*, 36, 193.

[44] Huntington, "Clash of Civilization," *Foreign Affairs* 72, no. 3 (1993):22–49.

observations. This is not surprising if we accept Short and Kambouri's claim that

> Huntington does not purport to judge the content of civilizational differences; rather, his point of departure is an acceptance of a general incompatibility of worldviews which is precisely why there is a broadly mutual need for the civilizational curtain. Huntington deems such a curtain necessary to avoid conflict and *to protect difference*.[45]

Interestingly it is this legitimacy of difference that is being catapulted to articulate 'a theory of contemporary neo-racism founded on a biologism that is presumably anti-racist.'[46] Short and Kambouri urge one to be vigilant toward manipulable 'neo-racist aesthetics' of visibility/invisibility in contemporary discourses on nationalism and civilization.[47]

This observation is significant because despite his rhetoric that an arms hold-down strategy will be subverted by the non-West, Huntington is surprisingly confident in proposing the idea of constituting a 'universal civilization.'[48] His work 'appeals to a sense of cosmopolitan tolerance while reasserting the dangerous nature of difference.'[49] In configuring the form of a universal civilization Huntington suggests that 'the emerging universal state of Western civilization is not an empire but rather a compound of federations, confederations, and international regimes and organizations.'[50] He further claims that a universal civilization is 'a distinctive product of Western civilization' deployed to achieve economic and cultural domination that is decried by non-Western civilizations as 'a threat' and denounced as 'nefarious imperialism.'[51] He acknowledges the need for a shared language in constituting a universal civilization but expresses his doubts about the language of human rights as a shared language.[52] Huntington claims, 'The non-West sees as Western what the

[45] Short and Kambouri, "Ambiguous universalism," 280.
[46] Short and Kambouri, "Ambiguous universalism," 281.
[47] Short and Kambouri, "Ambiguous universalism," 285.
[48] Huntington, *The Clash of Civilizations and the Remaking of World Order*, 56.
[49] Short and Kambouri, "Ambiguous universalism," 278.
[50] Huntington, *The Clash of Civilizations and the Remaking of World Order*, 53.
[51] Huntington, *The Clash of Civilizations and the Remaking of World Order*, 66.
[52] Huntington, *The Clash of Civilizations and the Remaking of World Order*, 59.

West sees as universal,'[53] thus providing a perfect example of 'the neo-racist politics of ambiguous universalism.'[54]

The 'neo-racist' logic of Huntington's work has been condemned for 'normalizing' the 'process of constructing foreign cultures as threatening and violence against people belonging to these cultures as legitimate.'[55] Huntington's prognosis of a 'clash of civilizations' is critiqued as an attempt to 'freeze the other non-Western civilizations … into fixed entities juxtaposed to a dynamic West.'[56] Cox argues that 'Huntington's metaphor for the "clash" was geological, the movement of tectonic plates, which emphasizes the solidity and impermeability of the entities in question: the impermeability of civilization.'[57] But Katzenstein concurs with Huntington on the existence of plural civilizations and that 'under specific conditions … political coalitions and intellectual currents can create ***primordial civilizational categories*** that are believed to be unitary and may even be believed to have the capacity to act.'[58] While it is explained that 'primordial civilizational discourse naturalizes particular institutional or practical arrangements, and thus it can create actorhood, validating dispositional theories of civilization,' the 'specific conditions' that 'create' these primordial civilizational categories are not elaborated at any great length.[59]

Katzenstein refutes Huntington's location of clash of civilizations in an anarchical international system to suggest that

> civilizations as configurations, constellations, or complexes … are not fixed in space or time. They are both internally highly differentiated and culturally loosely integrated. Because they are differentiated, civilizations transplant selectively, not wholesale. Because they are culturally loosely integrated, they generate debate and contestations. And, as social constructions of primordiality, civilizations can become political reifications, especially when encountering other civilizations.[60]

[53] Huntington, *The Clash of Civilizations and the Remaking of World Order*, 66.

[54] Short and Kambouri, "Ambiguous universalism," 292.

[55] Short and Kambouri, "Ambiguous universalism," 291.

[56] Robert Cox, "Consciousness and civilization: the Inside Story," paper presented at York University, Toronto, October 29, 2012.

[57] Cox, "Consciousness and civilization: the Inside Story."

[58] Peter Katzenstein, ed. *Civilizations in World Politics—Plural and Pluralist Perspectives* (London & New York: Routledge, 2010), 7 (italics inserted).

[59] Katzenstein, *Civilizations in World Politics,* 12, 7.

[60] Katzenstein, *Civilizations in World Politics,* 5–6 (italics inserted).

Thus for Katzenstein, civilizations exist in the plural and they coexist with each other within one '*civilization of modernity*, or what we often call today a global world.'[61]

A civilization of modernity is espoused to be 'a secular, technological social order based on a normative commitment to the expansion of human rights and the improvement of human welfare. This civilization of modernity interacts with and is constituted by a plurality of civilizations.'[62] It is important to temper this argument on plurality of civilizations and civilization of modernity by remembering that 'modernity—or more specifically, Western modernity and all of its inherent values'—is the condition to which all societies are expected 'to aspire if they are to be admitted into contemporary international society and afforded all its rights and privileges.'[63] The emphasis on a civilization of modernity generates a dilemma or a paradox for postcolonial people:

> On the one hand, (a Nonwestern state) has to root itself in the soil of its past, forge a national spirit, and unfurl this spiritual and cultural revindication before the colonialist's personality. But in order to take part in modern civilization, it is necessary at the same time to take part in scientific, technical, and political rationality, something which very often requires the pure and simple abandon of a whole cultural past. It is a fact: every culture cannot sustain and absorb the shock of modern civilization. There is the paradox: how to become modern and to return to sources; how to revive an old, dormant civilization and take part in universal civilization.'[64]

Katzenstein only suggests that 'silent spread, social emulation, self affirmation and explicit support' represent the 'inherent dynamism' of civilizations.[65]

While Katzenstein espouses social emulation as a strategy to strive toward a civilization of modernity and its concomitant particular rationality, other scholars suggest the possibility of mimetic maneuvers by

[61] Katzenstein, *Civilizations in World Politics*, 1.

[62] Katzenstein, *Civilizations in World Politics*, 10. Katzenstein cites Shmuel Eisenstadt (2001).

[63] Brett Bowden, *The Empire of Civilization: The Evolution of an Imperial Idea* (Chicago: University of Chicago Press, 2009), 17.

[64] Bowden, *The Empire of Civilization*, 98, see footnote 97, Bowden quotes Ricoeur to explain this paradox in an effort to explain how a postcolonial country struggles to find its personality.

[65] Katzenstein, *Civilizations in World Politics*, 35.

debating the significance of the struggle for 'personality' among postcolonial states.[66] It is these considerations of personality and not just rationality that can often play a critical role in the emphasis on the study of particular 'strategic cultures' and choice of military strategies of postcolonial states, as discussed in the following chapters. These differentialist practices of strategic culture are deemed to be significant even if the weapons technology is claimed to be imitated in practices of arms control and disarmament. It is even more difficult to accept Katzenstein's ideas on primordial civilizations and a civilization of modernity as he acknowledges that civilizations 'are not fixed in time and space.'

Katzenstein does not specify the conditions that create primordial categories except when different civilizations 'encounter' each other without any explication of encounters themselves. It is therefore more plausible to suggest that 'temporal movement' prevents 'identities from settling into primordial polarities.'[67] It can also be argued that instead of a 'civilization of modernity' suggested by Katzenstein, there exists 'a complex process of "minoritarian modernity" that seeks to normalize a culturally essentialist understanding of modernity.[68] This understanding of modernity as a Western phenomenon espouses a commitment to science, rationality and secularism in ordering human affairs. It is not interested in the question: 'what is modernity in those colonial conditions where its imposition is itself the denial of historical freedom, civil autonomy and the "ethical: choice of refashioning?"'[69]

Katzenstein continues to insist that 'the existence of plural and pluralist civilizations is reflected in transcivilizational engagements, intercivilizational encounters and civilizational clashes.'[70] There is a tacit assumption that cultural differences embody 'acquisition or accumulation of cultural knowledge' that will produce these exchanges.[71] There is no recognition that 'cultural difference … is the momentous, if momentary, extinction of the recognizable object of culture in the disturbed artifice of its signification at the edge of experience … Instead of cross-referencing there is an effective, productive cross-cutting across sites of cultural significance, that

[66] Bowden, *The Empire of Civilization*, 98.
[67] Bhabha, *The Location of Culture*, 5.
[68] Bhabha, *Location of Culture*, 5.
[69] Bhabha, *Location of Culture*, 46.
[70] Katzenstein, *Civilizations in World Politics*, 1.
[71] Bhabha, *Location of Culture*, 179.

erases the dialectical, disciplinary sense of cultural reference.'[72] Bhabha seeks to remind Katzenstein that cultural diversity as a 'category of comparative ethics' is a dangerous double-edged sword that represents a 'radical rhetoric of the separation of totalized cultures that live unsullied ... safe ... a mythic memory of unique collective identity' based on 'recognition of pre-given cultural contents and customs; held in a time-frame of relativism' that at the same time might permit liberals to champion 'cultural exchange or the culture of humanity.'[73]

Katzenstein stipulates that 'violent clashes occur for the most part within rather than between civilizations. Encounters and engagements, reflecting multiple traditions and practices, are typically peaceful forms of borrowing that run in one direction when the technological differences between civilizations is [*sic*] large, and in both directions when they are not.'[74] Thus by a deft sleight of hand, Katzenstein has provided a scheme of classification that emphasizes the possibility of 'violent clashes' as a result of intra-civilizational disputes and not inter-civilization conflicts. He further assumes that when significant 'technological differences' exist between civilizations, this results in encounters and engagements that are 'typically peaceful' and result in one-directional transfers of technology as a form of simple borrowing. But Bhabha contends that the '"transfer of technology" does not necessarily result in a transfer of power or the displacement of a neo-colonial tradition of political control.'[75]

This confident assumption of technological differences resulting in peaceful transfers is qualified by Katsenstein's suggestion of civilizational contestations generating different processes and outcomes. These are classified into three categories:

> *One* such outcome, cultural imperialism, describes the ***unilateral imposition*** of the norms and practices of one modernity or zone of prestige upon local norms and practices that it seeks to displace or destroy. A *second* outcome describes the ***wholesale adoption*** by local actors of the format but not the content of imported cultural products and practices. ... *Finally,* a third outcome describes a ***world of hybridization*** in which local norms and practices

[72] Bhabha, *Location of Culture,* 179–183.
[73] Bhabha, *Location of Culture,* 49–50.
[74] Katzenstein, *Civilizations in World Politics,* 7.
[75] Bhabha, *Location of Culture,* 347.

> are altered by selectively appropriating imported practices and thus reshaping civilizational processes.[76]

In other words, Katzenstein suggests three taxonomic possibilities from civilizational contestations: cultural imposition, cultural adoption and cultural hybridization.

While for Huntington 'conflict derives from the mixture of civilizations, from hybridity, from confusing the boundaries between different cultures,'[77] the concept of cultural hybridization articulated by Katzenstein is a process of selective alteration and appropriation of local norms and practices through importation. It is not an 'ambivalent space where the rite of power is enacted on the site of desire, making its objects at once disciplinary and disseminary.'[78] Thus, Katzenstein makes no effort to deliberate on 'hybridization of discourse and power' produced through a 'strategy of disavowal' that entails,

> a process of splitting as the condition of subjection: a discrimination between the mother cultureX and its bastards, the self and its doubles, where the trace of what is disavowed is not repressed but repeated as something *different*—a mutation, a hybrid.[79]

Bhabha suggests that the hybrid 'entertains difference' through negotiation and is 'uncontainable because it breaks down the symmetry and duality of self/other, inside/outside,' and 'destroys the logic of synchronicity and evolution which traditionally authorize the subject of cultural knowledge.'[80] Katzenstein does not engage with Bhabha's conceptualization of hybridity or even with those following Bhabha that see 'hybridity as something emergent from the necessary failures of colonial dichotomies' or view 'hybridity as precedent to (or, at least, coeval with) such dichotomies. New hybrids may be the result of novel colonial and postcolonial binaries, but hybridity itself is nothing new.'[81] Furthermore, if 'knowledge is hybrid,' it is important to recognize that 'not all hybrid

[76] Katzenstein, *Civilizations in World Politics,* 33 (italics inserted).
[77] Short and Kambouri, "Ambiguous universalism," 279.
[78] Bhabha, *The Location of Culture*, 159–160.
[79] Bhabha, *Location of Culture,* 159.
[80] Bhabha, *Location of Culture,* 5, 165.
[81] Seth, "Putting knowledge in its place," 378–379.

knowledges are made equal.'[82] The concept of 'differential hybridity' investigates 'how hybridity is enacted and regulated in transnational fields; fields in which "locality" both comes with and commands a price.'[83] It explores 'the ways in which the "same" hybrid knowledge is accorded different values in different contexts.'[84]

While Huntington and Katzenstein articulate the idea of 'universal civilization' and 'civilization of modernity,' respectively, Cox conceptualizes civilizations as forms of collective consciousness. To quote Cox,

> *Civilizations* … are historical phenomena, ways of looking at the world, *forms of collective consciousness* … Civilizations evolve through conflict within themselves and through borrowing from and resistance against encounters with other civilizations. They are forms of *consciousness malleable to the historical experiences of people*, not geological slabs crushing against one another.[85]

Cox advocates a historical perspective to consider the possibility of 'one unitary global civilization or as a plural world with a continuing diversity of civilizations.'[86] Cox seeks an interrogation of the possibilities and limitations of an all-embracing civilization led by the US or the feasibility of 'several constellations of world power working out a modus vivendi.'[87] He is troubled by the American 'myth of origin' as a 'shining city on a hill, a light to the world' with enormous military power.[88] He believes that a historical analysis will alert us to 'the illusion of assuming one's specific tradition has the quality of universality.'[89] Cox insists on an 'inter-civilizational dialogue' to understand differences between civilizations but cautions against a particular strand of Western thinking that has become 'fixated on the idea of transcending the state system … by some form of global governance, an empire that dare not speak its name.'[90] He insists that the lack of 'empathy' in an inter-civilizational dialogue will degenerate into a clash of civilizations.

[82] Seth, "Putting knowledge in its place," 380.
[83] Seth, "Putting knowledge in its place," 380.
[84] Seth, "Putting knowledge in its place," 380.
[85] Cox, "Consciousness and civilization: the Inside Story," 12.
[86] Robert Cox, "Consciousness and civilization: the Inside Story," 13.
[87] Robert Cox, "Consciousness and civilization: the Inside Story," 13.
[88] Robert Cox, "Consciousness and civilization: the Inside Story," 15.
[89] Robert Cox, "Consciousness and civilization: the Inside Story," 15–20.
[90] Robert Cox, "Consciousness and civilization: the Inside Story," 15, 18–20.

Civilizational Encounters in Africa

It is possible to suggest that this lack of empathy is because 'historians have rarely treated the civilizing mission as a serious ideology,' and little attention has been devoted to how its 'tenets were propagated by nineteenth century spokesmen for imperialism.'[91] Michael Adas in his study of European encounters with non-Western societies suggests that 'terms such as ethnocentrism, cultural chauvinism, and physical narcissism more aptly characterize European responses in the early centuries of overseas contact.'[92] It was as a result of these encounters between Europeans and non-Europeans that a sense of hierarchy surfaced in the minds of Europeans as they observed 'differences in material culture—which included science and technology.'[93] Adas is sentient in his observation that 'this hierarchy was not as explicitly delineated as it would be in the eighteenth century, when classification was the rage; nor was it as hard and fixed as it would become in the writings of racist writers, especially in the nineteenth century.'[94] But he insists that these attitudes of cultural chauvinism and hierarchy persist.

Adas notes how even while Europe itself was embroiled in numerous civil and religious wars in the sixteenth and seventeenth centuries it did not fail to disparage and deplore 'the seemingly incessant but small-scale wars waged by African coastal peoples.'[95] Furthermore, prior to the emergence of a more industrialized society in western Europe, there was also a pervasive sense of 'low esteem for African material culture,' and 'European observers considered the Africans deficient in the invention of tools and weapons and in their application to production and war.'[96] But other scholars insist on cultivating an understanding of the African 'warrior tradition' and are intrigued by the 'similarity of the military technology' in use across pre-colonial Africa.[97] Mazrui and Uzoigwe suggest that while in 'precolonial African military technology was very rudimentary' in waging

[91] Adas, *Machines as the Measure of Men*, 199.

[92] Adas, *Machines as the Measure of Men*, 12.

[93] Adas, *Machines as the Measure of Men*, 64.

[94] Adas, *Machines as the Measure of Men*, 65.

[95] Adas, *Machines as the Measure of Men*, 34.

[96] Adas, *Machines as the Measure of Men*, 39–40.

[97] G.N. Uzoigwe, "The Warrior and the State in Precolonial Africa: Comparative Perspectives," in *The Warrior Tradition in Modern Africa*, ed. Ali A. Mazrui (Leiden: E.J. Brill, 1977), 44–45.

offensive or defensive wars, other considerations, such as 'training, tactics, cohesion, leadership, discipline, martial spirit, numbers and geography in varying ways, would be more crucial than technology.'[98] Adas notes how European accounts acknowledged the Africans' ability to work iron, to produce forges, bellows, weapons and utensils, even of high quality in the Congo and Sierra Leone, but 'European contempt for African technological abilities' can be 'detected in tales of the dramatic effects of European firearms on "hostile natives" and the wonder shown by coastal peoples at even the simplest mechanical devices.'[99] It was not until the nineteenth century that 'firearms were fairly well spread' in Africa, and 'their use by no means discouraged the use of other weapons.'[100]

The Industrial Revolution in western Europe merely reinforced Orientalist tropes about the Africans lacking in scientific curiosity and inventiveness and mocked the precise scientific achievements of the Indians in South Asia as 'adulterated by flights of fantasy, mysticism, and mythology.'[101] According to the Orientalists, the Indians and the African rulers could receive weapons as 'gifts' from European explorers and envoys or could 'purchase' European arms but could not be expected to match the technological superiority of the Europeans. The Industrial Revolution helped establish 'Europe's material mastery' and machines as the most reliable measure of mankind.[102] This mastery enabled 'great advances in weapons design and production' and 'permitted the Europeans to subdue forcibly any overseas peoples who resisted their efforts to trade, convert, or explore.'[103] The expansion of colonial empires conflated science and technology as criteria for comparison, generated a discourse on the uniqueness and superiority of Western civilization and contributed to a significant polarization of cultures and societies as 'master-slave.'

This deployment of 'master-slave' technosocial metaphor was reinforced by an understanding of different conceptions of time in different cultures to the effect that 'no matter how complex and sophisticated non-Western modes of time might be, they were very different from the secular, clock-oriented time sense that had become dominant in industrializing

[98] Uzoigwe, "The Warrior and the State," 45.
[99] Adas, *Machines as the Measure of Men,* 40.
[100] Uzoigwe, "The Warrior and the State in Precolonial Africa," 45.
[101] Adas, *Machines as the Measure of Men,* 106–107.
[102] Adas, *Machines as the Measure of Men,* 134.
[103] Adas, *Machines as the Measure of Men,* 143.

Europe and North America,' as discussed in the previous chapter.[104] Landes observes, 'It was time, then, in combination with navigational imagination and courage, that opened the world. And so it was that the "barbarians" came to Asia, and not the reverse.'[105] In their interactions with other civilizations, this time difference and difference in instruments for measuring time were now deliberately exploited by the European missionaries and laymen to emphasize the superiority of Christian religion and European civilization vis-à-vis others. Landes argues that the Catholic priests were 'salesmen of a special kind.'[106] In their efforts at religious conversion the Jesuits used 'the wonders of western technology to charm their way' into other civilizations and did not hesitate to argue 'for the superiority of the Christian religion.'[107] They argued that those capable of making and possessing 'all kinds of special astronomical and geographical knowledge' were 'superior' and 'wiser' in the 'largest moral sense' and for this purpose conveniently adjusted 'the rules and rites of the Church to fit the premises and win the sympathy' of the cautious locals.[108] Landes observes, 'The Christian missionaries laid so much stress on the link between scientific knowledge and religious truth that any revision of the former implied a repudiation of the latter.'[109] It is helpful to remember this historical complicity of the Church as evangelical Christians try to revive a discourse on human rights as new standards of civilizations.

It was this sense of temporal and spatial differences that encouraged the Europeans to believe, 'African and Asian cultures promoted values that were antithetical to time thrift, punctuality, routinization, and other attitudes and patterns of behaviour that were believed essential to the successful functioning of "advanced" capitalist societies.'[110] The mastery of the Europeans was sought to be 'demonstrated by the fact that they were the inventors and manufacturers of modern weaponry,' and 'military prowess' constituted the key to conquest and rule.[111] The failure of the Asians to 'fully develop their early innovations in military organization and firearms'

[104] Adas, *Machines as the Measure of Men*, 250.
[105] Landes, "Clocks and the wealth of nations," 22–23.
[106] Landes, "Why Europe and the West? Why not China?" 12.
[107] Landes, "Why Europe and the West? Why not China?" 11–12.
[108] Landes, "Why Europe and the West? Why not China?" 12.
[109] Landes, "Why Europe and the West? Why not China?" 14.
[110] Adas, *Machines as the Measure of Men,* 250.
[111] Adas, *Machines as the Measure of Men,* 175.

was derided repeatedly.[112] A rhetorical emphasis was placed on the recruitment and training of Africans and Indian sepoys by the British and the French colonizers, as discussed in the next chapter. Adas shrewdly notes how the 'European colonizers made little attempt to propagate the civilizing mission ideology—as distinct from the work habits or the penchant for punctuality that it advocated … the civilizing mission was an ideology of dominance with a more limited scope than those aimed at achieving cultural hegemony.'[113] 'An understanding of and adherence to the principles of the civilizing mission' was to be carefully cultivated through practices of sly civility 'only among the Western-educated elites' to establish 'cultural hegemony.'[114] Any resistance or failure to emulate generated 'allegations of racial incapacity to suspicions of political machinations.'[115]

While the civilizing mission ideology is itself seldom suspect, efforts have been made on two fronts. One focuses attention on 'the extent to which African and Asian peoples were capable of acquiring the technological skills and mastering the scientific ideas that were the ultimate source of Western global dominance.'[116] The other makes an effort at understanding practices of socialization in these civilizational encounters between the West and the Rest in an effort to move beyond explanations based on 'gunboat diplomacy.'[117] However, such efforts are limited at present as African military history is still an 'underdeveloped field of study' with few written records available, and recourse to 'oral tradition' is often considered to be 'unreliable when dealing with the military exploits or martial spirit of a given society.'[118] But some representative samples of writings on civilizational encounters in Asia are available today.

[112] Adas, *Machines as the Measure of Men*, 175.

[113] Adas, *Machines as the Measure of Men*, 268.

[114] Adas, *Machines as the Measure of Men*, 269.

[115] Adas, *Machines as the Measure of Men*, 269.

[116] Adas, *Machines as the Measure of Men*, 272.

[117] Shogo Suzuki, *Civilization and Empire: China and Japan's Encounter with European International Society* (London & New York: Routledge, 2009), 11.

[118] Ali A. Mazrui, ed., *The Warrior Tradition in Modern Africa* (Leiden: E.J. Brill, 1977), 22.

Civilizational Encounters in Asia

In investigating civilizational encounters in the Asian context scholars insist that it is simplistic to focus only on the proclaimed universal standards of civilization and emphasize the need to devote attention to particular processes of socialization that led to the induction of non-Western societies 'into a Janus-faced European International Society.'[119] A study of civilizational encounters is considered to be of critical importance instead of resorting to attributing merely structural explanations of strategic interests, compliance and a 'reproduction of predetermined social practices, such as the "standard of civilization."'[120] Suzuki explicitly questions 'how non-European polities attempted to insert themselves into their new international environment.'[121] Several scholars like Landes, Gong, Suzuki, Ikuko and Bull offer varied accounts of these civilizational encounters in Asia.

Ikuko observes how Japan underwent 'a radical change in its temporal experience, moving from one following the rhythms of nature to one of mathematical precision, namely, the western time system.'[122] This change is attributed to 'Japan's desperate efforts to catch up with the western level of industry in the shortest possible time.'[123] Time discipline or regimentation of time in accordance with the mechanical clock is attributed to 'the international politics of the period.'[124] The adoption of 'two western systems of temporal measurement: the international meridian (the 24-hour system with twelve o'clock midnight as the beginning of the day) and the Gregorian calendar' was considered to be vital for 'being in harmony with all the civilized countries of the world.'[125] The Gregorian calendar to measure time 'ostensibly demonstrated the supremacy of western civilization' and served as economical schemes for 'civilizing' others.[126] These temporal metrics of civilization often represented a key moment of departure, a significant moment of 'no choice but to leave' the alternative frameworks

[119] Suzuki, *Civilization and Empire,* 14.
[120] Suzuki, *Civilization and Empire,* 7.
[121] Suzuki, *Civilization and Empire,* 14.
[122] Nishimoto Ikuko, "The Civilization of Time: Japan and the adoption of the western time system," *Time & Society* 6, no. 2/3 (1997): 237.
[123] Ikuko, "The Civilization of Time," 237.
[124] Ikuko, "The Civilization of Time," 245.
[125] Ikuko, "The Civilization of Time," 245.
[126] Ikuko, "The Civilization of Time," 246.

of time prevalent in Asia and Africa to arrive at the doorstep of Western modernity.[127]

Gerrit Gong claims, 'Wherever possible, the European countries sought to bring traditional, non-European countries into the international society in as orderly and humane a manner as possible.'[128] It is with this questionable assumption that Gong would like to initiate us into his study of standard of civilization by trying at the outset to suggest a level playing field where each contender viewed the other as less civilized due to different cultural systems. Gong argues further that 'many of the nineteenth century's military engagements, for example, the Opium Wars, were extensions of conflicting standards of "civilization" by other means.'[129] It appears that due to the different and conflicting standards of civilization at play, each side viewed the other as barbaric and uncivilized. Gong suggests that non-Western societies 'maintained their own standards of "civilization", based on and defined by their own cultural traditions and practices' and they felt threatened by the European standard of civilization as it challenged 'the legitimacy of their regimes, both domestically and internationally.'[130] The 'test and rule' pursued by European powers of recognizing whether a state was civilized or not rested on the premise 'whether its government was sufficiently stable to undertake binding commitments under international law and whether it was able and willing to protect adequately the life, liberty, and property of foreigners.'[131]

While the idea that 'Europe had the civilization most worth emulating' is traced back to 'Peter the Great's efforts to modernize ("civilize") Russia along European lines,' Gong insists it was 'Japan's essentially voluntary efforts to fulfil the European standard [that] vindicated it.'[132] While 'the Ottoman Empire was the first non-European country to gain provisional admittance into the European international society, it does not necessarily follow that it was admitted according to an explicit standard.'[133] Gong argues that it was the culmination of Japan's efforts to conform to the

[127] Ikuko, "The Civilization of Time," 245.

[128] Gerrit W. Gong, *The Standard of 'Civilization' in International Society* (Oxford: Clarendon Press, 1984), 6.

[129] Gong, *The Standard of 'Civilization,'* 8.

[130] Gong, *The Standard of 'Civilization,'* 7.

[131] George Schwarzenberger, 'The Standard of Civilization in International Law,' *Current Legal Problems*, 1955, p. 220, as cited by Gong, *The Standard of 'Civilization,'* 24, footnote 2.

[132] Gong, *The Standard of 'Civilization,'* 40.

[133] Gong, *The Standard of 'Civilization,'* 31.

standard of 'civilization' that made it 'necessary that the standard be articulated in specific legal terms.'[134] It was with the emergence of Japan as a powerful state that 'the standard of "civilization" took its place as a universally valid principle, applicable to all non-European countries seeking to enter the Family of Nations as "civilized states."'[135] But despite their long interaction with European state system, both Japan and the Ottoman Empire 'found the path to accreditation as a "civilized power long and difficult."'[136]

The difficulty lay in how a standard of civilization became a rubric in the nineteenth century which helped catalogue countries of the world into spheres of civilization, semi-civilization and barbarity. It was this stagist periodization that then led to the attribution of rights and duties of states. 'The authority to determine the jural capacity of the states in the barbarous and savage spheres belonged to the "civilized states" of Europe.'[137] The standard of civilization articulated by Europeans included some rights but 'what these basic "rights" were' and what constituted their guarantee was never well defined.[138] This problem was further compounded by 'differing conceptions of and demands for "civilized" rights' making them 'difficult to enforce.'[139] Gong makes a further effort to list the requirements of an European standard of civilization and suggests that it was codified as an explicit legal principle by 1905.[140] In these practices of codification of standards of civilization as international law it is interesting to note how there is an emphatic and consistent disciplinary note insisting on 'must,' 'accept,' 'apply,' 'consent' in order to be recognized as 'a legal member of the Family of Nations.'[141] It is this circulation of disciplinary tone and didactic language of compliance to meet the standards of civilization that becomes more acute and shrill and finds careful resonances in practices of arms control and disarmament agreements, as discussed further in succeeding chapters.

Any indication of lack of compliance compounded with positivist interpretations of 'civilized' rights under international law further 'facilitated

[134] Gong, *The Standard of 'Civilization,'* 29.
[135] Gong, *The Standard of 'Civilization,'* 29.
[136] Gong, *The Standard of 'Civilization,'* 10.
[137] Gong, *The Standard of 'Civilization,'* 56.
[138] Gong, *The Standard of 'Civilization,'* 14–15.
[139] Gong, *The Standard of 'Civilization,'* 14–15.
[140] Gong, *The Standard of 'Civilization,'* 14.
[141] Gong, *The Standard of 'Civilization,'* 30.

the rationalization of the use of force against non-European countries.'[142] The non-Western states realized that one could not vest blind faith in natural international law and its claims to universality and that positivist international law was subject to manipulation by the Europeans to safeguard their own sovereign interests. To quote Gong,

> The debate continues as to what extent the standard of "civilization" was intended to be, and was recognized as, a universal standard with objective, legal requirements and humanitarian aspirations, and to what extent it was simply an ethnocentric statement of European racial arrogance, or rationalization for colonial hegemony. A common "Third World" perception is that the standard of "civilization" symbolized an international legal system which was European-grown, reflected European cultural biases, and essentially codified European hegemony and imperial dominance. To argue, as some do, that international law discriminated against non-European countries simply because it originated in Europe is a *non sequitur*. To enquire how the social and intellectual assumptions inherent in European society influenced the standard's emergence is something else.[143]

In other words, some scholars contend that this shift from natural law to positivist law led to discarding of the 'principle of universality of the Family of Nations irrespective of creed, color, and continent' and encouraged crafting of a standard of civilization based on a Eurocentric understanding of rights of the civilized and practices of domination and discrimination against non Western societies. But other scholars claim that with this transition from natural to positivist law, the standard of civilization 'emerged not so much to ostracize the non-European countries from the Family of Nations as to include them within the domain of international law.'[144] Despite supporting this latter argument, Gong concedes that 'the standard was never much more than a fairly blunt, legal instrument ... subject to the admixture of contrasting elements—political and legal, subjective and objective, explicit and implicit—associated with any doctrine of recognition' with 'unspoken' 'subjective' and 'tacit' assumptions making it difficult to apply in practice but serving as a 'guide and stimulus for reform.'[145]

[142] Gong, *The Standard of 'Civilization,'* 42–43.
[143] Gong, *The Standard of 'Civilization,'* 45.
[144] Gong, *The Standard of 'Civilization,'* 44.
[145] Gong, *The Standard of 'Civilization,'* 21–22.

The international legal order was often conceived as a 'concentric circle model' or a 'charmed circle.'[146] This visual representation encouraged a positivist view of international law within which 'there existed two very different sets of norms that governed European International Society's relations with European states, on the one hand, and non-European states on the other.'[147] While adherence to international law served as a marker of 'civilized' identity, considerations of racial homogeneity guided the application of these norms in European and non-European societies.[148] Thus attendance at the late nineteenth-century Hague Conferences on disarmament and peace by the representatives of China, Persia and Siam did not automatically qualify or confer on them a "civilized" status,' but their attendance was seen only as efforts to populate the 'outer courts of the charmed circle.'[149] A more blatant exercise in discrimination, 'six African nations claimed sovereignty at the time, but none were invited to, or represented at, the first Hague Conference.'[150] The Hague Conferences were critical in codifying the laws of war based on distinctions between the 'civilized' and 'uncivilized' and the 'usages established between civilized nations' to conduct 'civilized' warfare.'[151] Gong claims, '[A]t least in theory, the standard of "civilization" was color-blind ... but applying the standard as an integral part of the international law was more difficult in practice.'[152]

The growing interactions with the Europeans made the Chinese and the Japanese increasingly conscious that the differential treatment accorded to them was based on 'civilizational' attainment as determined by the European International Society.[153] They sent several missions and delegations to Europe to learn more about the West. They were not willing to accept European institutions and standards uncritically without making an effort to learn more about them. The Iwakura mission from Japan visited the West in 1871 and they realized that in order to be considered civilized it would not be enough to only acquire the industry, technology and

[146] Gong, *The Standard of 'Civilization,'* 39.

[147] Suzuki, *Civilization and Empire,* 74.

[148] Suzuki, *Civilization and Empire,* 79–80, 85.

[149] Gong, *The Standard of 'Civilization,'* 19; Gerrit Gong quoting T.E. Holland, *Lectures on International Law* (London: Sweet and Maxwell, 1933), pp. 39–40.

[150] Gong, *The Standard of 'Civilization,'* 70.

[151] Gong, *The Standard of 'Civilization,'* 70–72, 74–76.

[152] Gong, *The Standard of 'Civilization,'* 53.

[153] Suzuki, *Civilization and Empire,* 55.

superior arms but that they would have to imbibe 'even seemingly unimportant differences of tradition and custom, such as dress or diet' to be accredited as a civilized state by the West.[154] The differential treatment meted out by the Europeans often on grounds of racial homogeneity served to sow the seeds of 'latent nationalism.'[155] The growth of Asian nationalism and anticolonialism contributed to a political climate in which apparently only science and technology accounted for whatever admiration non-Western peoples felt for European civilization and everything else was viewed with disdain and detested.[156]

The humiliation of the Opium Wars and experiences of racism made the Chinese question the 'semi-civilized' status accorded to them by the Europeans and to some extent resist adopting the wishful image of the apparently 'progressive' character of 'European-styled institutions.'[157] This resistance was embedded in a civilizational difference in outlook toward armaments and war. Landes suggests that 'the European may have thought that the purpose of war was to kill the enemy and win; the Chinese, strong in space and numbers, thought otherwise.'[158] This sense of difference played out further because while it was understood that

> military defeat was the technical reason why Western knowledge should be acquired, but it was also the psychological reason why it should not be. Instinctively, the Chinese preferred military defeat, which could be reversed, to entering a psychological crisis; people could stand humiliation but not self-debasement. … The mandarins sensed the threat to Chinese civilization irrespective of the economic and political issues, and they tried to resist this threat without regard to the economic and political dangers. In the past the Chinese had never had to give up their cultural pride: the foreign rulers always adopted the Chinese civilization. Hence there was nothing in their history to guide them through their modern crisis.[159]

[154] Gong, *The Standard of 'Civilization,'* 20.
[155] Suzuki, *Civilization and Empire,* 110.
[156] Adas, *Machines as the Measure of Men,* 203–204.
[157] Suzuki, *Civilization and Empire,* 112–113.
[158] Landes, "Why Europe and the West? Why not China?", 14.
[159] Landes, "Why Europe," 14. In this article Landes cites the above quote attributing it to the following sources: Carlo M. Cipolla, *Guns, Sails and Empires: Technological Innovation and the Early Phases of European Expansion, 1400–1700* (New York: Pantheon Books, 1966), 120; Fu-sheng Mu, *The Wilting of the Hundred Flowers: the Chinese Intelligentsia under Mao* (New York: Praeger, 1963), 76–77.

The Japanese were acutely aware that the Western wealth and prosperity was 'only a recent phenomenon' and 'the industrial revolution had come to the West only fifty years earlier.'[160] But when it came to armament 'the Europeans were maximizers. European technology was also monotonic-increasing; each gain was the basis for further gain.'[161]

A key lesson absorbed by China and Japan was that to secure survival it was imperative to strengthen one's military and acquire superior weapons. The existing literature on arms control and disarmament acknowledges gunpowder was invented in China and the latter 'pioneered the next improvement in fire arms also.'[162] But in China the traditional threat perception of attacks from Mongols on fortifications for centuries encouraged a defensive mindset that discouraged development of offensive weapons capabilities and considered shipbuilding a wasteful expenditure. On the contrary, Europeans with greater access to gunmetal, cannon-carrying ships, wealth garnered from overseas trade and willingness to engage in offensive wars,

> could afford to invest in technically proficient armies without fearing that the armed poor would challenge the class hierarchy upon which those governments rested. No other civilized society of the age enjoyed the same privilege. No other civilized state could arm the poorest classes of society with impunity.[163]

The Chinese 'copied objects at or near the frontier, but did not adapt or improve' upon the existing Western technology, and invested in their own sense of cultural superiority, failed to 'recognize the concurrent superiority of others,' especially in the area of armaments.[164] On the other hand it is claimed that 'European scientists rarely refused to learn or copy, and they were only too ready to revise their judgement when presented with the facts.'[165] These differences in cultural stereotypes notwithstanding, European colonial expansion was facilitated with their small superiority in

[160] Gong, *The Standard of 'Civilization,'* 180.

[161] Landes, "Why Europe and the West? Why not China?", 13.

[162] William McNeil Hardy, *The Age of Gunpowder Empires, 1450–1800* (Washington DC: American Historical Association, 1989), 3.

[163] McNeil Hardy, *The Age of Gunpowder Empires*, 45.

[164] Landes, "Why Europe," 20.

[165] Landes, "Why Europe," 21.

firearms and the susceptibility of non-Europeans to European diseases that often rapidly decimated their population.[166]

In Japan as early as 1868, 'fledgling newspapers such as *Yokohama shimpo mosihogusa* ran cartoons showing predatory foreigners selling arms to contending forces in the country.'[167] The Japanese elite experienced an acute 'desire to transform Japan into a strong military power that could defend itself from the 'civilizing face of European International Society,' and they were more willing to accept the dualistic character of the European International Society.[168] Suzuki observes, '[T]he audience for Japan's demonstration of "civilized" identity was primarily European International Society.'[169] While the Japanese acknowledged that race and technological considerations played an important role in the differential treatment meted out to non-Western societies, they also exhibited faith in attainment of 'a "civilized" identity on European International Society's terms that would greatly facilitate the protection of Japan's sovereignty.'[170] Thus their efforts at emulative learning were not confined to 'only the legalistic stipulations of the "standard of civilization", but also the "hidden" standard of introducing "Europeanized" systems of governance.'

Adas suggests that for centuries 'Japanese interest in European warfare and weaponry remained pronounced' and 'the Japanese were better informed about European civilization than any other non-Western people.'[171] The Chinese were emphatic in proclaiming 'the cultural neutrality of modern technology,' and in an effort at adaptation and strategic learning they began to appreciate the importance of industry and commerce in the 'production of advanced weapons.'[172] Gooday and Low, in their investigations of technology transfer and cultural exchange between Western scientists and engineers in late Tokugawa and Meiji Japan, debunk the existing myth that Japan's industrialization and modernization were a result of a 'forced entry' by US Navy Commodore Matthew Perry in

[166] Harding, *Is Science Multicultural?* 42–43.

[167] Peter Duus, "Weapons of the Weak, Weapons of the Strong—The Development of the Japanese Political Cartoon," *The Journal of Asian Studies* 60, no. 4 (2001): 983.

[168] Suzuki, *Civilization and Empire,* 117.

[169] Suzuki, *Civilization and Empire,* 141.

[170] Suzuki, *Civilization and Empire,* 117.

[171] Adas, *Machines as the Measure of Men,* 359.

[172] Suzuki, *Civilization and Empire,* 101.

1853–1854.[173] They insist that 'since Japan had not been closed to the rest of the world during the previous two hundred years, to claim that Perry opened it up is to acquiesce in the self-aggrandizing myth created by Perry and repeated uncritically by his biographers and their readers.'[174] On the contrary in meticulous detail they seek to undermine the 'ethnocentric emphasis on the agency of Westerners in developing Japanese science and technology' and showcase the importance of 'domestic processes of urbanization, industrial development, and trade during the preceding Tokugawa period (1600–1868).'[175]

It is undeniable that the threat of invasion from alien imperialist forces was a stimulus to Japanese acquisition and development of advanced technologies, but so were the efforts of Westerners to communicate their science and technology to Japan.[176] The imported 'hirelings' that came to work in Japan from Great Britain, France, the US and Germany 'developed particular lines of work consistent with their native industrial strength' and were 'budding imperialists sponsored by their nations and were linked to unequal treaties and trade agreements.'[177] Gooday and Low emphasize how 'the Tokugawa rulers selectively appropriated sources of foreign expertise to meet their own developmental agenda'; they also emphasize that the 'Japanese society exercised a significant degree of control over the "technology transfer" involved in this process' and that 'the distinct imperialist or neocolonial agendas involved on both sides were rather more often marked by friction or at least opacity' that occasionally led to mutual cross-cultural understanding.[178] It was the 'desire' of the Japanese to gain recognition and acceptance as a military power that helped them embark on a path of 'emulative learning' and generated a willingness to 'look beyond "Western" weapons and drill' and adopt practices of 'state centralization, adoption of technology and industry; and mass mobilization.'[179] It is helpful to note that these practices of 'emulative learning' or 'imitation' make significant changes in constituting one's

[173] Graeme J.N. Gooday and Morris F. Low, "Technology Transfer and Cultural Exchange: Western Scientists and Engineers Encounter Late Tokugawa and Meiji Japan," *Osiris* 13 (1998): 99, 101.

[174] Gooday and Low, "Technology Transfer and Cultural Exchange," 102.

[175] Gooday and Low, "Technology Transfer and Cultural Exchange," 102.

[176] Gooday and Low, "Technology Transfer and Cultural Exchange," 102–103.

[177] Gooday and Low, "Technology Transfer and Cultural Exchange," 104.

[178] Gooday and Low, "Technology Transfer and Cultural Exchange," 102.

[179] Suzuki, *Civilization and Empire*, 91, 125–126.

identities and interests based on one's growing desire for acceptance, power, prestige and legitimacy within the new international society.[180]

A change in 'the system of time was no exception' to the accelerated pace of industrialization demanded in societies threatened by the violence of colonization.[181] It was by taking recourse to rapid industrialization with time discipline that they could aspire to earn foreign currency necessary to establish 'munitions industry in order to raise Japan to world power status.'[182] This time consciousness with its emphasis on discipline and obedience in the service of the nation was inculcated in various ways such as introducing a 'new basic vocabulary' and 'guide books' to help with popular understanding.[183] This accelerated sense of time produced 'anxiety' and 'restlessness' about 'building a modern nation state.'[184] The Japanese in a 'similar fashion to the European states' passed the Conscription Edict in 1873 arguing that the 'Japanese citizens owed a duty to the state ... in return for their rights.'[185] The introduction of mass conscription and the willingness to equip it with advanced industrial and military technology were supplemented with measures that sought to 'suppress political dissent both through repressive legislation and a heavy dose of indoctrination in patriotism.'[186] Within a decade of their initial encounters with the Europeans, the Japanese were making 'Western style muskets of considerable quality' and improved 'the matchlocks they had originally imported from the West.'[187]

During the Russo-Japanese war, medical practitioners described the Japanese guns as a 'humanitarian weapon' and believed that the 6.5 mm bullets used by the Japanese vis-à-vis the 7.62 mm used by the Russians were of a far superior quality.[188] The International Red Cross observed,

> This weapon amazed the medical corps. The wounds it caused healed with incredible speed. Soldiers whose rib cage and lungs, sometimes even those

[180] Suzuki, *Civilization and Empire,* 138.
[181] Ikuko, "The Civilization of Time," 239.
[182] Ikuko, "The Civilization of Time," 246.
[183] Ikuko, "The Civilization of Time," 244.
[184] Ikuko, "The Civilization of Time," 254–255.
[185] Suzuki, *Civilization and Empire,* 133.
[186] Suzuki, *Civilization and Empire,* 136.
[187] Adas, *Machines as the Measure of Men,* 358–359.
[188] Olive Checkland, *Humanitarianism and the Emperor's Japan 1877–1977* (New York: St. Martin's Press, 1994), 54–55.

whose skulls and brains had been penetrated through and through could often return to the battle a few hours later.[189]

But in a somber tone of finality, Oliver Checkland observes, 'No further reference has been found to this extraordinary report of the Japanese bullet.'[190] This growing superiority in arms and the military defeat inflicted by the Japanese on the Russians came as a serious shock to the Europeans. To quote Adas, 'A non-white, non-European people had not only mastered Europe's science and technology, but it had proved more than a match, if somewhat backward, European empire.'[191] Those that were more receptive to the idea of reciprocity between Japan and the West faced competition from others chauvinistically proclaiming that 'we venture to doubt the existence of sufficient capacity in the Japanese mind for high original scientific work when unhelped.'[192] Some of them tried to communicate their condescending messages of Western superiority by claiming that the Japanese were more interested in 'learning science for military purposes than out of any desire for self-improvement.'[193]

The assumption of 'inherent asymmetry' and deliberate misrepresentation on the sensitive subject of transfer of technology informed Western ideas on the emergence of Japan as *Dai Nippon, the Britain of the East: A Study in National Evolution* and captured the imagination of the Western audiences.[194] This emphasis on 'evolution' signified the distance in time and technology that separated Europeans from Others. It was this sense of difference which was further reinforced by a racial prejudice that on the one hand grudgingly accorded Japan an 'exceptional' status among non-Western societies and applauded its efforts to 'remake their society in the image of industrial Europe,'[195] but on the other hand did not cease to

[189] Checkland, *Humanitarianism and the Emperor's Japan*, 54–55.

[190] Checkland, *Humanitarianism and the Emperor's Japan*, 55.

[191] Adas, *Machines as the Measure of Men*, 360–361.

[192] Graeme J.N. Gooday and Morris F. Low, "Technology Transfer and Cultural Exchange: Western Scientists and Engineers Encounter Late Tokugawa and Meiji Japan," *Osiris* 13 (1998): 106, 117.

[193] Graeme J.N. Gooday and Morris F. Low, "Technology Transfer and Cultural Exchange: Western Scientists and Engineers Encounter Late Tokugawa and Meiji Japan," *Osiris* 13 (1998): 104, 127.

[194] Gooday and Low, "Technology Transfer and Cultural Exchange," 108, 128; Henry Dyer, *Dai Nippon, the Britain of the East: A Study in National Evolution* (London: Blackie, 1904).

[195] Adas, *Machines as the Measure of Men*, 360–361, 310.

express doubt about the Japanese capacity to 'think scientifically or to invent new machines and methods of production.'[196] The Japanese were lampooned for 'borrowing machines and imitating European manufacturing techniques.'[197] The historical memory of a cartoon sketched by German Kaiser after Japan's victory over China in 1895 found resonance in Europe for several decades. This cartoon entitled "People of Europe Guard Your Most Precious Possessions!" depicted 'a buck toothed ogre, arising in the Far East and stretching menacing hands toward the West.'[198]

Japan was attracted to the idea of equality in the Janus-faced European International Society. For the Japanese, the idea that

> people could progress towards civilization was clear. Less clear was whether or not a hierarchy would persist as people at different points in their development progressed together. Whether the civilized would simply become more civilized remained an unanswered question.[199]

The Janus-faced European International Society carried within itself the promise of equality provided one met the standards of civilization with persistent efforts at 'emulative learning.' The Janus-faced European International Society encouraged younger aspirants to 'climb up the hierarchical ladder by attaining civilization.'[200] It failed to disclose that 'sovereign equality only operated within Europe, and European International Society in the nineteenth century was hierarchical vis-à-vis the "uncivilized" entities.'[201] Thus, 'progress toward "civilized" status was necessary and possible for the less "civilized" to achieve, but complete and perfect equality was not.'[202] It is little surprise that in this political climate of racial chauvinism and war mongering, Japan embraced the idea of a coercive civilizing mission toward its neighbors in its quest to acquire colonies and gain prestige in the eyes of the Europeans.

[196] Adas, *Machines as the Measure of Men,* 364.

[197] Adas, *Machines as the Measure of Men,* 364.

[198] Gene Weltfish, "American Racism: Japan's Secret Weapon," *Far Eastern Survey* 14, no. 17 (1945): 234.

[199] Gerrit W. Gong, *The Standard of 'Civilization' in International Society* (Oxford: Clarendon Press, 1984), 50.

[200] Shogo Suzuki, *Civilization and Empire: China and Japan's Encounter with European International Society* (London & New York: Routledge, 2009), 138–139.

[201] Suzuki, *Civilization and Empire,* 139.

[202] Gerrit W. Gong, *The Standard of 'Civilization' in International Society* (Oxford: Clarendon Press, 1984), 63.

Gong claims, 'Japan was naïve to assume that attaining "civilized" acceptance meant attaining equality.'[203] Japan embarked on a revisionist course only after it unsuccessfully tried to gain support from European powers to insert 'a racial equality clause in the Covenant for the League of Nations in 1919,' which was never accepted.[204] This led Japan to denounce the standards of civilization established by the Janus-faced European International Society smug in its own moral authority and embark on an alternative trajectory to constitute a Greater Asia Co-Prosperity Sphere in 'opposition' to the Anglo-American world order.[205] Gong insists,

> In the end, however, it was the Western "barbarians" and "infidels" who had the disposition and military capacity to impose their standard of "civilization." These foreigners insisted that "unequal treaty", "capitulation", and "protectorate" systems, all with extraterritorial provisions, be maintained until the non-European countries of Africa and Asia conformed to the "civilized" standards. European extraterritoriality thus became a badge of inferiority, for many non-European countries, a sign of "uncivilized" legal status.[206]

It is helpful to remember that this compulsive learning and accreditation took place in an increasingly coercive environment as the Europeans, in their imperial quest for colonies, trade and profit, wielded superior military clout, which made the non-European societies cognizant of the emphasis on 'survival,' 'competition' and 'the highly zero sum nature' of the Western world. [207]

Reciprocity and Rights in Standards of Civilization

A brief study of the civilizational encounters above shows how the Western powers did not hesitate to demonstrate their military might 'to enforce observance of the code of conduct as stipulated in the treaties and the standard of civilization.'[208] Europe's willingness to use force to impose a standard of civilization based on assertion of rights of the civilized was buttressed by its growing superiority in armaments such as breech-loading

[203] Gong, *The Standard of 'Civilization,'* 63.
[204] Suzuki, *Civilization and Empire,* 137.
[205] Suzuki, *Civilization and Empire,* 182.
[206] Gong, *The Standard of 'Civilization,'* 63.
[207] Suzuki, *Civilization and Empire,* 61–62.
[208] Suzuki, *Civilization and Empire,* 65.

rifles, canons, high explosives and the machine gun.[209] In the face of this military might, discourses on standard of civilization to some degree 'reflected Europe's need to explain and justify its overlordship of non-European countries in other than merely military terms.'[210] Suzuki claims,

> [A] common thread binding the otherwise loose coalition of states commonly called the "Third World" is their enduring sense of having been measured against a foreign standard of "civilization" and been found wanting. It was double insult. It was humiliating for non-European countries to have been declared "uncivilized", whether "barbarous" or "savage." Further, it was even more agonizing for them to have had their traditional standards of "civilization" cast aside as effete or inferior. The continued association of military and moral superiority—and of military and moral inferiority—lingers on.[211]

It is important to pay attention to these historically embedded civilizational encounters so as not to be deluded by twentieth-century Hedley Bull's sympathetic view emphasizing anarchical society and standards of civilization. Bull claims that 'the standard of "civilization" laid down by the Europeans in the late nineteenth and early twentieth centuries now appears to us part and parcel of an unjust system of domination and exploitation against which the peoples of Asia and Africa have rightly revolted.'[212] But any such sympathy is quickly qualified by assertions that deserve to be quoted at length here:

> the basic idea behind the requirement that governments aspiring to membership of international society should be able to meet standards of performance ... similar to those which European states expected of each other rested not upon ideas of superior right but on the need for reciprocity in dealings between European and non-European powers, which the latter in many cases were unable to meet. In the Ottoman Empire, in China and Japan, for example, the Europeans encountered powers in whose traditional understandings of diplomacy and international law the idea that relationships with outsiders could be based upon reciprocal interest and notions of equal right found no place. In the pre-literate and in some cases stateless political societies of black Africa (by contrast with the sophisticated Islamic

[209] Gong, *The Standard of 'Civilization,'* 42–44.
[210] Gong, *The Standard of 'Civilization,'* 42.
[211] Gong, *The Standard of 'Civilization,'* 246.
[212] Hedley Bull's foreword in Gong, *The Standard of 'Civilization,'* viii.

> or Islamicized kingdoms they also met in that continent, and with the Muslim and Hindu polities of south Asia) the European states encountered powers with which relationships of the kind they had with one another were not remotely possible.
>
> The arrogance of many Europeans, in equating civilization with the particular civilization of Europe, was no less than that of the Chinese, nor was the belief of Europeans that their religion was the one true faith any less than that of the Muslim peoples with whom they came into contact. The standard of 'civilization' on which the Europeans insisted did indeed lead to unjust treatment, but the demand of Asian and African peoples for equality of rights in international law was one that the latter did not put forward until they had first absorbed ideas of equal rights of states to sovereignty, of peoples to self-determination, and of persons of different race to individual rights, which before their contact with Europe played little or no part in their experience.[213]

Thus in a few ahistorical passages Bull would like us to believe that the idea of 'standard of civilization' articulated and determined by the West was not based upon the idea of 'superior right' but was imperative to educate and make the non-Western world appreciate the importance of ideas such as 'equality of rights' and 'reciprocity' in relationships. For Bull, how these ideas of standard of civilization based on rights and reciprocity are introduced and inscribed in the non-Western world in a coercive environment appears to be of secondary importance as these are 'preliterate,' 'stateless' societies in black Africa and sometimes 'sophisticated' polities of Asia.

The selective appropriation and emphasis on the idea of 'rights,' 'equality of rights,' 'reciprocity' to foreground justification for 'standards of civilization' and not 'superior right' are significant for Bull as a key exponent of maintaining order in an anarchical society, advocating expansion of international society and suggesting prescriptions for controlling arms race.[214] It is not intellect but the affect of emotions only such as 'arrogance' and 'faith' that Bull is willing to equate at par among the Europeans and non-Western population. But the meticulous historical research on civilizational encounters undertaken by Adas, Gong, Suzuki, Gooday and

[213] Bull's foreword in Gong, *The Standard of 'Civilization,'* viii–ix.

[214] Hedley Bull, *The Anarchical Society: A Study of Order in World Politics* (1977); *The Expansion of the International Society* (1984); *The Control of the Arms Race: Disarmament and arms control in the missile age* (1965).

Low mentioned above show it was not simply due to absence of reciprocity in the non-Western world but the emphasis on racial superiority and military superiority of the West that led to their reinforcement of a duplicitous standard of civilization in the world.

Suzuki insists that the contemporary International Society 'has been and still is a Janus faced one.'[215] This claim needs to be further investigated as some scholars now seek to make a distinction between old and new standards of civilization. They argue that the 'old standard of civilization' has been gradually phased out as it has fallen into disrepute but insist on 'new standards of civilization' based on modernity and human rights.[216] But other scholars, including me, argue that a classification of universalizing standards of civilization as old or new is problematic because the principle of universality generates a dilemma where on the one hand it creates 'legitimacy and prestige' but on the other encounters a dilution of 'the purity of the doctrines and increased the room for disagreement.'[217] While Huntington dismisses the idea of human rights as a new standard of civilization, Gong and Donnelly are intrigued to study 'the parallels between the old standard of "civilization" and a "new standard of human rights."'[218] Gong suggests that 'there is an easy and natural transition from the concern for "civilized" rights to concern for "human rights, as evidenced by the debate in the International Law Commission while the Universal Declaration of Human Rights was being drafted.'[219] He further argues that 'a common "standard of modernity" raises the possibility of a contemporary cosmopolitan culture' and 'vindicates the nineteenth-century assumption that the laws of science, being universal, undergirded a rational cosmology which would bring the "blessings of civilization" to all,'[220] a claim to be explored by studying civilizational practices of weapons control further rather than accepted at face value.

[215] Suzuki, *Civilization and Empire*, 183.

[216] Gerrit W. Gong, *The Standard of 'Civilization,'* 84–93.

[217] Gong, *The Standard of 'Civilization,'* 125; Mathur, "Human Rights as a New Standard of Civilization in Arms Control & Disarmament," *Alternatives; Global, Local, Political* (2018).

[218] Gong, *The Standard of 'Civilization,'* \92.

[219] Gong, *The Standard of 'Civilization,'* 91.

[220] Gong, *The Standard of 'Civilization,'* 92.

Critiques of Civilizational Discourses

A 'resurrection of the "civilization" discourse' has encouraged Mark Salter to suggest the surfing of a new 'civilizational realism' to reinscribe imperial cartographies on the post–Cold War order. The dual function of this move is to render the 'West' unproblematic and to 'barbarize' the multiple 'non-Wests.'[221] This represents a form of 'technological mentality' that demonizes the others and appropriates for itself the most advanced weapons of war as achievements of its own civilization.[222] It encompasses both 'civilizing process' of interdependence and expansion through mutual identification and is vulnerable to 'decivilizing processes' that pose a threat to the established status quo.[223] But instead of getting immediately swept up in these alarmist, polarizing assertions let us for a moment pause and rearticulate our rationale for engaging with civilizational discourses in the context of arms control and disarmament. This will help us to further gauge the significance of undertaking a civilizational analysis and to configure our approach toward such an undertaking.

It is for this purpose that it is insightful of Jackson to suggest that 'the language of "Western civilization", although powerful, is also historically and strategically pliable.'[224] He expresses an interest in 'the role of a rhetorical commonplace like "Western civilization" as an analytical category, a general framework or a wider context of struggle within which any agenda such as weapons regulation and control might be pursued or abandoned.[225] The particular manner of deployment of 'Western civilization' as a rhetorical commonplace is of interest as part of a 'process of legitimation.'[226] He therefore argues that

> tracing the history of a commonplace should not be the record of any intrinsic essence that the commonplace is purported to possess, but rather a record of how historical actors have sought to stabilize the commonplace,

[221] Mark B. Salter, *Barbarians & Civilization in International Relations* (London: Pluto Press, 2002), 4.

[222] Tzvetan Todorov, *Facing the Extreme: Moral Life in the Concentration Camps* (New York: Henry Holt, 1996), 43, 8–12.

[223] Maureen Montgomery, "Savage Civility: September 11 and the Rhetoric of 'Civilization,'" *Australasian Journal of American Studies* 21, no. 2 (2002): 63.

[224] Patrick Thaddeus Jackson, *Civilizing the Enemy – German Reconstruction and the Invention of the West* (Ann Arbor: University of Michigan Press, 2009), viii.

[225] Jackson, *Civilizing the Enemy,* 74–75, fn. 2.

[226] Jackson, *Civilizing the Enemy,* 241.

> and in doing so provided (perhaps unintentionally) the commonplace to the present actors as a resource.[227]

Jackson encourages us to 'focus on the language of "Western civilization"...to appreciate the kind of shaping effect that public debates about identity have on specific policy initiatives' such as arms control and disarmament.[228] A study that focuses on 'civilizational identity' helps one to grasp 'the dynamics and implications associated with claims to belong to a given civilization, and the political and social consequences of debates about what that membership *means* in practice.'[229] These meanings are crucial as they have an important bearing on efforts to regulate and prohibit weapons.

Bowden cautions us that the 'perpetuation' and not a mere 'revival' of the 'language of civilization' is a 'cause for concern' because 'the language of civilization comes with so much baggage' and 'the actions that all too often follow the language of civilization are anything but civilized.'[230] The concept of 'civilization' wields considerable power to 'commend and condemn,' and the implicit or explicit idea of a 'standard of civilization' sets the tone for differentiating between the '"civilized" and "uncivilized" nations or peoples in order to determine membership in the international society of states.'[231] Furthermore, the idea of a 'standard of civilization' and 'concomitant imperial civilizing missions' constitute a means toward realizing the ideal of a 'universal civilization.'[232] The perniciousness of this circulating language of civilization is reinforced by an observation that 'it is not a little characteristic of the structure of Western society that the watchword of its colonizing movement is "civilization."'[233] Bowden is troubled that 'the postcolonial moment and the demands of political correctness' might 'represent more of a blip on history's radar screen (granted a significant blip), than an altogether about-face or sea change in the nature of European/Western and Nonwestern relations.'[234]

[227] Jackson, *Civilizing the Enemy*, 44.
[228] Jackson, *Civilizing the Enemy*, x.
[229] Jackson, *Civilizing the Enemy*, 11.
[230] Bowden, *The Empire of Civilization*, ix.
[231] Bowden, *The Empire of Civilization*, 16.
[232] Bowden, *The Empire of Civilization*, 7.
[233] Bowden, *The Empire of Civilization*, 16, see footnote 37.
[234] Bowden, *The Empire of Civilization*, 7.

Helen Kinsella too urges us to be attentive to 'discourses of civilization' for the following functional reasons.[235] Firstly, discourses of civilization 'demarcate *static* differences, most frequently bounded by territorial distinctions.' Secondly, discourses of civilization 'denote processes of transformation—from barbarism to civilization—that immediately undermine the presumption of static or stable differences.' Thirdly, discourses of civilization 'set the limits of law (civilization vs. barbarism) and occasion the exercise of law (from barbarism to civilization). Fourthly, discourses of civilization are 'progressive and formative,' and 'set boundaries' and 'order an international hierarchy.' Fifthly, discourses of civilization regulate 'entry into the European state system' and legitimate 'an entirely different system of rules for those deemed outside the system.' Sixthly, discourses of civilization 'requires the participation and submission of all to propagate its future.' Seventhly, configuring the productive power of civilizational discourses allows for the possibility of indeterminacy and problems of compliance. Eighthly, discourses of civilization 'expose the temporality of any such hierarchies.' Thus Kinsella attributes much weightage to civilization discourses as constituting epistemological boundaries of learning but does not articulate how interventions with the help of civilization discourses are made to serve particular political projects such as arms control and disarmament.

This investigation is particularly important now that the resurrected language of civilization has at least 'two possible successors.'[236] These successors are understood to be the 'standards of modernity' and 'human rights as a new standard of civilization in weapons control.'[237] A careful exploration of these standards of civilization in practices of arms control and disarmament is imperative given the 'hysteria over weapons of mass destruction' and the potential power of civilizational discourses to wield disciplinary power in constituting the other as 'less than fully sovereign,' 'rogue,' 'predatory,' or 'uncivilized.'[238] It will not be amiss to suggest here that civilizational discourses under the guise of quest for modernity and

[235] Helen M. Kinsella, *The Image Before the Weapon—A Critical History of the Distinction between Combatant and Civilian* (Ithaca & London: Cornell University Press, 2011), 106–107, 126, 166, 189.

[236] Bowden, *The Empire of Civilization*, 166, see footnote 18. The idea of two successors of the classical standard of civilization is attributed by Bowden to Gerritt Gong.

[237] Ritu Mathur, "Human Rights as a New Standard of Civilization in Weapons Control?" *Alternatives: Global, Local, Political* 0.2, no. 42 (2018): 227–243.

[238] Bowden, *The Empire of Civilization*, 212.

defense of human rights can exacerbate threat perceptions, encourage arms races and problematize disarmament as humanitarian action. An investigation of civilizational discourses can no longer be reassuring if the Western right to bear arms and use force is 'legitimated in terms of a civilizing mission of one kind or another … the assumption is that it is the right of the West to bear arms to liberate the "natives."'[239] Barkawi and Laffey insist that 'this is and always has been the primary justification for imperialism in all its forms; it is about civilizing the barbarians.'[240]

This problem is compounded by a growing awareness that a 'Western security culture' has 'powerfully shaped the NACD policies and practices of states, and helped to define what it means for states to pursue their national interests.'[241] The 'conventional security studies rest on and reproduces Eurocentric histories and geographies of world politics.'[242] This is because

> Eurocentric accounts of great power competition tend to take the weak – the natives, the colonies, the periphery, the Third World, the global South—more or less for granted. They do so in the specific sense that agency, rationality, power and morality, as well as the fundamental dynamics of the world order, are assumed to reside in the global North. Alternatively, these various others are assumed to be just like us, only weaker. This generates a different problem, inasmuch as it denies their own history, their difference.[243]

A Eurocentric framework of analyses for security studies is claimed to provide 'few categories for making sense of the historical experiences of the weak and the powerless who comprise most of the world's population,' and 'by default these experiences are conceived in categories derived from great power politics in the North.' Secondly, it 'regards the weak and the powerless, as marginal and derivative elements of world politics, as at best the site of good liberal intentions or at worst a potential source of threats.' There is a failure to account for 'the multiple and integral relations between the weak and the strong. Failing to study the weak and the

[239] Tarak Barkawi and Mark Laffey, "The Postcolonial Moment in Security Studies," *Review of International Studies* 32, no. 2 (April 2006): 334, 343–344.

[240] Barkawi and Laffey, "The Postcolonial Moment," 334, 343–344.

[241] Keith Krause and Andrew Latham, "Constructing Non-Proliferation and Arms Control: The Norms of Western Practice," *Contemporary Security Policy* 19, no. 1 (1998): 23–24.

[242] Bhabha, *The Location of Culture* (London & New York: Routledge, 1994), 197.

[243] Barkawi and Laffey, "The Postcolonial Moment," 346.

strong together, as jointly responsible for making history.'[244] This framework of analyses also insists on a standard maneuver toward 'othering mass slaughter from the West and from modernity. It serves to preserve, in the face of any evidence to the contrary, the ethical character of the West and, in turn, underpins claims in liberal and security studies that the West is a force for the good in the world.'[245] It is therefore time to question the development of security studies in its 'modern form' and its efforts to represent itself as a 'seemingly neutral and timeless language of social science.'[246]

Conclusion

A quick survey of the existing literature on civilizational discourses above helps provide us with some signifiers pertaining to hierarchy, race, nationalism, technology and culture that might be useful to keep in mind as we further explore the effect of civilizational discourses in weapons control. Contemporary scholars championing civilizational discourses are caught in the midst of configuring the possibilities of a universal civilization reinforcing technological differences and danger of horizontal weapons proliferation to suggest a possibility of inter-civilizational violence. On the other hand, critical security studies and postcolonial scholars seek to bring center-stage the very language, categories and experiences that have produced and reproduced our understanding of arms control and disarmament as an exercise in modernity and a civilizing mission. This study takes note of these existing differences in scholarship.

A very small community of critical security studies scholars is empathetic toward the need for a more rigorous historical analysis of practices of arms control and disarmament and is very critical of the state-centric structure of the international system. But this scholarship has failed to seize the opportunity presented in the form of civilization discourses that subsume the sovereign state system to project civilization as the overwhelming identity that leads to confrontation on weapons issues and will be the source of inter-civilizational conflict. The existing postcolonial scholarship has not addressed the problem of weapons significantly but has

[244] Barkawi and Laffey, "The Postcolonial Moment in Security Studies," *Review of International Studies* 32, no. 2 (2006): 332–333.

[245] Barkawi and Laffey, "The Postcolonial Moment," 341–342.

[246] Barkawi and Laffey, "The Postcolonial Moment," 334, 344.

taken issue with civilizational bias in security studies more generally. The commitment of both these approaches toward articulating the concerns of the marginalized and question hegemonic practices makes them suitable for articulating a critique of civilization discourses in the context of weapons. It is therefore the contributions from both critical security studies and postcolonial studies that are deployed to undertake a further critique of civilization discourses in the context of arms control and disarmament.

Going forward, this study seeks to navigate the problematique of difference articulated by Huntington, by cultivating Cox's suggestion of need for empathy and Barkawi and Laffey's awareness of the difficulties encountered in undertaking empirical, contrapuntal analyses of the integral relations existing between the West and the Rest in addressing problems of weapons. The following account does not claim to be comprehensive but is illustrative in its effort to make visible the circulating power of civilizational discourses, embedded in an understanding of civilizational time, a time that carefully deploys practices of stereotyping, sly civility and mimesis to administer a civilizing therapy on practices of arms control and disarmament. These practices are the micro-capillaries of power wielded in the temporal dynamic of 'West and the Rest' in everyday practices that can only be made visible and disrupted with a postcolonial disposition toward time and temporality to regulate and prohibit weapons.

* * *

CHAPTER 3

Colonial Consciousness and Civilizing Therapy

Civilizational Consciousness

While Cox talks about civilizational consciousness, Nandy asserts that colonialism is 'first of all a matter of consciousness' and that 'colonialism minus a civilizational mission is no colonialism at all.'[1] But in the 'slender narratives' tracing the history of arms control and disarmament since the late nineteenth century, there is scarcely any acknowledgment of practices of colonialism, colonial consciousness and civilizational mission. In recent articles, Neil Cooper and I observe how the period of the late nineteenth century is often studied in an ahistorical, fragmented and cursory manner by scholars and policymakers devoted to the study of arms control and disarmament.[2] In these often policy-oriented accounts there is an overt emphasis on delineating the 'drivers of production and trade' of arms and a visible 'manic repetition' of the 'the Hague conference (s)' as an originary moment of practices of arms control and disarmament.[3] It will not be a mistake to argue that the late nineteenth-century European practices of multilateral arms control and disarmament with their careful

[1] Ashis Nandy, *The Intimate Enemy—Loss and Recovery of Self under Colonialism*, 2nd Edition (New Delhi: Oxford University Press, 1983), 63, 11.

[2] Ritu Mathur, "Sly Civility and the Paradox of Equality/Inequality in the Nuclear Order," *Critical Studies on Security* 4, no. 1 (2016): 57–72; Neil Cooper, "Race, Sovereignty, and Free Trade: Arms Trade Regulation and Humanitarian Arms Control in the Age of Empire," *Journal of Global Security Studies* 3, no. 4 (2018): 444–445.

[3] Cooper, "Race, Sovereignty, and Free Trade," 445; Bhabha, *The Location of Culture*, 286.

R. Mathur, *Civilizational Discourses in Weapons Control*,
https://doi.org/10.1007/978-3-030-44943-8_3

and pretentious deployment of the language of civilization and humanitarianism are an exercise in writing, administering, a civilizing therapy to the rest.

Keith Krause in tracing the history of arms trade for several centuries identifies a significant ideological shift from mercantilism to laissez-faire in late nineteenth-century Europe that henceforth guided technology and arms transfers.[4] Krause observes the following:

> [I]n the sixteenth to eighteenth centuries, the mirror image of "military self sufficiency (as) … an aspect of autarchy in the mercantilistic sense" would be the belief that weapons, being the source of power (analogous to specie), should not be traded except for strictly political reasons. This would result in direct intervention in (control of) the arms trade. With the shift from mercantilist to laissez-faire thought, however, trade is seen as the source of wealth and power and the engine of growth for sustained and enhanced productive capacity; this would logically result in fewer direct restrictions on arms transfers. A shift to indirect political intervention in the market also follows from this, and objections to the trade in technology may even diminish, as long as the wellsprings of technological innovation are not directly threatened.[5]

This shift from mercantilism to laissez faire in arms trade helped Europeans profit from selling arms to Africans. During the period 1885–1902 this trade was voluminous and facilitated by the arms race in Europe that created a market for obsolete arms that could then be sold in Africa. Beachey notes,

> The arms trade in East Africa was linked with the development and use of new types of fire-arms in Europe … By 1878 all the European powers had rearmed their infantry with the Chassepot, Snider, and Martini-Henry breech-loaders, all using metallic cartridge cases and steel barrels instead of iron as in the old muskets. The result of this change-over was that a great supply of obsolete weapons, chiefly percussion guns using caps instead of the flintlock mechanism, was thrown on the market. In East Africa—a large unpoliced territory—there was an avid demand on the part of Arab and African alike for any type of fire-arm.[6]

[4] Krause, *Arms and the State,* 211.

[5] Krause, *Arms and the State,* 15, also see footnote 5.

[6] R.W. Beachy, "The Arms Trade in East Africa in the Late Nineteenth Century," *The Journal of African History* 3, no. 3 (1962): 452.

An unregulated arms trade in obsolete arms for profit was not a matter of much concern to the Europeans as long as the 'arms so imported were cheap and worthless weapons manufactured to last for a maximum period of some two or three years and after that time becoming useless and worn out.'[7] But trade in large quantities and sophistication of imported arms flooding the interior of Africa generated much concern among the Europeans.

The Europeans were perplexed with 'indiscriminate arms trade' that was arming the natives engaged in mutinies and uprisings against the colonizers.[8] Cooper notes how 'the extension of European influence in Africa in the 1880s produced a backlash from Arab traders, particularly in Central and East Africa where life became more dangerous for missionaries and colonial settlers.'[9] Furedi observes that there existed a tacit agreement at the outbreak of the Anglo-Boer War that 'blacks should not be armed,' an understanding that was 'outweighed by the demands of military survival.'[10] Beachey notes how 'the Boers had strenuously opposed British slackness in allowing the arming of the natives and this had been one of the major issues of dispute between the British and Boers in the Transvaal.'[11] The competing spheres of influence of the Europeans on the continent of Africa made tentative measures such as required licensing, registration, stamping, gun tax and naval blockade more expensive and difficult to enforce. The trade in slaves and ivory had generated a lucrative trade in arms-running.

Ironically, the problem of arms transfers to Africa was framed by the as a 'great question' demanding 'prompt measures' to regulate 'import of arms' into Africa without which 'the development and pacification of this great continent will have to be carried out in the face of an enormous population, the majority of whom will probably be armed with first-class breech-loading rifles.'[12] This shared sense of fear and vulnerability among the European powers encouraged the signing of the Brussels Declaration

[7] Euan Smith, the British Counsul General at Zanzibar, quoted by R.W. Beachy in "The Arms Trade in East Africa," 453.

[8] Beachy, "The Arms Trade in East Africa," 454–455.

[9] Cooper, "Race, Sovereignty, and Free Trade," 450.

[10] Frank Furedi, *The Silent War—Imperialism and the Changing Perception of Race* (New Brunswick, New Jersey: Rutgers University Press, 1998), 31–32.

[11] Beachy, "The Arms Trade in East Africa," 454.

[12] Euan Smith, the British Counsul General at Zanzibar, quoted by R.W Beachy in "The Arms Trade in East Africa," 453.

of 1890. It was under the humanitarian pretext of ending slave trade and protecting the aboriginal people of Africa that the Brussels Declaration was signed among European powers as an international agreement for securing 'benefits of peace and civilization' to the vast continent of Africa.[13] Cooper cautions against 'a narrow (but incomplete) interpretation of the Brussels Conference' that it 'represented an attempt to both consolidate an established antislavery norm and graft prohibitory norms on the provision of arms and liquor to Africans onto this established norm.'[14] He insists that 'as far as firearms were concerned, this meant formalizing the transformation of trading arms for slaves from a compelling national interest to a venal activity.'[15] The Brussels Declaration institutionalized a 'dual regime of regulation: the application of a liberal export norm for peacetime exports *from* imperial metropoles combined with extensive attempts to manage arms flows *into, within, and between* colonial spaces.'[16] This regime helped Europeans maintain a 'qualitative military advantage over native populations' and rendered the Africans powerless in their resistance to European conquest.[17]

This becomes more visible as we read the text of the Brussels Declaration at length. Article 1 of the Brussels Declaration argues that 'progressive organization' and 'gradual establishment' of the African territories can take place most effectively 'under the sovereignty or protectorate of civilized nations.'[18] Article 1 (7) imposes 'restriction of the importation of firearms, at least those of modern pattern, and of ammunition throughout the entire extent of the territory in which the slave-trade is carried on.'[19] Articles VIII of the Brussels Declaration states,

> The experience of all nations that have intercourse with Africa having shown the pernicious and preponderating part played by firearms in operations connected with the slave-trade as well as internal wars between the native tribes; and this same experience having clearly proved that the preservation

[13] Treaty text of the Brussels Declaration (1890) formally known as *Slave Trade and Importation into Africa of Firearms, Ammunition, and Spirtual Liquors (General Act of Brussels)*, July 2, 1890.

[14] Cooper, "Race, Sovereignty, and Free Trade," 449.

[15] Cooper, "Race, Sovereignty, and Free Trade," 449–450.

[16] Cooper, "Race, Sovereignty, and Free Trade," 445.

[17] Cooper, "Race, Sovereignty, and Free Trade," 452–453.

[18] Treaty text of the Brussels Declaration (1890).

[19] Treaty text of the Brussels Declaration (1890).

> of the African population whose existence it is the express wish of the powers to protect, is a radical impossibility, if measures restricting the trade in fire-arms and ammunition are not adopted, the powers decide, so far as the present state of their frontiers permits, that the importation of firearms, and especially of rifles and improve weapons, as well as of powder, balls and cartridges, is, except in the cases and under the conditions provided for in the following Article, prohibited in the territories comprised between the 20th parallel of North latitude and the 22nd parallel of South latitude, and extending westward to the Atlantic Ocean and eastward to the Indian Ocean and its dependencies, including the islands adjacent to the coast within 100 nautical miles from the shore.[20]

Articles VIII to Article XIII of the Brussels Declaration focus on the problem of regulating arms trade in Africa more specifically and at length. Article XII stipulated express provision 'to secure the punishment of infringers of the prohibitions' and their accomplices 'by fine or imprisonment, or by both of these penalties, in proportion to the importance of the infraction and in accordance with the gravity of each case.'[21]

The Brussels Declaration argues that it would be impossible to safeguard African populations from 'intestine war between indigenous tribes' without addressing 'the pernicious role of firearms,' a 'radical impossibility if restrictive measures on the commerce in firearms and munitions are not established.'[22] But 'restricting the flow of arms' was presented as only an underlying measure to end slave trade in Africa 'under the sovereignty or the protectorate of civilized nations' and ensuring stability of European possessions.[23] Cooper claims that the Brussels Act 'was consistent with the broader approach to arms trade restrictions adopted by the major powers in all the spaces of empire' and how 'the spaces of empire were increasingly subject to intensive and extensive efforts to restrict the trade in arms via import controls, internal regulation of colonial spaces, and export controls instituted at key nodal points in regional arms markets.'[24] David Stone observes, 'The European powers, motivated by concern about the stability

[20] Treaty text of the Brussels Declaration (1890).

[21] Treaty text of the Brussels Declaration (1890).

[22] David R. Stone, "Imperialism and Sovereignty: The League of Nations' Drive to Control the Global Arms Trade," *Journal of Contemporary History* 35, no. 2 (2000): 215.

[23] Stone, "Imperialism and Sovereignty," 215, quoting from Brussels Convention of 2 July 1890, chap. 1, art. 1, point 7, in Nouveau Recueil General de Traites, 2nd series, vol. 16, 5–6, 8. Text in French.

[24] Cooper, "Race, Sovereignty, and Free Trade," 453–454.

of their colonial empires , agreed on the need to control arms trafficking, and the USA concurred.'[25] It is helpful to note that 'calls for arms trade regulation in the spaces of empire were rarely located in broader critiques of militarism in Europe' or in 'any emerging humanitarian law of war tradition.'[26] In fact, 'neither activists nor officials actively sought to frame the Brussels Act in relation to earlier initiatives such as the 1868 Declaration of St. Petersburg banning the use of explosive and fulminating bullets or the 1874 Brussels Declaration on the Laws and Customs of War.'[27]

This lack of attention is palpable and presents an interesting contrast to 'the invocation of an institutional tradition' during this period to help institutionalize a norm against the use of asphyxiating shells and deleterious gases under the Hague Laws.[28] Price argues that 'chemical weapons were considered an international issue of concern ' at the time of the Hague conference in 1899 and there was much debate on the application of customary restraints to regulate and prohibit the use of such weapons.[29] In these debates, there was an effort underway to constitute 'a common identity among the great powers as civilized nations' and asphyxiating shells played a 'symbolic role' in articulating 'laws of civilized warfare.'[30] In these struggles, one finds voices articulating their awareness of this 'cursed comedy' of humanizing warfare that carried within itself the paradox of cherishing civilization while nurturing militarism and therefore the need to 'tear the mask off.'[31]

Despite a vociferous debate on customary restraints, 'the discipline of civilization' was exercised selectively with regard to the Hague ban on asphyxiating gases.[32] It is argued that this arbitrary exercise of discipline became manifest in an environment of 'growing awareness of a standard of civilization during this period.'[33] It was articulated in the language of the Hague Laws, banning the use of asphyxiating shells 'among Contracting

[25] Stone, "Imperialism and Sovereignty," 214.

[26] Cooper, "Race, Sovereignty, and Free Trade," 454.

[27] Cooper, "Race, Sovereignty, and Free Trade," 454.

[28] Richard Price, *The Chemical Weapons Taboo* (Ithaca & London: Cornell University Press, 1997), 90.

[29] Price, *Chemical Weapons Taboo*, 31.

[30] Price, *Chemical Weapons Taboo*, 37, 54–55.

[31] Leo van Bergen, 'The poison gas debate in the inter-war years,' *Medicine, Conflict and Survival* 24, no. 3 (2008): 182–183.

[32] Price, *Chemical Weapons Taboo*, 35.

[33] Price, *Chemical Weapons Taboo*, 35.

Powers in the case of war between two or more of them' with the qualifier that 'it shall cease to be binding from the time when, in a war between the Contracting Powers, one of the belligerents shall be joined by a non-Contracting Power.'[34] Price acknowledges, 'the Hague Declaration established a discriminatory regime,' as 'those contracting powers were the nations that would count as the members of an emerging society of civilized states,'[35] but at the same time is cognizant of circulating contentions that 'a violation of this norm by these nations could painfully negate their own common and supposedly superior standard of civilized identity.'[36]

Price is emphatic in his assertion, '[T]here was no suggestion during the Hague conferences that the use of asphyxiating shells was to be regarded as legitimate against "uncivilized" nations.'[37] Price insists, '[T]here was no active establishment by those present that this contractual language simultaneously legitimized and positively sanctioned certain uses of asphyxiating shells (for example, against nonparticipants) against those outside the ken of the civilized family of nation.'[38] On the contrary, there is a suggestion that 'one of the qualifications of a civilized nation was to partake in the regulation of warfare that began among the European society of states in the mid-nineteenth century' and 'the contractual language of the prohibition was a legitimizing inducement to join the society of civilized states, an invitation to self-discipline.'[39]

The irony of such an 'invitation to self-discipline' is succinctly captured by Albert Memmi as he observes how a deliberately constituted, asymmetrical relationship of power between the colonizers and the colonized emerged during this period:

> While it is pardonable for the colonizer to have his little arsenals, the discovery of even a rusty weapon among the colonized is cause for immediate punishment. The Arab fantasia has become nothing more than the act of a trained animal which is asked to roar, as he used to, to frighten the guests. But the animal roars extremely well; and nostalgia for arms is always present, and is part of all ceremonies in Africa, from north to south. The lack of implements of war appears proportional to the size of the colonialist forces;

[34] Price, *Chemical Weapons Taboo,* 35.
[35] Price, *Chemical Weapons Taboo,* 35.
[36] Price, *Chemical Weapons Taboo,* 43
[37] Price, *Chemical Weapons Taboo,* 36.
[38] Price, *Chemical Weapons Taboo,* 36.
[39] Price, *Chemical Weapons Taboo,* 36.

> the most isolated tribes are still the first to pick up these weapons. This is not a proof of savagery, but only evidence that the conditioning is not sufficiently maintained.[40]

These limitations were imposed by experiences of vulnerability and fear that the colonial subjects might use these weapons against their own colonial masters.[41] This sense of fear and vulnerability in the West was further reinforced with nineteenth-century memories of the African 'primary resistance' and Indian 'mutinies for independence' which fundamentally altered colonizers' attitudes toward their colonies.[42]

The defeat of the Italians by the Ethiopians in 1896 represented 'the first decisive victory gained by troops that may be reckoned as oriental over a European army in the open field, for at least three centuries.'[43] The Japanese victory in the Russo-Japanese war in 1905 was much publicized and 'presented not as a local triumph of one nation over another, but as a victory with global implications, of the Mongolian people over the European.'[44] The military victories of the non-European powers were touted to rouse racial anxieties to 'hold the racial line.'[45] Gunther et al. in their exploration of 'The West: a securitizing community?' argue that 'the performative effects of a security semantics in which "the West" figures as the threatened, yet notoriously vague referent object that has to be defended against alleged challenges' generate a 'rhetorical heat' that sanctions a culture of 'self-assertion, self-authorization and self-immunization.'[46]

It is through these practices of 'rhetorical instrumentalization' that 'the West' exercises a 'performative power to construct politically relevant distinctions' between 'the West' and the 'non-West' and at the same time encourages allusive references to the impending threats from the

[40] Albert Memmi, *The Colonizer and the Colonized* (Boston: Beacon Press, 1967), 93–94.

[41] Neil Cooper, "Race, Sovereignty, and Free Trade," 453.

[42] Ali. A. Mazrui, "Gandhi, Marx and the Warrior Tradition – Towards Androgynous Liberation," in *The Warrior Tradition in Modern Africa*, ed. Ali A. Mazrui (Leiden: E.J. Brill, 1977), 179.

[43] Furedi, *The Silent War*, 29, see footnote 10.

[44] Furedi, *The Silent War*, 30, see footnote 11.

[45] Furedi, *The Silent War*, 26.

[46] Gunther Hellman, Benjamin Herborth, Gabi Schlag and Christian Weber, "The West: a securitising community?" *Journal of International Relations and Development* 17, no. 3 (2013): 367, 389.

'non-West.'[47] There was a need for 'constant preparedness,' and weapons technologies 'considered too horrific to use against Europeans' such as 'the notorious Maxim gun and dumdum bullet or the French Coloniale bomber' were 'developed specifically for colonial use.'[48] Salter argues that 'the imperial origin of the machine gun and strategic bombing is not insignificant' as 'aerial bombing was first conducted in the colonial context' and Asia and Africa had been 'pacified' with the help of the machine gun.[49] It was the necessity of maintaining order and exercising control over colonial possessions that constituted 'a specific colonial form of *arms control as governmentality*, whereby mechanisms of prohibition and prescription were *both* put to the service of governing which peoples could legitimately use what kind of arms.'[50] For example, successive legislation was enforced in British India in 1858, 1860, 1878 and 1909 to constantly refine and revise 'who had the right to own, import, export, and produce what kind of arms, where they could be transferred to, and under what conditions.'[51]

These 'regulations were not just about the effective management of arms flows but also an intrinsic part of the process by which imperial gradations of race, culture, and threat were actually produced.'[52] They were 'predicated on a moral economy in which European norms of racial superiority and imperialism framed the standards of appropriate behavior of the era and the fluid but always subordinate identities of the other.'[53] These imperial practices of prohibition and prescription were fluid in their efforts to 'manage arms flows according to where people were placed in the racially inflected triple hierarchies of civilization, loyalty, and utility to imperial power.'[54] The desire of the West to maintain 'imperial influence and imperial order' produced discourses on free trade, sovereignty, development and civilization within which arguments on prohibition and prescription of weapons could be situated.[55] Paternalistic and Orientalist

[47] Salter, *Barbarians & Civilization in International Relations*, 39
[48] Salter, *Barbarians & Civilization in International Relations*, 39.
[49] Salter, *Barbarians & Civilization*, 84.
[50] Cooper, "Race, Sovereignty, and Free Trade," 455.
[51] Cooper, "Race, Sovereignty, and Free Trade," 456.
[52] Cooper, "Race, Sovereignty, and Free Trade," 456.
[53] Cooper, "Race, Sovereignty, and Free Trade," 456.
[54] Cooper, "Race, Sovereignty, and Free Trade," 456.
[55] Cooper, "Race, Sovereignty, and Free Trade," 455.

discourses on humanitarianism and disarmament were selectively deployed to disarm the savages.[56]

This civilizational consciousness was further reinforced with the publication of Darwin's *Origin of the Species* (1859), which promised to offer a coherent and scientifically respectable way to replace monogenetic accounts of human physical difference with effectively polygenetic ones. This work generated an entire body of dubious literature on scientific evolutionism to justify racial hierarchies. Kelley notes how 'an entire generation of "enlightened" European scholars facilitated 'racial boundary policing' by wiping out the cultural and intellectual contributions of other cultures and engaging in practices of 'fabrication of Europe as a discrete, racially pure entity, solely responsible for modernity, on the one hand, and the fabrication of the Negro on the other.'[57] These practices of erasure 'stripped all of Africa of any semblance of "civilization", using the printed page to eradicate their history and thus reduce a whole continent and its progeny to little more than beasts of burden or brutish heathens.'[58] It generated a forgetfulness that Africans belonged to 'a race that had already been working in gold and silver two thousand years ago.'[59] At this juncture, it is helpful to pause and reflect on Ali A. Mazrui's observation:

> [W]ith the coming of statehood the warrior tradition becomes absorbed into a large complex of military organization. Sometimes the individual warrior becomes no more than a cog in a military machine. But the warrior tradition as a sub-system of norms and perspectives may continue to condition military behavior in spite of the enlargement of organization scale.[60]

[56] Cooper, "Race, Sovereignty, and Free Trade," 454.

[57] Robin D.G. Kelley, "A Poetics of Anticolonialism," in *Discourses on Colonialism*, Aime Cesaire, translated by Joan Pinkham (New York: Monthly Review Press, 2000), 22.

[58] Kelley, "A Poetics of Anticolonialism," 22.

[59] Franz Fanon, *Black Skin, White Masks*, translated by Charles Lam Markmann (New York: Grove Press, 1967), 130.

[60] Ali A. Mazrui, ed., *The Warrior Tradition in Modern Africa* (Leiden: E.J. Brill, 1977), 2.

Martial Races

Under practices of mercantilism the use of colonies for the extraction of resources for the development of weapons was acceptable but transfer of weapons to the colonial sepoys themselves was subject to limitations.[61] The problem of integration of native soldiers to serve imperial military ambitions was a major preoccupation of imperial powers during this period. How to maintain control over their imperial possessions without arming the native soldiers assumed great significance. A military that could be used by the imperial powers in the colonies as a first line of defense for internal security, serve as an imperial expeditionary force and engage in probing expeditions. A professional military that will be obedient and loyal and enjoy a very visible presence in the colonies. The role of the military in the modern nation-building projects undertaken in the colonies is not to be ignored.

Stephen Cohen insists that the terms such as 'sepoy' (derived from sipahii, meaning soldier) and later 'jawan' (youth) were deliberately deployed by the British in India.[62] These terms conveyed a relationship of paternalism and helped distinguish native soldiers as being 'trained and organized according to European military standards' and 'led in the field by European officers.'[63] The recruitment of the sepoys was 'transformed from a territorial to a racial and caste basis' in India.[64] This was facilitated by implanting the idea of a "martial race" to sow the seeds of difference and set the 'Natives against Natives.'[65] The idea of a martial race was grounded in various explanations based on cultural and psychological differences between castes and regions in India that were 'exaggerated and systematized' by the colonizers.[66] They further tried to ground their explanations in scientific terms by seeking to establish 'direct correlations between climate and martial character.'[67] These efforts were compounded

[61] Deepak Kumar, *Science and the Raj – A Study in British India*, 2nd edition (Oxford: Oxford University Press, 2006), 40, 43; Itty Abraham, *The Making of the Indian Atomic Bomb – Science, Secrecy and the Postcolonial State* (London & New York: Zed Books, 1998), 57–58.

[62] Stephen P. Cohen, *The Indian Army—Its Contribution to the Development of a Nation* (Los Angeles, London: University of California Press, 1971), 7, 50.

[63] Cohen, *The Indian Army*, 7.

[64] Cohen, *The Indian Army*, 41.

[65] Cohen, *The Indian Army*, 39.

[66] Cohen, *The Indian Army*, 51.

[67] Cohen, *The Indian Army*, 47–48.

by romanticization of the 'long-term historical theory of Aryan conquest' to argue that 'only certain races were permitted to bear arms, and in course of time only certain races remained fit to bear arms.'[68] Interestingly, 'the fighting ability and loyalty of many classes was first determined, and later an ancestry was "discovered"' by the colonizers to justify the rationale of martial races as a criterion for recruitment.[69] While 'great care was taken to avoid violation of the troops' religious scruples,' to avoid any rebellion, it was imperative that 'groups recruited into the military were from the politically most backward regions of India.'[70]

Similarly, in the context of Africa, 'persistent in the imperial mentality was the simple assumption that martial prowess was ethnically distributed.'[71] This assumption grounded in the indigenous 'warrior tradition' of Africa was supplemented with other considerations such as literacy, organization and political consciousness of local communities. The imperial powers made it a deliberate practice to recruit from 'some of the least privileged ethnic communities in Africa and from some of the most peripheral regions,' and 'illiterate or semi-literate Africans' were considered to be 'better soldiers than the better educated.'[72] The better educated were 'distrusted as "cheeky" and not adequately obedient.'[73] Mazrui observes how 'once the young rustic is himself in the army, he becomes subject to certain westernizing influences,' but the better educated, politically conscious African became in a fundamental sense a 'rural misfit in his own village,' lacking in suitable employment opportunities.[74]

These practices of 'cultural relativity' in the recruitment of martial races based on ethnic differences soon fostered a 'beguiling fantasy' of a 'prototypical image of the noble savage.'[75] These images considered to be a 'part

[68] Cohen, *The Indian Army*, 47.

[69] Cohen, *The Indian Army*, 49.

[70] Cohen, *The Indian Army*, 52–53.

[71] Ali A. Mazrui, "Soldiers as Tradionalizers—Military Rule and the Re-Africanization of Africa," in *The Warrior Tradition in Modern Africa*, ed. Ali A. Mazrui (Leiden: E.J. Brill, 1977), 247.

[72] Ali A. Mazrui, "The Warrior Tradition and the Masculinity of War," in *The Warrior Tradition in Modern Africa*, ed. Ali A. Mazrui (Leiden: E.J. Brill, 1977), 80.

[73] Mazrui, "The Warrior Tradition," 80.

[74] Ali A. Mazrui, "Armed Kinsmen and the Origins of the State—An Essay in Philosophical Anthropology," in *The Warrior Tradition in Modern Africa*, ed. Ali A. Mazrui (Leiden: E.J. Brill, 1977), 243.

[75] Aidan Southall, "The Bankruptcy of the Warrior Tradition," in *The Warrior Tradition in Modern Africa*, in ed. Ali A. Mazrui (Leiden: E.J. Brill, 1977), 166–170.

of the genre' of 'colonial stereotypes' served as 'psychological props' perpetuating the colonial system.[76] Thus an emphasis on 'martial valour' as the 'first differentia' between the ruler and the ruled 'perfectly fitted the dominant structure of colonialist thought.'[77] It received a tacit endorsement among the colonized trying to reform and stake a claim in belonging to the martial races. Nandy suggests that '[i]n doing so they identified the West with power and hegemony, which in turn they identified with a superior civilization.'[78] The idea of a martial race based on these ambiguous scientific explanations was exercised so rigorously that it soon acquired the status of 'scriptural authority.'[79] It carefully inculcated a process of cultural co-optation that psycho-analysts describe as very nuanced processes of 'identification with the aggressor.'[80] Thus it is barely a surprise that 'no harm' was perceived in 'one martial race adopting in part the outlook of the other' as 'it was a common belief among the British that the British officers themselves represented a martial race.'[81]

These seemingly innocuous practices of naturalization processes tie the colonizer and the colonized in an 'unbreakable dyadic-relationship' in which the colonized seek to emulate the West. But those that were excluded and marginalized from these processes and ridiculed by the colonial powers for 'their alleged nonmartial, unmanly traits' and 'lack of opportunities' to receive 'military training or participate in the defense of India' resented and mocked these practices of inclusion and exclusion perpetrated by the colonizers.[82] The encouragement of the martial races by the colonial powers to fight imperial wars presents a stark contradiction to the ridicule meted out to the rebels in the colonies that wore khaki uniforms in an effort to represent themselves as nationalist soldiers seeking treatment in accordance with the laws of war.[83] These practices were the subject of parody and ridicule among the African people in Niger who did not hesitate to be 'dressed in pith helmets and carrying their swagger

[76] Southall, "The Bankruptcy of the Warrior Tradition," 170–171, 172–173; Mazrui, "Soldiers as Tradionalizers," 247–248.

[77] Ashis Nandy, *The Intimate Enemy*, 24.

[78] Nandy, *The Intimate Enemy*, 24.

[79] Cohen, *The Indian Army*, 46.

[80] Nandy, *The Intimate Enemy*, 7.

[81] Cohen, *The Indian Army*, 52.

[82] Cohen, *The Indian Army*, 99–100.

[83] Albert Memmi, *The Colonizer and the Colonized* (Boston: Beacon Press, 1967), 95.

sticks … take the roles of European army generals who speak to their troops in pidgin French or pidgin English.'[84]

The internalization of Western values and efforts to constitute an understanding of the West based on indigenous experiences of the colonized generated a perception that their own subordination was due to 'emasculation and defeat in legitimate power politics.'[85] They shared the aspirations of modernity toward 'the application of science for the betterment of the human condition, and committed to rationality in ordering human affairs,' but how to engender this 'modernity—as a Western thing' in a postcolonial state?[86] Abraham observes how the '*condition* of the postcolonial emerges from its moment in world space and time, into a world whose dominant rules and values appear already defined.'[87] How to 'come to terms with a global condition where the rules were set by someone else?'[88] How to 'internalize the norms of science and technology that are fundamental to change'?[89] How to use time for development of indigenous technologies or importation to assert a place in modernity?[90] Is the subaltern's quest for modernity and progress subject to a paternalistic and condescending imperial power granting a measure of freedom to the 'crypto-barbarians' in need of further civilization?[91]

In response to these questions, it is suggested that the subalterns' quest for civilization and modernization is to be only 'at the pace tolerated by the military'[92]—a military that is interested in only 'modeling' the 'sepoys' and 'jawans' after their European officers and equips them only with 'second hand equipment' to deliberately maintain and nurture a 'technical gap' to foster a relationship of subordinate dependence and not equality;[93] a military that was 'not geared to receiving and absorbing technological innovations' in 'communications and engineering technologies as well as increasingly complex weaponry' but was expected to

[84] Michael Taussig, *Mimesis and Alterity*, 241, see footnote Peter Stoller quoted in the text.

[85] Nandy, *The Intimate Enemy*, 10.

[86] Abraham, *Indian Atomic Bomb*, 66.

[87] Abraham, *Indian Atomic Bomb*, 18–20; The reference to rules is to the already defined conditions of political subjectivity, statehood and sovereignty.

[88] Abraham, *Indian Atomic Bomb*, 19.

[89] Abraham, *Indian Atomic Bomb*, 20.

[90] Robert S. Anderson, *Nucleus and Nation—Scientists, International Networks and Power in India* (Chicago & London: The University of Chicago Press, 2010), 476.

[91] Ashis Nandy, *The Intimate Enemy*, 7.

[92] Cohen, *The Indian Army*, 2.

[93] Cohen, *The Indian Army*, 2, 30–31, 49, 121.

serve in imperial wars.[94] The significant dependence of the Indian army for 'any new type of equipment, or any new weapon of considerable sophistication from abroad, or else a laborious effort had to be made to manufacture the item in India' became a serious bone of contention for those serving in the military.[95] Cohen observes how the lack of equipment, humiliation endured in military defeats and 'racial discrimination' had the effect of 'provoking the few contacts that were made between Indian officers and nationalist politicians.'[96] He concludes that 'racial discrimination' had the 'net effect' of intensifying the professional outlook of Indian soldiers demanding better equipment and the need for respect and trust that ultimately swayed them with nationalist ideas, as discussed in the next section.[97] It was the First World War that served a blow to the 'martial races theory' as the colonial armies 'suffered inordinate losses due to its obsolete equipment' and presented an opportunity to the 'returning sepoys' to 'compare British and French treatment of their colonials.'[98]

The principle of racial equality was not recognized even as military conscription was introduced in Western and colonized societies during the Great Wars. The non-Whites, especially the Blacks, were humiliated as they were assigned only to 'transport, engineer and other services in which the soldiers did not carry arms' but observed the 'soldiers from India operating infantry weapons, artillery and armour' even if they were of an inferior quality.[99] It was only with the outbreak of the First World War that the colonial state enabled the establishment of 'ordnance factories to produce defence goods' in the colonies.[100] Frank Furedi suggests that the colonial soldier represented 'a classical Marginal Man, but one in possession of a weapon' and therefore a subject of produced and reproduced alarming reports on how 'the returning colonial soldier' would be 'potentially a force of subversion.'[101] But it is questionable whether 'the use of

[94] Cohen, *The Indian Army,* 56–57.
[95] Cohen, *The Indian Army,* 131.
[96] Cohen, *The Indian Army,* 123.
[97] Cohen, *The Indian Army,* 121–123.
[98] Cohen, *The Indian Army,* 69, 71.
[99] Hugh Tinker, *Race, Conflict and the International Order – From Empire to the United Nations* (London & Basingstoke: The Macmillan Press Ltd., 1977), 47.
[100] Abraham, *Indian Atomic Bomb,* 55.
[101] Furedi, *The Silent War,* 153.

colonial troops against other whites violated the racial hierarchy that is central to the ideology of imperialism. … The willingness of colonial subjects to die patriotically for the European undid this hierarchy.'[102]

Nationalism

Partha Chatterjee argues that the 'nationalist imagination in Asia and Africa is posited not on an identity but rather on a difference with the "modular" forms of the national society propagated by the modern West.'[103] It is the 'rule of colonial difference' that enables strategic and tactical 'deployment of the modern forms of disciplinary power.'[104] Chatterjee suggests that Eastern nationalism possesses an acute awareness that the standards of civilization 'have come from an alien culture, and that the inherited culture of the nation did not provide the necessary adaptive leverage to enable it to reach those standards of progress. The "Eastern" type of nationalism, consequently, has been accompanied by an effort to "re-equip" the nation culturally, to transform it. But it could not do so simply by imitating the alien culture, for then the nation would lose its distinctive identity. The search therefore was for a regeneration of the national culture, adapted to the requirements of progress, but retaining at the same time its distinctiveness.'[105]

Similarly, in the context of Latin America, Hymans too seeks to make a distinction between 'oppositional' nationalism and 'nonoppositional' nationalism.[106] Hymans conceptualizes 'nonoppositional nationalism' as being invested in the cultivation of 'a national identity that produces great national pride without also producing fear and loathing of an external "other."'[107] Nonoppositional nationalism is seen as an exercise in prudence. This finds resonance with the ideas articulated by Bhabha above. The idea of 'oppositional nationalism' is grounded on a dynamic of differ-

[102] Salter, *Barbarians & Civilization*, 86.

[103] Partha Chatterjee, "The Nation and Its Fragments: Colonial and Postcolonial Histories," in *The Partha Chatterjee Omnibus* (New Delhi: Oxford University, 1999), 5.

[104] Chatterjee, "The Nation and Its Fragments," 18.

[105] Partha Chatterjee, "Nationalist Thought and the Colonial World," in *The Partha Chatterjee Omnibus* (New Delhi: Oxford University, 1999), 2.

[106] Jacques E.C. Hymans, "Of gauchos and gringos: Why Argentina never wanted the bomb, and why the United States thought it did," *Security Studies* 10, no. 3 (2001): 155–156.

[107] Hymans, "Of gauchos and gringos," 154.

ence 'seen as threatening and inimical to values and interests.'[108] Civilizational discourses inflaming oppositional nationalism evoke ' a sense of cognitive and emotional predispositions that form an explosive psychological cocktail.'[109] In the context of African nationalism in particular, that 'extremism of political language' needs to be traced back to an initial 'distrust of violence as a strategy of liberation.'[110] But 'the nationalist struggle taught the politicians that no phrase and no trick was too mean to use against the political enemy' and 'as long as the "enemy" was a colonial government or institution, it did not seem to matter what language, tactics, or weapons were used.'[111]

This is not surprising after reading the text of the Brussels Declaration (1890) earlier and the Convention for the Control of the Trade in Arms and Ammunition signed at St. Germain-en-Laye, a Paris suburb, on September 10, 1919.[112] In the preamble to this Convention, it is observed that the First World War had 'led to the accumulation in various parts of the world of considerable quantities of arms and munitions of war, the dispersal of which would constitute a danger to peace and public order.'[113] It was further noted that earlier restrictions on the supply of arms to Africa 'no longer meet present conditions, which require more elaborate provisions applicable to a wider area in Africa and the establishment of a corresponding regime in certain territories of Africa.'[114] These concerns led to more stringent measures such as introducing a system of licensing arms exports that effectively curtailed 'the world of arms trading to a limited circle of recognized governments signatory to St. Germain, cutting off all those outside that restricted set.'[115]

This Convention for the Control of the Trade in Arms and Ammunition (1919) further required states party to the treaty to 'publish an annual report showing the export licenses which it may have granted, together

[108] Hymans, "Of gauchos and gringos," 154.

[109] Hymans, "Of gauchos and gringos," 156.

[110] Ali A. Mazrui, "The Warrior Tradition," 105–106.

[111] Mazrui, "The Warrior Tradition," 105–106.

[112] David R. Stone, "Imperialism and Sovereignty: The League of Nations' Drive to Control the Global Arms Trade," *Journal of Contemporary History* 35, no. 2 (2000): 217; "Convention for the Control of the Trade in Arms and Ammunition," in *League of Nations Treaty Series*, Vol. 7, 331.

[113] Stone, "Imperialism and Sovereignty," 217.

[114] Stone, "Imperialism and Sovereignty," 217.

[115] Stone, "Imperialism and Sovereignty," 217; "Convention for the Control of the Trade in Arms and Ammunition," in *League of Nations Treaty Series*, Vol. 7, 332–333.

with the quantities and destinations of the arms and ammunition to which the export licenses referred.'[116] It further restricted arms to the non-Western world by banning shipments to 'any country which refuses to accept the tutelage under which it has been placed.' It declared Africa (except for Libya, Algeria and South Africa), the Arabian Peninsula through Iran and north to Transcaucasia, and all Asian sections of the Ottoman Empire to be prohibited areas fearing arming of insurgent movements. To quote Stone, 'There was little doubt among representatives in Paris that keeping arms out of African and Asian hands was St. Germain's chief task.'[117] It was considered to be 'the moral duty of all civilized states' that 'can only be efficiently performed by agreement between the principal Powers.'[118] These provisions were implemented informally even before the treaty was ratified. The League of Nation's Temporary Mixed Commission on Armaments acknowledged in September 1921 that 'the main purpose of the (St. Germain) Convention was not to promote disarmament as among civilized States, but to prevent arms from getting into the hands of private persons or organizations, or of certain barbarous or semi-civilized peoples' and that the only effect of the St. Germain agreement was on arms trafficking in the 'prohibited areas.'[119]

The extremism of nationalist language can also be traced back to Abyssinians (Ethiopians) suffering as the victims of chemical warfare waged by the Italians in 1935–36, a usage that is often described as a 'rupture' or an 'exception' to an 'attenuated' universal norm prohibiting chemical warfare.[120] It is significant to note how a proclaimed universal chemical weapons taboo exalted for being invoked on grounds of 'institutional tradition' to establish superior standards of civilizational identity, to nurture laws of civilized warfare, to serve as an exercise in self-discipline and an invitation to induce others to join is now considered to be 'attenuated by its embeddedness in these more diffuse norms of international society' that draw upon a colonial legacy of hierarchy, demarcation and inequality.[121] Price suggests,

[116] Stone, "Imperialism and Sovereignty," 217.
[117] Stone, "Imperialism and Sovereignty," 217.
[118] Stone, "Imperialism and Sovereignty," 217.
[119] Stone, "Imperialism and Sovereignty," 217.
[120] Price, *Chemical Weapons Taboo*, 105–106, 108.
[121] Price, *Chemical Weapons Taboo*, 91, 108.

> This rupture was manifested in the demarcation of distinct zones of warfare—war among the "civilized" advanced industrialized countries was a different matter from conflicts involving other areas such as colonies ... And the use of chemical weapons might be less unacceptable in one area than another.[122]

A lack of attention and study of these more 'diffuse norms' that persist and wield performative power to discriminate in the use of weapons is an interesting legacy in practices of arms control and disarmament, a legacy that persists in deriding the efforts of the subaltern to acquire these weapons as 'poor man's bomb' and considers their acquisition 'an insufficient entry fee into the club of "civilized" warfare manned by industrial/technological powers.'[123]

These imperial wars and the outbreak of the First World War generated a climate in the colonies of acute nationalist consciousness and recognition of 'the value of the military as a national universal solvent; as an expression of the national will.'[124] The nationalists now began to appreciate the importance of gradually transforming a mercenary army into an effective citizen army. They questioned the burden of taxation incurred by the colonies in supporting troops to wage imperial wars and the training, position and equipment of the natives in the military. The nationalists in the colonies no longer felt the need to 'slavishly' model their institutions after the European powers or that the 'technical and organizational prerequisites of nationhood' belonged only to the Europeans.[125] On the contrary, they were inspired by the Japanese and recognized that 'the military is the ultimate sanction available to a government.'[126] The Great War had demonstrated that 'a nation that did not possess military strength could not hope to preserve its independence.'[127]

Despite these significant developments, it is pertinent to pause and question,

[122] Price, *Chemical Weapons Taboo,* 107.
[123] Price, *Chemical Weapons Taboo,* 144.
[124] Cohen, *The Indian Army,* 58.
[125] Cohen, *The Indian Army,* 91.
[126] Cohen, *The Indian Army,* 93.
[127] Subhas Chandra Bose, an Indian nationalist and founder of the Indian National Army, quoted by Cohen, *The Indian Army,* 100.

> why is it that non-European colonial countries have no historical alternative but to try to approximate the given attributes of modernity when that very process of approximation means their continued subjection under a world order which only sets their tasks for them and over which they have no control?[128]

Kelley responds by observing how 'colonial domination required a whole way of thinking, a discourse in which everything that is advanced, good and civilized is defined and measured in European terms.'[129] The answer can be further understood in terms of the 'epistemic privilege' asserted by the West representing a 'framework of knowledge which proclaims its own universality; its validity, it pronounces, is independent of cultures.'[130] Thus the condition for nationalist thought to be considered 'modern' is to accept the claim to universality of this 'modern' framework of knowledge.[131] Ironically, it is in this acceptance that while

> Nationalism denied the alleged inferiority of the colonized peopke; it also asserted that a backward nation could "modernize" itself while retaining its cultural identity. It thus produced a discourse which, even as it challenged the colonial claim to political domination, it also accepted the very intellectual premises of "modernity" on which colonial domination was based.[132]

This acceptance is not without contestation of the epistemic privilege exercised by the West in articulating 'what counts' as universal.[133]

In spite of the 'passive revolution' that in general characterizes the transition from colonial to postcolonial nation-states, it is important to note that 'nationalist thought is selective about what it takes from Western rational thought.'[134] It is selective as it opposes colonial rule and argues in favor of political possibilities 'which colonialist thought refuses to admit.'[135] Chatterjee observes that the nationalist 'quarrel with colonialist thought will be necessarily carried into the domain of justification.'[136] It will 'question the veracity of colonialist knowledge, dispute its arguments, point out

[128] Partha Chatterjee, "Nationalist Thought and the Colonial World," 10.

[129] Robin D.G. Kelley, "A Poetics of Anticolonialism," in *Discourses on Colonialism*, Aime Cesaire, translated by Joan Pinkham (New York: Monthly Review Press, 2000), 27.

[130] Chatterjee, "Nationalist Thought and the Colonial World," 10–11.

[131] Chatterjee, "Nationalist Thought and the Colonial World," 10–11.

[132] Chatterjee, "Nationalist Thought and the Colonial World," 30.

[133] Price, *The Chemical Weapons Taboo*, 150–151.

[134] Chatterjee, "Nationalist Thought and the Colonial World," 50, 41.

[135] Chatterjee, "Nationalist Thought and the Colonial World," 41.

[136] Chatterjee, "Nationalist Thought and the Colonial World," 41.

contradictions, reject its moral claims.'[137] It is therefore more pertinent to question whether the colonial nationalist issued an alarm and alert against 'race-thinking' experienced as an 'ever-present shadow which accompanied the development of the comity of European nations' and cautioned against the dangers of 'racism being a kind of exaggerated nationalism' that could be mobilized to wage chemical warfare by the Italians against the Abyssinians.[138]

This sense of caution becomes apparent with colonial scientists being repeatedly urged 'by activists in the national movement to stay out of jail,' 'keep their head down' and 'keep away from politics.'[139] This advice is not only political but strategic as politics of a scientist often had an impact on his ability to work, nurture associations, travel overseas, and gain a scientific reputation and international recognition in securing a fellowship with the Royal Society of Great Britain. The particular politics of a colonial scientist was always under careful scrutiny by Western scientists as they wielded power over decisions regarding access to laboratories and bestowing fellowships on colonial scientists.[140] A colonial scientist had to exercise prudence in articulating his political views in encounters with scientists in the West. The particular politics of a scientist in the West was often significant in determining whether a colonial scientist would get access to their laboratories or not. If a scientist in the West was deemed sympathetic to the nationalist struggles waged in the colonies, access could be facilitated, but if a scientist in the West was not sympathetic to these revolutionaries, then access could be obstructed. During the colonial period and for a long time thereafter the colonial scientists too were suspect by their own populations as 'being too oriented to Europe to be *real* Indians in a cultural sense.'[141]

An acute sense of alarm about this lack of authenticity could be effectively raised at a time when nationalist consciousness encounters 'frameworks of knowledge created by post-Enlightenment rationalist thought.'[142] These encounters encourage nationalist thought to make allowances for

[137] Chatterjee, "Nationalist Thought and the Colonial World," 41.

[138] Hannah Arendt, "Race thinking before Racism", *The Review of Politics* 6, no. 1 (1944): 41–42.

[139] Robert S. Anderson, *Nucleus and Nation—Scientists, International Networks and Power in India* (Chicago & London: The University of Chicago Press 2010), 16, 27, 108.

[140] Anderson, *Nucleus and Nation,* 43–44.

[141] Anderson, *Nucleus and Nation,* 534.

[142] Partha Chatterjee, "Nationalist Thought and the Colonial World," 50.

'modern attributes of European culture' that can be acquired but also generate confident assertions that 'true modernity for the non-European nations would lie in combining the superior material qualities of Western cultures with the spiritual greatness of the East.'[143] This elitist 'act of cultural synthesis' was expected to be performed by the 'supremely refined intellect' of scientists and lawyers in the colonies.[144] But some lawyers and doctors in the colonies such as Gandhi in India tried to expose the demonic face of Western sciences as they maneuvered to mobilize the masses and sought 'historical consolidation of the "national" by decrying the "modern."'[145] Fanon in Algeria and Aime Cesaire in Martinique cautioned against the 'rise of a new ruling class mimicking the colonial masters' and demanded an 'overthrow of a master class's ideology of progress, one built on violence, destruction, genocide.'[146]

A master ideology of imperialists emphasizes that 'arms tend to shorten and prevent wars' and acquisition of the 'best arms' is imperative for 'enhancement of national power through technological innovation and the legitimation of advanced technology as the currency of domination.'[147] A master ideology pursued by imperialists resists any 'restriction on the invention and construction of new types of arms' on grounds that such regulations and prohibitions 'would place civilized peoples in a disadvantageous position in time of war with nations less civilized or with savage tribes.'[148] A master ideology that is unrelenting in its discursive strategy of advocating weapons ban as a strategy for 'discipling "uncivilized nations."'[149] A master ideology that cunningly evokes the language of civilization as a classic trigger for a hyper-state of patriotic fervor and antagonism toward the enemy to wage wars and resist disarmament. Despite the iteration and reiteration of this master ideology with its emphasis on arms and civilization, experts such as Stuart Hall are content to note in a neutral tone that the purpose of arms control and disarmament during this period is 'at the end of conflicts to create a new balance … to develop and perpetuate stability between states … to develop norms of behaviour in international relations … control the proliferation of weapons … and

[143] Chatterjee, "Nationalist Thought and the Colonial World," 51.
[144] Chatterjee, "Nationalist Thought and the Colonial World," 51.
[145] Chatterjee, "Nationalist Thought and the Colonial World," 51.
[146] Kelley, "A Poetics of Anticolonialism," 27.
[147] Price, *Chemical Weapons Taboo*, 42.
[148] Price, *Chemical Weapons Taboo*, 42.
[149] Price, *Chemical Weapon Taboo*, 42.

international control.'[150] They do not acknowledge that circulation of this pernicious master ideology embedded in racial consciousness has the effect of generating counter-discourses on Pan-Africanism and Pan-Asianism.

Jean Allman claims, '[I]n the US there was an efflorescence in Black Internationalism in the wake of Italy's invasion of Ethiopia in 1935—an internationalism that continued to insist on the inextricable connections between struggles for equality and racial justice in the US and anticolonial resistance in Africa and Asia,'[151] thus demonstrating that 'the principle of territoriality behind the emergence of nations has simply transformed the mythology of kinship; it has not obliterated such mythologies.'[152] Aime Cesaire insists that 'the Negritude movement between the two world wars' is 'a concrete rather than an abstract coming to consciousness' to engage with experiences of difference, denial, alienation and assimilation, and assert Africa's contribution and accomplishment at a time when a 'history of world civilization' could be written without 'devoting a single chapter to Africa, as if Africa had made no contribution to the world.'[153] This nationalist consciousness often found voice in the form of poetry 'plumbed from the depths of the unconscious' to give voice to 'experience as a whole' of life in the colonies where 'poetic knowledge is born in the great silence of scientific knowledge.'[154] To quote Aime Cesaire, 'It is poetry and therefore revolt.'[155]

An expression of revolt visible in nationalist thought that condemned the race-thinking of the West and asserted the right to self-determination and right to sovereign statehood on the international stage. To quote Chatterjee,

> Nationalism has arrived: it has now constituted itself into a state ideology; it has appropriated the life of the nation into the life of the state. It is rational

[150] Stuart Croft, *Strategies of Arms Control – A History and Typology* (Manchester & New York: Manchester University Press, 1996), 32.

[151] Jean Allman, "Rethinking Power and Politics in the African Diaspora: Nuclear Imperialism and the Pan-African Struggle for Peace and Freedom – Ghana 1959–1962," *Souls* 10, no. 2 (2008): 85.

[152] Ali A. Mazrui, "Armed Kinsmen and the Origins of the State—An Essay in Philosophical Anthropology," in *The Warrior Tradition in Modern Africa*, ed. Ali A. Mazrui (Leiden: E.J. Brill, 1977), 19.

[153] Aime Cesaire, *Discourses on Colonialism*, translated by Joan Pinkham (New York: Monthly Review Press, 2000), 91–92.

[154] Cesaire, *Discourses on Colonialism*, 17–18.

[155] Cesaire, *Discourses on Colonialism*, 28.

and progressive, a particular manifestation of the march of Reason; it has accepted the global realities of power, accepted the fact that World History resides Elsewhere. Only it has now found its place within that universal schema of things.[156]

It is helpful to supplement this moment of 'arrival' of nationalist thought in the colonies with an acute observation that 'when nationality is defined in "racial terms" the issue of presumed consanguinity asserts its immediacy.'[157] This is because 'territory has not replaced kinship as a basis of allegiance; it has simply introduced a new way of defining kinship. ... Territoriality provides a broader definition of kinship, but by no means supplants it.'[158] Nationalism in the colonies is experienced as a 'discourse of order, of the rational organization of power' that claims to incorporate all dissent and is 'actualized in the unified life of the state' that expresses itself in a 'single, consistent, unambiguous voice.'[159] This voice insists on autonomy of state as its central organizing principle and social justice as its legitimizing principle.[160] It represents a 'national marriage between the ideas of progress and social justice.'[161]

The promise of progress and justice to be realized in postcolonial states is premised on the assertion of there being 'nothing organic or essential in European civilization which has made it dynamic and powerful' but that 'every civilization, it is now argued, has its periods of growth and periods of decay' explained by a host of 'conjunctural factors: "economic, political, intellectual, whatever."'[162] Thus, 'the cultural values, or the "spirit", which go with a particular sort of growth are capable of being extracted from their civilizational context and made universal historical values. Then they are no longer the "property" of any particular culture, nor are they essentially or organically tied with that culture.'[163] It is the colonial powers that are held responsible for impeding 'the growth of the forces of modernity' in colonial societies, and with the removal of alien power these

[156] Chatterjee, "Nationalist Thought and the Colonial World," 162.
[157] Ali A. Mazrui, "Armed Kinsmen and the Origins of the State," 13.
[158] Ali A. Mazrui, "Armed Kinsmen and the Origins of the State," 12.
[159] Chatterjee, "Nationalist Thought and the Colonial World" 51.
[160] Chatterjee, "Nationalist Thought and the Colonial World," 132.
[161] Chatterjee, "Nationalist Thought and the Colonial World" 132.
[162] Chatterjee, "Nationalist Thought and the Colonial World," 137.
[163] Chatterjee, "Nationalist Thought and the Colonial World," 137.

societies could resume their course of technological development.[164] In this endeavor, postcolonial states 'must learn from the West.'[165]

Colonial Science and Heroic Scientists

However, any effort to learn is discouraged by colonial masters, especially in areas of scientific education, fundamental research in sciences or development of indigenous sciences in the colonies.[166] The problem was not simply in terms of differences in pay, lack of scientific infrastructure in the colonies and resistance to appointments of natives to teach sciences in the universities.[167] Adas observes,

> Few of the colonized, and virtually none beyond the Western educated elite, had any appreciation for the theoretical breakthroughs and technical accomplishments that were responsible for the European dominance. But nearly all were only too aware of the Europeans' unprecedented capacity for the application of scientific knowledge to production, communications, and above all, military technology.[168]

The colonial scientists themselves were acutely aware of 'where the metropolitan centers of science were located,' and this knowledge was significant in the colonies because

> the absence of knowledgeable consumers of modern scientific research in India forced them to look westwards to find such consumers and protect their self-image as scientists. Their country respected them mainly as grand successes without appreciating the content of their work. Even this success was defined in terms of bureaucratic status, degrees, wealth, and the opinion of established scientists outside India.[169]

[164] Chatterjee, "Nationalist Thought and the Colonial World," 137.

[165] Chatterjee, "Nationalist Thought and the Colonial World," 138, see footnote 23.

[166] An excellent discussion on colonial science as a dependent science is provided by Deepak Kumar, *Science and the Raj – A Study in British India*, 2nd edition (Oxford: Oxford University Press, 2006), 1–18, 26–28.

[167] Ashish Nandy, *Alternative Sciences – Creativity and Authenticity in Two Indian Scientists*, 2nd edition (Delhi: Oxford University Press, 1995), 38–39; Abraham, *Indian Atomic Bomb*, 41–42.

[168] Adas, *Machines as the Measure of Men*, 268.

[169] Ashish Nandy, *Alternative Sciences*, 60.

This dependence generated among some colonial scientists an experience of suffering evoked from real or imaginary sense of hostility toward Western scientists. Some were reluctant to acknowledge the help that they received from Westerners in terms of funding or editorial work. Others were suspicious and feared that their innovative research could be plagiarized by the Westerners.[170] Nandy observes that it was their colonial status, their vulnerable 'sensitivity to issues of dominance and submission, and not any actual interference in the processes of research, which was often the main contribution of colonialism to intellectual decay.'[171] Other scholars disagree and argue that while the colonial government often promised to build laboratories and provide staff, it did not support this process 'in proportion to the commitment of private individuals.'[172] They also argue that it was often very difficult for colonial scientists to gain any practical work experience in the laboratories and factories located in the West.

While the 'norm of modern science' proclaims itself to be 'a universal practice' accessible to anyone 'as long as they are good enough,' the practices of 'colonial science' deliberately made the colonies dependent on metropolitan institutions and scientists.[173] It is therefore important to study the 'cultural context of individual creativity in science in the non-Western world' and engage in 'site-specific and context-sensitive' research.[174] The discriminatory practices of colonial science encouraged the perception that 'the science practiced in most non-Western settings is derivative, inferior, and has yet to reach acceptable—read Western—levels of quality.'[175] Some colonial scientists were careful in demonstrating to the domestic audiences how their work was celebrated abroad while often maintaining 'an image of neglected and isolated genius ignored by Western scientists.'[176] In order to secure the sympathy and support of scientists in the West, some even represented themselves as 'a poor transient whose fate was to return to a distant and ill-equipped outpost in his native

[170] Nandy, *Alternative Sciences,* 113.

[171] Nandy, *Alternative Sciences,* 142.

[172] Anderson, *Nucleus and Nation,* 37–38.

[173] Abraham, *Indian Atomic Bomb,* 40, see footnote 19; "Who Gets to do Science" in *The 'Racial' Economy of Science: Toward a Democratic Future*, ed. Sandra Harding (Bloomington: Indiana University Press, 1993), 197–200.

[174] Nandy, *Alternative Sciences,* ix; Anderson, *Nucleus and Nation,* 2–3; Mallard, Paradeise and Peerbaye, *Global Science and National Sovereignty,* 32.

[175] Abraham, *Indian Atomic Bomb,* 35.

[176] Anderson, *Nucleus and Nation,* 31.

land.'[177] Another image cultivated was one of a 'heroic scientist' working alone in a lab against a hostile world and was particularly inspiring during the inter-war period of growing nationalism.[178]

It was difficult for European scientists to accept 'colonial scientists in Western laboratories' as the problem of race generated an unspoken norm of 'firm boundaries between metropolis and colony.'[179] They were unsure how to deal with these colonial scientists in their 'hybrid form' representing a 'colonial body' but possessing a 'mind — fully expressive of Western culture and arts as well as the upper reaches of physics.'[180] The body served as a racial signifier and generated a sense of 'ambivalence' in the reception colonial scientists received in the metropole working with other scientists that could not accept them as equals.[181] This ambivalence was often attributed to a perception among Western scientists that a 'secret complex' was harbored by colonial scientists, a 'secret complex' that made the colonial scientists at once the subject of envy and intrigue by compatriots and at the same time suffer from an acute anxiety of 'not being taken quite seriously by Englishmen.'[182] These everyday insecurities and uncertainties with regard to being 'colonial,' 'hybrid' scientists subject to vagaries of reception in the civilized West reinforced an acute civilizational consciousness. These experiences reinforce an understanding that '"Western" science cannot be known unambiguously by location or personality; it depends on an act of power in order to know that it is dominant.'[183] Several other portraits of sensitivity experienced by colonial scientists in their encounters with Western scientists are further sketched by Anderson as he notes how often colonial scientists emphasized that some of their groundbreaking work was done in the impoverished colonies but was only met with 'incredulity' by the Europeans.[184] The publication of their research in local journals did not gain them much recognition or merit.[185] It was irksome for colonial scientists to encounter the pervasive assumption that their most creative work was undertaken only when they went

[177] Anderson, *Nucleus and Nation*, 35.
[178] Anderson, *Nucleus and Nation*, 138.
[179] Abraham, *Indian Atomic Bomb*, 40.
[180] Abraham, *Indian Atomic Bomb*, 40.
[181] Abraham, *Indian Atomic Bomb*, 40–41.
[182] Anderson, *Nucleus and Nation*, 67.
[183] Abraham, *Indian Atomic Bomb*, 41.
[184] Anderson, *Nucleus and Nation*, 31.
[185] Anderson, *Nucleus and Nation*, 31.

abroad. It is important to recognize the 'anguish of being a dissenting scientist' standing 'outside the perimeters of the "civilized world" engaging in 'the psychological costs of confronting an imperial system of knowledge.'[186] The crushing poverty and colonial status associated with 'defeated systems of knowledge' often 'enter a person's or group's self-definition and become psychological forces' manifest in their nationalism.[187] To quote Nandy,

> By conceding the cultural and psychological determination of science, in places and times when both cultural and personal systems are in flux, one exposes uncertainties that can lead to crippling anxiety and to a self-examination that can be particularly painful.
>
> Nowhere does this social determination of scientific creativity create so much anxiety and confusion as in the societies self-consciously trying to draw up new blueprints for their futures. In such societies, science becomes a battleground where the society's new ambitions confront its "backlogs", and the scientist becomes a microcosm where the community's adaptive capacities challenge the creativity of the individual. In the process itself, sometimes science itself is distorted and some scientists are destroyed. The society, too, may pay a heavy price, swinging between the extremes of total acceptance of exogenous models of science in society and a doomed search for absolute autonomy in the area of knowledge.[188]

The colonial scientists often had to deal with Western prejudices regarding Indians as being 'bright but impractical people.'[189] These prejudices maintained that 'Indians could be excellent at metaphysics and languages but not in the exact sciences.'[190] Another persistent prejudice was 'Indians would not be capable of good experimental science.'[191] The politics of the scientists in the West encouraged them to think that the colonies could not survive without the imperial presence of the Europeans. They failed to acknowledge 'how the default mechanisms of macroeconomic colonial policy were always privileging British industry and technology and spare parts imports, thus implicitly steering Indians toward theoretical or more

[186] Ashish Nandy, *Alternative Sciences*, viii, ix.
[187] Ashish Nandy, *Alternative Sciences*, ix, 8.
[188] Nandy, *Alternative Sciences*, 18–19.
[189] Anderson, *Nucleus and Nation*, 81.
[190] Nandy, *Alternative Sciences*, 38.
[191] Anderson, *Nucleus and Nation*, 37.

research-oriented kinds of work and away from practical applications.'[192] It was only with the outbreak of the Great War that any possibility of Indians engaging in new applications of technical knowledge was even considered a possibility but even then it was difficult for them to get 'practical training after completing their theses.'[193]

The Europeans prioritized their claim that 'the natural sciences were more important than other disciplines' and insisted that 'in the more crucial disciplines Indians were not as good as Englishmen.'[194] This emphasis on 'sciences of nature' as the 'paradigm of all rational knowledge' to serve human 'interests' is not innocent but smacks of 'cultural essentialism' deployed to assert 'domination of the world.'[195] It is this 'epistemic privilege' of 'rationality as an ethic' that has 'become the last bastion of global supremacy for the cultural values of Western industrial societies. It is a privilege which sanctions the assertion of cultural supremacy while assiduously denying at the same time that it has anything to do with cultural evaluations.'[196] It is extremely difficult for Western scientists to acknowledge and 'distinguish between the culture of science, as something that could be parochial and ideologically colored, and the formal text of science, as something more universal and objective.'[197] The Western sense of superiority entrenched in 'the scientific achievement of the West' ridiculed the Indian for being fixated with medieval technology.[198] Thus science became a 'symbol of western intrusion' and scientists in the colonies felt compelled to develop 'techniques of coping with the intrusion.'[199]

Nandy analyzes the techniques pursued by the 'first generation of modern scientists' in India in the following words:

> The first was to separate the culture and the content of science and, then, fight for pluralizing the existing culture of science in such a way that it would accommodate the Indian worldview. The second was by dismantling the dominant culture of science and replacing it by a new culture more congruent with Indian values. Neither was truly practicable … a third device …

[192] Anderson, *Nucleus and Nation,* 81.
[193] Anderson, *Nucleus and Nation,* 151.
[194] Nandy, *Alternative Sciences,* 38.
[195] Chatterjee, "Nationalist Thought and the Colonial World," 14.
[196] Chatterjee, "Nationalist Thought and the Colonial World," 16–17.
[197] Nandy, *Alternative Sciences,* 119.
[198] Nandy, *Alternative Sciences,* 38.
[199] Nandy, *Alternative Sciences,* 19.

> build an entirely new Indian structure of science ... battle against the formidable edifice of modern science. All the responses were consistent with the logic of a colonial situation, and one must judge for oneself which was the more tragic end.[200]

These responses of colonial scientists as elites of a subject society were lock in step with the development of nationalist thought in the colonial world, as discussed above. The problem of intellectual decay in the colonies was more deep seated and could be attributed to practices of 'colonial racism.'[201] The practices of colonial racism deliberately emphasize and exploit the differences between the colonized and the colonizers. They further seek to sustain these differences, transforming them into irrefutable standards of fact that correspond with concrete realities to the benefit of the colonial powers. It was these explicit practices of colonial racism that made it impossible for the colonized to cultivate any taste for 'mechanized civilization and a feeling for machinery.'[202] Thus, a sense of 'technical inadequacy' was deliberately cultivated as 'the colonizer pushed the colonized out of the historical and social, cultural and technical current.'[203] To reiterate, the difficulties involved in conditioning the colonized to a sense of technical inadequacy is compounded with the politics involved in labeling of particular natives as belonging to the 'martial races' and the problems of supplying inferior weapons to the native soldiers even as they fought in the imperial wars of Europe.

Hybrid Scientists

But as Itty Abraham claims, 'knowledge of the conditions prevalent in advanced states' percolates in the colonies with the help of 'hybrid' scientists and the soldiers returning home after fighting imperial battles overseas.[204] The search for self-esteem not devoid of cultural roots motivates the colonial scientists to join forces with the nationalist leadership in colonial societies. Some colonial scientists from India, China, Brazil, Argentina

[200] Nandy, *Alternative Sciences*, 19–20.

[201] Memmi, *The Colonizer and the Colonized*, 71.

[202] Memmi, *The Colonizer and the Colonized*, 117.

[203] Memmi, *The Colonizer and the Colonized*, 114–115.

[204] Abraham, *Indian Atomic Bomb*, 19, 40; to name a few hybrid scientists, Homi Jehangir Bhabha from India, Shiro Ishii from Japan.

and Japan studying and working in Europe returned to their home countries to develop their own indigenous national science and technology programs.[205] The inter-war period was a time for 'heroic scientists' to work 'alone in a lab against a hostile world.'[206] Shiro Ishii proposed 'speeding-up of Japanese work on germ warfare and hoped that if human experiments could be sanctioned Japan would have an unassailable lead.'[207] Homi Bhabha, a nuclear physicist, considered it his 'duty' to remain in India to help build scientific research institutions and work on a secretive nuclear program.[208] The West focused more on the racial origins than on scientific capabilities and, on these grounds, consistently rejected participation by colonial scientists in the Allied war efforts. As the war efforts demanded 'science in the service of the state,' the 'nationality of scientists now acquired a meaning that could not be divorced from politics.'[209]

The 'contradiction between the powerful consensual myth of the universality of science in theory and its parochiality in practice' became increasingly visible to the colonized.[210] It was their frustrated nationalism and desire to emulate that was resisted by the West. A sense of fear and vulnerability engulfed the West that the colonized will in future become 'counterplayers' that question the civilizational status quo and seek to create an alternative frame of reference.[211] 'The Allies other than the Americans (that is, the Dutch, French as well as the British) believed that the end of the war would enable them to re-establish their colonial empires' and 'found it difficult to accept' the declaration of independence by their colonies.[212] This feeling of vulnerability and threat encouraged a 'false sense of cultural homogeneity,' aggressive nationalism and a hyper-masculinity that 'openly sanctified—in the name of such values as competition—new forms of institutionalized violence and ruthless social Darwinism' against

[205] John Lewis and Xue Litai, *China Builds the Bomb* (Stanford: Stanford University Press, 1988), 44–45; Matias Spektor, "The evolution of Brazil's nuclear intentions," *The Nonproliferation Review* 23, no. 5–6 (2016): 640.

[206] Anderson, *Nucleus and Nation,* 138.

[207] Checkland, *Humanitarianism and the Emperor's Japan*, 127.

[208] Anderson, *Nucleus and Nation,* 105.

[209] Abraham, *Indian Atomic Bomb,* 42.

[210] Abraham, *Indian Atomic Bomb,* 43.

[211] Nandy, *The Intimate Enemy,* 11.

[212] Checkland, *Humanitarianism and the Emperor's Japan,* 155.

the Other represented as 'devious, effeminate and passive-aggressive' that needed to mature and be disciplined.[213]

But as mentioned earlier, the significant role of professional scientists in nation-building was appreciated by activist nationalists, encouraging the colonial scientists to quietly undertake research work and cultivate their professional networks.[214] In an effort to wear 'the garb of modernity' the nationalists were eager to recruit scientific experts capable of 'marshaling the latest knowledge made available by science and technology.'[215] This sentiment was further enriched with the presence of 'refugee scientists' from Europe living in the colonies during the inter-war period.[216] These refugee scientists often brought intellectual stimulation through their teaching and research in the colonies. It was an era of 'scientocracy' in the colonies when colonial scientists and activist nationalists linked 'science with civilization.'[217] Colonial scientists questioned the status and purpose of their civilization and accepted opportunities to 'tour research facilities in Great Britain, Canada and the US to learn about "models" for organizing military-oriented research.'[218]

Anderson notes how often Indian scientists were in close contact and communication with scientists in the West working on weapons programs. These associations were formed as colonial scientists circulated within the formal and informal international networks of scientists.

Anderson observes the 'intellectual sophistication' of 'more than a handful' of Indian scientists that quickly grasped 'the potentials and risks of nuclear weapons and nuclear power' prior to the nuclear explosion in Hiroshima and Nagasaki.[219] They read scientific journals and kept abreast of latest scientific discoveries and during their visits to Europe were aware of scientists working on secret weapons development programs in service of the state. Anderson mentions that one particular Indian scientist S. Chandrasekhar was urged by Western scientists to join the Manhattan Project at Los Alamos but declined.[220] The reasons for his decision to

[213] Nandy, *The Intimate Enemy,* 37.

[214] Anderson, *Nucleus and Nation,* 108.

[215] Jawaharlal Nehru, *The Discovery of India* (New York: John Day, 1946), p. 38; Chatterjee, "Nationalist Thought and the Colonial World," 158.

[216] Anderson, *Nucleus and Nation,* 70.

[217] Anderson, *Nucleus and Nation,* 91.

[218] Anderson, *Nucleus and Nation,* 105–106, 114–115, 118.

[219] Anderson, *Nucleus and Nation,* 1.

[220] Anderson, *Nucleus and Nation,* 116.

decline are not explored at any length by Anderson, but several references are made to show how during the inter-war period informal professional networks were cultivated between the colonial scientists and scientists in the West. Meghnad Saha and Shanti Bhatnagar's association with Fritz Haber and Walther Nernst, scientists responsible for the invention of the nerve gas, is notable.[221] Similarly, Homi Bhabha's friendship with Heisenburg in Germany, James Chadwick in the UK and Oppenheimer in the US as scientists involved with nuclear weapons programs in their countries is also noteworthy.[222] The colonial scientists were expected to be nationalists while also maintaining a cosmopolitan outlook that would enable them to circulate within international networks of scientists. They were often lampooned as 'the mimic men.'[223]

While one does not get any direct evidence of how these individual relationships were exploited to advance the weapons development program by the colonial scientists, there is evidence to suggest how the growing rivalry and competition among the European powers during the inter-war period and in the aftermath of the Second World War were carefully exploited by the colonial scientists to gain scientific equipment. On the other hand efforts were being made by the imperial powers to 'reposition an empire science network, soon to be called a commonwealth network at a new center of power in Washington.'[224] In this effort it was imperative to reach out to scientists in the colonies that were not entirely 'disaffected' by the colonial rule.[225] These efforts at outreach by the weakening imperial powers were designed to maintain their access to important minerals such as beryl ore, thorium and uranium from the colonies in Asia and Africa. The colonial scientists recognized the sly civility behind these practices of the West and would shrewdly use their mineral resources as bargaining chips with the West to purchase military equipment, nuclear reactors and heavy water.[226] A revolution in military nuclear technology 'became a standard for the education of world cultures to Western technology' and put an end to colonial territorial expansion.[227] It forced a realization that 'there may be no way out of the present danger, than an

[221] Anderson, *Nucleus and Nation,* 34–36.
[222] Anderson, *Nucleus and Nation,* 100, 178–179.
[223] Ashish Nandy quoted by Anderson, *Nucleus and Nation,* 560, footnote 58.
[224] Anderson, *Nucleus and Nation,* 116.
[225] Anderson, *Nucleus and Nation,* 114.
[226] Anderson, *Nucleus and Nation,* 201–202.
[227] Derrick De Kerckhove, "On Nuclear Communication," *Diacritics* 14, no. 2 (1984): 71.

accelerated access to nuclear maturity, precisely through technological improvement.'[228]

These feelings of insecurity were compounded in the inter-war period with the publication of Oswald Spengler's *The Decline of the West*. For the purpose of our study we will focus on his two main arguments. He argued that every civilization 'passes through the age-phases of the individual man. Each has its childhood, youth, manhood, and old age.' He then developed this argument further to the effect that the decline of the West is inevitable 'because the West has developed machine technology to an extent previously unknown and spread it over the entire planet.'[229] The ideas contained in this book 'disseminated around the world in almost no time' and were 'critically important to the dissemination of the occidentalist common place' until the end of the Second World War.[230] These ideas were to shape the thinking of American policymakers as they grappled with the problem of nuclear weapons, discussed further along in the text. George Kennan 'read him and found much that was congenial,' and Paul Nitze 'steeped himself in Spengler,' and these were policymakers that became the key architects of the post-1945 constitutional order of arms control and disarmament.[231] The regulation and control of the weapons technology, especially nuclear weapons technology, was of paramount importance to them to prevent the decline of the West and to maintain its superiority. These ideas also influenced others that seemed to be arriving on the international scene with the tide of nationalism gaining in strength, raising demands for sovereign statehood. These ideas found resonance as the colonized tried to comprehend and negotiate a new constitutional nuclear order espoused in a language of standards of civilization.

Constitutional Order

James Crawford argues that 'the concept of "civilization" was used as a form of exclusion of non-Western values, of non-Western identity, and even of legal personality.'[232] He insists that 'from the beginning international law was not exclusively concerned with the relations between states,

[228] Mark Sanders, "Remembering Apartheid," *Diacritics* 32, no. 3/4 (2002): 75.

[229] Jackson, *Civilizing the Enemy*, 107.

[230] Jackson, *Civilizing the Enemy*, 107.

[231] Jackson, *Civilizing the Enemy*, 105.

[232] See preface by James Crawford in Antony Anghie's *Imperialism, Sovereignty and the Making of International Law* (Cambridge: Cambridge University Press, 2004), xii.

but more importantly with the relations of domination.'[233] These observations are borne out from the discussion above demonstrating how the 'laws of warfare and the treaties of international organizations' were carefully based on 'the tacit or explicit value consensus which "European civilization" represented.'[234] The concept of civilization gained currency as it 'provided the legal title to the position of dominating Power' and 'determined the circle within which the law of nations applied.'[235] This understanding of international law premised on the concept of civilization empowered the sovereign state to do 'as it wishes with regard to the non-sovereign entity which lacks the legal personality to assert any legal opposition.'[236]

The 'consent' of the sovereign to treaties as 'expression of sovereign will' and 'customs' of a society assumes a significant role.[237] Anghie suggests, 'At the simplest level, the connection between sovereignty and culture was embodied by the fundamental positivist proposition that only European states could be sovereign. ... Not only was the non-European excluded from the realm of sovereignty but European culture and society were naturalized.'[238] It became common knowledge in the West that international law was applicable only between 'the civilized and the Christian people of Europe or to those of European origin.'[239] The colonies struggled to gain recognition as independent sovereign states from their imperial masters. Anghie asserts,

> [C]olonialism was central to the constitution of international law in that many of the basic doctrines of international law—including, most importantly, sovereignty doctrine—were forged out of the attempt to create a legal system that could account for the relations between the European and non-European worlds in the colonial confrontation.[240]

[233] See preface by James Crawford in Anghie's *Imperialism, Sovereignty and the Making of International Law*, xi.

[234] Salter, *Barbarians & Civilization in International Relations*, 15.

[235] R.P. Anand, *New States and International Law* (Delhi: Vikas Publishing House Pvt. Ltd., 1972), 21–22.

[236] Anghie, *Imperialism, Sovereignty and the Making of International Law*, 34.

[237] Anghie, *Imperialism, Sovereignty and the Making of International Law*, 44.

[238] Anghie, *Imperialism, Sovereignty and the Making of International Law*, 102.

[239] Anand, *New States and International Law*, 17–18.

[240] Anghie, *Imperialism, Sovereignty and the Making of International Law*, 3.

Anghie further insists that it is pretentious to assume that 'international law came fully formed and ready for application' in the colonies and the latter had only to assimilate them to become a part of an 'existing, stable, "Eurocentric" system.'[241] The rhetorical emphasis on maintenance of international order conceals the problem of 'dynamic of difference.'[242]

The problem of 'dynamic of difference' encounters 'different cultural orders, each with its own ideas of propriety and governance' and engages in an 'endless process of creating a gap between two cultures, demarcating one as "universal" and civilized and the other as "particular" and uncivilized, and seeking to bridge the gap by developing techniques to normalize the aberrant society.'[243] These techniques involve a complex process of 'characterization of the personality of the Indians' and 'elaboration of a novel system of universal natural law.'[244] The personality of the Indian is one that is capable of reason but is 'unredeemable' as 'violators of the law' and that can only by being subject to a civilizing mission be brought to follow apparently universal norms and standards of international law that are in effect European.[245] The Indian is therefore 'excluded from the sphere of sovereignty' and the Indian 'acts as the object against which the powers of sovereignty may be exercised in the most extreme ways.'[246] This violence of constituting universal international law vis-à-vis colonialism persisted in the late nineteenth century as the positivists 'sought to reconstruct the entire system of international law as a creation of sovereign will.'[247]

R.P. Anand argues that 'it was only during the nineteenth century, as the European countries came to develop their power, that under the influence of positivism, they began to question the legal personality of the Asian states ... Might has indeed become right.'[248] Africa was totally unrepresented, and only five Asian states—Turkey, China, Japan, Persia and Siam—attended the first Hague Conference in 1899. Kinsella observes that the invitations to the conference were extended premised on distinctions between civilized and barbarian rather than on the possession of

[241] Anghie, *Imperialism, Sovereignty and the Making of International Law*, 4–5.
[242] Anghie, *Imperialism, Sovereignty and the Making of International Law*, 4.
[243] Anghie, *Imperialism, Sovereignty and the Making of International Law*, 4, 16.
[244] Anghie, *Imperialism, Sovereignty and the Making of International Law*, 19.
[245] Anghie, *Imperialism, Sovereignty and the Making of International Law*, 26–27.
[246] Anghie, *Imperialism, Sovereignty and the Making of International Law*, 27–30.
[247] Anghie, *Imperialism, Sovereignty and the Making of International Law*, 33.
[248] Anand, *New States and International Law*, 18.

sovereignty.[249] This conference deliberated on arguments pertaining to the regulation and prohibition of dumdum bullets in the following terms:

> In civilized war a soldier penetrated by a small projectile is wounded, withdraws to the ambulance, and does not advance any further. It is very difficult with a savage. Even though pierced two or three times, he does not cease to march forward, does not call upon the hospital attendees, but continues on and before anyone has time to explain to him that he is flagrantly violating the decisions of the Hague Conference, he cuts off your head.[250]

Although the Hague conference banned the use of dumdum bullets, the imperial powers persisted in their use against the Afro-Asians. They insisted on their use, arguing that they engaged in 'wars with men, who although poorly armed, did attack in great numbers' and therefore 'needed bullets with "stopping power."'[251] Thus, 'while European powers claimed to derive rights from treaties they entered into with non-European states, they refused to accept the obligations arising from them,' and often these treaties created only 'obligations of "honour" on the part of European states,' leaving much to their own 'discretion and not International Law.'[252] Kinsella notes, 'The barbarian was said to wage war unconstrained and without discipline. … Yet, against the barbarian, civilized entities were allowed to wage a war unconstrained and without discipline.'[253] Ironically, 'although the barbarian was presumed to demarcate a clear opposite or absolute limit of civilization, the barbarian was, in fact, immanent to civilization.'[254]

The 'Hague ban was absolute, it was not unreservedly universal' and the 'Hague Declaration established a discriminatory regime' by stipulating that the terms of these agreements were binding only on the contracting parties and 'shall cease to be binding from the time, in a war between the Contracting Powers, one of the belligerents shall be joined by a non-Contracting Power.'[255] The agreements negotiated in the form of St.

[249] Kinsella, *The Image Before the Weapon*, 107.

[250] Kinsella, *The Image Before the Weapon*, 108.

[251] Jeff Guy, *Remembering the Rebellion – The Zulu Uprising of 1906* (Scottsville, South Africa: University of KwaZulu-Natal Press, 2006), 85–86.

[252] Antony Anghie, *Imperialism, Sovereignty and the Making of International Law*, 80–81, see footnotes 153 and 154.

[253] Kinsella, *The Image Before the Weapon*, 108.

[254] Kinsella, *The Image Before the Weapon*, 108.

[255] Price, *Chemical Weapons Taboo*, 35.

Petersburg Declaration (1868), Washington Treaty (1921) and Geneva Protocol (1925) were considered to be agreements among the civilized.[256] While the St. Petersburg Declaration 'prohibited the use of certain projectiles among *civilized nations*,' the Geneva Protocol emphasized how 'the general opinion of the *civilized world*' had 'justly condemned … the use in war of asphyxiating, poisonous or other gases.'[257] Similarly the Washington Treaty stated,

> The use of asphyxiating, poisonous or other gases and all analogous liquids, material or devices, having been fully condemned by the general opinion of the civilized world and a prohibition of such use having been declared in treaties to which a majority of the civilized Powers are parties.[258]

These agreements and imperial wars simply reinforced the significance of membership in a society of civilized, sovereign states. This 'society constituted law and law constituted society.'[259] This body of law 'distinguished between civilized states and non-civilized states and asserted further that international law applied only to sovereign states which comprised "family of nations."'[260]

The problem then confronted by the non-European states was, how to seek admission into the international society? Anghie is emphatic in his insistence that we recognize 'society's operational role as a mechanism by which cultural assessments can be transformed into a legal status.'[261] The concept of society 'enables a distinction to be made between different types of states,' and 'the effect of the distinction is to exclude non-European states from the family of nations and hence from the realm of sovereignty itself.'[262] Nandy suggests that this is possible through subtle and sophisticated 'means of acculturation' that beget 'models of conformity' and 'models of dissent.'[263] These modes of conformity and models

[256] Price, *Chemical Weapon*, 84; Croft, *Strategies of Arms Control – A History and Typology*, 25.

[257] Croft, *Strategies of Arms Control*, 25, 29; Japan and the Unites States did not sign the Geneva Protocol of 1925

[258] Price, *Chemical Weapons Taboo*, 84.

[259] Anghie, *Imperialism, Sovereignty and the Making of International Law*, 47.

[260] Anghie, *Imperialism, Sovereignty and the Making of International Law*, 35.

[261] Anghie, *Imperialism, Sovereignty and the Making of International Law*, 98.

[262] Anghie, *Imperialism, Sovereignty and the Making of International Law*, 99.

[263] Nandy, *The Intimate Enemy*, xii.

of dissent include 'codes which both the rulers and the ruled can share.'[264] These codes in the form of social norms and cognitive categories are enforced with overt socioeconomic and psychological rewards and punishment and also through the inner momentum of violence 'in which the ruled are constantly tempted to fight their rulers within the psychological limits set by the latter.'[265]

The figures of alterity to the West, the stereotypical representations of the noble savage and the dirty dog, as discussed in Chap. 1, are thus to be accommodated or disciplined with the help of these legal codes. Some non-European countries initially pursued the path of acculturation, through conformity, such as China, Japan and Ethiopia. In the late nineteenth century, they sought membership within the Red Cross movement, but their requests did not always meet with immediate success. Their requests were often denied on grounds of not being sufficiently civilized. The proclamations of universality by humanitarian organizations too remain 'captive to the colonial definitions of the universal.'[266] The International Committee of the Red Cross (ICRC) as a humanitarian organization embedded in the political culture of the West invoked conditions of 'sufficiently civilized' and 'national character' prior to granting any recognition to the non-Western societies. The initial reply of the Red Cross to requests for membership by China was as follows:

> We cannot officially recognize the existence of a Red Cross Society in a State which is not a signatory of the Geneva Convention. ... We do not believe that the Chinese people are sufficiently civilized, from the point of view of the laws of war, to observe faithfully the Geneva Convention, even after their Emperor has signed it. ... We can only recognize a single society per state, and this society must have a national character; yours being composed exclusively of foreigners would not satisfy this essential condition.[267]

Japan was the first non-Western country to become a fully recognized member of the Red Cross on June 6, 1886.[268] Olive Checkland questions whether Japan's haste to join the Red Cross organization based in Geneva

[264] Nandy, *The Intimate Enemy*, 2.
[265] Nandy, *The Intimate Enemy*, 3.
[266] Nandy, *The Intimate Enemy*, 123.
[267] Checkland, *Humanitarianism and the Emperor's Japan*, 45.
[268] Checkland, *Humanitarianism and the Emperor's Japan*, 8.

was based on an 'urgent need to join a world club.'[269] He suggests that it was a strategic move by the Japanese government 'determined to legitimize itself as far as possible on the world stage' and seek 'recognition' in a discriminatory world.[270] It was only through participation in the International Red Cross that the Japanese could hope to persuade the Western powers of their 'maturity' and convey 'a standard early sign of statehood.'[271] It is also helpful to recollect how the ICRC refused to provide gas masks to the people of Abyssinia experiencing aero-chemical warfare waged by the Italians citing legal texts.

While the non-European states have to await recognition by the European states, the latter themselves were established as sovereign European states 'through reliance on the concept of society' which is explicitly European.[272] To quote Anghie, 'Once constituted, however, the sovereign asserts supremacy by presenting itself as the means by which society operates and comes into being. ... A structure of power and decision-making is implicit in the doctrine because the power to "recognize" new states is vested in the states that are already sovereign.'[273] Thus 'sovereignty is explicitly identified with particular cultural characteristics and a particular cultural process: that of Europe' and 'the story of the "expansion of international society"—an ambiguous, euphemistic and somewhat misleading term when it is understood that this refers not to an open process by which the autonomy and integrity of non-European states were accepted, but to the colonial process by which Asian and African societies were made to accept European standards as the price of membership.'[274]

The non-European societies enjoyed no recognizable rights under international law, while the European sovereign states enjoyed 'virtually no legal restrictions' on their actions with respect to the non-European people.[275] The non-European societies were therefore confronted with the

[269] Checkland, *Humanitarianism and the Emperor's Japan*, xvii.

[270] Checkland, *Humanitarianism and the Emperor's Japan*, 8, 173. Subsequently, other Asian countries such as Siam (1895), Korea (1903) and China (1904) joined the Red Cross movement.

[271] Checkland, *Humanitarianism and the Emperor's Japan*, 70, 8, 174.

[272] Antony Anghie's, *Imperialism, Sovereignty and the Making of International Law* (Cambridge: Cambridge University Press, 2004), 99.

[273] Anghie, *Imperialism, Sovereignty and the Making of International Law*, 99–100.

[274] Anghie, *Imperialism, Sovereignty and the Making of International Law*, 100–101.

[275] Anghie, *Imperialism, Sovereignty and the Making of International Law*, 103.

'fundamental contradiction of having to comply with authoritative European standards in order to win recognition and assert themselves.'[276] Japanese 'admission' into the 'charmed circle of European great powers' was made possible with the Anglo-Japanese alliance of 1902, and she signaled her 'promotion' by challenging and defeating Russia.[277] It was only with Japan's military ascendancy and defeat of Russia in 1905 that it could secure its acceptance into the family of nations. To quote a Japanese diplomat, 'We show ourselves at least your equals in scientific butchery, and at once we are admitted to your council tables as civilized men.'[278]

In Japan there was a celebratory mood that 'unleashed a flood of self-congratulatory cartoons' in newspapers depicting a 'stylishly dressed Japan throwing a reception for the family of "civilized" nations, to which it now belonged.'[279] The Japanese celebrated their recognition as a civilized nation by disparaging their 'half-civilized' Asian neighbors. Japanese cartoons depicted 'a plucky little Japan pulling ahead of its fat and clumsy neighbor China in a footrace towards "civilization."'[280] Japan's proposal that the principle of racial equality be included in the Covenant of the League at the Peace Conference of 1919 was soundly rejected by the Anglo-American powers. This reinforced the message that in order to be recognized as sovereign, a state must construct a modern military and procure weapons. Peter Duus observes how in Japan 'the satirical boundary the cartoonists drew between "us" and "them" not only marked domestic political divisions but also traced the contours of national identity.'[281]

War of Civilization

To claim a place in the international order, some of the newly independent colonies through their rhetoric of nationalism constituted their own 'security imaginary,' asserting significance of their 'civilizational identity' and 'civilizational subjecthood' to claim greatness that could not be based only

[276] Anghie, *Imperialism, Sovereignty and the Making of International Law*, 107.

[277] E.H. Carr, *What Is History?* (Middlesex, England: Penguin Books, 1961), 147.

[278] Quote seen in R.P. Anand, *New States and International Law* (Delhi: Vikas Publishing House Pvt. Ltd., 1972), 21, see footnote 60; B.V.A. Roling, *International Law in an Expanded World* (Amsterdam: Djambatan, 1960), 10.

[279] Duus, "Weapons of the Weak, Weapons of the Strong," 984.

[280] Duus, "Weapons of the Weak, Weapons of the Strong," 984.

[281] Duus, "Weapons of the Weak, Weapons of the Strong," 984.

on their material capabilities.[282] The West too persisted in its efforts to 'universalize' and 'enrich its ethnic stereotypes by appropriating the language of defiance of the victims.'[283] It confronted the need to devise an alternative schema for retaining power to civilize and control the barbarians. The West tried to propagate the idea that the Second World War was a 'war of civilization' and tried to rebuild an international order that is governed 'through a system of double standards, but this time its form is moral not racial.'[284] The moral choices presented a stark 'cultural choice: civilization or the threat of chaos—either one or the other.'[285]

The use of nuclear weapons in Japan reinforced the message that 'locations in the hierarchy of states are marked off in part by specific weapons, so the possession of certain weapons is considered the sine qua non for claiming places higher up the international order. Perhaps of central importance in this regard are nuclear arms.'[286] Kerckhove argues that 'the nuclear bomb was an American solution to World War II and it continues to be a typically "American" and "technological" solution to world peace.'[287] He argues that the consequence of this 'nuclear oneupmanship' is that the 'structuring principle of the whole planet is now subjected to a single Western technology.'[288] Furthermore 'it is highly doubtful that China, India, and all the non-Western countries which are courting nuclear technology would have ever been prompted to embark in that venture on their own accord,' and in doing so 'they are fast losing the identity and self-regulating principles of order invested in their individual cultures and traditions.'[289]

The use of nuclear weapons in Hiroshima and Nagasaki, an 'exhibitionist' exercise of the colonizers, fueled a sense of panic.[290] The widespread circulation of rumors under imperial conditions of colonialism and censorship regarding the unprecedented destructive power of this particular

[282] Himadeep Muppidi, "Postcoloniality and the Production of Insecurity," in *Cultures of Insecurity: States, Communities and the Production of Danger*, ed. Jutta Weldes, Mark Laffey, Hugh Gusterson and Raymond Duvall (Minneapolis: University of Minnesota Press, 1999).

[283] Nandy, *The Intimate Enemy,* 32.

[284] Furedi, *The Silent War,* 46.

[285] Bhabha, *The Location of Culture,* 189.

[286] David Mutimer, *The Weapons State—Proliferation and the Framing of Security* (London & Boulder: Lynnie Rienner Publishers, 2000), 137.

[287] Derrick De Kerckhove, "On Nuclear Communication," *Diacritics* 14, no. 2 (1984): 75.

[288] De Kerckhove, "On Nuclear Communication," 76.

[289] De Kerckhove, "On Nuclear Communication," 76.

[290] Bhabha, *Location of Culture,* 166.

weapon reawakened the barely hidden anxieties of being left behind. This 'pseudo-petrification' both 'incites and excites' as there is an uncertain 'colonial silence.'[291] This silence does not question the perpetuated colonial bias of the state system itself but projects the subaltern state as the mimetic model for redressal of inequalities and injustices perpetuated with the use of superior weapons. It is unwilling to encounter any possibility that suggests the 'assimilationist language of statism, even if it is to make a case for granting a standard of recognition to the third world against the assumption of its inherent savagery,' might 'end up reproducing a colonial dynamic that ill-serves the colonized.'[292]

A 'language of colonial nonsense' that is 'inscriptions of an uncertain colonial silence' surfaces, baffling the verities of culture with their refusal to answer, translate questions: 'what does the colonial power want?' or 'He is saying this to me, but what does he want?'[293] These questions are suggestive of 'setting up (of) another specifically colonial space of the negotiations of cultural authority.'[294] But in this space 'one silence repeats the other' and 'the threatened "loss" of meaningfulness in cross-cultural interpretation, which is as much a problem of the structure of the signifier as it is a question of cultural codes (the *experience* of other cultures), then becomes a hermeneutic project for the restoration of cultural "essence" or authenticity.'[295] The language of colonial nonsense was articulated by President Truman in response to the atomic bombing of Hiroshima and Nagasaki when he stated,

> Nobody is more disturbed over the use of the atomic bombs than I am but I was greatly disturbed over the unwarranted attack by the Japanese on Pearl Harbour and their murder of our prisoners of war. The only language they seem to understand is the one we have been using to bombard them. When you have to deal with a beast you have to treat him as a beast. It is most regrettable but nevertheless true.[296]

[291] Bhabha, *Location of Culture,* 177.

[292] Shampa Biswas, Nuclear Desire- Power and the Postcolonial Nuclear Order, (London & Minneapolis, Minnesota University Press, 2014), 196.

[293] Homi K. Bhabha, *The Location of Culture* (London & New York: Routledge, 1994), 166, 177.

[294] Bhabha, *Location of Culture,* 169.

[295] Bhabha, *Location of Culture,* 179.

[296] Barton J. Bernstein, "Understanding the Bomb," *Diplomatic History* 19, no. 2 (1995); Bruce Cumings, "On the Strategy and Morality of American Nuclear Policy in Korea – 1950 to the Present," *Social Science Japan Journal* 1, no. 1 (1998): 67.

Truman has been critiqued for his explicit racism against imperial Japan and the inability to make a distinction 'between leadership by fanatical militarists and the Japanese people, or between combatants and innocent civilians.'[297] Truman appears to be completely unaware that the nuclear bomb is not a mere object but constituted an information environment that penetrated and evoked 'deep-seated feelings and attitudes.'[298] It was this kind of racism that became the subject of Japanese anti-American propaganda during the war. The Japanese argued,

> Not only in the Southern States, but throughout the United States, the rule of White Supremacy has apparently become the blind, bigoted creed of American Whites. ... So intolerant, arrogant and selfish are American whites proving to be in their attitude toward colored people within their borders, that it is too much to expect them to accord any better treatment to the peoples of the world in the future.'[299]

It was in this atmosphere of war that the Japanese calls for Pan-Asianism to foster an Asian civilizational identity vis-à-vis the Western civilizational identity gained currency.

The fluid atmosphere of war and its shifting terrain of conquests and defeats that held the promise of changing the terms of dominance and servitude encouraged the subalterns to 'invoke the language of humiliation' at the hands of the imperial powers experienced by the colonies.[300] It was in this fluid atmosphere of war propaganda that strategies of othering gathered monumental force, empowering the idea of 'American exceptionalism' as a 'particular type of Orientalism.'[301] American exceptionalism championed the idea of the 'West' in asserting 'positional superiority of Western countries in relation to the Othering of the non-West.'[302] An

[297] Cumings, "On the Strategy," 68.

[298] De Kerckhove, "On Nuclear Communication," 78.

[299] Gene Weltfish, "American Racism: Japan's Secret Weapon," *Far Eastern Survey* 14, no. 17 (1945): 236.

[300] Sanjay Palshikar, "Understanding Humiliation," in *Humiliation: Claims and Context*, ed. Gopal Guru (Oxford, New Delhi: Oxford University Press, 2009), 83.

[301] Meghana V. Nayak and Christopher Malone, "American Orientalism and American Exceptionalism: A Critical Rethinking of US Hegemony," *International Studies Review* 11, no. 2 (2009): 253.

[302] Nayak and Malone, "American Orientalism and American Exceptionalism," 254.

investigation of the particular practices of American exceptionalism 'to provide order to the world' can help unravel 'the fiction of a coherent Western civilization,' but it does not detract from the shared 'discursive deployment of ontological differences and epistemological claims' of Orientalism and Exceptionalism that justify a 'racial hierarchy that prioritizes Anglo-Saxons.'[303]

It is helpful to note that 'the othering of Europe' necessary to the exercise of American Exceptionalism as a particular type of Orientalism is 'different from the othering of the non-West.'[304] In the process of othering, 'the Western Other' there is a sense of differentiation to induce a distinctiveness that is 'familiar and recognizable to the Western self even in moments of fierce disagreement and rivalry.'[305] But in the process of othering 'the non-Western' there is a sense of disavowal, the 'over there' is a signifier of fear and danger as 'potential similarities to the non-Western Other are beyond the realm of imagination.'[306] This nuanced process of othering permits 'a mutual complicity in violence against non-Western Others.'[307] Thus American exceptionalism joined forces with European exceptionalism to produce a particular type of post–Second World War constitutional legal order and specialized international regimes pertaining to nuclear non-proliferation. The production of this nuclear order is premised on a reactionary European desire to retain its power and prestige in the nuclear order and an 'anxious' American desire to be 'both a beneficiary of centuries of Western civilization' and at the same time represent the US as 'more humane and more successfully liberal than Europe.'[308]

Conclusion

This ambivalence sets the stage for further power play trumpeting the West and the Rest. This problem is compounded by a circulating totalitarian nuclear discourse that is premised on a pretentious assumption that all sovereign states compete with each other to possess nuclear weapons and

303 Nayak and Malone, "American Orientalism and American Exceptionalism," 254, 253.
304 Nayak and Malone, "American Orientalism and American Exceptionalism," 262.
305 Nayak and Malone, "American Orientalism and American Exceptionalism," 262.
306 Nayak and Malone, "American Orientalism and American Exceptionalism," 263.
307 Nayak and Malone, "American Orientalism and American Exceptionalism," 263.
308 Nayak and Malone, "American Orientalism and American Exceptionalism," 260.

obsesses over the problem of proliferation to the exclusion of all other 'competing frames of nuclear reference.'[309] In this totalitarian nuclear discourse, 'the African continent—with the singular exception of South Africa—is not considered part of the nuclear world.'[310] Jean Allman notes, '[W]hat is often missing from historical reflections on Pan-Africanism, African nationalism, and movements for independence is the relationship between struggles for the liberation of the continent from colonial rule and pacifist movements in opposition to nuclear armament.'[311] This neglect is consistent with the colonial mindset that is willing to extract uranium from African countries but due to their lack of possession of technical means and political will to build nuclear weapons is ignored. The visibility of a country in this totalitarian discourse is premised on its ability to wrest the status of a nuclear weapon state. Thus problems of postcolonial science persist as it now struggles with the meaning of 'nuclearity.'[312]

No effort is made among the arms control and disarmament experts toward acknowledging that the idea of 'progress of civilization' was not universal in the early twentieth century even as it was mobilized toward 'alleviating as much as possible the calamities of war.'[313] But it is this lack of universality in the laws of war that is expressed time and again by international lawyers seeking to regulate and prohibit the use of aero-chemical warfare.[314] The lack of attention to these normative claims of civilizational practices, the problems of inclusion and exclusion in constituting arms control and disarmament agreements and imperial concerns with the

[309] Itty Abraham, "What really makes a country nuclear? Insights from nonnuclear Southeast Asia," *Critical Studies on Security* 4. no. 1 (2016): 2, 14.

[310] Abraham, 'What really makes a country nuclear?' 24.

[311] Jean Allman, "Rethinking Power and Politics in the African Diaspora: Nuclear Imperialism and the Pan-African Struggle for Peace and Freedom – Ghana 1959–1962," *Souls* 10, no. 2 (2008): 83.

[312] Gabrielle Hecht, *Being Nuclear: Africans and the Global Uranium Trade* (Cambridge: MIT Press, 2012); Abraham, "What really makes a country nuclear?" 24–41.

[313] See text of The Declaration of St. Petersburg, December 11, 1868, in *A Documentary History of Arms Control and Disarmament*, Trevor N. Dupuy and Gay H. Hammerman (New York & London: T.N. Dupuy Associates in association with R.R. Bowker Company, 1973), 48.

[314] Ritu Mathur, *The International Committee of the Red Cross & Humanitarian practices of Arms Control & Disarmament* (Ph.D. Dissertation, York University, 2011), chapter on chemical weapons.

transfer of weapons generate a historical legacy that underscore the significance of understanding how practices of arms control and disarmament have been deployed as civilizational practices since the late nineteenth century and comprehending practices of neo-racism or racial etiquette practiced in a nuclear world order.

* * *

CHAPTER 4

Sly Civility and Institutionalized Humiliation

Racial Etiquette

The use of nuclear weapons in Hiroshima and Nagasaki is representative of a crisis of modernity. The use of this weapon of mass destruction is seen as an 'index in the crisis of learning' and an 'emblematic refutation of illusions about historical progress tied to progress in science and technology.'[1] It is observed how

> the actual and potential destructiveness of military technology is one case of technical powers that are out of appropriate social control, reflecting a deficit in the social learning required to regulate evolving human powers. The inability to come to terms with Hiroshima, then, suggests an ethical and cultural deficit that has general significance.[2]

Hiroshima is considered to be not only a temporal marker dividing the old and new epoch in weapons technologies but representative of a 'cultural crisis,' an 'impasse that can be measured in cultural and institutional terms.'[3]

Peterson insists that efforts to address this impasse are not simply a matter of 'providing ethical guidelines to the cultivation and use of new

[1] Richard J. Peterson, "Human Rights: Historical Learning in the Shadow of Violence," *The American Journal of Economics and Sociology* 68, no. 1(2009): 258.

[2] Peterson, "Human Rights," 259.

[3] Peterson, "Human Rights," 259, 266.

R. Mathur, *Civilizational Discourses in Weapons Control*,
https://doi.org/10.1007/978-3-030-44943-8_4

technological powers.'[4] On the contrary, there is an urgent need to be attentive to practices that are 'rooted in reconstructions of the social relations presently constituted in part by violence' and 'the institutional problem of the processes and relationships in which such regulation would take place.'[5] In being attentive to these practices and institutions, it is imperative to note how 'race is implicated in the constitution of the "national" and race is 'central to the "fictive ethnicity" around which nationalism is organized.[6]Racism as an 'internal supplement' contributes to the tensions between nationalism's 'quasi-"universalist" aspirations to unite heterogeneous individuals in a common identity (a cultural or ethnic supplement to territorial control) and the particularist ideal type around which such an identity is constructed.'[7]

Balibar suggests,

> [A]ll contemporary states are racial states in this sense—they harbor inequalities and conflicts that are legitimized in terms of race differences or some practical equivalent—but they are also legally and politically committed to establishing equality, at least at the formal and juridical level, and therefore to combating racism or banning it from the public sphere and the political community.[8]

Thus neo-racism constitutive of practices of sly civility 'contains past racisms and transcends them by finding new foundations for social difference and obscuring their most unacceptable elements with an aesthetic of tolerance.'[9]

It can be argued that this obscurity is particularly feasible at a time when 'the nuclear predicament—the result of the invention of a single device—sprang into the world full-fledged, offering little time for reflection or adjustment.'[10] A 'conspiracy of silence' with astounding 'speed' formalized racial equality as a principle of order in the new international

[4] Peterson, "Human Rights," 261.

[5] Peterson, "Human Rights," 261, 259.

[6] Short and Kambouri, "Ambiguous universalism," 274; Etienne Balibar, "Racism and Nationalism," 50.

[7] Short and Kambouri, "Ambiguous universalism," 274.

[8] Etienne Balibar, "Racism Revisited: Sources, Relevance, and Aporias of a Modern Concept,"*PMLA* 123, no. 5(2008): 1636.

[9] Short and Kambouri, "Ambiguous universalism," 274.

[10] Jonathan Schell, "The Abolition I—defining the great predicament,"*The New Yorker*, January 2, 1984, 444, quoted and cited by Kerckhove, "On Nuclear Communication," 71–81.

system.[11]Arendt argues that it was now possible to speak in racial terms while still professing faith in the equality of all peoples.[12]Furedi observes, 'The shift in attitude was so swift and apparently so widely endorsed that the previous longevity of anti-egalitarian and racist sentiments can and was easily lost sight of.'[13] This 'silent war' has 'produced, over time, social formations and even world orders that were macrostructural systems of inclusion and exclusion' as experienced during the Cold War.[14] It is therefore pertinent to explore further, how in an era of nuclear weapons, this silent war wields the disciplinary power of civilizational discourses?

It is possible to address this question by taking note of some key assumptions at play in the constitutional nuclear order. Ideational representations of this nuclear order as articulated by scholars suggest that it is a negotiated 'constitutional order' that fosters 'institutionalized processes of participation and decision-making that specify rules, rights, and limits on power holders.'[15] These ideational representations make some implicit assumptions regarding time and race. One is that the feasibility of a constitutional order is dependent on the 'difference in the two time horizons' that factor into the calculations of the powerful states and the weaker states. The latter realize that in the absence of an institutional arrangement bargaining will be based on power capacities and they will lose. On the other hand, powerful states are more 'willing to trade off gains today for gains tomorrow.'[16]A further assumption claims, 'the question of race has been "resolved" in international relations through decolonization and sovereignty.'[17] These implicit assumptions facilitate periodization and reorganization of scholarship 'around national rather than racial differences' and contribute to marginalization of study of race in constituting the new nuclear order.[18]

[11] Bhabha, *The Location of Culture*,175; Furedi, *The Silent War*, 14.

[12] Hannah Arendt, "Race thinking before Racism", *The Review of Politics* 6, no. 1(1944): 49.

[13] Furedi, *The Silent War*, 15.

[14] Randolph B. Persaud and R.B.J. Walker, "Apertura: Race in International Relations,"*Alternatives: Global, Local, Political* 26, no. 4(2001): 373–374; Furedi, *The Silent War*, 5.

[15] G. John Ikenberry, *After Victory—Institutions, Strategic Restraint and the Rebuilding of Order after Major Wars*(Princeton & Oxford: Princeton university Press, 2001), 29.

[16] Ikenberry, *After Victory*,56–57.

[17] Short and Kambouri, "Ambiguous universalism," 270.

[18] Short and Kambouri, "Ambiguous universalism," 271; R.J. Vincent, "Race in International Relations,"*International Affairs* 58, no. 4(1982): 331–356; Robert J. Vitalis,

The idea of political mastery is further reinforced in the consciousness of the West in the nuclear age with the possession of these weapons even as the use of these weapons evoked a 'growing sense of moral unease' and possibility of 'fear of revenge' by Others.[19] A 'second form of colonization' epitomized as racial etiquette gained ground through practices of sly civility in the nuclear order,[20] a form of psychological colonization that alters cultural priorities within colonized societies and induces one to generalize that 'the modern West' is not just 'a geographical and temporal entity' but a 'psychological category.'[21] It encourages a sense of omnipresent, omnipotent, 'The West is now everywhere, within the West and outside; in structures and in minds.'[22] The racial etiquette accompanying this psychological orientation is now subtly imbricated in a new 'political order' premised on a 'norm against noticing' race,[23] Thus a misplaced emphasis on theory-building through simulation, abstraction and deliberate marginalization of 'descriptive or historical analysis of the kind that can highlight the racialized practices constitutive of the current global order' but which are castigated for lacking in rigor.

A sense of vulnerability and tolerance is reinforced with the emergence of a 'new racial etiquette' that makes it difficult to be overtly racist.[24] Practices of sly civility now cloaked neo-racism, racial etiquette or racial pragmatism at play in the new constitutional order and served to emphasize the need to 'neutralize the development of race consciousness,' and to be 'racially conscious was to be disruptive if not threatening.'[25] These practices of sly civility did not represent any serious commitment to anti-racism but simply sought to depoliticize race relations by considering them a matter of representation. An effort was made to evade any

"The Graceful and Generous Liberal Gesture: Making Racism Invisible in American International Relations," *Millennium* 29, no. 2(2000): 331–356; Robert Vitalis, "Birth of a Discipline," in *Imperialism and Internationalism in the Discipline of International Relations*, ed. David Long and Brian C. Schmidt (Albany: State University of New York Press, 2005).

[19] Furedi, *The Silent War,* 19; Checkland, *Humanitarianism and the Emperor's Japan,* 179.

[20] Nandy, *The Intimate Enemy,* xi.

[21] Nandy, *The Intimate Enemy,* xi.

[22] Nandy, *The Intimate Enemy,* xiii.

[23] Ikenberry, *After Victory,* 23. Ikenberry defines 'political order' as a governing arrangement comprising of rules, principles and institutions that define the core relationships between states that are party to the order; Short and Kambouri, "Ambiguous universalism," 270.

[24] Furedi, *The Silent War,* 23–24.

[25] Furedi, *The Silent War,* 110.

questions of discrimination and equality by carefully crafting practices of sly civility without giving up on the idea of political mastery. The 'imperial cycle began anew, with atomic bombing—more palatably referred to as "nuclear testing"—of the Marshall Islands, the Sahara, the Navajo Nation, Maralinga, Moruroa and other colonized spaces.'[26]

Nuclear Tests and Nuclear Blackmail

The promise of constitutionalism as the antidote to asymmetrical power relations did not undermine the sense of vulnerability, fear articulated in a particular vision of a 'Cold War reinforced Western order.'[27] It was in fact considered to be a war waged 'against the subjects of their military empires,'[28] an 'asymmetric war between the technologically enabled and the technologically uninitiated.'[29] Any effort to forge a new constitutional order with its practices of racial etiquette could not erase the memory of atomic bombs deliberately used against Japan and not Germany during the Second World War. The atmosphere of suspicion and distrust was not conducive toward negotiating a post-war constitutional order but encouraged an understanding of race consciousness being interchangeable with 'national consciousness.'[30] It generated concern that

> [t]he resentment of Asia's democrats against racial discrimination is so profound that it can easily become a kind of racial chauvinism directed against Westerners.…This consciousness of racial discrimination provoked many Indians to believe that we used the atom bomb in Japan and not in Germany because much as we hated the Germans they were, after all, white men.[31]

This sense of distrust was further reinforced when US conducted nuclear tests in its trust territories such as the Pacific Islands and France conducted its nuclear tests in Algeria.[32] Bolton argues, '[R]acism was not

[26] Gabrielle Hecht, "Introduction," in *Entangled Geographies: Empire and Technopolitics in the Global Cold War*, ed. Gabrielle Hecht (Cambridge: MIT Press, 2011), 4–5.

[27] Ikenberry, *After Victory*, 163.

[28] Robert Jacobs, "Nuclear Conquistadors: Military Colonialism in Nuclear Test Site Selection during the Cold War,"*Asian Journal of Peacebuilding* 1, no. 2(2013): 160.

[29] Jacobs, "Nuclear Conquistadors," 173.

[30] Furedi, *The Silent War*, 114.

[31] Furedi, *The Silent War*, 209, see footnote 39.

[32] Tilman A. Ruff, "The Humanitarian Impact and Implications of Nuclear Test Explosions in the Pacific Region,"*International Review of the Red Cross* 97, no. 889 (2015):

incidental to nuclear testing—it provided the political scaffolding on which the testing program was built.'[33]

It is observed that 'in 1945, the aircraft that dropped nuclear bombs on both Hiroshima and Nagasaki took off from the Tinian in the Mariana Islands in the Pacific; and US nuclear tests in the Pacific began as early as 1946.'[34] These tests in the Pacific were conducted without the 'prior knowledge or consent' of the local inhabitants as 'their lands and seas have been used for and contaminated by the development, testing and deployment of nuclear weapons by distant powers—France, the United Kingdom and the United States.'[35] It is estimated that 'more than 315 atmospheric, underground and underwater nuclear tests were conducted in the region by Britain, France and the United States between 1946 and 1996.'[36] Ruff claims, '[T]he overall priority was nuclear weapons development, whatever the cost,' and 'in the headlong rush to develop, test and deploy the world's most destructive weapons, safety, environmental and health considerations were often irresponsibly sidelined, even by the available knowledge and standards of the time.'[37]

The emerging literature on nuclear and missile tests in the Pacific from declassified archival resources is now being studied by scholars. They comment on the attitudes of those authorizing and conducting the test explosions as inserting typologies based on racial and cultural differences to rearticulate stereotypes. These scholars suggest that 'a variation of the civilization discourse was deployed by Western powers, counterintuitively, to legitimate nuclear colonialism in the Pacific, by portraying test sites as "remote", "primitive" and even "savage" places.'[38] They observe a sense of differentiation was deliberately maintained between '"civilized" personnel and "primitive" indigenous people.'[39] A stereotypical imaginary of the Polynesian as 'exotic, enchanted, docile and primitive, far from "civilization"' cultivated during the colonial era perpetuated itself to now help

777–778, 793.

[33] Matthew Bolton, "The '-Pacific' part of 'Asia-Pacific': Oceanic diplomacy in the 2017 treaty for the prohibition of nuclear weapons," *Asian Journal of Political Science* 26, no. 3(2018): 376.

[34] Ruff, "The Humanitarian Impact," 776.

[35] Ruff, "The Humanitarian Impact," 776.

[36] Ruff, "The Humanitarian Impact," 779.

[37] Ruff, "The Humanitarian Impact," 799.

[38] Bolton, "The '-Pacific' part of 'Asia-Pacific,'" 372.

[39] Ruff, "The Humanitarian Impact," 778.

nurture nuclear fantasies of colonial powers like France in pursuit of recognition as a nuclear weapons state.[40] The 'nuclear subaltern was identified, marginalized, and brutalized' and 'their marginality, their powerlessness, was the resource that drew their imperial occupiers to focus on their lands and their seas.'[41] The nuclear test sites were 'generally located in the far reaches of their military empires or domestic landmasses, displacing and contaminating marginalized populations with little recourse, information, or compensation.'[42] The differences in race, ethnicity, religion, class and 'lack of technological modernism' made the safety and security of subalterns a secondary consideration.[43]

It was only the weapons designers in the metropole and their complaints about the 'long amount of time that it took to travel back and forth' and how these temporal and spatial distances between nuclear test sites 'were delaying advances in weapons design' of a 'functional thermonuclear weapon' that could prompt a change of decision in nuclear test site selection.[44] The decision to establish a domestic nuclear test site in the US was considered a possibility only to accommodate the considerations of time weighing on weapons designers and in areas considered to be inhabited by a 'low-use segment of the population' such as the 'Native Americans and Mormons' living close to Nevada test site in the US.[45] The timing of a nuclear test could be subject to temporal experiences of imperial masters such as the French president Charles de Gaulle visiting French Polynesia to observe a nuclear test. The wind was blowing in the wrong direction, as a result of which the test was getting 'delayed,' but the imperial master simply 'tired of waiting' ordered the test to proceed, 'resulting in significant contamination of the populations of French Polynesia, the Cook Islands, Samoa and Fiji.'[46]

A study of the British Report on the 'Danger Area' for the 1957 Grapple Nuclear Tests on Christmas Island shows that there was no sense of

[40] Bolton, "The '-Pacific' part of 'Asia-Pacific,'" 377; N. Maclellan and J. Chesneauix, *After Moruroa: France in the South Pacific*(Melbourne, Australia: Ocean Press, 1998).

[41] Jacobs, "Nuclear Conquistadors,"160.

[42] Jacobs, "Nuclear Conquistadors," 159.

[43] Jacobs, "Nuclear Conquistadors," 160.

[44] Jacobs, "Nuclear Conquistadors," 165.

[45] Jacobs, "Nuclear Conquistadors," 166; Carole Gallagher, *American Ground Zero: The Secret Nuclear War* (New York: Random House, 1993), xxiii.

[46] Jacobs, "Nuclear Conquistadors," 171; Stewart Firth, *Nuclear Playground*(Honolulu: University of Hawaii Press, 1987).

hesitation in prescribing 'maximum radiation dose limit for "primitive" Pacific people exceeding that recommended internationally and different from that of the British personnel.'[47] In this test the radiation dosage was about 'fifteen times higher (for primitive peoples) than which would be permitted by the International Commission on Radiological Protection (ICRP).'[48] In military assessment reports of this particular test a 'culturally distinct' understanding of radiological doses becomes manifest:

> For civilized populations, assumed to wear boots and clothing and to wash, the amount of exposure necessary to produce this dosage is more than necessary to give an equivalent dosage to primitive peoples who are not assumed to possess these habits....It is assumed that in the possible regions of fallout at Grapple there may be scantily clad people in boats to whom this criteria of primitive people should apply.[49]

Such evaluations were later officially abbreviated to 'only very slight health hazards to people would arise, and that only to primitive peoples.'[50] Similarly, the 'total explosive yield of US nuclear test explosions in the Pacific locations—Bikini and Enewetak Atolls in the Marshall Islands, Johnston Atoll in the Central Pacific, and Kiritimati (Christmas Island, lent for this purpose by the British)—at 152.8 megatons (Mt) dwarfs the 1.05 Mt yield of atmospheric tests conducted in the continental US at the Nevada Test Site (land of the Western Shoshone people).'[51] In the official representations of the Atomic Energy Commission (AEC) the Marshallese were referred to as 'savages by our standards,' and this sense of discrimination was reinforced with statements to the effect, 'While it is true that these people do not live, I would say, the way Westerners do, civilized

[47] Ruff, "The Humanitarian Impact," 778.

[48] Ruff, "The Humanitarian Impact," 778, see footnote 12; "Danger Area," paper by Air Vice-Marshal W. E. Oulton, November 19,1956, No. GRA/TS.1008/1/Air; minutes of meeting on November 27,1956, marked Top Secret – UK Eyes Only, XY/181/024, cited in NicMaclellan, "Grappling with the Bomb: Opposition to Pacific Nuclear Testing in the 1950s", in the *Proceedings of the 14th Biennial Labour History Conference*,eds. Phillip Deery and Julie Kimber (AustralianSociety for the Study of Labour History, Melbourne, 2015), 11.

[49] Jacobs, "Nuclear Conquistadors," 168–169.

[50] Jacobs, "Nuclear Conquistadors," 169.

[51] Frederick Warner and René J.C. Kirchmann(eds), Scientific Committee on Problems of the Environment (SCOPE) of the International Council for Science, *SCOPE 59. Nuclear Test Explosions: Environmental and Human Impacts* (John Wiley & Sons, New York, 1999), 19–22; Ruff, "The Humanitarian Impact," 777–778.

people, it is nevertheless also true that these people are more like us than mice.'[52]

The imperial powers tried to justify the conduct of nuclear tests to the subalterns by insisting on the necessity of testing to 'put an end to war';'for the good of mankind and to end all wars'; for the defense of the 'Free World'; in the 'interests of general peace and security'; and 'peaceful applications of nuclear energy.'[53] It will not be amiss to suggest that the deliberate and staged deployment of this language to sustain and strengthen the 'New Look' defense policy of the US is representative of practices of sly civility. These pious expressions of intent to conduct nuclear tests in trust territories and former colonies did not extend to conducting tests in 'populationcentres of US' or 'New Caledonia' in close proximity to Australia and New Zealand where'political opposition could not be contained through colonial mechanisms.'[54] On the contrary, decisions to conduct the tests 'overseas until it could be established more definitely that continental detonations would not endanger the public health and safety'were the explicit advice given by the Atomic Energy Commission to the US Congress prior to conducting BRAVO, a thermonuclear explosion, in the Pacific.[55] Henry Kissinger, on being questioned about missile testing at Kwajalein, did not hesitate to claim, 'There are only 90,000 of them out there. Who gives a damn?'[56] This callous misrepresentation of the number and suffering of the subalterns was accompanied by denials that their actions were 'irresponsible.'[57]

In an attempt to forge 'special nuclear relationship' among themselves, the major Western powers were willing to make allowances to France to

[52] Matthew Bolton, "The '-Pacific' part of 'Asia-Pacific,'" 376; Robert Jacobs, "Nuclear Conquistadors," 157–177.

[53] Jacobs, "Nuclear Conquistadors," 158; Jack Neidenthal, *For the Good of Mankind: A History of the People of Bikini and Their Islands* (Majuro: Bravo Publishers, 2001), 2; Martha Smith-Norris, "'Only as Dust in the Face of the Wind': An Analysis of the BRAVO Nuclear Incident in the Pacific,1954,"*The Journal of American-East Asian Relations* 6, no. 1(1997): 18, 20.

[54] Jacobs, "Nuclear Conquistadors," 158, 170–172; Jane Dibblin, *Day of Two Suns: US Nuclear Testing and the Pacific Islanders*(New York: New Amsterdam Books,1988), 20.

[55] Smith-Norris, "'Only as Dust in the Face of the Wind,'"6.

[56] Bolton, "The '-Pacific' part of 'Asia-Pacific,'"376; W. Hickel, *Who Owns America?* (Englewood Cliffs, New Jersey: Prentice Hall, 1971), 208; Jacobs, "Nuclear Conquistadors," 174; David Vine, *Islands of Shame: The History of the US Military Base on Diego Garcia* (Princeton: Princeton University Press, 2009), 183.

[57] Smith-Norris, "'Only as Dust in the Face of the Wind,'" 12.

conduct its own nuclear tests in Algeria and initiate a 'strict nonproliferation policy towards third countries.'[58] They pursued a 'tacit' strategy to 'cajole, coax, but never threaten France' to abandon its nuclear tests.[59] France proceeded to conduct its nuclear tests on the grounds that any effort to agree on a test ban discriminated against the nuclear have-nots and insisted that nuclear tests were vital to the restoration of France to great power status. France insisted it 'would only subscribe to a nuclear test ban agreement if the three existing nuclear Powers agreed at the same time to suspend production of nuclear weapons and to destroy their existing stocks.'[60] It conducted these nuclear tests at a time when nuclear weapon states were negotiating a test ban and despite vehement opposition from African and Asian states that 'construed prospective French testing as a new form of European domination—a form of imperialism that exposed adjacent African states to radioactive contamination.'[61]

The diplomatic protests lodged did not generate any concerted effort among the Western powers to compel France 'to heed rising African anxieties.'[62] On the contrary, the British tried to placate the Nigerians for being 'highly emotional' on the subject of nuclear testing, and the Japanese protests against nuclear tests in the Pacific were similarly dismissed by the US on grounds that the Japanese were 'emotional, ignorant, pathologically sensitive' and could be silenced with some monetary compensation.[63] Another master diplomatic stroke was to prevent the isolation of France by proposing and dividing votes with a 'carefully worded alternative resolution' to the one proposed by Morocco in the UN General Assembly condemning French nuclear tests.[64] India's proposal for a 'Standstill Agreement' prohibiting nuclear testing by all nuclear powers to the UN

[58] Mervyn O'Driscoll, "Diplomatic Triangles, the United Nations and the Problem of French Nuclear Testing, 1959–1960", *Journal of Cold War* Studies 11, no. 1(2009): 28–56, retrieved from https://muse.jhu.edu/article/259184

[59] O'Driscoll, "Diplomatic Triangles."

[60] Richard Scott, "A Ban on Nuclear Tests: The Course of Negotiations, 1958–1962," *International Affairs* 38, no. 4(1962): 503.

[61] O'Driscoll, "Diplomatic Triangles," retrieved from https://muse.jhu.edu/article/259184

[62] O'Driscoll, "Diplomatic Triangles." retrieved from https://muse.jhu.edu/article/259184

[63] O'Driscoll, "Diplomatic Triangles." Martha Smith-Norris, "'Only as Dust in the Face of the Wind'" 33.

[64] O'Driscoll, "Diplomatic Triangles." retrieved from https://muse.jhu.edu/article/259184

Disarmament Commission could not be dismissed so easily. This proposal argued that the destructive potential of nuclear weapons in respect of time and space was a subject of anxiety and, in the absence of 'effective protection,' posed a serious threat to the 'existence of man and civilization as we know it.'[65] This proposal received attention and support within the Non-Aligned Movement (NAM) and the UN.

The voice of the NAM gained further strength in disarmament conferences convened at the UN as it proposed constructive measures to address issues regarding verification of nuclear test ban. For instance:

> What they proposed was that an international commission composed of scientists from nonaligned nations, should be set up, and that national detection systems should report to this commission all relevant seismic information throughout the world. If the commission could not determine whether any particular event was nuclear or natural it would call for further information from the country in whose territory the event had been located. If after receiving that information the neutral commission was still unsatisfied it would seek permission from the country concerned to send an inspection team to the area. If this permission was refused the country concerned would have drawn upon itself the suspicion of having violated the treaty and the other signatories would then have the right to withdraw from it.[66]

There was an awareness that the proposal mentioned above to address the 'problem of inspection is certainly the best that has so far been suggested…if agreement is ever to be reached on the ending of the nuclear weapons tests it is probable that it will be found along the lines of these neutralist proposals.'[67] It was further observed how neutralist representation largely from the Third World 'did not mean impartiality in sentiment' but one of conduct.[68] The neutralists harbored few illusions of power themselves but sought only to mediate, remain 'impartial' and 'prod the

[65] Ministry of External Affairs India, *'Stand-still Agreement' Statement*, Jawaharlal Nehru in the Indian Lok Sabha, April 2, 1954, document retrieved from meaindia.nic.in; see Office of the Special Assistant for National Security Affairs, White House Office, *Memo,* June 23, 1954, NSC Series, DDE Library.

[66] Richard Scott, "A Ban on Nuclear Tests: The Course of Negotiations, 1958–1962,"*International Affairs* 38, no. 4(1962): 509.

[67] Scott, "A Ban on Nuclear Tests," 509.

[68] Joseph L. Nogee, "The Neutralist World and Disarmament Negotiations,"*The Annals of the American Academy of Political and Social Science* 362, no. not available (1965): 75. The neutralist representation at the UN Eighteen-Nation Disarmament Conference, comprised

nuclear powers when negotiations bogged down.'[69] Their conduct is described at length by Joseph Nogee as one of 'caution and reserve,' a 'technique of non-involvement' while issuing 'balanced criticism and praise' in the form of 'innocent and innocuous questions'and oblique compliments.[70] It is acknowledged that the moderate tone of their interventions prevented negotiations from collapsing but then 'at no time was the Eighteen-Nation Conference the locus of genuine negotiations.'[71] Their exclusion is stated as a matterof fact that the 'partial test-ban agreements were negotiated either bilaterally between the Soviet Union and the United States or by the three nuclear powers at Moscow.'[72]

Global protests and demonstrations, diplomatic resolutions and proposals to ban nuclear tests and secure verification from subalterns persistently met with practices of resistance and exclusion on terms similar to the imperial logic articulated in the nineteenth century, as discussed in the previous chapter. A more trenchant attempt to articulate and recycle this imperial logic is now presented under the guise, 'we must be sensitive to world opinion. But we have also an obligation to contribute to shaping it.'[73] In a visible attempt to shape this world opinion, imperial logic now becomes visible as an argument in sly civility, posing a question, 'whether a complete suspension of nuclear testing is desirable, whatever the possibilities of inspection'?[74] This question, posed by Kissinger in his article'Nuclear Testing and the Problem of Peace,' is a significant example of an exercise in imperial resistance to practices of arms control.[75] Kissinger in an earlier statement did not give a damn to the victims of nuclear testing in the Pacific but now adopts a tone emphatic in its desire to draw attention to the 'intense,' 'yearning' and 'deepest aspirations of the free world' to suggest, 'we have been ready to stigmatize as more immoral than other weapons the weapon around which we have built our defense of that

of Brazil, Burma, Ethiopia, India, Mexico, Nigeria, Sweden and the United Arab Republic (UAR).

[69] Nogee, "The Neutralist World," 74.

[70] Nogee, "The Neutralist World," 74.

[71] Nogee, "The Neutralist World," 79.

[72] Nogee, "The Neutralist World," 79.

[73] Henry A. Kissinger, "Nuclear Testing and the Problem of Peace,"*Foreign Affairs* 37, no. 1(1958): 8.

[74] Kissinger, "Nuclear Testing,"2.

[75] Kissinger, "Nuclear Testing,"1–18.

world. But the very intensity of our desire for peace may increase our peril.'[76]

In mouthing these claims for peace, Kissinger, as US Secretary of State and National Security Advisor, is acutely aware that 'the issue of nuclear testing is a touchstone of our sincerity.'[77] But this does not prevent him from resorting to issuing a rhetorical civilizational signal, 'There is no doubt that the Western world is in deep trouble.'[78] Kissinger is adamant that 'even in the military field we are inadequately prepared to deal with most of the issues with which we are likely to be confronted.'[79] The threat of a nuclear test ban is exaggerated and deliberately depicted as a 'first step' toward'increased campaign to outlaw nuclear weapons altogether,' a measure conceived as being 'tantamount to unilateral disarmament' and as a design to 'paralyze the free world rather than to bring about peace as we understand the word.'[80] These observations are reinforced with a statement that this sense of peril arising from the possibility of 'complete ban on nuclear tests' has 'political and psychological implications.'[81]

An appearance of reasonableness is displayed by Kissinger as he suggests that 'if inspection was found to be technically feasible, we would be willing to discuss a complete ban,' but then proceeds to caution that 'the best inspection system can guard only against presently known methods of evasion. In the nature of things it is difficult to protect against a contingency not yet imagined.'[82] This play of psychosis about the uncertainty of future developments is reinforced with statements insisting 'once nuclear tests have been banned the free world will not abrogate its agreement easily, even in the face of strong provocation' and that 'in the West a ban on nuclear testing will be largely self-policing' but 'evasion will be easier to attempt and to conceal in the Soviet Union than in the West.'[83] It is further suggested that a nuclear test ban 'will contribute to a psychological attitude in the West making it impossible for any of our allies to acquire nuclear weapons' and that 'of possible methods to prevent the spread of

[76] Kissinger, "Nuclear Testing,"1.
[77] Kissinger, "Nuclear Testing," 17.
[78] Kissinger, "Nuclear Testing," 18.
[79] Kissinger, "Nuclear Testing," 17.
[80] Kissinger, "Nuclear Testing,"7,8.
[81] Kissinger, "Nuclear Testing,"1.
[82] Kissinger, "Nuclear Testing,"3.
[83] Kissinger, "Nuclear Testing,"3.

nuclear weapons, a test ban is the most disadvantageous to the free world.'[84]

This sense of fear and uncertainty experienced by a 'status-quo power' is reinforced with abstract hypothetical claims that a nuclear test ban will lead to the 'attrition of our weapons laboratories'and present 'great difficulty reassembling testing machinery' and it might be years 'before tests could be resumed,' resulting in a 'serious disadvantage' and 'weakening of the will of the free world.'[85]An initial skeptical yet willing attitude to engage with technical shortcomings for a nuclear test ban is soon discarded to state explicitly, 'there is a great difference between obtaining information which is technically reliable, and establishing a similar degree of political and psychological clarity.'[86] While inserting a temporal and spatial clause for political and psychological ambivalence, Kissinger adamantly persists in advocating, 'We require more conventional forces. We must have a wider spectrum of nuclear weapons.'[87] Kissinger insists a 'premium' be placed on 'weapons development' and demands more 'time for a careful study of this problem' pertaining to nuclear testing.[88] This demand for more time, a standard civilizational ploy, to secure a strategic deferral produced after almost two decades only a Partial Test Ban Treaty (PTBT) in 1963 that 'prohibited all but underground nuclear explosions,' thereby 'making it more difficult for countries to try out nuclear weapons by prohibiting the relatively easy tests in the atmosphere.'[89]

Despite these blatant temporal and spatial exercises of power by the West, the governments of the Marshall Islands in their long struggle to bring some compensation and treatment to the victims have had to agree to renounce all claims 'past, present and future…(that are) based on, arise out of or are in any way related to the Nuclear Testing Program, and which are against the United States.'[90] Bolton argues that in their efforts

[84] Kissinger, "Nuclear Testing," 14.

[85] Kissinger, "Nuclear Testing,"4,6.

[86] Kissinger, "Nuclear Testing,"4.

[87] Kissinger, "Nuclear Testing,"9.

[88] Kissinger, "Nuclear Testing," 16.

[89] Bertrand Goldschmidt, "A Historical Survey of Nonproliferation Policies,"*International Security* 2, no. 1(1997): 76.

[90] Ruff, "The Humanitarian Impact," 796–797, see footnote 106; NicMaclellan, "The Long Shadow of Bravo,"*Inside Story*, February 24, 2014, http://insidestory.org.au/the-long-shadow-of-bravo; Human Rights Council, Report of the Special Rapporteur on the Implications for Human Rights of the Environmentally Sound Management and Disposal of Hazardous Substances and Wastes, CalinGeorgescu, Addendum, Mission to the Marshall

to stigmatize nuclear weapon states the Oceanic states have been compelled to flip the civilizational script and resort to resistance through practices of 'hybridizing and creolizing' civilizational discourses that tend to invest nuclear weapons as an indicator of 'status and civilization.'[91] In their practices of resistance against 'nuclear racism' the survivors claim, 'as victims we are not begging for favor, we are just standing up for our rights and our dignity.'[92]

They offer resistance to being used as 'guinea pigs' and strive to merge a 'hidden transcript' of grievances with the 'public transcript' of the rulers on standards of civilization legitimating their rule.[93] This weaving of transcripts is undertaken without necessarily accepting the legitimacy of the hegemon but is an insistent 'faithful repetition'of expectations to maintain standards of civilization through respect for international humanitarian law, human rights and sovereignty of states.[94] The agonizingly 'slow pace of disarmament negotiations' has encouraged them to bring lawsuits against nuclear-armed states for not fulfilling their legal obligations toward nuclear disarmament.[95] These practices of resistance sometimes accompanied by public demonstrations of protest and rioting 'surprised foreign journalists accustomed to stereotypes of Tahitian docility.'[96] Despite these practices of resistance and representation of the victims of nuclear tests, it is argued, 'too much time has passed. The ranks of these survivors are rapidly thinning....Too many men—our fellow Fijians have gone to their graves without justice. ...There is a saying that justice delayed is justice denied.'[97]

Islands (27– 30 March 2012) and the United States of America (24–27 April 2012), UN Doc. A/HRC/21/48/Add.1, September 3, 2012, p. 4, para. 10, pp. 10–15.

[91] Bolton, "The '-Pacific' part of 'Asia-Pacific,'" 373.

[92] Bolton, "The '-Pacific' part of 'Asia-Pacific,'" 383.

[93] J.C. Scott, *Domination and the Arts of Resistance: Hidden Transcripts* (New Haven, Connecticut: Yale University Press, 1990), 55.

[94] Bolton, "The '-Pacific' part of 'Asia-Pacific,'" 373.

[95] Alicia Sanders-Zakre, "Marshall Islands Lose Nuclear Cases,"*Arms Control Today* 46, no. 9(2016): 32.

[96] Matthew Bolton, "The '-Pacific' part of 'Asia-Pacific,'" 381.

[97] Ruff, "The Humanitarian Impact," 788.

National Science and International Law

It is not difficult to surmise that these experiences of suffering from nuclear tests and struggles for justice generated and reinforced in the public mind of the subalterns an association of atomic energy with national defense. It is possible to suggest without laying claim to any universalizing principle that the possession of nuclear weapons technology now became a symbol of power, protection and prestige among both colonial and postcolonial states. This new technology now gave rise to 'modern myths' about the impact of science and technology in international politics and generated an awareness of the timelag between 'lead time' needed to develop a new weapon or weapons systems and 'use time' when a weapon can be actually put to use.[98] It generated a demand that national science be subordinated to the state interests defined in terms of national security.

Abraham observes that'[f]or Nehru, the scientific object, the atom, is the sign of a new era of human civilization.'[99] It is with 'the atom and the scientific knowledge' that an independent nation can be transformed into a modern state.'[100] Zoppo notes,

> Faced with the immense problems of building new societies, the political leaders of Africa, Asia, and Latin America seek the traditional optimism of science and see the atoms as the midwife of economic and social development.…What differs from country to country is the awareness about indigenous capabilities, the degree of commitment todevelop and exploit nuclear energy in the immediate future, and the intensity of attachment to national independence in pursuing this goal.[101]

But the desire to transform 'colonial science' into 'national science' did not undermine the sense of dependency and knowledge that the latter was a by-product of Western scientific advances that had 'spread over the world as a by-product of Western expansion and imperialism.'[102]

It was therefore important that postcolonial states be no longer content with reiteration of the past in terms of 'national time' that seeks to

[98] Karl W. Deutsch, "The Impact of Science and Technology on International Politics,"*Daedalus* 88, no. 4(1959): 669, 672.

[99] Abraham, *Indian Atomic Bomb,* 28.

[100] Abraham, *Indian Atomic Bomb,* 29.

[101] CiroZoppo, "Nuclear Technology, Weapons, and the Third World,"*Annals of the American Academy of Political and Social Science*, no. 386 (1969): 119.

[102] Abraham, *Indian Atomic Bomb,* 35.

reconcile 'scientific knowledge held both by Indian sages and Western scientists.'[103] There was an urgent and insistent need for 'arguing for the existence of a "world time", a time that is marked by the material form of energy that societies use' and is 'located in a world-historical space, where it is one among many, and where the historical epoch is marked by a non-human entity—the atom.'[104] It is this technology that can transform a 'state-in-the-making.'[105] The nationalist sentiments informing the postcolonial state 'consciously denied Western authority as the font of modern science and technology' by deliberate omission and elision in public speeches in an attempt to suggest that these were 'universal phenomena that could have emerged from anywhere.'[106] They insisted that 'atomic energy had been made available to the people of the world through the efforts of "scientists of many nations working in full and free collaboration" with each other.'[107] They justified their quest for atomic energy by establishing a direct correlation between the rate of energy used for development and the degree of 'civilization' achieved.[108] In this desire for nuclear energy and nuclear weapons there is a 'menace of mimicry' in pursuit of strategic objectives.[109]

The Western powers persisted with their 'manifest tendency to regard postcolonial states as underdeveloped European states.'[110] The postcolonial states were deemed to have simply moved from the control of European states to that of the superpowers. This encouraged 'the diminution of the particularity of the postcolonial state and the use of traditional models, images and stereotypes to characterize these states.'[111] This new racial etiquette persisted in its lack of respect for the different experiences of the postcolonial states and encouraged a generic understanding of the state as a mimetic unit of analysis within which all understanding of culture and identity is subordinated. This problem of mimesis was further complicated by the assertions of US foreign policy officials such as George

[103] Abraham, *Indian Atomic Bomb*, 29.
[104] Abraham, *Indian Atomic Bomb*, 29.
[105] Abraham, *Indian Atomic Bomb*, 29.
[106] Abraham, *Indian Atomic Bomb*, 100.
[107] Abraham, *Indian Atomic Bomb*, 101.
[108] Abraham, *Indian Atomic Bomb*, 100.
[109] Bhabha, *The Location of Culture*, 126.
[110] Salter, *Barbarians & Civilization*, 118. Also see Roxanne Doty for exact quotation as cited by Salter in footnote 22.
[111] Salter, *Barbarians & Civilization*, 125–126.

Kennan in 1948 that '[o]ur real task in the coming period is to devise a pattern of relationships which will permit us to maintain this position of disparity without positive detriment to our national security.'[112] Karl Deutsch claimed, 'It would certainly not be a policy of one-sided disarmament. The purpose of our policy is to preserve the Western way of life and its defensive strength, not to abandon it.'[113] Among the Western powers there was a shared understanding of a joint responsibility for the 'preservation of the only truly valuable civilization' and to 'reinforce the physical barriers which still guard Western civilization.'[114]

The principle of inequality that had helped cultivate race-thinking along national lines was not to be eroded so easily. It was now to be nurtured to foster a 'kind of nobility among nations.'[115] America and England were the first nations to 'deal with the race-problem in practical politics'for centuries, and as an imperial power England had long professed to be the supreme guarantor for humanity.[116] Jackson observes that 'in the years immediately following the Second World War the discourse in the West shifted towards a more exclusive "Western civilization."'[117] The idea of 'Western civilization' that had been so obscure during the century and a half preceding the Second World War now became identifiable as a rhetorical resource with three basic characteristics:"the West" as a supranational entity that is superior, larger and older than its component states and '"civilizational" concerns trump merely national ones'; 'the West is an 'exclusive' community and 'the West' is 'linked to a series of other commonplaces such as the defense of liberty.'[118] This became more pronounced in post-war US policy statements evoking 'traditional American exemplarism' with its 'two commitments: the metageographical (almost ontological) distinctiveness of America' and 'the notion of heliotropism' carrying

[112] Quote cited in G. John Ikenberry, *After Victory,* 169, fn10; "Memorandum by the Director of the Policy Planning Staff (Kennan) to the Secretary of State and Under Secretary of State (Lovett),"February 24,1948, Office of the Historian, *Foreign Relations of the United States,*Vol.1, 1948, 524.

[113] Karl W. Deutsch, "The Impact of Science and Technology on International Politics,"*Daedalus* 88, no. 4(1959): 681.

[114] Ikenberry, *After Victory,*193, 195.

[115] Arendt, "Race-Thinking," 62.

[116] Arendt, "Race-Thinking," 63, 70.

[117] Jackson, *Civilizing the Enemy,* 56–57.

[118] Jackson, *Civilizing the Enemy,* 110.

the 'vague notion that history follows the path of the sun and that the destiny of (human) civilization consists in a march to the west.'[119]

Among the imperial powers there was a sense of bemusement at the absence of any 'noticeable tendency amongst the Asian and African states to regard international law as a product of the Western civilization or reject it on that basis.'[120] It was not without a certain degree of ridicule and mockery at the

> evidence of the lasting dependence of non-Western nations in the conduct of their international affairs upon fundamental concepts of the Western world from which their political leaders nevertheless so ardently crave to liberate their states without, however, being able either to derive any different workable principle of international law from data of their own national history or to develop independent legal principles susceptible of replacing the traditional standard principles of existing international law.[121]

This sense of mockery was reinforced by bombastic allegations against the new states and their attitude toward international law. It was alleged, 'Afro-Asian nations are incapable of understanding the present system of law and justice as it is based on Christian values,' and their attempts to extract legal concepts from modern international law 'without having first duly mentally digested them' result in 'distortion and misunderstanding of elementary legal issues such as the limitations of national sovereignty.'[122] There was denial that the nineteenth-century practices of legal positivism that had excluded the non-Europeans from the protection of international law could have any 'retroactive effect' in the present.[123] An adamant insistence that the new states instead of being considered as 'new comers to the family of nations' must be 'considered as a continuous community of states irrespective of the change of law or of doctrine.'[124]

[119] Jackson, *Civilizing the Enemy*, 57.

[120] Anand, *New States and International Law*, 52.

[121] Anand, *New States and International Law*, 8, see footnote 10; J.H.W. Verzijl, "Western European Influence on the Foundations of International Law," in his *International Law in Historical Perspective* (Leyden, 1968), 435–436.

[122] Anand, *New States and International Law*, 9. see footnote 14; Verzijl, "Western European Influence," 443.

[123] Anand, *New States and International Law*, 20.

[124] Anand, *New States and International Law*, 20, see footnote 53; C.H. Alexandrowicz, "Grotius and India,"*Indian Yearbook of International Affairs* 3, no. 30 (1954): 164.

It was claimed that the attitude of the new countries toward international law 'is not caused by any inherently unique characteristic of Asian or African civilization as such; it is a product of a phase of development through which many, if not all, nations pass at some time or the other' and these attitudes toward international law are modified 'not as a matter of basic values but according to the national interest prevailing at a particular period.'[125] It was emphasized that 'national interest' rather than 'cultural traditions' determined the attitude of new states toward international law.[126] It was suggested that 'the price of the expansion of international law from the law of European Christendom to the law applicable to the universal community of nation' entailed 'a continuous dilution of its content, as it is reinterpreted for the benefit of the newcomers,' and 'a new conceptual synthesis grounded on the basic fact of ideological and cultural pluralism' could serve as the basis of a new world law.[127] This would help accommodate the cultural differences that made the new states 'intransigent' in their attitude toward judicial settlement of international disputes.[128]

The 'myth of universality' facilitated the automatic inclusion of new states in international law, but their demands for disarmament were seen as eroding international law and order. It was claimed that their inclusion had reduced the United Nations from an organization that represents civilized people to an organization in which 'barbarians and semi-barbarians have the upper-hand.'[129] These 'heretics,' 'primeval entities,' obstructed and impeded the development of international law and therefore cannot

[125] Anand, *New States and International Law*, 51; W. Friedman, "United States Policy and the Crisis of International Law,"*American Journal of International Law* 59(1965): 858; W. Friedmann, "Half a Century of International Law,"*Virginia Law Review* 50, no. 8(1964): 1377.

[126] Anand, *New States and International Law*, 51, see footnote 24; O.J. Lissitzyn, "International Law in a Divided World,"*International Conciliation*, no. 542 (1963): 57–58; Wolfgang Friedmann, *The Changing Structure of International Law* (New York: Columbia University Press; London: Steven & Sons, 1964), 302; A.A. Fatouros, "Participation of the 'New' States in the International Legal Order of the Future," in *The Future of the International Legal Order*, Vol. I, R.A. Falk and Cyril E. Black(Princeton: Princeton University Press, 1969), 349–350.

[127] Anand, *New States and International Law*, 49; F.S.C. Northrop, *Taming of the Nations*(New York, 1952), pp. 80–81,88.

[128] Anand, *New States and International Law*, 49–50.

[129] Anand, *New States and International Law*, 67, see footnote 85; B.V.A. Roling, *International Law in an Expanded World* (Amsterdam, 1960), 68.

be 'taken seriously by the old states.'[130] These allegations gave rise to growing suspicion and skepticism that the 'criterion' of "civilized nation" as a basis of participation in the community of nations has been abandoned.'[131] The subalterns denied that they have 'abused their power of numbers to unnecessarily harass the Western countries' in the General Assembly of the UN.[132] They insisted their use of the General Assembly was as a 'popular forum for repudiating some of the old norms and creating new law.'[133] But there was an unwillingness to allow new states to question the existing norms and practices of international law as it was believed that

> [i]n asserting the faculties of statehood, the new state is accepting the structure and the system of Western international law, and it may not, without offending all juristic doctrine, pick and choose the acceptable institutions, if only because its next door neighbour, also a new state, will also claim a like privilege.[134]

It was of considerable import for the West led by the US to win the ideological battle of the Cold War to deliberately eliminate any possibility of the other cultivating an insight into its reduction, servility and offer resistance.[135]

The problem of universalizing existing international law from its parochial and Eurocentric origins consumed legal scholarship and treaty-making processes to regulate and prohibit weapons. Afro-Asian legal scholars recognized that they could not in practice dispense with international legal principles 'by force of circumstances.'[136] There is no alternative means of protection available outside the scope of international law.[137] Their acceptance of the principles of 'sovereignty, recognition, territorial

[130] Anand, *New States and International Law*, 66–67.

[131] Anand, *New States and International Law*, 25.

[132] Anand, *New States and International Law*, 77.

[133] Anand, *New States and International Law*, 75.

[134] Anand, *New States and International Law*, 70; D.P. O'Connel, "Independence and Problems of State Succession," in *The New Nations in International Law and Diplomacy*, William V.O'Brien (New York, 1965), 12–13.

[135] Gopal Guru, "Rejection of Rejection," in *Humiliation-Claims and Context*, ed. Gopal Guru (Oxford, New Delhi: Oxford University Press, 2009), 216.

[136] Anand, *New States and International Law*(Delhi: Vikas Publishing House Pvt. Ltd.,1972), 62.

[137] Anand, *New States and International Law*, 84.

integrity, non-aggression, non-intervention, sovereign equality, reciprocity, peaceful settlement of dispute and diplomatic and consular relations' was premised on the understanding that 'they cannot disengage themselves from pre-existing rules and situations, or at least they cannot do so immediately and forever.'[138] There was an insistent note that international law must be 'adapted' to represent the interests of the new states in the new world order' and that 'certain well-developed principles of inter-state conduct' existed in ancient civilizations such as India, China, Egypt but that 'each system of international law disappeared with the disappearance of the civilization (or civilizations) under which it flourished.'[139] The subalterns decried the 'unequal treaties' signed during the colonial era and asserted the right of the new states to address the problem of treaty obligations anew. These obligations would be undertaken from a principle of equality.[140]

Amnesia, Denials and Abstractions

Despite these assertions of rights and equality from the subalterns, Hedley Bull insists that it is cooperation between the superpowers that serves 'universal purposes' even as 'it inevitably serves special or bilateral purposes also. These special or bilateral purposes reflect the preference of the two great powers for a world order in which they continue to enjoy a privileged position.'[141] Bull, a notable representative of the 'English School' on issues of arms control and disarmament, attempts to 'rationalize the existing distribution of power.'[142] Priority is given to maintenance of stability, and questions pertaining to justice and change are marginalized without any explicit reason and therefore susceptible to bias. There is a reluctance to consider 'goals such as the promotion of just international and internal change, which in the view of a large section of international society requires an assault on the prevailing distribution of power, and should be pursued even at the price of reduced security, an increased economic burden of

[138] Anand, *New States and International Law*, 62–63.

[139] Anand, *New States and International Law*, 11–12, 116.

[140] Anand, *New States and International Law*, 75.

[141] Robert O'Neil and David N. Schwartz, *Hedley Bull on Arms Control* (New York: St.Martin's Press, 1987), 192 (italics inserted); Hedley Bull, "Arms control and World Order,"*International Security* 1, no. 1(1976): 3–36.

[142] O'Neil and Schwartz, *Hedley Bull on Arms Control,* 192; Bull, "Arms control and World Order,"3–36.

armaments and a greater militarization of society.'[143] A bias that deems any change and quest for equality and justice in practices of arms control and disarmament as susceptible to generating an 'assault,' 'reduced security' and 'greater militarization.'[144]

Bull acknowledges that 'the set of assumptions about world order which at present underlies the enterprise of arms control commands little support outside the circle of the United States and the Soviet Union and their closest allies.'[145] This lack of support is further reinforced by an observation that 'there has been little discussion of the question whether the assumptions about world order that are so central to our present approach to arms control, and are so decisively rejected by China and the aspirant powers of the Third World, are valid.'[146] Despite recognition of this lack of consensus in the study of arms control and disarmament practices, Bull is confident that

> the objection of the third world countries is not to the quality of order in the present international arrangements; it is rather to the way in which these arrangements discriminate against them. Once these changes they are seeking have been effected, andnew arrangements have replaced the old ones, it is possible they will come to sense a stake in them.[147]

Thus the efforts of the Third World states to question the existing practices of arms control and disarmament are conceived as only a temporal exercise that can be addressed. No further attempt is made to investigate how the 'arrangements that discriminate' can be changed except the suggestion that 'those who have special interests recognize the special responsibilities that go with them, and conduct themselves in such a way as to engage general support for the system whose custodians and guarantors

[143] O'Neil and Schwartz, *Hedley Bull on Arms Control* (New York: St.Martin's Press, 1987), 192–193; Bull, "Arms control and World Order,"3–36.

[144] O'Neil and Schwartz, *Hedley Bull on Arms Control*,192–193; Bull, "Arms control and World Order,"3–36.

[145] O'Neil and Schwartz, *Hedley Bull on Arms Control*,191; Bull, "Arms control and World Order,"3–36.

[146] O'Neil and Schwartz, *Hedley Bull on Arms Control*,195 (italics inserted); Bull, "Arms control and World Order,"3–36.

[147] O'Neil and Schwartz, *Hedley Bull on Arms Control*,196 (italics inserted); Hedley Bull, "Arms control and World Order,"3–36.

they are.'[148] Any consideration that the exercise of special responsibilities had been devolved upon the very powers that have used nuclear weapons does not receive due consideration.

Nevertheless, in a gesture of benign liberal openness Bull urges us to question,

> What assumptions concerning a desirable and feasible world order are implicit in our presenttheory and practice of arms control and disarmament?
>
> What assumptions about world order should inform our approach to arms control?
>
> Given answers to the above questions, what consequences follow for our arms control policy?[149]

Bull suggests that 'what we should notice about this theory and practice is the extent to which it assumes or implies that world order can and should be founded upon the present political structure of the world and the existing distribution of power within it.'[150] Despite this liberal encouragement toward enquiry, Bull is dismissive of practices that seek to question this structuring of the world order and distribution of power to address the problem of weapons. This is evident from his observation:

> But the vision of world order that is projected by our present arms control arrangements is one against which the majority of states are in revolt. It is true that among countries such as China, India, Iran, Indonesia, Egypt, Libya, Saudi Arabia, Brazil, Argentina, Nigeria, one finds different degrees of opposition to these arrangements, deep mutual divisions without any agreement about an alternative conception of world order. However, they all see the emphasis on Soviet-American bilateral goals—in arms control, in the treatment of security as the commanding value, in the preoccupation with stabilization of the great power balance, in the efforts to control proliferation, and in the network of tacit understandings between the great

[148] O'Neil and Schwartz, *Hedley Bull on Arms Control,* 214 (italics inserted); Hedley Bull, "The Role of the Nuclear Powers in the Management of Nuclear Proliferation," in *Arms Control for the Late Sixties*, ed. James Ed. Dougherty and J.F. Lehman Jr.(D.Van Nostrand Co, 1968), 143–150.

[149] O'Neil and Schwartz, *Hedley Bull on Arms Control,* 191; Bull, "Arms control,"3–36.

[150] O'Neil and Schwartz, *Hedley Bull on Arms Control,* 191; Hedley Bull, "Arms control and World Order,"*International Security* 1, no. 1(Summer 1976): 3–36.

powers—as part of a system of hegemony which they wish to break down in spite of the fact they have nothing in mind with which to replace it.[151]

To reiterate, Bull recognizes the 'majority of states are in revolt' against the existing structure of arms control and disarmament, but instead of investigating the raison d'être of this revolt in a systematic manner, he is content to argue that those revolting suffer from 'deep mutual divisions'and 'have nothing in mind to replace it.' He does not make any allowances for the historical circumstances of these revolting states that enable them to take these positions or investigate the particular demands of the revolting states but demands the need for a coherent 'alternative conception of a world order' that can substitute the existing statusquo. He lists colonialism, racialism, distribution of wealth, consumer, good or technology as the sources of Third World alienation but insists that this alienation is 'rooted also in the Third World's lack of power, including military power—its sense of impotence and vulnerability in relation to the Western countries and the Soviet Union.'[152] This decrying of the practices of the Third World, the halfhearted attempt to trace these to a list of causal categories, the lack of historicity and demanding demeanor underscores the importance of historical engagement articulating the particular conditions of discrimination in the nuclear order.

The insistence on preservation of the statusquo reduced all other efforts to question the existing international order into a failure to adjust, and the problem of 'maladjustment' was used to further reframe racial consciousness.[153] It became increasingly difficult to address problems of equality and justice in practices of arms control and disarmament as growing 'technostrategic' practices of arms control and disarmament encouraged a crisis of memory, an intellectual amnesia that enabled a forgetfulness of past history and generated assertions that '[t]he history of arms control is quite short.'[154] Little heed was paid to E.H. Carr's exhortations to historians'to take account of the widening horizon of history outside this country and outside western Europe' and his warning, 'what disturbs and alarms me is

[151] O'Neil and Schwartz, *Hedley Bull on Arms Control*,196 (italics inserted); Bull, "Arms control and World Order,"3–36.

[152] O'Neil and Schwartz, *Hedley Bull on Arms Control*, 201–202 (italics inserted); Bull, "Arms control and World Order,"3–36.

[153] Furedi, *The Silent War*, 134, 153.

[154] Barry Buzan, *An Introduction to Strategic Studies* (London: Macmillan for the International Institute for Strategic Studies, 1987), 253; Croft, *Strategies of Arms Control*, 34.

not the march of progress in Asia and Africa, but the tendency of dominant groups in this country—and perhaps elsewhere—to turn a blind or uncomprehending eye on these developments, to adopt towards them an attitude oscillating between mistrustful disdain and affable condescension, and to sink back into a paralysing nostalgia for the past.'[155] The superpower arms race and the emphasis on 'stability' effectively marginalized all historically informed efforts to reflect on questions of equality and justice in practices of arms control and disarmament.

These practices of sly civility in the form of denial and crisis of historical memory are buttressed with structural theories and their abstract assumptions that seek to naturalize order, stability and balance in the creation and maintenance of a nuclear world.[156] Mutimer claims that 'naturalisation of the balance of power reached its zenith' with Kenneth Waltz's *Theory of International Politics'* arguing:

> The theory, then, is built up from the assumed motivations of states and the actions that correspond to them. It describes the constraints that arise from the system that those actions produce, and it indicates the expected outcome: namely, the formation of balances of power. Balance-of-power theory is microtheory precisely in the economist's sense. The system, like a market in economics, is made by the actions and interactions of its units, and the theory is based on assumptions about their behaviour.[157]

These efforts at naturalization and theorization based on ahistorical assumptions often 'project' the 'decision-making rationales' pursued 'notably' in the US 'onto all other states regardless of all the contradictory historical evidence.'[158]

Furthermore, the metaphors of stability and balance that underpin international order derive their strength from 'dyadic relationships.'[159] These metaphors marginalize 'those outside the central "balance", rendering non-European states or regions either as invisible or as mere appendages to the superpower confrontation.'[160] Furthermore,'once a stable balance is achieved' there is 'no guarantee that any reduction in arsenals,

[155] E.H. Carr, *What Is History*?148–149.

[156] Mutimer, *The Weapons State,* 37–43.

[157] Kenneth Waltz, *Theory of International Politics* (Reading: Addison-Wesley, 1979), 118.

[158] Abraham, "'Who's Next?'", 50.

[159] Mutimer, "Reimagining Security," 28.

[160] Mutimer, "Reimagining Security," 29.

even a "symmetrical" reduction, would produce a similarly stable balance at the lower level of arms. Indeed, building on the received wisdom of the Cold War, there might even be a case to be made for high level of arms, as a "balance" at high levels is more resistant to small changes—that is, it is more "stable."'[161] The neo-realists 'make no apologies for inequalities' but accept them as a 'structural fact.'[162] The assumption of anarchy and inequality marginalizes any genuine concern with 'how that inequality is perceived by those who are on the short end of it' and makes it 'a problem only insofar as it may affect great power security, balance of power and stability.'[163] There is little accounting for the 'historically contingent and culturally inflected content of the national interest' articulated in reference to particular countries.[164] To maintain the performative power of the structure, some neo-realists willingly advocate the spread of nuclear weapons as another crudely ritualistic exercise in mimesis.

It will therefore not be amiss to argue that the problem of humiliation looks 'endemic when understood from the structural point of view. It is going to be there as long as structures that underlie and renew the need for inequality and subordination/servility exist.'[165] Hagan observes that'structural theories allows [*sic*] limited conceptual space for reflection on the role of the West as a civilizational identity' and notes in particular how 'authors in the realist tradition, therefore, incorporate conceptions of the West into their commentary on International Relations but not into their theoretical structure.'[166] To quote Hagan,

> If states were self-seeking, self-regarding units, one would expect that associations on the basis of a transnational form of identity such as the civilizational would have little or no relevance. However, assumptions of transnational identities such as the West slip into realist discussions of world politics... Morgenthau's references to the West make assumptions about its nature, constitution, and its centrality. Such assumptions are not accounted for in his state-centric model of power politics.[167]

[161] Mutimer, "Reimagining Security," 33.
[162] Biswas, *Nuclear Desire*, 179.
[163] Biswas, *Nuclear Desire*, 179.
[164] Latham, "Constructing national security," 130.
[165] Guru, "Theorizing Humiliation," 11.
[166] O'Hagan, *Conceptualizing the West,* 32, 24.
[167] O'Hagan, *Conceptualizing the West,* 22–23.

This realist logic persists despite Toynbee's critique of 'national-state structure' and insistence on 'civilizations or "societies" rather than nations or periods as the intelligible units of historical studies.[168] Thus, 'racism, the greatest killer of the human race since time immemorial, is still the strong force' deliberately unattended by discourses on balance of power and stability in arms control.[169] It is neglected because the nuclear bomb generated 'a phase of fetishistic-narcissistic fascination with the object itself' in the West.[170] It marginalized consideration of the idea that 'until the advent of nuclear technologies, human inventions were considered as mere adjuncts to culture.'[171]

The normalized context of structural competition among equal sovereign states 'leaves little scope for the feeling of humiliation for those who have lost in such a competition,' and 'the relatively less competent' states 'through their instrumental rationality can avoid humiliation by staying away from the competition.'[172] To quote Gopal Guru,

> Ironically, "common agreed upon rules' force people to moderate their aspiration to a subsidized level where they tend to "reason out" their exclusion as a natural fallout of their inability to participate and hence nobody is to blame but themselves. This individualization of blame removes the possibility of making claims for humiliation that is internal to such rules.[173]

Humiliation is also rendered more palatable through 'the complex process of mediation and moderation that works as its processes.'[174] The emphasis on balance and stability further helped to foster a distinction between arms control and disarmament. While arms control is considered stabilizing, disarmament is 'seen to be destabilizing,' carrying 'entailments of vulnerability and weakness.'[175]

Nuclear deterrence, the bulwark of managerial practices of arms control, is now projected as an exercise in rationality and 'abstraction' to

[168] O'Hagan, *Conceptualizing the West*, 87, 103–104.

[169] James G. Ferguson, "Of Mimicry and Membership: Africans and the 'New World Society,'" *Cultural Anthropology* 17, no. 4(2002): 561.

[170] De Kerckhove, "On Nuclear Communication," 78.

[171] De Kerckhove, "On Nuclear Communication," 79.

[172] Guru, "Theorizing Humiliation," 12.

[173] Guru, "Theorizing Humiliation," 12.

[174] Guru, "Theorizing Humiliation," 11.

[175] Mutimer, *The Weapons State*, 40.

guide practices toward vertical arms control among the superpowers.[176] In practicing deterrence 'it is out of the question for the sides involved to "really" mean what they say, for doing what they say would seem to dispossess the action of a discernible meaning.'[177] Deterrence, according to Derrida, is purely 'rhetorical—strategic escalation or nothing at all.'[178] It is 'pure mimesis.'[179] The technostrategic practices of arms control and disarmament based on abstract assumptions of deterrence and balance of power delimit the terrain of questions that can be raised and 'serve as an 'important boundary marker' so that those without access to nuclear weapons cannot be taken seriously.'[180] There is no real desire to question or critique 'the ethnocentrism of those who rely on nuclear deterrence for great power security but deny its significance for third world states.'[181] This denial evokes an 'angry reaction from the rest of the world—in particular, in the former colonies that aimed at great-power status.'[182]

This anger circulates as 'the image of proliferation' is constructed among '(particularly western) states and is invoked as a threat to international order and stability to further "strengthen controls on the spread of technology related to the research for or production" of weapons.'[183] The metaphor of proliferation signifies 'the "other"' and is 'grounded in biology.'[184] Practices of proliferation entail that the supplier states 'police the circulation of technology' and the recipients accept these policing measures at the risk of being identified as 'immature,' 'backward,' 'nuclear outlaw' or 'rogue state' that is 'unwilling to conform to the rules of civilized behaviour.'[185] An outlaw, outlier or a rogue is deemed to be 'hostile

[176] For an understanding of the concept of abstraction and its deployment in international relations, seeSankaran Krishna, "Race, Amnesia, and the Education of International Relations," in *Decolonizing International Relations*, ed. BranwenGruffydd Jones (Plymouth: UK: Rowman & Littlefield Publishers, Inc., 2006), 91–95.

[177] NecatiPolat, *International Relations, Meaning and Mimesis* (New York: Routledge, 2012), 36.

[178] Polat, *International Relations,* 36.

[179] Polat, *International Relations,* 36.

[180] Biswas,*Nuclear Desire,* 70.

[181] Biswas,*Nuclear Desire,* 179.

[182] Gregoire Mallard, *Fallout: Nuclear Diplomacy in an Age of Global Fracture* (Chicago: University of Chicago Press, 2014), 246.

[183] Anghie, *Imperialism, Sovereignty and the Making of International Law*, 67, 55; Mutimer, "Reimagining Security,"1; David Mutimer, *The Weapons State*, 4.

[184] Mutimer, "Reimagining Security," 22.

[185] Mutimer, *The Weapons State,* 8, 97.

or seemingly hostile Third World states with large military forces and nascent Weapons of Mass Destruction (WMD) capabilities' that exists outside 'a larger, settled community' or civilization 'whose rules the outlaws refuse to follow.'[186] It is argued that the West could only be persuaded to accept 'legal proscriptions' against these nuclear weapons based on the dreaded possibility that these weapons could be used as 'powerful force multipliers' by 'poor and weak countries.'[187]

Security Culture and Decorative Savages

The Western powers completely failed to empathize with 'multiple valences of atomic energy' that had found resonance in postcolonial societies.[188] The US, enamored with its exceptional status within the Western civilization as a responsible superpower, sought to contain the threat of communism and waged wars in Korea and Vietnam 'to bring the light of civilization to Asia.'[189] The new superpower was so preoccupied with building its own nuclear arsenal that it was unthinkable for it to envisage that any of the new sovereign postcolonial states 'would be in a position to develop an independent atomic energy project—military or civil—for many decades to come.'[190] Gusterson observes, '[C]olonial overtones' in the 'collective common sense' of the West represented especially by the 'US defense intellectuals, politicians and pundits—leaders of opinions on nuclear weapons.'[191] This collective consciousness failed to take note that atomic energy signified'a source of cheap electrical energy to developmentalists, a means of overcoming neo-colonial domination to nationalists, a sign of masculinity and intellectual prowess to scientists, a resource for state power to socialists, and an instrument of foreign policy to realists and militarists.'[192]

The West persisted in its outlook of considering them as mere suppliers of raw materials such as thorium, monazite, beryllium and manganese. The efforts by these postcolonial countries to use the sale of these

[186] Michael Klare, *Rogue States and Nuclear Outlaws: America's Search for a New Foreign Policy*(New York: Hill and Wang, 1995), p.14; Mutimer, *The Weapons State*, 95.

[187] Price, *Chemical Weapons Taboo*, 144.

[188] Abraham, *Indian Atomic Bomb*, 104.

[189] Jackson, *Civilizing the Enemy*, 57.

[190] Abraham, *Indian Atomic Bomb*, 81.

[191] Gusterson, "Nuclear weapons and the Other in the Western Imagination," 111–112.

[192] Abraham, *Indian Atomic Bomb*, 104.

materials in exchange for expertise that could directly benefit their atomic energy programs were strongly resisted by the West. The acquisition of 'modern technology' and especially nuclear technology by the postcolonial states perturbed the West,which then resorted to claims that these technologies were 'always marked with the trace of the foreign.'[193] They questioned the 'purely national origins of atomic energy' in the postcolonial states that had benefitted from the detailed plant designs, drawings and advice that they had received from the West. These dangerous attempts by the West to represent the postcolonial states as 'decorative savages' depict how the West denounces the performative modernity of the other.[194]

The 'decorative savages' according to the West are capable of nothing more than a crude attempt at mimicry, a 'savage aping' at a superficial level of technological prowess that is 'in fact in the service of deeper levels of "primitive", "tribal," or magical thinking.'[195] Any Third World country's desire to acquire nuclear weapons was condemned as an act of national chauvinism. It was further subject to ridicule and caricature. Said observes,

> As momentous, generally important issues face the world—issues involving nuclear destruction… popular caricatures of the Orient are exploited by politicians whose source of ideological supply is not only the half-literate technocrat but the superliterate Orientalist.[196]

Said suggests that this period was ripe to produce 'military-national-security possibilities of an alliance, say, between a specialist in "national character analysis" and an expert in Islamic institutions… for expediency's sake if for nothing else.'[197] Questions were raised, 'how to reach a less culture-blind study of international relations (?)' and 'how to approach and represent otherness (?)'[198] It was now claimed that the neglect of culture in international security studies needed to be remedied as 'strategic culture' gives meaning to 'objective' variables such as technology.[199] It was

[193] Abraham, "The Ambivalence of Nuclear Histories," 58.

[194] I borrow the term 'decorative savages' from James G. Ferguson, "Of Mimicry and Membership: Africans and the 'New World Society,'" *Cultural Anthropology* 17, no. 4(2002): 557.

[195] Ferguson, "Of Mimicry and Membership," 557.

[196] Said, *Orientalism*,107–108.

[197] Said, *Orientalism*,107–108.

[198] Valbjorn, "Before, during and after the cultural turn," 62.

[199] Johnston, "Thinking about Strategic Culture," 34.

further reinforced that 'if strategic culture changes, it does so slowly, lagging behind changes in "objective" conditions.'[200]

The extremely technocratic and specialized discourse on 'strategic analysis' based on 'extreme forms of certain generalizations' is now to be complemented with an understanding of 'security culture.'[201] Security culture is to be understood as a 'sub-set of political, diplomatic and strategic/military culture.'[202] This simple yet carefully crafted scholarly maneuver facilitated'[t]he return of culture and identity in IR theory,' and scholars debated how to navigate this 'cultural turn in IR' with the avowed objective of redressing 'some of the weaknesses inherent in the dominant realist literature.'[203] A consensus definition of security culture in the context of weapons control was now proposed in the following terms:

> Culture, as it refers to non-proliferation, arms control, disarmament and security-building issues, consists of those enduring and widely-shared beliefs, traditions, attitudes, and symbols that inform the ways in which a state's/society's interests and values with respect to security, stability and peace are perceived, articulated and advanced by political actors and elites.[204]

To study practices constitutive of 'identity' and 'culture,' scholars now promised to provide 'coherent' and 'sensible' accounts of 'security culture' to emphasize how 'security culture can be expected to exercise a powerful influence on a state's nonproliferation, arms control and disarmament policies and practices.'[205] They sought to explore the differences in 'language' and 'thought' between different national security cultures to gauge their 'orientations' toward violence and gauge prospects for 'development of the arms control and security-building dialogue' in an effort to ameliorate 'us-them' differences.[206]

[200] Johnston, "Thinking about Strategic Culture," 34.

[201] Johnston, "Thinking about Strategic Culture," 32.

[202] Keith Krause, "Cross-cultural dimensions of multilateral non-proliferation and arms control dialogues: An overview,"*Contemporary Security Policy* 19, no. 1(1998): 14.

[203] Yosef Lapid and FrederichKratochwill, eds, *The return of culture and identity in IR theory* (Boulder, Colorado: Lynne Rienner, 1996); Valbjorn, "Before, during and after the cultural turn,"55–82; Latham, "Constructing national security," 130–131.

[204] Krause, "Cross-cultural dimensions," 14.

[205] Latham, "Constructing national security," 131–132.

[206] Johnston, "Thinking about Strategic Culture," 38–41; Krause, "Cross-cultural dimensions,"3.

But Johnson admits there is 'a great deal of confusion over what it is that strategic culture is supposed to explain, how it is supposed to explain, and how much it does explain.'[207] Krause concurs to argue that culture is a 'residual phenomena that do not seem at first glance to have a "rational" explanation.'[208] This problem is compounded as a narrow focus on similarities among various actors may follow from a universalistic standpoint but be embedded in Eurocentric ethnocentrism.[209] In practices of strategic culture there is great difficulty in 'exporting or translating the fundamental concepts of the Western nonproliferation, arms control and disarmament experience to regional contexts.'[210] By focusing excessively on the differences between cultures one produces a 'narrow focus on how the Other is fundamentally different from (the perception of) oneself.'[211] Thus, Walker cautions against the 'seductive rhetoric' of discourses that try to display their cultural 'sensitivity to other civilizations.'[212] Valbjorn insistson a 'blind/blinded stalemate' that makes scholars within the field of international relations (IR)

> blind to the diversity of forms of international relations as well as blind to IR's own peculiar cultural standpoint—the alternatives suggested have in different ways often replaced a problematic culture-blind position with approaches that in turn most of all appear as culture-blinded.[213]

Johnston cautions against practices of strategic analysis that seek to 'reinforce stereotypes about strategic predispositions of other states' and urges 'care' as 'American policy attention shifts to, for instance, the Asia-Pacific region, an area where US images of the "other" have been rife with stereotyped generalizations about particular "strategic styles."'[214]

Others caution against practices of revived 'Occidentalism' or 'Orientalism in reverse,' a sly strategy of redeploying 'representations previously employed to legitimize Western imperialism' that 'were later on

[207] Johnston, "Thinking about Strategic Culture," 63.
[208] Krause, "Security Culture,"220.
[209] Valbjorn, "Before, during and after the cultural turn," 64.
[210] Krause, "Conclusions: Security Culture," 231.
[211] Valbjorn, "Before, during and after the cultural turn," 64.
[212] R.B.J. Walker, ed., *Culture, ideology and world order*(Boulder, Colorado: Westview, 1984), 7–8.
[213] Valbjorn, "Before, during and after the cultural turn," 56.
[214] Johnston, "Thinking about Strategic Culture," 64.

reversed and used by local groups calling for an end of Western interference by reference to an allegedly unique culture.'[215] The seeds of this cultural strategy were sowed during the transition from colonial to postcolonial, independent status, when some Afro-Asian elites 'internalized' and 'mimicked' racially defined 'civilizational' thinking that 'did not go beyond Western colonial thought.'[216] To quote Abraham at length,

> the reliance on civilizational categories for understanding global differences was not restricted to Europeans alone. Generations of local political elites in the colonies had grown up internalizing these categories and they remained potent means by which to understand the world.
>
> This **slippage** should not come as a surprise. Modern Asian elites had long been steeped in the knowledge-systems of Europe; indeed, such expertise was a condition of having political voice and being taken seriously within colonial societies. Hence, that Asian elites would adopt and internalize the tacit and explicit conditions of distinction embedded in authoritative social and political institutions is to be expected. Asian articulations of their own differences worked by inverting the familiar hierarchy, but were not able to transcend it, as Gandhi among others would have hoped. This new articulation of difference did little more than relocate Asian civilization in global hierarchies, seeking to make it pre-eminent rather than subordinate; it did not go further and offer a critical appraisal of the idea of civilization. …Asian elites were not able to think *outside* the category of race and civilization as a way of thinking beyond colonial categories, we find Asian elites had internalized entirely the racial logics through which the world was seen and its hierarchy naturalized, a practice that would have important implications for foreign policy decision-making.[217]

This was foreseen by Gandhi and therefore his urgent insistence on the need for 'the rewriting of "civilization" and its conversion from a source of domination to a means of political empowerment.'[218] However, this rewriting of civilization is not an easy task.

[215] Valbjorn, "Before, during and after the cultural turn," 66, see reference2; S.al-Azm, "Orientalism and Orientalism in reverse," in *Orientalism—a reader*, ed. A.L. Macfie(Edinburgh: Edinburgh University Press, 2000).

[216] Itty Abraham, "From Bandung to NAM: Non-alignment and Indian Foreign Policy, 1947–65,"*Commonwealth & Comparative Politics* 46, no. 2(2008): 198, 200.

[217] Abraham, "From Bandung to NAM," 200, 202.

[218] Abraham, "From Bandung to NAM," 200.

Johnston notes the persistent dilemma faced by scholars regarding 'how is strategic culture transmitted through time' and 'from what time periods should these sources be taken?'[219] The problem of timelag is further explicated by understanding how particular 'ideas long ago left within the "mother discipline" still reside within the receiving disciplines.'[220] It is difficult to address these temporal questions as 'the alleged homogeneity of a society's strategic culture across time is problematic.'[221] The problem of timelag persists and raises questions regarding continuity and interruption of strategic cultural practices. Furthermore, there is pervasive ambiguity as 'much of the strategic culture literature does not really specify what exactly should be analyzed when looking for culturally-based ranked set of grand strategic preferences.'[222] Nevertheless, studies have been pursued to investigate'Western security culture' and efforts made at critiquing the 'universalizing' cultural myths perpetuated by Western security practices that concealed 'a diversity of culturally derived identities, aspiration and styles.'[223]

There are studies that bring attention to 'unique security culture' of particular non-Western countries and claim how often they are 'at odds with the principles and norms underpinning Western approaches to non-proliferation, arms control and disarmament.'[224] This problem is compounded by an awareness that recourse to discourses on strategic culture is constitutive of master-slave maneuvers in 'instruction or imitation' to 'obscure or mask strategic choices' and can be deployed in an effort to 'pre-empt challenges to the status-quo.'[225] It is argued that 'the principle of cultural diversity does not necessarily ensure better understanding of the *specific Other*' and such practices of strategic culture 'appear to be about "positioning" rather than "uncovering."'[226] This carries the 'risk of giving rise to a less *internationalized* than *renationalized* discipline,' reinforcing the state-centric dynamic of difference and produce productive

[219] Johnston, "Thinking about Strategic Culture,"39.

[220] MortenValbjorn, "Before, during and after the cultural turn," 68.

[221] Johnston, "Thinking about Strategic Culture," 38.

[222] Johnston, "Thinking about Strategic Culture," 49.

[223] Latham, "Constructing national security," 133.

[224] Latham, "Constructing national security," 147; Itty Abraham, "'Who's Next?'"48–56.

[225] Jack L. Snyder, *The Soviet Strategic Culture: Implications for Nuclear Options, R-2154-AF* (Santa Monica, California: Rand Corporation, 1977), 9; Johnston, "Thinking about Strategic Culture," 36, 43–44.

[226] Valbjorn, "Before, during and after the cultural turn," 63.

myths idealizing the past.[227] This reinforces the message that the 'most profound legacy' with which Western leaders and promoters of nuclear arms control and disarmament agenda have to address is that of colonialism, discrimination, dependence and subordination.[228]

It is suggested that it would therefore be more feasible to engage in multilateral and regional practices of confidence building measures and weapons control to 'mute' cultural specificities and inter-civilizational rhetoric that cripple forums such as the Conference on Disarmament.[229]But any effort at addressing 'ethnocentric standpoint' is further crippled as 'most analysts ofarms control and disarmament issues are people who are steeped in the European history of arms control and security-building, and who wish to make the best use of this expertise in other regional or multilateral security building projects.'[230] These studies on strategic culture often try to articulate 'ideal types' of strategic 'dyads' constituted in terms of democratic security community and those outside it.[231] They seek to demonstrate to varying degrees how 'a wide variety of disparate societies may share a similar realpolitik strategic culture.'[232] Some studies try to showcase at length a hybridization of particular non-Western cultural security scripts with the 'universalized and globally institutionalized' security script articulated through the 'mechanism of imperialism' by the West.[233]

These diverse tactics to ameliorate 'hegemonic monologues' with 'hybrid dialogues' can 'mute' but do not necessarily address the dangers associated with practices of strategic culture as indicated above.[234] There is an emphatic insistence 'that cultural realpolitik is a hardy norm in international relations' and 'that in addition to focusing on "needs, interests and objectives", attention should be paid to "norms, accounts and social definitions."'[235] This atmosphere of cultivated scholarly ambivalence about

[227] Valbjorn, "Before, during and after the cultural turn," 72–73.

[228] Krause, "Security Culture,"224.

[229] Krause, "Security Culture," 235.

[230] Keith Krause, "Cross-cultural dimensions of multilateral non-proliferation and arms control dialogues: An overview,"*Contemporary Security Policy* 19, no. 1(1998): 4.

[231] Johnston, "Thinking about Strategic Culture," 61.

[232] Johnston, "Thinking about Strategic Culture," 33, 35.

[233] Latham, "Constructing national security," 136–137.

[234] Valbjorn, "Before, during and after the cultural turn," 66.

[235] Johnston, "Thinking about Strategic Culture," 63; Latham, "Constructing national security," 131.

the significance of culture in security studies is compounded with Huntington's infamous prediction about a 'clash of civilization' based on an essentialized understanding of cultural differences. It is these differences in culture of different civilizations that are considered to be the premise of failure to control horizontal nuclear weapons proliferation. An urgent intervention to mitigate this prophetic apocalypse is made by Krause,who suggests that'cultural factors can be used to explain the origins of and (different reactions to) chemical and nuclear weapons taboos.'[236]

Taboos and Norms of Civilization

There is a growing awareness of the difficulties experienced in universalizing particular norms such as 'equality' in nuclear arms control and disarmament negotiations.[237] In the existing security studies literature on diffusion of norms there are references to a growing 'arms control community' of experts that can provide 'clarification and education' in a 'technical' and 'apolitical' manner to policymakers representing the superpowers.[238] But at the same time there is an understanding that 'complex ideas that may have strong cultural or social roots mattered, and could be shared or learned—a lesson that should not be lost on those locked in seemingly intractable confrontations in other regional contexts.'[239] Thus, there is a sense of advocacy of superpower model exchanges during the Cold War that can now be deployed in attempts at socialization, in other regional contexts such as South Asia.

While there is much advocacy of nuclear weapons taboo, it is interesting to note how social constructivist scholars such as Price and Tannenwald observe and acknowledge the interplay of different 'standards of civilization' in the use and non-use of chemical and nuclear weapons, respectively. Tannenwald observes but does not question the significance of 'taken-for-granted norms such as "civilization"' in her study of the nuclear weapons taboo.She is more interested in how the emergence of a nuclear taboo has an effect on US policy and how 'new interpretations of hegemony could give rise to a discourse that seeks to

[236] Krause, "Cross-Cultural Dimensions,"1.
[237] Krause and Latham, "Constructing Non-Proliferation," 30.
[238] Krause and Latham, "Constructing Non-Proliferation," 27–28.
[239] Krause and Latham, "Constructing Non-Proliferation," 34.

legitimize the use of nuclear weapons by the United States to enforce norms against so-called barbarians.'[240] The circulation of racist arguments preceded the institutionalization of the nuclear weapons taboo in treaty texts such as the Nuclear Nonproliferation Treaty (NPT). But Tannenwald does not explore the possibilities of 'racial' contestation of the nuclear taboo and its institutionalization in the NPT as an 'unequal treaty' among sovereign states at length.

There is marginalization of studying possibilities of enforcement of nuclear norms to maintain the 'standards of civilization' against the 'barbarians' and their effects. There is a need for more reflexivity to question whether by expounding norms against weapons of mass destruction this scholarship is in fact subscribing and reinforcing a particular set of civilizational practices. Their interest in the problem of weapons can be ascribed as 'thematic,' confined to 'epistemological as well as ethical system which provides a framework of elements and rules for establishing relations between elements' but does not go further in investigating the 'problematic' of possibilities for transformation.[241] There is an element of disinterest in investigating how the emphasis on internalization of norms by the subalterns is another deliberate attempt to eliminate any consciousness of the subaltern 'developing an insight into reduction' and question the conditions of servility to the West.[242] This is in keeping with the practices of maintaining ideological supremacy of the West vis-à-vis others in the field of arms control and disarmament. There is a failure to explicitly acknowledge that 'racism is the parade ground where the civilized rehearse this love-hate relation' against the savages that 'spill out, escape the grid of the normative, and therefore conceptuality itself.'[243]

On the contrary, postcolonial scholars such as Abraham and Gusterson argue that the NPT's grounding of 1964 as the dividing time-line between proliferators and non-proliferators suggests the possibility that 'there is something altogether different about post-1964 proliferators: somehow they are seen to embody a distinct threat to the prevailing order.'[244] They are conceived as a threat because of their 'unwillingness to play by the

[240] Nina Tannenwald, "Stigmatizing the Bomb: Origins of the Nuclear Taboo," *International Security*, 29, no. 4, 2005: 5–49.

[241] Chatterjee, "Nationalist Thought and the Colonial World," 38–39.

[242] Gopal Guru, "Rejection of Rejection," in *Humiliation—Claims and Context*, ed. Gopal Guru (Oxford, New Delhi: Oxford University Press, 2009), 219.

[243] Taussig, *Mimesis and Alterity*, 67.

[244] Abraham, *Indian Atomic Bomb*, 14.

"rules of the game."'[245] These allegations are made with scarcely any engagement or scrutiny about the 'nuclear pasts of most states other than the pre-1964 proliferators.'[246] There is, however, a degree of caution to the possibility that the 'rhetoricof progress' can be deployed to 'subvert the cultures of societies' that have experienced 'external colonialism' and that can encourage the growing forces of nationalism within these societies to argue for acquisition of weapons themselves, claiming the existence of an 'external threat to legitimize and perpetuate' their own presence.[247]Gusterson notes,

> Although the Non-Proliferation Treaty divided the countries of the world into nuclear and nonnuclear by means of a purely temporal metric—designating only those who had tested nuclear weapons by 1970 as nuclear powers—the treaty had become the legal anchor for a global nuclear regime that is increasingly legitimated in Western public discourse in racialized terms.[248]

In a further attempt to explicate this observation, Gusterson suggests the deployment of 'subtle orientalist ideologies' by the West in an effort to essentialize the Otherness of the Third World vis-à-vis the West.[249] This is facilitated by the efforts of the West to represent itself as a collective ideological front that

> (1) makes the simultaneous ownership of nuclear weapons by the major powers and the absence of nuclear weapons in the Third World seem natural and reasonable while problematizing attempts by such countries as India, Pakistan, and Iraq to acquire these weapons; (2) it presents the security needs of the established nuclear powers as if they were everybody's; (3) it effaces the continuity between Third World countries' nuclear deprivation and other systematic patterns of deprivation in the underdeveloped world in order to inhibit a massive North-South confrontation; and (4) it legitimates the nuclear monopoly of the recognized nuclear powers.[250]

[245] Abraham, *Indian Atomic Bomb,* 15.

[246] Abraham, *Indian Atomic Bomb,* 16.

[247] Nandy, *The Intimate Enemy,* xii.

[248] Hugh Gusterson, "Nuclear Weapons and the Other in the Western Imagination," *Cultural Anthropology* 14, no. 1(1999): 113 (italics inserted).

[249] Gusterson, "Nuclear Weapons," 114 (italics inserted).

[250] Gusterson, "Nuclear Weapons," 115.

The struggle for legitimacy to acquire nuclear weapons is fought further on the grounds that

> (1) Third World countries are too poor to afford nuclear weapons; (2) deterrence will be unstable in the Third World; (3) Third World regimes lack the technical maturity to be trusted with nuclear weapons; and (4) Third World regimes lack the political maturity to be trusted with nuclear weapons.[251]

In this struggle for legitimacy 'the claim to rational decision-making is frequently used by great powers to justify the possession of nuclear weapons. Conversely, the *purported lack of rationality*,on the part of other states, particularly revolutionary regimes like Cuba or Iran, is routinely invoked to explain why they cannot be trusted with nuclear weapons.'[252] These countries are time and again hectored by the West and complain of 'being tired of being lectured to by American officials on the priority of Iran's economic progress over the development of its military potential.'[253]

The existing literature on arms control and disarmament is replete with rhetorical polarizations that depict the West as the trustworthy and responsible actor that needs to police the rebellious and recalcitrant Third World that is not up to the task, whose science and technology is not even capable of addressing their basic population and food problems and is constantly seeking attention. All these 'recurrent images and metaphors...*pertain in some way to disorder*.'[254] The West persists with 'a broadly paternalistic approach' of 'Papa knows best' and resists the idea of 'political maturation' of postcolonial states.[255] But these representations heighten subaltern 'sensitivities about any restrictions that might perpetuate or increase the technological gap' that already exists between the West and the Rest.[256] These representations awaken fear of 'atomic colonialism'

[251] Hugh Gusterson, "Nuclear Weapons," 115.

[252] Barkawi and Laffey, "The Postcolonial Moment in Security Studies," 338; Hugh Gusterson, *People of the Bomb: Portrait of America's Nuclear Complex*(Minneapolis, MN: Minnesota University Press, 2004), ch.2.

[253] Mustafa Kibaroglu, "Iran's Nuclear Ambitions from a Historical Perspective and the Attitude of the West,"*Middle-Eastern Studies* 43, no. 2(2007): 227.

[254] Gusterson, "Nuclear Weapons," 129.

[255] Stephen McGlinchey, "Lyndon B. Johnson and Arms Credit Sales to Iran, 1964–1968,"*The Middle East Journal* 67, no. 2(2013): 238.

[256] CiroZoppo, "Nuclear Technology, Weapons, and the Third World,"*Annals of the American Academy of Political and Social Science,* no. 386 (1969): 120.

and 'space age colonialism.'[257] There is an unwillingness among the developing countries to merely 'become a nuclear market comparable to the old-semi-colonial markets, in the sense that those countries would supply raw materials to advanced States, from which they would acquire finished industrial products.'[258] The postcolonial states are cognizant of nuclear weapons as the currency of power and 'differential standards of national security—a sort of nuclear apartheid.'[259]

Nuclear Apartheid

The struggle for equality cannot be waged without grasping the problem of nuclear apartheid position as it

> quite starkly and compellingly points to the material inequities in the distribution of global nuclear resources—inequities that are written into, for interrogating the invocation of 'race' institutionalized, and legitimized through some of the major arms control treaties, creating an elite club of 'nuclear haves' with exclusive right to maintain nuclear arsenals that are denied to the vast majority of the nuclear "have-nots."[260]

Biswas insists that, 'to use the word apartheid is clearly to use a racial signifier and one that carries within it a certain contemporary political resonance…the nuclear apartheid argument is in one sense an attempt to point to the continuing exclusions and marginalizations faced by people of colour in Third World countries in a global order dominated and controlled by privileged Whites in the First World countries.'[261] Biswas ponders on how to locate China in the racial cartographies of the nuclear order, but Subramanyam is clear that, '[w]hile China may continue to show some defiance, against the policies of the West on occasion, the nuclear distribution indicated the continuing domination of the traditional White imperialists in an overwhelmingly non-White world.'[262] The Chinese did not share fears generated by 'the statistical argument about

[257] Zoppo, "Nuclear Technology," 119.

[258] Zoppo, "Nuclear Technology," 120.

[259] Jaswant Singh, "Against Nuclear Apartheid," *Foreign Affairs* 44, no. 5(1998): 48.

[260] Shampa Biswas, "'Nuclear Apartheid' as Political Position: Race as a Postcolonial Discourse," *Alternatives* 26, no. 4(October–December 2001): 486, 485–522.

[261] Biswas, "Nuclear Apartheid," 485–522.

[262] Quoted in Biswas, "Nuclear Apartheid," 497, see footnote 37.

the dangers of nuclear proliferation which is extremely common in the West.'[263] On the contrary, they initially trivialized the atom bomb as a 'paper tiger' and asserted that the West's efforts to 'halt proliferation' would be tantamount to 'an abdication of the right of self-defence on the part of other countries.'[264] The Chinese insisted,

> They have it and you don't and so they are very haughty. But once those who oppose them also have it, they would no longer be so haughty, their policy of nuclear blackmail and nuclear threat would no longer be effective, and the possibility for a complete prohibition and thorough destruction of nuclear weapons would increase.[265]

China insisted on breaking this nuclear monopoly of the West as it reminisced how during the the 'Forgotten War' waged by the US in Korea, President Truman, General Douglas McArthur and Air Force General Curtis LeMay had threatened to use atomic weapons. The European powers had to restrain the US by issuing a reminder that the use of the atom bomb would suggest that 'Europeans and Americans have a low regard for the value of Asiatic lives.'[266] These rhetorical reminders from the Chinese on experiences of nuclear threat and nuclear blackmail and its position on nonproliferation led the West to argue, 'less plausible but still conceivable is the possibility that the Chinese might favour spreading nuclear weapons to non-white peoples as an appeal to racism. But available evidence suggests that such Chinese racism as does exist would be unlikely to operate along these lines.'[267]

Similarly, in exploring the motives for India's decision to make a transition from its ambivalent position as a nuclear-capable state to a nuclear weapon state, Biswas suggests that this is best represented in a nationalism that is emphatic in its refusal 'to be blackmailed and treated like oriental blackies.'[268] Prior to the Indian nuclear test in 1974, the West persisted with its practices of stereotyping India as 'a pacifist culture fostered by

[263] Oran R. Young, "Chinese Views on the Spread of Nuclear Weapons," *The China Quarterly*, no. 26 (1966): 144.

[264] Young, "Chinese Views," 149,151.

[265] Young, "Chinese Views," 146.

[266] Bruce Cumings, "On the Strategy and Morality of American Nuclear Policy in Korea—1950 to the Present," *Social Science Japan Journal* 1, no. 1(1998): 59.

[267] Young, "Chinese Views," 158.

[268] Biswas, "'Nuclear Apartheid,'" 497, see footnote 39.

Mahatma Gandhi's philosophy' and Indian nuclear strategists sought to disabuse the subalterns of their 'conditioning by the West' in the following terms:

> [T]he present generation of decision makers and elite marks a marginal improvement over the previous generation in regard to Indocentricity...still they are too much influenced by their conditioning by the liberal West....But this attitude is bound to change as the newer generation of decisionmakers move into positions of influence. Mrs. Gandhi is at present the only practitioner of realpolitik among a whole lot of confused Westernisedelite.[269]

Pant argued that India's refusal to sign the NPT was 'a response to its discriminatory structure— separating nuclear haves from have-nots—not a result of India wanting nuclear weapons— yet.'[270] This emphasis on 'not-yet' is significant and buttressed by an understanding that 'the mighty and the weak do not get humiliated the same way.'[271] Palshikar suggests that 'a close reading of the vocabulary deployed shows that the powerful speak of slight, offence, rudeness, temerity, whereas the subalterns complain of callousness, neglect, and inhuman treatment.'[272] This becomes most visible during 'a sudden and momentary reversal of relations of hierarchy' such as India's nuclear tests.[273]

The rhetoric of 'nuclear apartheid' is a 'rhetoric of humiliation' that is instrumentally deployed as 'a technique of political mobilization and consolidation' to shame the West.[274] It will not be a mistake to suggest that postcolonial states harbor feelings of 'resentment' toward the mindset of the West as a trustee that can 'preach' to the have-nots to have even less.[275]

[269] K. Subramanyam quoted in article by Richard K. Betts, "Incentives for Nuclear Weapons: India, Pakistan, Iran,"*Asian Survey* 19, no. 11 (1979): 1068–69.

[270] K.C. Pant, "Rajya Sabha Extensive Debate on India's Peaceful Nuclear Explosion," August 21, 1974, *Indian Nuclear History collection*, Wilson Center Digital Archive, 251–253, retrieved from http://digitalarchive.wilsoncenter.org/document/119760, cited by VipinNarang, "Strategies of Nuclear Proliferation: How States Pursue the Bomb,"*International Security* 41, no. 3(2016/17): 139, footnote 72.

[271] Sanjay Palshikar, "Understanding Humiliation," in *Humiliation—Claims and Context,* ed. Gopal Guru (Oxford, New Delhi: Oxford University Press, 2009), 82.

[272] Palshikar, "Understanding Humiliation," 82.

[273] Palshikar, "Understanding Humiliation," 82.

[274] Ashish Nandy, "Humiliation—Politics and the Cultural psychology of the Limits of Human Degradation," in *Humiliation—Claims and Context*,ed. Gopal Guru (Oxford, New Delhi: Oxford University Press, 2009), 51.

[275] Jaswant Singh, "Against Nuclear Apartheid,"*Foreign Affairs* 44, no. 5(1998): 43.

They seek to demonstrate to the West their 'scientific, technological and organizational abilities' that they claim to have acquired decades ago in their quest for nuclear weapons.[276] Goldschmidt observes how the Indians could claim that in conducting their first nuclear test,

> the plutonium they used had been extracted in a nationally built reprocessing plant and came from Indian natural uranium which had been irradiated in the first exported research reactor offered for peaceful purposes by Canada to India in the mid-1950s before international safeguards were introduced.[277]

They further insist on their capacity for careful deliberation that has led to a calibrated strategy of 'moral' dissuasion, 'covert' possession and 'overt' declaration of being a nuclear weapons state.[278] They even appear to be cognizant and respectful of the international legal framework as they argue,

> Since it is now argued that the NPT is unamendable, the legitimization of nuclear weapons implicit in the unconditional and indefinite extension of the NPT is also irreversible. India could have lived with a nuclear option but without overt weaponization in a world where nuclear weapons had not been formally legitimized. That course was no longer viable in the post-1995 world of legitimized nuclear weapons.[279]

The very careful effort to present these arguments suggests an attempt to counter a '"politics of cultural representation"—a general perception of the unstated assumption in global nuclear discourse that "the subcontinent is full of unstable people with deep historical resentments, incapable of acting rationally or managing a technologically sophisticated arsenal."'[280] While there is a sense of denial from recanting, subscribing to or reinventing the sterile doctrines of Cold, there is simultaneously an expression of faith in constituing a 'universal security paradigm for the entire globe' based on disarmament or equal and legitimate security

[276] Singh, "Against Nuclear Apartheid," 43–44.

[277] Bertrand Goldschmidt, "A Historical Survey of Nonproliferation Policies," *International Security* 2, no. 1(1997): 78.

[278] Singh, "Against Nuclear Apartheid," 43.

[279] Singh, "Against Nuclear Apartheid," 44–45.

[280] Quote cited in Shampa Biswas, "'Nuclear Apartheid' as Political Position: Race as a Postcolonial Discourse," *Alternatives* 26, no. 4(October–December 2001): 497, see footnote 44.

for all.[281] There is also an emphasis on the need to 'address the unfinished agenda of the centuries.'[282]

Their is an assertion of equivalence that argues if 'deterrence' is the product of 'state rationality,' then the horrific production of 'mutual destruction' should operate as smoothly to prevent nuclear war in the Indian subcontinent (where contiguous territory only magnifies the horror) as it does in the European theater.[283] The demand for respectand assertion of equivalence that accompany postcolonial discourses of disarmament constitute a 'plea for change.'[284] They represent a desire to bring to the fore an understanding that

> it is not a PROLIFERATION problem—that is, a spread of weapons technology from those who have to those who do not presently have. Rather, the problem needs to be imagined as a (DIS)ARMAMENT problem—the possession of nuclear and other arms, regardless of who has them.[285]

But acceptance of this argument requires 'changing the mindset toward the problem' to 'a changed reality.'[286] This is a difficult exercise as the entrenched mindset of the imperial master galvanized by the 'dynamic of difference' continues to dictate practices of regimes based on technology denial, forcible disarmament and counter-proliferation, as discussed in the next chapter.[287]

The problem of nuclear apartheid can be made more visible by taking note, in writing, of another visible sample of colonial nonsense proliferating practices of sly civility while attempting to question the logic of inequality embodied in the NPT.[288] Joseph Nye describes the allegations of discrimination, hypocrisy and failure to live up to commitments levied by the diplomats of nonnuclear weapons states against the superpowers as a 'drama' and then poses the question,'should this drama be taken seriously?'[289] At the very outset itself his answer is an ambivalent 'no and

[281] Singh, "Against Nuclear Apartheid," 50–52.
[282] Singh, "Against Nuclear Apartheid," 52.
[283] Quoted cited in Biswas, "'Nuclear Apartheid,'" 496, see footnote 43.
[284] Mutimer, "Reimagining Security," 36.
[285] DavidMutimer, "Reimagining Security," 36.
[286] DavidMutimer, "Reimagining Security," 36.
[287] Charles Krauthammer, "The Unipolar Moment," *Foreign Affairs* 70, no. 1(1991): 32–33.
[288] Joseph S. Nye Jr., "NPT: The Logic of Inequality," *Foreign Policy*, no. 59 (1985): 123.
[289] Nye, "The Logic of Inequality," 123.

yes.'[290] The answer is premised on a deliberation undertaken as an exercise in abstraction to insist that 'it is quite possible to justify nuclear inequality.'[291] Nye suggests that there is a 'basic intuitive compact underlying the NPT' and describes the NPT itself as an 'imaginary compact.'[292] He then suggests that 'under certain conditions' and 'other things remaining equal,' nuclear inequality is acceptable.[293] This reluctance to engage with historical circumstances and inserting ceteris paribus clauses to advance seemingly abstract conditions of arguments is a questionable exercise. This becomes even more specious as it is followed by an outright assertion that 'nuclear inequality has nothing to do with racism on the part of weapons states or with the irrationality that some claim to see in Third World leaders.'[294] This outright mockery and dismissal to take seriously the allegation of racialism in addressing the problem of inequality suggests an acutely shrewd political mindset wary of displacement of power relations in the practices of arms control and disarmament.

This mindset as represented by Nye in the field of arms control and disarmament deliberately seeks to justify the problem of inequality. It is wary of any attempt to question it by issuing a warning that this could lead to the possibility that 'deterrence will fail.'[295] It deliberately splits the problem of inequality, discouraging any investigation of its racial roots, and foregrounds it as only a technical problem susceptible to failure. The failure of deterrence, it is argued, 'is likely to be much higher in most regional situations because of the shaky political conditions found in most states seeking nuclear weapons as well as their limited experience with nuclear command and control systems.'[296] The existing inequality is further justified on grounds that with 'new proliferators' the threat of breaking 'nuclear taboo becomes that much more likely.'[297] The maintenance of inequality is proposed in the following terms: 'under many circumstances the introduction of a single bomb in some non-nuclear states may be more likely to lead to nuclear use than the addition of a thousand more

[290] Nye, "The Logic of Inequality," 123.
[291] Nye, "The Logic of Inequality" 124.
[292] Nye, "The Logic of Inequality," 124, 129.
[293] Nye, "The Logic of Inequality," 124–126.
[294] Nye, "The Logic of Inequality," 126.
[295] Nye, "The Logic of Inequality," 126.
[296] Nye, "The Logic of Inequality," 126.
[297] Nye, "The Logic of Inequality," 127.

warheads to the US and Soviet stockpiles.'[298] This particular statement reignites the trauma of the subaltern that is to be severely penalized should even a single rusty weapon be discovered in its possession by the colonizer.

Despite these claims Nye is confident in his assertion, 'nonproliferation is not an inconsistent or hypocritical policy if it is based on impartial and realistic estimation of relative risks.'[299] But he is oblivious to the consideration that risk of failure of deterrence and violation of taboo are all sourced to 'new proliferators' that need to be policed. It is assumed that 'the police function is traditionally the domain of great powers in international politics.'[300] Any resistance to this policing function from other states is circumscribed by polarized choices between 'some ordered inequality in weaponry'and 'anarchic inequality,' an oxymoron that is described by Nye to be 'more dangerous.'[301] Nye casually entertains the possibility that 'third countries may hold the superpowers similarly accountable' but fails to provide any account of how this might be undertaken as he insists on 'alliance guarantees' to stem proliferation and readily concludes that the NPT's 'Article VI obligations cannot be interpreted as simple disarmament.'[302] The transfer of nuclear technology even for energy programs is also to be grounded in an 'evolutionary approach' and susceptible to additional deliberation on a 'region's stability and of the susceptibility of the technology to safeguards.'[303]

It is this entrenched mindset that is displayed by Nye four decades into the Cold War. He displays little desire to question the legacy of attitudes that he has inherited from those that have been revered and are woven into the traditional discourses on arms control and disarmament. Nye completely ignores the warning issued by Betts that the 'discussion of the danger of nuclear proliferation has suffered too much abstraction and too little specification.'[304] Betts observes an 'international "diffusion of power"' and is critical of the West that 'seldom' appreciates the 'national power' of others but persists in stereotyping others as 'basket

[298] Nye, "The Logic of Inequality," 128.
[299] Nye, "The Logic of Inequality," 127.
[300] Nye, "The Logic of Inequality," 131.
[301] Nye, "The Logic of Inequality," 130.
[302] Nye, "The Logic of Inequality" 128.
[303] Nye, "The Logic of Inequality" 130.
[304] Richard K. Betts, "Incentives for Nuclear Weapons: India, Pakistan, Iran,"*Asian Survey* 19, no. 11 (1979): 1053.

cases,''primitive, hopelessly poor, dependent' and 'arrogant.'[305] Betts encourages the West to acknowledge,

> while the desire for a degree of technical or economic autonomy is understandable for formerly colonized nations, and is not beyond the realm of possibility...near autonomy in at least *one* important area—nuclear energy—might therefore be all the more important as a symbol of national sovereignty.[306]

Mallard seeks to focus our attention on the historical specificity of the conditions under which the nuclear legal order came into existence. He acknowledges the anger of postcolonial states is in response to the 'exclusive rights' and 'European nuclear settlement' gained while negotiating 'the broader global NPT regime.'[307] Mallard argues that it was 'European exceptionalism' that set the framework for nuclear non-proliferation negotiations and that the 'strongest tension' was rooted in securing the 'survival of the European system of control of nuclear activities' set up by the European Community of Atomic Energy (Euratom) Treaty in 1957.[308] The Euratom is composed of six European states (France, West Germany, Italy, the Netherlands, Belgium and Luxembourg).[309] In his detailed exploration of how Europe weighted East-West negotiations of the NPT, Mallard emphasizes the significance of the US-Euratom Treaty (1958). The US-Euratom Treaty of 1958

> did not prohibit military use of imported (or locally produced) source and special fissionable materials by Euratom member states as long as such was declared to Euratom; it did not grant to nuclear importers (such as the United States) a "right to pursuit" over degraded fissile materials (for instance, plutonium extracted from the waste of nuclear fuels imported by Euratom); and it did not authorize foreign inspections on its soil—instead, the United States was granted a right to "verify"(or rather, to read) the accountancy books of nuclear materials in Euratom territory.[310]

[305] Betts, "Incentives for Nuclear Weapons," 1054.

[306] Betts, "Incentives for Nuclear Weapons," 1061–1062(emphasis by Betts).

[307] Gregoire Mallard, *Fallout: Nuclear Diplomacy in an Age of Global Fracture* (Chicago: University of Chicago Press, 2014), 246.

[308] Mallard, *Nuclear Diplomacy*, 7–8.

[309] Mallard, *Nuclear Diplomacy*, 7.

[310] Mallard, *Nuclear Diplomacy*, 220.

It was European desire to protect the provisions of this treaty that shaped its position during negotiations of the statute of the International Atomic Energy Agency (IAEA) and the NPT. During these negotiations, 'the West made it clear that the Euratom Treaty would trump any new soft or hard law as far as the application of safeguards was concerned in Europe.'[311] At the same time meetings of 'Ottawa Powers' comprising of Anglophone countries 'insisted that not only among themselves but also between themselves and Euratom countries, they would not require the impositions of IAEA safeguards on their nuclear trade.'[312] The significance of access to nuclear technology and the possibility of integrated markets based on this technology were defended as a matter of European community's 'rights' against nuclear safeguards.[313]

The desire to safeguard these interests led to advocacy of an incremental approach toward IAEA safeguards that would first be imposed on research reactors before any imposition of comprehensive safeguards on all kinds of nuclear facilities. This visibility of 'the double (triple) standards regarding the US approach to controls' was denounced by the Third World countries as they 'saw in it a neocolonial mindset at work, which divided the world between the white-dominated Western nations (whose nuclear trade would be excluded from safeguards by the IAEA) and the rest (whose nuclear trade, especially concerning research reactors, would be strictly controlled by the IAEA).'[314] It was European desire for 'Euratom's exclusive control of nuclear activities in Europe' that

> forced the IAEA to design a new global NPT safeguards system that was based on the Euratom system. The Euratom control system shaped how the IAEA, charged with the responsibility of ensuring compliance with the NPT, was to function in the global nonproliferation regime.[315]

Ratification of the NPT itself was held hostage by all Euratom members 'until after the date (when they signed the IAEA-Euratom Agreement),' giving Euratom 'increased bargaining power in its negotiation.'[316] Mallard reinforces the significance of this observation by iterating how 'European

[311] Mallard, *Nuclear Diplomacy*, 224.
[312] Mallard, *Nuclear Diplomacy*, 220–221.
[313] Mallard, *Nuclear Diplomacy* 231–232.
[314] Mallard, *Nuclear Diplomacy*, 221.
[315] Mallard, *Nuclear Diplomacy*, 14.
[316] Mallard, *Nuclear Diplomacy*, 14.

lawmakers… have long used international law to enslave instead of empower the non-European world' and concurred with Forland's observation to the effect that, 'in spite of the global orientation of the negotiations and the global problem that the NPT was addressing, it (wa)s in fact striking to what extent the European context set the framework for the negotiations.'[317]

Despite acknowledging the historical practices of European exceptionalism in the nuclear order, Mallard appears to be only interested in suggesting 'conditions that would make it possible' to 'include…outliers in a way that would *emulate* the *harmonization* between Europe's regional and global treaty rules.'[318] The concept of 'harmonization' was introduced by European jurists to address fear that the strengthening of the IAEA 'would sooner or later force the United States to adapt the Euratom controls to fit IAEA controls, if only to respond to criticisms of doublestandards.'[319] The concept of harmonization was therefore a stratagem pursued to accommodate 'preexisting treaties and agreements between the United States and Europe' to retain their privileged state of exceptionalism in the nuclear order.[320]

Ironically despite this admission, it is 'the story of Europe's nuclear opacity and its evolution' that is still championed as offering 'new lessons to deal with the issue.'[321] It is claimed that failure to emulate and harmonize accordingly will generate the possibility of 'double or triple standards' in the international legal system that will eventually generate a 'state of chaos.'[322]The postcolonial states accuse the Western powers of practicing 'international neo-colonialism' and insist that 'any regime seeking to control the spread of nuclear technologies had to be applied equally to all states.'[323] They further insist that these efforts of the Western powers to regulate the behavior of non-nuclear weapons states were attempts to dictate 'what they could and could not do to further their own national goals and objectives.'[324] These efforts were an affront to the principle of sovereign equality under international law and that no 'self-respecting' state

[317] Mallard quoting Astrid Forland in *Nuclear Diplomacy,* 8.
[318] Mallard, *Nuclear Diplomacy,*15(italics inserted).
[319] Mallard, *Nuclear Diplomacy*, 225, 228.
[320] Mallard, *Nuclear Diplomacy,* 228.
[321] Mallard, *Nuclear Diplomacy*, 15.
[322] Mallard, *Nuclear Diplomacy*, 15.
[323] Abraham, *Indian Atomic Bomb,* 138–139.
[324] Abraham, *Indian Atomic Bomb,* 138.

could accept.[325] But as Victor Villanueva observes, there is 'a difference between speaking and being heard, that if one is constantly speaking but is never heard, never truly heard, there is, in effect, a silence, a silencing… how racism seems always to be an appendage…but not quite integral, even when race is the issue.'[326]

Interestingly while it is common knowledge that France and Germany have played a significant role in the expansion and development of nuclear programs, including infrastructure, technology and training of nuclear scientists from the developing countries throughout the Cold War, they have never been described as pariah or rogue states engaged in nuclear proliferation. On the contrary, their efforts are rationalized in the following manner: The US decision in 1974 to suspend the supply of low enriched uranium for low enriched uranium reactors created an opportunity for European competitors to develop their own fuel-producing technologies and merchandise them overseas.[327] While France maintained a policy of 'ambivalence' and 'abstention from the NPT,' Germany 'openly defied the US,' insisting that it was 'allowed to develop, produce and operate technologies encompassing the whole nuclear cycle' and was 'anxious to sell to whoever might be suitable.'[328] For decades, these European countries did not exhibit 'deep anxiety' about 'horizontal proliferation,' were 'ready to sell sensitive enrichment and reprocessing technologies' and were reluctant to 'impose strict conditions of sale, especially the requirement that all of the recipients' nuclear facility be placed under safeguards.'[329] Therewas only a rhetorical reiteration of the fear that 'transfer of such technologies…could lead to an erosion of Nuclear Non-Proliferation Treaty.'[330]

There has been no outcry against these European proliferators of nuclear technology. The spread of nuclear technology by European powers is 'conceived and acted on as an autonomous technologically driven process,' and their ambivalence toward the NPT is further rationalized.[331] It is argued that their fear of the NPT stems from it being cast 'as an

[325] Abraham, *Indian Atomic Bomb,* 138.

[326] Victor Villanueva, "On the Rhetoric and Precedents of Racism,"*College Composition and Communication* 50, no. 4(1999), p. 653.

[327] Mustafa Kibaroglu, "Iran's Nuclear Ambitions from a Historical Perspective and the Attitude of the West,"*Middle-Eastern Studies* 43, no. 2(2007): 231.

[328] Kibaroglu, "Iran's Nuclear Ambitions," 232.

[329] Kibaroglu, "Iran's Nuclear Ambitions," 232–233.

[330] Kibaroglu, "Iran's Nuclear Ambitions."

[331] Mutimer, *The Weapons State,* 141.

instrument as well as a sign of Europe's second-rate status' and their struggle and resistance toward the NPT is justified in terms of 'their position in world politics.'[332] It is further modestly suggested it was only due to 'a lack of coherence in the nuclear non-proliferation strategies of the West, and disharmony in their export control policies,' that the Others were able to exploit these differences and gain access to sensitive technology.[333] The exclusive responsibility of exploiting 'to the utmost the opportunity to gain access to sensitive technologies' is placed on a number of Third World countries often castigated as the 'Axis of Evil.'[334] In the contemporary discourses specifically targeting Third World countries, Mutimer observes,

> What is more, the miscreants in the "proliferation" image are seen as acting in an excessive or aggressive manner and are constructed as outlaws—those who step beyond the established rules of the international game. There is absolutely no recognition that rather than the behaviour of outlaws, the acquisition of the trappings of modern state power is central to admission to the game in the first place, that states behave this way precisely because that is what it means to be a state.[335]

Conclusion

It is questionable if acquisition of power demonstrated through the visible trappings of a sovereign state is sufficient for postcolonial states to engage with the disciplinary power exercised by the West through the practices of normalization deliberately maintained in the nuclear order.[336] It is difficult to address this question without taking note of how supplier-oriented export controls problematize movement of technology instead of arms production and possession, as discussed in the next chapter. The emphasis

[332] Harald Muller cited by Kibaroglu, "Iran's Nuclear Ambitions," 233, see footnote 90; Harald Muller, "Non-Proliferation Policy in Western Europe: Structural Aspects," in *A European Non-Proliferation Policy, 1988–1992*, Muller (European Interuniversity Press, 1993), 86.

[333] Kibaroglu, "Iran's Nuclear Ambitions," 231.

[334] Kibaroglu, "Iran's Nuclear Ambitions," 231.

[335] Mutimer, *The Weapons State*, 141, 156–157.

[336] Michel Foucault, *Discipline and Punish: the Birth of the Prison* (New York: Pantheon Books, 1977). Foucault engages with the question of power by making a subtle distinction between sovereign power (publicly exhibited) and disciplinary power (everyday practices of normalization).

on proliferation discourages engagement with the full range of meanings of a nuclear program and it is only at the critical stage of mimicry of a nuclear explosion and weaponization that a postcolonial country is considered to have moved 'closer into line with received interpretations of what a "typical" nuclear programme does and signal its entry into the exclusive nuclear club.'[337]

This suggests that the idea of moral progress enunciated as 'a significant distance from both civilizational imperialism and the politics of pristine sovereignty' cannot be traversed without being cognizant of mimetic maneuvers and temporal practices of sly civility. The principle of formal equality is still relevant because it is based on the twin ideas of non-discrimination and procedural fairness.[338] Both of these principles are the subject of intense debate and discussion to create a level playing field of arms control and disarmament as shown above. This has given rise to deliberations on how the principle of formal equality needs to be supplemented with principles of egalitarianism.

The idea of egalitarianism is closely associated with humanitarian practices of arms control and disarmament. It is argued that egalitarianism acknowledges diversity of experiencesand inequalities in societies and seeks to redress them. It is this egalitarian approach that has helped humanitarian actors to bring center stage the sufferings of the victims and gained much traction in the last decade of the Cold War. But given the colonial legacy of imperialism and humanitarianism, scholars caution that it might be presumptuous to assume that practices of humanitarian arms control and disarmament will 'question the structuration of society along the axis of power and domination' or 'lead to the generalization of respect for all.'[339] Humanitarian narratives of arms control and disarmament often 'read as a narrative of collective guilt and collective complicity on the one hand and collective victimization and collective harm on the other.'[340] These narratives seek 'restitution for historical wrongs' that generate

337 Abraham, "The Ambivalence of Nuclear Histories," 55.

338 NeeraChandhoke, "Equality for What? Or the Troublesome Relation between Egalitarianism and Respect," in *Humiliation—Claims and Context*, ed. Gopal Guru (Oxford, New Delhi: Oxford University Press, 2009), 146.

339 NeeraChandhoke, "Equality for What?"150.

340 Chandhoke, "Equality for What?," 151.

'spiralling claims of victimhood on the one hand, and demands for compensation on the other.'[341] The efforts 'where the victim is the hero, suffering has been trivialized because it has been reduced into an index for compensation.'[342]

These humanitarian efforts fail to foster respect but reproduce feelings of humiliation and inequality because

> there is considerable conceptual difference between participating in the reconstruction of a society that has been unequally and unfairly organized by asking for an equalization of resources, and demanding compensation because one has been victimized. The first road to egalitarian democracy may reinforce confidence that one is an equal shareholder in the stakes of a society.The second may just reinforce feelings that one approaches the entire system as a complainant.[343]

The systematized inequality and institutionalized humiliation in practices of arms control and disarmament 'prohibits equality of status because it permits one group to ritually exploit another.'[344] Nandy suggests that 'while civilization as a process means the gradual abolition or dilution of master-slave relationships, it also means a growing awareness that it is more honourable to be slave than a master.'[345] The slave is presumed to be 'morally and cognitively superior' engaged in 'a constant effort to beat the master at his own game.'[346]

A game in which the West does not hesitate from decrying the efforts of 'countries that do not usually sit at the top tables' as 'obstructive' and dismisses their efforts for 'not being in a position to do something about it.'[347] The logic being that these countries have 'less of a stake in arms control and nonproliferation outcomes; because they have less of a stake;

[341] Chandhoke, "Equality for What?," 153.

[342] Chandhoke, "Equality for What?," 153.

[343] Chandhoke, "Equality for What?," 155.

[344] Chandhoke, "Equality for What?," 157.

[345] Ashish Nandy, "Humiliation—Politics and the Cultural Psychology of the Limits of Human Degradation," in *Humiliation—Claims and Context*,ed. Gopal Guru (Oxford, New Delhi: Oxford University Press, 2009), 45.

[346] Nandy, "Humiliation—Politics," 45.

[347] Amanda Moodie and Michael Moodie, "Alternative Narratives for Arms Control,"*The Nonproliferation Review* 17, no. 2(2010): 315, 318.

they should have less of a voice in the process.'[348] This condescending attitude and 'lack of equal respect'among participants toward the engagement of developing countries in addressing the problem of weapons persist as the Western powers allege that developing countries 'had limited understanding of the issues' and 'had no "equity" in influencing negotiations.'[349] There is growing resistance to this perception as 'multilateralism is more than just putting additional chairs around the table and then telling people sitting in them what's what.'[350]

Thus scholars now concede that 'the Cold War was a civilizational conflict. Public discourse and behaviour drew sharp civilizational boundaries between East and West—before and after the Cold War.'[351] Katzenstein insists,

> [A]t the origin of the Cold War a clash of civilizations, created and maintained by public rhetoric, helped create, reflect and reinforce the division of the world. This civilizational dimension of the Cold War politics has largely been lost in the realist and liberal reconstructions that conceive of international politics as a game played by actors with given identities and fixed interests.[352]

The civilizational rubric reiterates itself in the sublimation of formal racial discourses to discreet practices of sly civility. These practices authorized special responsibilities of the Western powers vis-à-vis the others. They ascribed universal motives of victory, wealth and power despite suffering from a crisis of memory and dismissed any alternative demands for justice as rhetorical. This became possible through the possession of powerful weapons technologies and practices of amnesia, denial and abstraction in addressing the problem of weapons. The practices of sly civility facilitated development of international law without acknowledging its historical complicity in constituting arbitrary standards of civilization. The attempts to resist these practices by the alienated faced the disciplinary

[348] Moodie and Moodie, "Alternative Narratives," 315.

[349] Margarita H. Petrova, "Rhetorical Entrapment and Normative Enticement: How the United Kingdom Turned from Spoiler into Champion of the Cluster Munition Ban,"*International Studies Quarterly* 60, no. 3(2016): 394.

[350] Moodie and Moodie, "Alternative Narratives for Arms Control," 315.

[351] Katzenstein, *Civilizations in World Politics,* 11.

[352] Katzenstein, *Civilizations in World Politics,* 11.

power of ridicule through caricature of national character and denunciation as nationalist chauvinism. It is therefore a colossal mistake to assume Huntington's 'civilizational analysis as an innovation at the end of the Cold War when in fact it was only a repetition of what had happened at the Cold War's outset.'[353]

* * *

[353] Katzenstein, *Civilizations in World Politics,* 13.

CHAPTER 5

Mimesis and Weapons Control

Introduction

A reading of the previous chapter suggests, 'modernity plays an important role in generating among the servile a critical consciousness about actual and possible forms of humiliation.'[1] It is therefore pertinent to consider 'what insights might we gain, as scholars of international relations, from interrogating the invocation of "race" through the deployment of the nuclear-apartheid position?'[2] It is also imperative to question whether 'the language of rights makes assertion against humiliation possible.'[3] But Huntington ignores these significant questions premised on race and rights and on the contrary encourages us to pause and dwell on another question, 'Can the Rest copy the West?'[4] The bold and facile articulation of this question is not an innocent exercise. It is evocative of an emotion of 'disdain in the mainstream imagination.'[5] It is a deliberately provocative question premised on an awareness that 'the established thinking,' 'the bulk of conventional explanations of international politics,' is dismissive of

[1] Gopal Guru, "Theorizing Humiliation," 5.

[2] Biswas, "'Nuclear Apartheid,'" 486.

[3] Guru, "Theorizing Humiliation," 5.

[4] Samuel Huntington, "The West Unique, Not Universal," *Foreign Affairs* 75, no. 6 (1996): 35.

[5] Polat, *Meaning and Mimesis*, viii.

R. Mathur, *Civilizational Discourses in Weapons Control*,
https://doi.org/10.1007/978-3-030-44943-8_5

a study of mimesis as 'subordinate,' 'insignificant,' 'secondary and irrelevant.'[6]

The temporal significance of this question and its resurgent seductive power can be traced back to the European history of Enlightenment. Huntington articulates it in more mundane terms. Huntington argues that 'from time to time' leaders of developing countries have faced the imperative of the need to 'modernize' but their efforts have 'created "torn" countries, unsure of their cultural identity. Nor did Western cultural imports significantly help them in their pursuit of modernization.'[7] He then insists that 'more often, leaders of non-Western societies have pursued modernization and rejected westernization.'[8] In this pursuit for autonomy and modernization, 'scientific advancement is associated with modernity' and 'there is a powerful symbolism associated with mastering the technical demands of nuclear science.'[9] This makes it 'increasingly difficult to renegotiate or replace the constitutional order,' and the 'costs of disruption or change in this system have grown steadily over the decades.'[10]

The threat to this constitutional nuclear order has become more apparent with a further shift in discourses reinforcing nuclear export control regimes, expressing concern with scientific mercenaries navigating the nuclear order, and meeting the challenges of dealing with the rogue or outlier states. In addressing these nuclear proliferation challenges at length, it might be helpful to ponder briefly on the idea of 'copy' articulated by Huntington. Alternative terms for 'copy' are 'imitation,' 'mimicry' and 'mimesis.' Taussig suggests that in 'relation to the civilizing process' it is interesting to note 'the wonder of mimesis lies in the copy drawing on the character and power of the original, to the point whereby the representation may even assume that character and play.'[11] Polat argues mimesis is 'focal to processes of meaning formation in thematic grasps of international politics and therefore constitutive of reality.'[12] In other words, practices of mimesis as 'conscious play-acting' constitute 'sticky webs of copy and contact' involving two layers of 'a copy or imitation, and

[6] Polat, *Meaning and Mimesis*, viii, 2.

[7] Huntington, "The West Unique, Not Universal," 35.

[8] Huntington, "The West Unique, Not Universal," 35.

[9] Wyn Bowen and Matthew Moran, "Iran's Nuclear Programme: A Case Study in Hedging?" *Contemporary Security Policy* 35, no. 1 (2014): 38.

[10] Ikenberry, *After Victory*, 253.

[11] Taussig, *Mimesis and Alterity*, 2.

[12] Polat, *International Relations*, 2.

a palpable, sensuous connection between the very body of the perceiver and the perceived.'[13] It is a sensate knowledge 'adhering to the skin of things' both cognitive and compulsive in its desire to reproduce.[14] It is therefore imperative to not only question 'Can the rest copy the West?' but more significantly question: how does the copy, 'the representation shares in or acquires the properties of the represented'?[15]

Taussig reinforces the weight of this question by asking, 'How much of a copy does the copy have to be to have an effect on what it is a copy of? How "real" does the copy have to be?'[16] These questions are pertinent if we want to explore 'what it is to be an image of some thing, most especially if we wish not only to express but to manipulate reality by means of its image.'[17] This possibility of manipulation exists because

> the mimetic basis remains, dependent, above all, on an alterity that follows the ideological gradient decisive for world history of savagery vis-à-vis civilization … we must needs [*sic*] be sensitive to the crucial circulation of imageric power between these sorts of selves and these sorts of anti-selves, their ominous need for and their feeding off each other's correspondence—interlocking dream-images guiding their reproduction of social life no less than the production of sacred powers.[18]

It is suggested that the mimetic faculty is 'resurgent' and 'mobile,' and is able to traverse a 'two way street' with the advent of mimetic machines.[19] It is further observed that in practices of copying attention must be paid not only to 'correspondence,' 'similarity,' the 'tyranny of the visual notion of image' but also to the relations of 'contact' that can produce an 'imperfect ideogram.'[20] These relations of contact have resurfaced: 'From the mid-point of the twentieth century with the final dissolution of formal colonial controls there emerged a sort of reversal of contact, a "second contact," with the birth of a radically different border between the West and the rest, between civilization and its Others.'[21]

[13] Taussig, *Mimesis and Alterity*, 21, 241.
[14] Taussig, *Mimesis and Alterity*, 44–45.
[15] Taussig, *Mimesis and Alterity*, 47–48.
[16] Taussig, *Mimesis and Alterity*, 51.
[17] Taussig, *Mimesis and Alterity*, 57.
[18] Taussig, *Mimesis and Alterity*, 65.
[19] Taussig, *Mimesis and Alterity*, xiv, 20.
[20] Taussig, *Mimesis and Alterity*, 57, 65.
[21] Taussig, *Mimesis and Alterity*, 251.

Enlightened Nuclear Order

The condition of civilization (meaning Western civilization—the civilization of Capital) since the era of Enlightenment is premised on the ability to regulate and dismiss mimesis.[22] It is the 'civilized eye' that provides this 'staging,' this 'drawing-out' of the 'space between' the colonized and the colonizer, infused and permeated with 'colonial tension.'[23] In this 'intersubjective staging,' 'meaning is mimetic through and through' as meaning of utterances such as 'national security,' 'proliferation' and 'deterrence' is to be gathered from an intersubjective exchange of 'repetitions, imitations and habits' without which it 'would be impossible to conceive of rights even literally.'[24] The 'organization of mimesis' understood as 'mimesis of mimesis' is critical to 'Enlightenment civilization' to help classify, regulate and police legal and illegal practices of mimesis such as nuclear proliferation.[25] This is because 'what's being mimicked is mimicry itself—within its colonial shell.'[26]

It is in this context, the quest for nuclear weapons by Others can be interpreted as an unintended 'parody of Western technology' that encourages others to 'enter into a chamber of endlessly reflecting mirrors without resolution.'[27] It is therefore not surprising that there is now an attempt by some scholars in the West to hark back to an Enlightenment-inspired nuclear order complemented with suggestions to forge ahead with a more revolutionary 'rights-based order.' The emphasis on a rights-based nuclear order is intriguing given that 'the very idea that rights are universal conflicted with the imperative of building a nation' and discourses on rights were traditionally deployed to contend the legitimacy and illegitimacy of a particular rule-based order.[28] This development coincides with a growing concern regarding questions of justice and fairness in the nuclear nonproliferation regime and expresses trepidation at the vanishing nuclear taboo.[29]

[22] Taussig, *Mimesis and Alterity*, 215; Polat, *Meaning and Mimesis*, viii, 10–11.

[23] Taussig, *Mimesis and Alterity*, 78–79.

[24] Polat, *Meaning and Mimesis*, 23.

[25] Taussig, *Mimesis and Alterity*, 47, 200, 215.

[26] Taussig, *Mimesis and Alterity*, 241.

[27] Taussig, *Mimesis and Alterity*, 248.

[28] Eric A. Posner, *The Twilight of Human Rights Law* (New York: Oxford University Press, 2014), 12.

[29] Nina Tannenwald, "Justice and Fairness in the Nuclear Nonproliferation Regime," *Ethics & International Affairs*, 27, no. 3 (2013) 299–317; Nina Tannenwald, "The Vanishing Nuclear Taboo," *Foreign Affairs*, 97, no. 6 (2018), 1624.

There is a growing sense of 'moral outrage' about the declining non-proliferation regime that needs to be situated in a 'wider moral context of the crisis' of the international nuclear order.[30]

This moral outrage is further attributed to 'a striking lack of intellectual curiosity about most of the developments that account for the "second nuclear age."'[31] Furthermore, while the 'second nuclear age' is being problematized, there is no accounting for 'trumpeting triumphalism' at the initial acquisition of nuclear weapons technology and its monopolistic possession by the West.[32] On the contrary, there is a 'monumental show of "imperial nostalgia"' associated with 'the decline of national grandeur and the international power politics connected to economic and political hegemony.'[33] This sense of imperial nostalgia is complemented with 'colonial nostalgia' as regrettable 'loss of sociocultural standing or, more precisely, the colonial lifestyle.'[34] In these experiences of nostalgia there is visible an acute desire, a yearning to recover prestige and institutionalize 'hegemonic advantages' of imperialism in an effort at stamping the historical past on to the present in unpredictable ways.[35]

It is to this purpose that the time after the end of the Cold War is now described as 'a potential moment of rebirth of the "ordering project."'[36] It is considered to be an opportunity to mull on the question, 'what new order should we be seeking?' In undertaking this exercise it is notable that the 'we' is often not all inclusive but is constrained in its imagination courting attention of the US as the dominant actor in the ordering strategies of the international nuclear order. The international nuclear order is distinguished as 'America's "special project."'[37] These discourses signify renewed attempts to provide an ideological clout to the dominant actor to help it maintain the existing international order within which the NPT is

[30] Michael Ruhle, "Enlightenment in the second nuclear age," *International Affairs* 83, no. 3 (2007): 519; Paul Schulte, "Universal vision or bounded rationality," *International Affairs* 83, no. 3 (2007): 501.

[31] Ruhle, "Enlightenment in the second nuclear age," 519.

[32] Patricia M.E. Lorcin, "Imperial Nostalgia; Colonial Nostalgia—Differences of Theory, Similarities of Practice," *Historical Reflections/Reflexions Historiques* 39, no. 3 (2013): 99.

[33] Lorcin, "Imperial Nostalgia," 97–111.

[34] Lorcin, 'Imperial Nostalgia," 97.

[35] Lorcin, 'Imperial Nostalgia," 103, 106.

[36] Brad Roberts, "All the king's men? Refashioning global nuclear order," *International Affairs* 83, no. 3 (2007): 523.

[37] Roberts, "Refashioning global nuclear order?" 528.

particularly enshrined as an 'Enlightenment project.'[38] These discourses signify nuclear weapons as a prerequisite for an enlightened order as these weapons are considered the 'most efficient weapons to defend the West' and 'the final line of defence.'[39] It is argued that a nuclear order controlled and maintained by the West is a requisite for 'political breathing space for Enlightenment.'[40] It is asserted that 'an ordering strategy founded on Enlightenment values … has become increasingly hard to sustain as weaponry has diffused within and beyond the NPT's confines.'[41]

The 'philosophical roots of the nonproliferation project' are traced back with token reference to eighteenth-century Enlightenment in Europe that is often critiqued for an unparalleled degree of 'myth-making,' simplification, overstatement and 'misleading' imposition of power vis-à-vis others.[42] In this harking back to Enlightenment, there is a convenient amnesia on how the tools of the Enlightenment deployed as 'modern capitalist mode of production, in absorbing all other social systems and establishing itself as the only world system,' deliberately promoting the West as the 'only form of civilization … the West, or Western civilization, came to absorb or replace the plurality of civilizations that preceded it.'[43] This shrinkage of social space is key to configuring how historical practices of mimesis are marginalized and suppressed by advocates of European Enlightenment. It is therefore more pertinent to question scholars harking back to Enlightenment practices, whether the mimetic medium of the state and the regulations on transfer of weapons technology have resulted in the transfer of power or the displacement of a 'neo-colonial tradition of political control' in the field of arms control and disarmament?[44] This question has gained a sense of temporal urgency with the indefinite extension of the NPT.

[38] William Walker, "Nuclear Enlightenment and counter-enlightenment," *International Affairs* 83, no. 3 (2007): 431–453.

[39] Joachim Krause, "Enlightenment and nuclear order," *International Affairs* 83, no. 3 (2007): 495.

[40] J. Krause, "Enlightenment and nuclear order," 495.

[41] Walker, "Nuclear Enlightenment and counter-enlightenment," 433.

[42] Pierre Hassner, "Who killed nuclear Enlightenment?" *International Affairs* 83, no. 3 (2007): 455; David S. Yost, "Analysing international nuclear order," *International Affairs* 83, no. 3 (2007): 551–552.

[43] O'Hagan, *Conceptualizing the West*, 31.

[44] Bhabha, *The Location of Culture*, 347.

Compliance Discourse

The indefinite extension of the NPT has accompanied rhetorical trumpet calls alerting the West on an impending 'crisis of the system' and has generated appeals for re-establishing 'political mastery' in the international system.[45] It is argued that the international nuclear order possesses 'hallmarks of a grand Enlightenment project.'[46] Any effort to question this Enlightenment project itself is conceived to be possible only through a 'counter-enlightenment' movement 'rooted in American political culture.'[47] The invocation of 'progressive Enlightenment values' is justified on three grounds.[48] First, this made it 'easier to draw states into a *rule based order* that could moderate the power play that nuclear weapons encouraged.' Secondly, it helped banish 'romantic politics inimical to restraint.' Finally, it helped 'erect guards against the "unreasonable rationality" that always lurks where politics and technology meet in a competitive and interest-driven environment.' The idea of threat from 'romantic politics' with its allusive references to disarmament and 'unreasoned rationality,' as those struggling for equality and justifying their right to nuclear weapons, is further burnished with assertions of 'inherent superiority' of the ordering strategy and fearful prognosis of an alternative that is perpetually vulnerable to catastrophe.[49]

The emphasis is no longer on recruitment of new members but on compliance of members to the existing constitutional nuclear order. The problem of compliance is that the others 'may not have the power to create order but they do have the power to cause some disorder.'[50] The problem of 'acceptance' of the existing international order in a manner that upholds 'the existing structure of obligations' is now a central preoccupation of the West.[51] It is now being acknowledged that 'inequality is seen by the have-nots as less inevitable and acceptable.'[52] There is concern that 'power and legitimacy' of the international order 'have been profoundly

[45] Walker, "Nuclear Enlightenment and counter-enlightenment," 431, 440.
[46] Walker, "Nuclear Enlightenment and counter-enlightenment," 431.
[47] Walker, "Nuclear Enlightenment and counter-enlightenment," 432.
[48] Walker, "Nuclear Enlightenment and counter-enlightenment," 433.
[49] Walker, "Nuclear Enlightenment," 433.
[50] Roberts, "Refashioning global nuclear order," 529.
[51] Henry Kissinger, *A World Restored* (Boston: Houghton Mifflin, 1957), 172–173.
[52] Hassner, "Who killed nuclear Enlightenment," *International Affairs*, 463.

modified in a direction unfavourable to the West.'[53] It is observed that 'the authority of the West' has 'considerably weakened' and 'given rise to a general feeling in the "rest" that they no longer have to accept and follow rules which they have not created and which they feel are intended to perpetuate a domination which belongs to the past.'[54]

A perceived desire for 'new rules' and the insistence that 'these rules should be written less by a declining "West" than by an ascending "Rest"' have generated a sense of vulnerability in the West.[55] The West is now perplexed that the rest in their quest for nuclear weapons is 'bound to think that the American strategic establishment saw nothing wrong with nuclear weapons as long as they were confined to the developed world and has discovered their madness when they have become accessible to newcomers.'[56] The West now admits that the NPT is an 'unfair treaty' with unequal obligations but is unwilling to address the problem of disarmament as it continues to voice a threat from those it nomenclatures as the rogue states.[57] The politics of debunking any disarmament bargain struck between the nuclear haves and have-nots in the 1960s as a 'myth' is rooted in fear, expressed in the following words:

> If the continued existence of the NPT is made contingent upon the readiness of the five nuclear weapons states to eliminate their nuclear weapons, this would give the most problematic actors within the regime not only an open invitation to denounce the treaty, but also ample opportunities to control the political non-proliferation agenda.[58]

The responsibility for this myth-making is primarily attributed to states from the Non-Aligned Movement whose delegations at the NPT Review Conference in 1995 are dismissed as being 'full of polemic and emotion but devoid of any reasonable substance.'[59] Any consideration of disarmament is further mocked based on the lack of 'positive acknowledgement,' 'little evident domestic or overseas sympathy' and improbability of 'gratitude and restraint' from the non-Western countries toward the British

[53] Hassner, "Who killed nuclear Enlightenment," 463.
[54] Hassner, "Who killed nuclear Enlightenment," 463.
[55] Hassner, "Who killed nuclear Enlightenment," 463.
[56] Hassner, "Who killed nuclear Enlightenment," 465.
[57] J. Krause, "Enlightenment and nuclear order," 492.
[58] J. Krause, "Enlightenment and nuclear order," 491.
[59] J. Krause, "Enlightenment and nuclear order," 491.

experience of reductions in its nuclear arsenal.[60] An impatience with a 'passive' US administration has generated strident appeals on the impending sense of crisis of survival of the existing international nuclear order.[61] This is repeatedly articulated in an alarming manner. To quote Pierre Hassner, 'In the long run (if we survive the short and middle term), a renegotiation of the Nuclear Non-proliferation Treaty on a basis which overcomes its present hierarchical and unbalanced character may be undertaken.'[62]

The champions of an enlightened nuclear order present two interesting perspectives on the NPT. On the one hand it is argued that the 'true bargain' on the NPT was struck between the US and the 'silent majority of states' and that this 'basic' bargain between the US and 'the weak is still alive.'[63] On the other hand the 'NPT's constitutionalism' is either credited with reconciling the contrasting rights and obligations of the nuclear 'haves' and 'have-nots' or debunked as dangerous 'myth-making'[64] It is suggested that the NPT, to maintain pretensions of universalism, facilitated a compromise that placed a 'temporary trust' among the acknowledged nuclear weapons states but at the same time insisted that this trust 'could not be extended to other states.'[65] In this reconciliation 'the NPT served great powers' interests and 'coercive diplomacy was involved in bringing states into the fold' to endow 'the settlement magnetic authority and legitimacy.'[66] The NPT accorded the 'possibility of greater mastery of the political sphere and of reining in forces which, if states were left to their brutish ways, could result in a lethal nuclear anarchy.'[67] China and Russia are decried for apparently not sharing the same sense of 'special responsibility' vested in the US leading the West in its effort to 'handle' the 'difficult cases' against proliferation of weapons.[68] The possibility that nuclear proliferation is now seen as a 'US problem,' with other states reluctant to join these efforts due to their discomfiture and unwillingness

[60] Paul Schulte, "Universal vision or bounded rationality," *International Affairs* 83, no. 7 (2007): 505–506.

[61] J. Krause, "Enlightenment and nuclear order," 491.

[62] Hassner, "Who killed nuclear Enlightenment," 467.

[63] J. Krause, "Enlightenment and nuclear order," 490.

[64] Walker, "Nuclear Enlightenment and counter-Enlightenment," 490.

[65] Walker, "Nuclear Enlightenment and counter-enlightenment," 436.

[66] Walker, "Nuclear Enlightenment and counter-enlightenment," 437–438; Roberts, "Refashioning global nuclear order," 529.

[67] Walker, "Nuclear Enlightenment and counter-enlightenment," 437.

[68] Michael Ruhle, "Enlightenment in the second nuclear age," *International Affairs* 83, no. 3 (2007): 519.

to take 'political direction from Washington,' is not seriously considered.[69]

On the contrary, a spate of exhortatory statements insist on representing 'arms' control as 'the expression of the best of Enlightenment.'[70] There is now a concerted effort to 'forget or downplay … the hypocrisy which prevailed almost without exception among nuclear powers, and to a large extent also among non-nuclear states, about getting rid of their own nuclear weapons and reaching nuclear disarmament.'[71] There is a self-congratulatory mood in the West at the maintenance of 'a certain balance of hypocrisy' that has yielded 'positive results.'[72] These positive results are described by Hassner in the following words: 'The official designation of nuclear weapons as illegitimate, the commitment to get rid of them in an ideal world, the need to justify their possession by some kind of alibi was a positive factor.'[73] However these positive results are now qualified by fears of an erosion of an international political order based on 'mutual interests and shared myths' that is now being 'poisoned by absolute hostility, or a search for revenge, or at least an ever-deepening distrust and contempt.'[74]

These fears are compounded by a growing realization that 'the traditional instruments of technology denial were becoming less and less effective.'[75] The policing of the international system by the West is further endorsed to the effect,

> It is not necessary to assert that "unreasonable" or "rogue" actors with nuclear ambitions are invariably "evil" or psychopathic, or that there will be many of them. But such actors do currently exist and the unpreventable possibility of others emerging cannot be omitted from any consideration of the nuclear future.[76]

[69] Arturo C. Sotomayor, "Brazil and Mexico in the Nonproliferation Regime," *The Nonproliferation Review* 20, no. 1 (2013): 87.

[70] Hassner, "Who killed nuclear Enlightenment," 459.

[71] Hassner, "Who killed nuclear Enlightenment," 462.

[72] Hassner, "Who killed nuclear Enlightenment," 463.

[73] Hassner, "Who killed nuclear Enlightenment," 463.

[74] Pierre Hassner, "Who killed nuclear Enlightenment," 463.

[75] J. Krause, "Enlightenment and nuclear order," *International Affairs*, 496.

[76] Paul Schulte, "Universal vision or bounded rationality," *International Affairs* 83, no. 7 (2007): 502.

The magnitude of these problems is underscored by narratives recounting the 'large number of nuclear physicists and other experts educated in the West and the former Soviet Union' and the emergence of nuclear smuggling networks that undermine the assumption that 'a state with nuclear ambitions would be dependent on the assistance of the established nuclear powers.'[77]

The apparent unwillingness of the so-called rogue states or weapons states to comply with the existing norms of the NPT has encouraged a range of arms control measures such as export controls, sanctions, preemption, missile defense, counter-proliferation and so forth. These varied responses exist because

> states do not easily reach agreement on how to address compliance issues, relying as they do on different standards of evidence, types of information, and varying definitions of "significant" noncompliance. Lack of agreement means lack of action, lack of action means no penalties; no penalties means that unacceptable behaviour continues.[78]

The perpetuation of enlightened hypocrisy makes it permissible for the West to take recourse to stereotypical distinction in crafting a response to mimetic alterity as distinguishing between 'good' and 'bad' proliferators even if this runs 'counter to the very logic of universal arms control regimes.'[79] This 'Janus-faced sense of the savage corresponds to the great mythologies of modern progress' and helps sustain the realpolitik of these situations, as mentioned earlier in Chap. 1.[80]

Finnemore explicitly states how the US's arms control policy is in a 'time warp.'[81] There is evidence to demonstrate 'in cases such as Israel, South Africa and Pakistan, the United States did not prevent proliferation.'[82] On the contrary, it has shown much 'tolerance' and 'complicity' with its willingness to make 'deals' and 'exceptions to the principle of

[77] Ruhle, "Enlightenment in the second nuclear age," 518.

[78] Moodie and Moodie, "Alternative Narratives for Arms Control," 308.

[79] Ruhle, "Enlightenment in the second nuclear age," 520.

[80] Taussig, *Mimesis and Alterity*, 142.

[81] Nina Tannenwald, "US Arms Control Policy in a Time Warp," *Ethics & International Affairs*, 15, no. 1 (2001): 51.

[82] Or Rabinowitz and Nicholas L. Miller, "Keeping the Bombs in the Basement: US Nonproliferation Policy toward Israel, South Africa, and Pakistan," *International Security* 40, no. 1 (2015): 47.

nonproliferation' toward states friendly to the US.[83] In securing these deals a great deal of emphasis is placed on secrecy.[84] This secrecy often 'entailed a non-testing and non-declaring guarantee' so as not to be seen as an overt act of defiance against the NPT.[85] The secrecy also helped to 'limit the damage to US credibility on nonproliferation.'[86] The US does not hesitate from supplying advanced weaponry and nuclear fuel to these friendly states as a trade-off measure to get them to accept some safeguards.[87] It even went so far as to 'downplay the intelligence' based on evidence showing that 'Pakistan was smuggling dual-use components out of both the United States and Europe.'[88]

To reiterate, these rhetorical practices of 'strategic Orientalism' are premised on the 'pervasive' and 'axiomatic belief that the West (or occasionally the United States) as a civilization has a special role to play in global security affairs' and the rogue or outlier states are 'beyond the pale of 'civilized' international relations (that does not respect generally accepted global norms regarding state conduct) and is therefore a danger to international peace and security.'[89]

It is observed,

> While the end of the Cold War and the evolution of a new discourse of danger have modified aspects of Western Nuclear Arms Control & Disarmament (NACD) culture, this transformation has not marked a radical break with past beliefs. Rather, the new interpretative matrix is marked by elements of both change and continuity. This highlights the fact that NACD cultures change only slowly, and even when shocked adapt in ways consistent with established interpretative patterns.[90]

In fact as the practices of 'strategic Orientalism' generate consensus and demands for 'unity' in the West, there is a growing emphasis on how 'new enemies need to be eliminated and denied access to WMD.'[91] Traditional

[83] Avner Cohen, *Israel and the Bomb* (New York: Columbia University Press, 1999), 193; Rabinowitz and Miller, "Keeping the Bombs in the Basement," 50, 59, 60.

[84] Rabinowitz and Miller, "Keeping the Bombs in the Basement," 51.

[85] Rabinowitz and Miller, "Keeping the Bombs in the Basement," 60.

[86] Rabinowitz and Miller, "Keeping the Bombs in the Basement," 51, 79.

[87] Rabinowitz and Miller, "Keeping the Bombs in the Basement," 53–54, 67, 71–72.

[88] Rabinowitz and Miller, "Keeping the Bombs in the Basement," 82.

[89] Krause and Latham, "Constructing Non-Proliferation," 41, 37.

[90] Krause and Latham, "Constructing Non-Proliferation," 38.

[91] Gawdat Bhagat, "Nuclear Proliferation: The Islamic Republic of Iran," *International Studies Perspectives* 7, no. 2 (2006): 127.

nonproliferation measures understood in terms of demand-side measures such as security assurances and supply-side measures such as denial of access to nuclear materials are no longer deemed enough. But now counter-proliferation strategies have gained momentum, as 'there does appear to exist a Western consensus that denial strategies are the most important first line of defence against rogue states.'[92] This underpins what to non-Western countries often appears to be an overzealous commitment to 'discriminatory' Western export control regimes that seek to 'prevent technology flows to non-Western states.'[93]

Export Controls

It is important to note that the West did not always exhibit such fervent commitment toward nuclear technology denial and export controls. On the contrary, in an effort to expand its sphere of influence and profit during the Cold War, the US championed an 'Atoms for Peace' program encouraging the sale of nuclear fuel and nuclear reactors to the developing countries. Sarah Bidgood observes, 'The US was matched in its enthusiasm for the peaceful atom—as well as its disregard for its proliferation potential—by the Soviet Union.'[94] France and Germany exported 'sensitive nuclear material and equipment to aspiring proliferators with minimal assurances of its peaceful applications.'[95] These states were opposed to 'making full-scope safeguards for enrichment and processing facilities and technology,' and US appeared to be 'flexible' to accommodate their demands.[96] The NPT provisions codifying the inalienable right of signatory states to peaceful nuclear energy and their obligation to conclude safeguards agreements with the International Atomic Energy Agency (IAEA) were deemed acceptable only after much jockeying for power among these countries, as discussed in the previous chapter. Thus, any need for stringent export controls to contain proliferation was to be calculated vis-à-vis commercial interests as these states competed with each other. To quote Hymans, 'the efforts of the North to stem the tide of weapons proliferation were still secondary to their efforts to promote

[92] Rabinowitz and Miller, "Keeping the Bombs in the Basement."

[93] Krause and Latham, "Constructing Non-Proliferation," 40.

[94] Sarah Bidgood, "The establishment of the London Club and nuclear export controls," *Adelphi Series* 56, (2016): 136.

[95] Bidgood, "The establishment of the London Club," 138.

[96] Bidgood, "The establishment of the London Club," 149–150.

nuclear exports.'[97] This problem was further compounded as 'not all countries were considered equal as "recipients" of nuclear technologies.'[98] Any possibility of safeguards was resisted unless there was a tentative possibility of diversion of aid for military purposes.

The mimetic flash of Indian nuclear tests in 1974 shocked and threatened to destabilize the existing nuclear order. It immediately galvanized the Western powers to 'make nuclear technology sales and transfer dependent on adherence to the nonproliferation regime.'[99] A spate of technology control regimes such as the Nuclear Suppliers Group (NSG), Zangger Committee, Australia Group, Missile Technology Control Regime and Wassenaar Arrangement emerged. These regimes, unlike the NPT, are non-treaty-based weapons technology export control regimes. These regulatory regimes with coordination of 'control lists' and exchange of information on states of 'serious concern' instituted stringent control measures premised on the condition that they do not interfere with the commercial exchange of relevant technology, material, or equipment.'[100] These export control regimes with their practices of technology denial reinforced and contributed toward a growing sense of both procedural and substantive injustice.[101]

These measures further vitiated the political discourse by deploying 'human rights' discourses to claim that the other could not be trusted with dual use technologies.[102] The selective deployment of these civilizational discourses hand in hand with the institutionalization of these exclusionary regimes by the West is justified on the grounds that,

> treaty-based export control regimes are not sufficiently developed, that many states do not have adequate national export control systems, and that such arrangements are needed to fulfil treaty obligations not to transfer materials or equipment that could be used to develop banned weapons.[103]

[97] Hymans, "Why Argentina never wanted the bomb," 162.

[98] Gisela Mateos and Edna Suarez-Diaz, "'We are not a rich country to waste our resources on expensive toys': Mexico's version of Atoms for Peace," *History and Technology* 31, no. 3 (2015): 246.

[99] Hymans, "Why Argentina never wanted the bomb," 162.

[100] Moodie and Moodie, "Alternative Narratives for Arms Control," 309.

[101] Tannenwald, Nina. "Justice and Fairness in the Nuclear Nonproliferation Regime," 313.

[102] Matias Spektor, "The evolution of Brazil's nuclear intentions," *The Nonproliferation Review* 23, no. 5–6 (2016): 641; Hymans, "Of gauchos and gringos," 167.

[103] Moodie and Moodie, "Alternative Narratives for Arms Control," 309.

This assumption that all states will try to acquire weapons of mass destruction is refuted by developing countries, emphasizing the provision in most agreements, especially the NPT, for 'cooperation and assistance in the promotion of relevant science and technology for peaceful purposes.'[104] These developing countries argue that export control arrangements hamper their desire for technological autonomy and economic development and contend that 'such arrangements represent efforts of the technological "haves" to retain their economic, commercial and scientific dominance and prevent those without access to such technology from changing their "have not" status.'[105] They insist that their national resistance is to 'defend the principle of equality of sovereign states and to protect pathways for development.'[106] Duarte argues that,

> [w]hile faithful to the principles and basic tenets of Western European values and civilization, Brazil believed that the pursuit of its interests did not entail automatic adherence to all policy postures of the Western bloc. Since its resources and capabilities were still limited, Brazil wanted to be able to take independent decisions and keep its hands as free as possible until the time would come to take further steps in the field of its nuclear development.[107]

But the sudden insistent demand by Western powers to supply nuclear fuel and nuclear reactors contingent to a country's adherence with the non-proliferation regime and full scope of safeguards came as a rude shock to developing countries such as Argentina and Brazil.

It threw their relationship with supplier states into 'disarray' as previously agreed contracts were now unilaterally violated.[108] Spektor notes how 'the United States unilaterally suspended existing nuclear-fuel supply contracts.'[109] Hymans demonstrates this abuse of power when 'the United States blocked the transfer of a Canadian heavy water plant to Argentina, on the grounds that it had not agreed to allow Argentina to acquire heavy water technology, but rather only the means to obtain heavy water.'[110] Any

[104] Moodie and Moodie, "Alternative Narratives for Arms Control," 308.

[105] Moodie and Moodie, "Alternative Narratives for Arms Control," 308.

[106] Hymans, "Why Argentina never wanted the bomb," 157.

[107] Sergio de Queiroz Duarte, "Brazil and the nonproliferation regime: a historical perspective," *The Nonproliferation Review* 23, no. 5–6 (2016): 551.

[108] Hymans, "Why Argentina never wanted the bomb," 166.

[109] Matias Spektor, "The evolution of Brazil's nuclear intentions," *The Nonproliferation Review* 23, no. 5–6 (2016): 640.

[110] Hymans, "Of gauchos and gringos," 169.

effort by Argentina to 'offer financial incentives to the Western suppliers in order to weaken their nonproliferation fervor' or to 'blackmail' them by threatening to 'develop unsafeguarded sensitive nuclear technologies' did not serve much purpose and only provided more fodder to discredit its reputation as a 'nuclear rogue.'[111] The pursuit of these arbitrary and discriminatory practices by the US made these countries realize that 'belonging to the Western bloc did not imply integration with the developed world,' and this contributed to their identification with the Third World.[112]

It was only when these countries complied with the NPT and abandoned their ballistic-missile projects that they were accepted as members of export control regimes such as the Nuclear Suppliers Group (NSG) and the Missile Technology Control Regime (MTCR).[113] However, this present act of compliance by these states is no guarantee that the criteria for membership to export control regimes will not change again in the future.[114] While the US takes pride in transforming Argentina from a nuclear 'rogue' to a nuclear 'choirboy' and uses 'the Latin American case of nuclear rollback as a key justification for retaining traditional approaches to fighting proliferation,' the Argentines refer to these nonproliferation measures as 'disarming of the disarmed.'[115] Spektor's investigation reveals that 'at no point were Brazil's nuclear policies primarily motivated by the goal to build nuclear weapons' and that it has embraced nonproliferation norms 'while believing that the existing regime is unfair, selective, and skewed in favor of the strong.'[116] The repetitive exercise of coercive diplomacy by an imperial power to compel a state to 'accept second class nuclear status, the greater the risk that its nuclear policies will become vehicles for nationalist self-expression.'[117]

Despite this persistent dispute, members of these export control groups, in order to implement export controls in a similar way, are 'identifying states outside their number for sanction,' and these measures are 'directed

[111] Hymans, "Of gauchos and gringos," 170–171.

[112] Arturo C. Sotomayor, "Brazil and Mexico in the Nonproliferation Regime," *The Nonproliferation Review* 20, no. 1 (2013): 89; Mario E. Caranza, "Rising Regional Powers and International Relations Theories: Comparing Brazil and India's Foreign Security Policies and Their search for Great Power Status," *Foreign Policy Analysis* 13, no. 2 (2014): 255–277.

[113] Spektor, "Brazil's nuclear intentions," 645.

[114] Caranza, "Rising Regional Powers," 13.

[115] Hymans, "Of gauchos and gringos," 153–154, 184.

[116] Spektor, "Brazil's nuclear intentions," 636.

[117] Hymans, "Why Argentina never wanted the bomb," 158.

against a very large group of states.'[118] Hymans 'suggests a need for a major overhaul in the assumptions of both sides of the Washington debate over nuclear proliferation' and insists there is a 'need for more sensitivity in US assessments of the goals of burgeoning nuclear states.'[119] Mutimer notes with credulity, the 'arrogance of the suppliers on the inside—the authority that they arrogate to themselves, which translates into the common meaning of the term—is staggering.'[120] Arnett issues a cautionary note against the 'anti-arms control crowd' in the West that represents an anachronistic worldview and maintains a 'relentless drumbeat of public doubt' regarding compliance by those designated as rogue states.[121] Betts insists that the West 'will have to offer these countries something better than the moralistic homilies or heavy-handed threats professed so far.'[122]

The West's discriminatory sense of caution is buttressed by 'a simple logic' being advanced to argue that 'sensitive nuclear assistance is an important determinant of nuclear proliferation.'[123] What is being deliberately problematized is the 'ongoing, often contentious dispute regarding provisions in most agreements that oblige state parties to offer cooperation and assistance in the promotion of relevant science and technology for peaceful purposes.'[124] Concerted efforts are being made to reinterpret and constrain the rights of developing countries to possess an indigenous nuclear fuel cycle in an effort to proclaim a new 'non-enrichment' norm exerting pressure on these countries 'to forgo (once again!) domestic enrichment and reprocessing of nuclear fuel in exchange for ready access to fuel provided by multilateral fuel banks.'[125] To quote Matthew Kroenig,

> states that receive sensitive nuclear assistance can better overcome the common obstacles that states encounter as they attempt to develop a nuclear weapons arsenal. They can leapfrog technical design stages, acquire tacit knowledge from more advanced scientific communities, economize on the

[118] Mutimer, *The Weapons State*, 85.

[119] Hymans, "Why Argentina never wanted the bomb," 184–185.

[120] Mutimer, *The Weapons State*, 85.

[121] Eric Arnett, "Iran is not Iraq," *Bulletin of the Atomic Scientists*, 54, no. 1 (1998): 14.

[122] Richard K. Betts, "Incentives for Nuclear Weapons: India, Pakistan, Iran," *Asian Survey* 19, no. 11 (1979): 1072.

[123] Matthew Kroenig, "Importing the Bomb: Sensitive Nuclear Assistance and Nuclear Proliferation," *The Journal of Conflict Resolution* 53, no. 2 (2009): 162.

[124] Moodie and Moodie, "Alternative Narratives for Arms Control," 308.

[125] Tannenwald, Nina. "Justice and Fairness in the Nuclear Nonproliferation Regime," 306–307.

costs of nuclear development, and avoid international pressure to abandon a nuclear program.[126]

Instead of confronting the West's persistent and growing fear of increased expertise of the Other there is a 'cynically mischievous' attempt to present dodgy intelligence and engage in vociferous speculation on deploying alternative strategies of preemption and military intervention, as seen in the case of Iraq.[127] These 'hysterical' practices of fearmongering generate further 'alienation' and carry a presentiment of the dangerous possibility that US policy will bear the burden of unravelling arms control.[128]

Contemporary efforts to suggest that these countries follow the 'Japanese model' of acquiring nuclear materials and technology but 'not cross the line to nuclear weapons' are increasingly advocated by the West.[129] The Japanese model represents the limits of mimicry acceptable to the West. These appeals have fallen on deaf ears, compounding the problem with recognition that 'nonproliferation policy cannot rely on popular pressure' to 'dissuade' countries from 'building a nuclear force.'[130] These persistent strategies of non-proliferation that have divided 'the world into nuclear-haves and nuclear have-nots' undermine 'whatever self-imposed normative restrictions upon such "nuclear sharing" that may exist.'[131] An interesting dyadic relationship is emerging between the legitimized export control and sanction based regimes controlled by the West on the one hand and on the other hand the 'pariah international', 'gray market' for nuclear technologies and the availabiility of 'scientific mercenaries willing to sell their services to any country seeking to develop nuclear weapons.'[132] The potential availability of these measures to the rest is sometimes considered a 'legitimate response to the perceived Western domination.'[133]

[126] Kroenig, "Importing the Bomb," 162.

[127] Arnett, "Iran is not Iraq," 13, 14.

[128] Arnett, "Iran is not Iraq," 14.

[129] Gawdat Bhagat, "Nuclear Proliferation," 135; Wyn Bowen and Matthew Moran, "Iran's Nuclear Programme: A Case Study in Hedging?" *Contemporary Security Policy* 35. no. 1 (2014): 26; George Perkovich, *Universal Compliance: A Strategy for Nuclear Strategy* (Washington: Carnegie Endowment for International Peace, 2005).

[130] Richard K. Betts, "Incentives for Nuclear Weapons: India, Pakistan, Iran," *Asian Survey* 19, no. 11 (1979): 1068.

[131] Lewis A. Dunn, 'Gray Marketeering,' *International Security*, Vol. 1, No. 3, 1977, 112.

[132] Lewis A. Dunn, 'Gray Marketeering,' 109, 112.

[133] Lewis A. Dunn, 'Gray Marketeering,' 109, 112.

The Western practices of technology denial often confirmed the Others' mistrust that 'the West was not going to give sensitive technology to Iran.'[134] It reinforced fears of discrimination that 'from the perspective of the US, especially in the nuclear field, what was good for the Shah was not good for the Imam' and that 'had the Islamic republic possessed nuclear weapons capacity, the US may have thought twice about interjecting its navy into the Persian Gulf and engaging Iranians.'[135] This distrust is explicit in public statements of victimization by the West to the effect that

> [i]t is obvious that the West and the anti-revolutionary forces do not want Iran to possess this valuable technology even at a peaceful level. It is also obvious that not only no other country can forego the rights of its nation and sign an agreement to that effect. Such a thing cannot happen.[136]

It is further observed that 'countries with a nuclear fuel cycle will export energy around the world in the future, gaining a very high income by doing so' and 'every country equipped with a complete fuel cycle will be able to stand on its feet in securing energy and not be forced to become dependent.'[137] Meyer argues that the act of acquiring nuclear weapons is sometimes seen as an act of 'arriving on the nuclear front' to bolster 'national power and success.'[138] However, it is not easy to meet this couched desire as,

> [w]hile the NPT allows for the transfer of nuclear technology and materials for civilian nuclear energy program among signatory states, in practice, however, most nuclear-states have prevented non-nuclear weapon states … from developing an indigenous mastery of nuclear technology for peaceful purposes by imposing a virtual embargo on suppliers for nuclear industries.[139]

The continued imposition of sanctions on Iran despite it being a signatory to the NPT and 'prohibiting it from developing safeguarded uranium-enrichment technologies under IAEA supervision' generate an

[134] Kibaroglu, "Iran's Nuclear Ambitions," 235.
[135] Kibaroglu, "Iran's Nuclear Ambitions," 234.
[136] Bowen and Moran, "Iran's Nuclear Programme," 38.
[137] Bowen and Moran, "Iran's Nuclear Programme," 37.
[138] Stephen M. Meyer, *The Dynamics of Nuclear Proliferation* (Chicago: University of Press, 1984), 50, cited by Mario E. Caranza, "Rising Regional Powers," 11.
[139] Sotomayor, "Brazil and Mexico in the Nonproliferation Regime," 84–85.

'unacceptable precedent' conveying the blatant message of the master that 'the United States will only adhere to nonproliferation as long as they justify punishing any country that refuses to align itself with US strategic interests.'[140]

The deliberate manipulation and subordination practices pursued by the master to serve its own particular sovereign interests are seen as undermining universal aspirations of arms control disarmament. The calculated efforts of the West at technology denial, coupled with more insistent demands that developing countries accept more intrusive verifications under the IAEA Additional Protocol, are met with deep distrust and resistance. These practices of sly civility stoke dormant 'tensions and synergies between modernity and nationalism' in the Third World.[141] Zoppo acutely observes how 'each denial of nuclear information or reticence by the protagonist powers in giving nuclear aid awakens memories of the colonial past and, correspondingly, strengthens that nationalism that strives for nuclear status in the new states.'[142]

National Scientists to Rogue Scientists

This resurgent nuclear nationalism is to be further situated in a 'psychological operations campaign' waged by the West, especially targeting nuclear scientists via threat, intimidation and assassination.[143] Nuclear scientists in Iraq, Syria, Egypt and Iran are regular targets of assassination.[144] This tragic development is compounded with the growing use of terror as a 'tool for intimidating or eliminating scientists (for working or not working) on nuclear programs.'[145] These threats further decimate and erode the idea of universal science vis-à-vis national science and shrink the 'very pockets of civility that must be reached to deal with complex nuclear issues.'[146] The resurgence of nuclear nationalism and national science is

[140] Spektor, "The evolution of Brazil's nuclear intentions," 647.

[141] Mateos and Suarez-Diaz, "Mexico's version of Atoms for Peace," 253.

[142] Zoppo, "Nuclear Technology, Weapons, and the Third World," 116.

[143] William Tobey, "Nuclear Scientists as assassination targets," *Bulletin of the Atomic Scientists* 68, no. 1 (2012): 65.

[144] Terrence Henry, "The Covert Option: Can sabotage and assassination stop Iran from going nuclear?" *The Atlantic Monthly* 296, no. 5 (2005): 54–55.

[145] Siegfried S. Hecker and Abbas Milani, "Iranian nuclear scientists," *Bulletin of the Atomic Scientists* 71, no. 1 (2015): 49.

[146] Hecker and Milani, "Iranian nuclear scientists," 50.

prompted in an environment of cyber attacks and targeted assassinations to kill nuclear scientists in Iran.[147] The assassination attempt on the life of Fereydoun Abbasi-Davani and killing of other nuclear scientists, such as Ardeshire Hassanpur, Masoud Ali Mohammadi, Darious Rezaeinejad and Majid Shahriari, are understood as persistent attempts by the West to sabotage Iran's nuclear program.[148] These experiences further confound any resistance or rescue of other Iranian scientists, being subject to detention and imprisonment, such as Omid Kokabee and his refusal to participate in Iran's nuclear program.[149]

Tobey critiques these attempts by arguing, 'nuclear scientists are different from terrorists. They do not pose an immediate threat of violence against another nation. Presumably, they are acting against the laws of their country. Unless their nation is at war, they are not obviously legitimate military targets.'[150] Hecker and Milani argue that 'killing nuclear scientists makes reducing the threat of nuclear war harder, not easier' and is contrary to the 'scientific spirit' necessary for international collaboration 'to deal with the nuclear risks facing the world today.'[151] This particularly violent strategy of denial signals diplomatic hardening of stance and 'no credible possibility of a diplomatic solution.'[152] But those advocating for pursuit of such a strategy of denial and sabotage in the US remain undeterred and insist that such covert operations are useful psychologically in undermining the confidence of these nuclear scientists and sow seeds of doubt regarding their people and equipment.[153] The diminishing pool of nuclear scientists further extends the time horizon for mastering the nuclear fuel cycle in a developing country.

Those advocating for a rigorous pursuit of 'pre-emption' measures only pause to question 'to what extent this would be regarded as barbarous, uncivilized, and destabilizing by the international community.'[154] It is

[147] Hecker and Milani, "Iranian nuclear scientists," 47.

[148] Tobey, 'Nuclear Scientists as assassination targets," 68–69; Declan Butler, "Iranian nuclear scientists attacked: Murder and Cyber-Assault Target Nuclear Programme," *Nature* 468 (2010): 607.

[149] Hecker and Milani, "Iranian nuclear scientists," 47.

[150] William Tobey, "Nuclear Scientists as assassination targets," 67.

[151] Hecker and Milani, "Iranian nuclear scientists," 46.

[152] Tobey, "Nuclear Scientists as assassination targets," 67.

[153] Terrence Henry, "The Covert Option: Can sabotage and assassination stop Iran from going nuclear?" *The Atlantic Monthly* 296, no. 5 (2005): 55.

[154] Henry, "The Covert Option," 56.

helpful to note here that there are efforts underway in the West that acknowledge the assassination of nuclear scientists is a violation of existing norms under international laws of war. But they do not hesitate from arguing that these norms cannot be absolute and indulge in abstract thought experiments that could justify assassinations of nuclear scientists as a strategy of denial. These attempts at justification are of course made by taking recourse to offering revisionist accounts of Just War theory to conceive these targeted assassination measures as an 'exception.'[155] These circuitous efforts to find possible exceptions appear to be oblivious to the immense suffering of the subaltern 'national scientists' and only succeed in facilitating a subtle shift in civilizational discourses that now seeks to absorb history further to typologize them as 'rogue scientists' engaged in proliferation.

Tobey observes that 'nuclear scientists—even those in suspected illicit weapons programs—are different from terrorists' and that strategies of denial can delay a nuclear program but make it even more difficult to monitor a 'covert nuclear program.'[156] Hecker and Milani similarly argue, '[F]ear and bullets do not stop nuclear programs; they beget ever more secrets and ever more hidden nuclear sites.'[157] Taussig suggests that '"secret" equals slippage.'[158] It is possible to suggest that a slippage in mimesis results in an 'imperfect ideogram' such as the A.Q. Khan network.[159] The emergence of Khan network is attributed to 'exploiting weaknesses in export control systems and recruiting suppliers, including some in states that were members of the Nuclear Suppliers Group (NSG).'[160] It is 'hostility' toward Western controls on nuclear technology that has motivated the rise of transnational proliferation networks.[161]

[155] Tamar Meisels, "Assassination: Targeting Nuclear Scientists," *Law and Philosophy* 33, no. 2 (2014): 204–234.

[156] Tobey, "Nuclear Scientists as assassination targets," 61–62.

[157] Hecker and Milani, "Iranian nuclear scientists," 51.

[158] Taussig, *Mimesis and Alterity*, 116.

[159] Taussig, *Mimesis and Alterity*, 115.

[160] David Albright and Corey Hinderstein, "Unraveling the A.Q. Khan and Future Proliferation Networks," *The Washington Quarterly* 28, no. 2 (2005): 112.

[161] Albright and Hinderstein, "Unraveling the A.Q. Khan and Future Proliferation Networks," 112; Christopher Oren Clary, "The A.Q. Khan Network: causes and implications" (Thesis, Naval Postgraduate School, Monterey: California, 2005), 46–47. Retrieved from http://hdl.handle.net/10945/1833

These networks have shattered 'any complacency' that the West may have enjoyed as guardians of export control regimes.[162] It is suggested that

> [t]he network's key customers were states contemptuous of NSG controls and committed to violating the Nuclear Non-Proliferation Treaty (NPT) in their quest for secret nuclear capabilities. In essence the network adapted to and benefitted from the discriminatory and voluntary export control regime that was embodied in the NSG and complementary export control systems. There is little confidence that other networks do not or will not exist or that elements of Khan network will not reconstitute themselves in the future.[163]

Thus, it is not to the credit of the expertise of national scientists such as A.Q. Khan that the emergence of these proliferating networks is attributed but rather to the feelings of 'hostility,' 'weakness' and 'contemptuousness' toward a 'discriminatory' regime. It is the power of growing counter-narratives questioning the norm of nuclear non-proliferation as 'nuclear apartheid' and the subaltern's struggle to wrest power from this regime that have given rise to Khan network, a clandestine global supply chain. This network demonstrated that 'nuclear components designed in one country could be manufactured in another, shipped through a third (which may have appeared to be a legitimate user), assembled in a fourth, and designated for eventual turnkey use in a fifth.'[164] In the last decade of the twentieth century, Pakistan emerged not simply as a nuclear power but as a nuclear broker. Khan, a nuclear scientist, is hailed as a 'national hero' enjoying the protection and patronage of his country.[165]

We are reminded that 'Khan and his network were working against time' and 'what Khan did was to shorten timelines, perhaps dramatically.'[166] The success of Khan is lauded in the following text: 'A country which

[162] Albright and Hinderstein, "Unraveling the A.Q. Khan and Future Proliferation Networks," 120.

[163] Albright and Hinderstein, "Unraveling the A.Q. Khan and Future Proliferation Networks," 112.

[164] Mohamed ElBaradei, Director General of IAEA, quoted Albright and Hinderstein, "Unraveling the A.Q. Khan and Future Proliferation Networks," in "Nuclear Non-Proliferation: Global Security in a Rapidly Changing World." IAEA. IAEA, June 20, 2004. https://ww.iaea.org/newscenter/statements/nuclear-non-proliferation-global-security-rapidly-changing-world

[165] Albright and Hinderstein, "Unraveling the A.Q. Khan and Future Proliferation Networks," 116–117.

[166] Clary, "The A.Q. Khan Network," 26, 88.

could not making sewing needles, good bicycles or even ordinary durable metalled roads was embarking on one of the latest and most difficult technologies.'[167] But in the West this national scientist is considered to be 'at least as dangerous as Osama bin Laden,' a terrorist.[168] He is considered to be a scientist that returned from Europe with 'stolen centrifuge designs and, perhaps more importantly, a list of dozens of companies that supplied centrifuge parts and materials.'[169] Khan contends that he 'took advantage of the willingness of western companies to do business and decided to make purchases from the open market.'[170] He seeks to make visible European greed to the effect, 'they literally begged us to buy their equipment. We bought what we considered suitable for our plant and very often asked them to make changes and modifications according to our requirements.'[171] There is further resistance to accept 'that what occurred was illegal.'[172] The porosity of the export control regimes and the nuclear enterprise of Khan network to transform itself from 'importing into exporting organization' proved to be a critical point in practices of sly civility and mimesis in proliferation studies.[173]

The practices of mimetic maneuvering appear to have come full circle with India and Pakistan declaring themselves to be nuclear weapons states. A subtle shift in the master-slave narrative is increasingly discernible with practices of mimesis. In copying the master, the subaltern is now willing to demonstrate its own scientific prowess in building and testing nuclear weapons. It is further wielding its entrepreneurial skills at establishing a transnational proliferation regime and justifying it on grounds of commercial practices followed in the West. The practices of 'strategic defiance' against the West have escalated to threatening demands and blackmail of sharing nuclear technology and nuclear bomb–making expertise with other postcolonial states.[174] There is a conscious need to acknowledge the

[167] Clary, "The A.Q. Khan Network," 26; Peter Edidin, "Pakistan's Hero: Dr. Khan Got What He Wanted, and He Explains How," *New York Times*, February 15, 2004.

[168] Doughlas Jehl, "CIA Says Pakistanis Gave Iran Nuclear aid," *New York Times*, November 24, 2004.

[169] Clary, "The A.Q. Khan Network," 23.

[170] Clary, "The A.Q. Khan Network," 24.

[171] A.Q. Khan, "Uraniuam Enrichment at Kahuta," in *Dr. A.Q. Khan and the Islamic Bomb*, Zahid Malik (Islamabad: hurmat, 1992), 96; Clary, "The A.Q. Khan Network," 27.

[172] Zahid Hussein, interview with Mirza Aslam Beg, 'There is a Conspiracy Against me by the Jewish lobby,' *Newsline*, March 3, 2004; Clary, "The A.Q. Khan Network," 44.

[173] Clary, "The A.Q. Khan Network," 35.

[174] Clary, "The A.Q. Khan Network," 42–43.

'series of manoeuvres' that continuously produce and reproduce the 'dynamic of difference' that generates 'rebellion and opposition' to the status quo.[175] The careful mimetic maneuvers have turned the clock in a cyclical manner that it is no longer only the West capable of threatening the Rest.

Remapping Nonproliferation

In the face of this challenge, there is an attempt to articulate new concepts such as hedging and encourage remapping of nonproliferation strategies. Hedging, a relatively new concept used to describe proliferation behavior, is often characterized as a strategic exercise in gauging the 'intent' between 'nuclear pursuit and nuclear rollback.'[176] This intent is based on the assessment of 'an indigenous technical capacity' and involves 'nuclear fuel-cycle facilities capable of producing fissionable materials (by way of uranium enrichment and/or plutonium separation)' and offers a political choice whether to 'package their final product into a nuclear explosive charge.'[177] The exercise of this choice is critical in an era when the NPT regime has 'delegitimized nuclear weapons among nations,' but 'this does not mean that nations have lost interest in the acquisition of nuclear weapons.'[178] It is only that in an atmosphere surfeit with practice of sly civility 'nations cannot voice their interest publicly in the international arena.'[179]

Walker makes another attempt at remapping strategies of nonproliferation on the basis of the relationship between great powers and proliferating states, which he describes in the following manner:

> *assisted proliferation* (e.g. Iran-North Korea, China-Pakistan); *protected proliferation*, whereby the protecting and protected state act in quasi-alliance (e.g. US-Israel, US-India) or the protector shelters the proliferators against strong intervention by others (e.g. Russia-Iran, China-North Korea); and *combated proliferation*, whereby a state or states set out to enforce change by military or other means.[180]

[175] Anghie, *Imperialism, Sovereignty and the Making of International Law*, 311–312.

[176] Bowen and Moran, "Iran's Nuclear Programme," 27–28.

[177] Bowen and Moran, "Iran's Nuclear Programme," 29; Ariel Levite, "Never Say Never Again: Nuclear Reversal Revisited," *International Security* 27, no. 3 (2002): 69, footnote 3.

[178] Bowen and Moran, "Iran's Nuclear Programme," 30.

[179] Bowen and Moran, "Iran's Nuclear Programme," 30.

[180] Walker, "Nuclear Enlightenment and counter-enlightenment," 450.

These practices of typologization do little to address 'how far along the path toward developing nuclear weapons a state can go while remaining technically in compliance with the NPT's Article IV, which permits access to atomic energy technology.'[181] There is more legal hairsplitting on different types of proliferation relationships. These carefully crafted practices of taxonomy do not account for how a historical change in these relationships is taking place and fail to articulate how 'past failures to disclose the importation of nuclear material and the construction of a heavy water production plant and facilities for uranium enrichment, processing and storage' can now be represented as a 'failure' and not a 'violation' in practices of nonproliferation.[182] This 'hedging' of meaning between 'violation' and 'failure' represents an exercise in power by the subaltern vis-à-vis the West.

Bowen and Moran suggest that hedging once again encourages a 'veritable obsession with time.'[183] Time is spent 'debating timelines to acquisition,' and 'timelines offer a means of positioning a state's nuclear programme in relation to the bomb.'[184] Hedging complicates articulation of a timeline as it involves undertaking political and technical calculations that need validation. This effort at validation is often an international exercise in 'conjecture' and 'projections' of existing stockpiles of enriched fissile material and involves varying assessments of 'scale and speed' of enrichment programs.[185] These technical issues are then qualified by political assessments of hedging by 'default' or hedging by 'design.'[186] To ascertain this difference, scrutiny of variables such as evidence of fuel cycle, domestic narratives and international diplomacy is suggested to grapple with the problem of a proliferating state.[187] This circuitous discourse once again generates ambiguity and leaves one grappling with the problem wondering whether 'hedging by default' constitutes a 'failure' and 'hedging by intent' is an act of 'violation' of the NPT.

As these problems persist, European powers appear to be 'less shy about offering inducements for good behaviour' but the US administration is

[181] Shahram Chubin and Robert Litwak, "Debating Iran's Nuclear Aspirations," *The Washington Quarterly* 26, no. 4 (2003): 101.

[182] Chubin and Litwak, "Debating Iran's Nuclear Aspirations," 100.

[183] Bowen and Moran, "Iran's Nuclear Programme: A Case Study in Hedging?" 31.

[184] Bowen and Moran, "Iran's Nuclear Programme," 31.

[185] Bowen and Moran, "Iran's Nuclear Programme," 34–35.

[186] Bowen and Moran, "Iran's Nuclear Programme," 26, 40.

[187] Bowen and Moran, "Iran's Nuclear Programme," 28.

emphatic that it 'will not tolerate the construction of a nuclear weapon' in Iran.[188] The 'US administration officials repeat the policy mantra that all options are on the table' and resort to the 'combination of axis of evil rhetoric' that includes not succumbing to nuclear blackmail, military pre-emption and striking a grand bargain.[189] In making these claims there is anxious recognition that 'excessive focus on punishment' through imposition of sanctions for decades has been counter-productive and has only succeeded in isolating the US, compelling it to rely on its European allies as 'we've sanctioned ourselves out of influence.'[190] The 'US ability to take out a regime without inflicting unacceptable collateral damage to the civilian population may have priced US security assurances to Iran out of the market.'[191] It is also to be noted that the 'broader nuclear narrative ... places the blame for diplomatic failure on the shoulders of Western powers, particularly the United States.'[192] The US stands accused of diplomatic 'malpractice' for unilateral withdrawal from the Joint Comprehensive Plan of Action (JCPOA) negotiated with Iran.

Conclusion

In these humbling circumstances there is a need to show respect that 'the best nonproliferation decision is one that is made indigenously.'[193] It is also possible to consider that 'alteration of the political landscape, domestically, regionally, internationally, or a combination of all, can persuade states not to seek NW.'[194] But instead of acknowledging the limitations and possibilities of these practices, the efforts of the West are to 're-establish control,' meet the 'pressures to expand civil nuclear commerce' and urgently draw 'a line around the states which may possess nuclear arms and discourage others ... from crossing it.'[195] Allowances are made to suggest that this 'grave duty now falls on nine nuclear-armed states' and to generate 'awareness of the dangers of conceding normality' to nuclear weapons. But these gestures represent a facile attempt at 'reconciliation'

[188] Chubin and Litwak, "Debating Iran's Nuclear Aspirations," 108.
[189] Chubin and Litwak, "Debating Iran's Nuclear Aspirations," 110.
[190] Bhagat, "Nuclear Proliferation," 133.
[191] Chubin and Litwak, "Debating Iran's Nuclear Aspirations," 110.
[192] Bowen and Moran, "Iran's Nuclear Programme," 41.
[193] Chubin and Litwak, "Debating Iran's Nuclear Aspirations," 113.
[194] Bhagat, "Nuclear Proliferation," 126.
[195] Walker, "Nuclear Enlightenment and counter-enlightenment," 450–451.

that uncritically endorses Enlightenment and modernity and accepts inequality as the condition for maintenance of the international order.[196] These exercises represent the paucity of imagination to conceptualize the institutionalized humiliation of the other and an illusory attempt to address their experiences of abject humiliation. There is a rhetorical and insistent demand, 'they need to tell us where else there is to go, and how to go there, together.'[197]

In this demand articulated by Walker, one hears a resonance of Hedley Bull's insistence that the others, in engaging with the problem of the nuclear order, have nothing in mind with which to replace it and that their efforts down the road can be reduced to a spate of rhetoric that cannot be meaningful unless and until they are willing to join a pre-constituted 'rule-based' nuclear order that moderates the nuclear power play and is representative of an Enlightened nuclear order.[198] It will not be amiss here to suggest that Walker and his colleagues championing the nuclear order as Enlightened and ruled based are suffering from 'rule naivete.'[199] Rule naivete refers to the view that 'good' in the nuclear order can be 'reduced to a set of rules that can be impartially enforced.'[200] Rule naivete vests too much confidence in legal interpretations on questions pertaining to dangerous weapons but law is often silent in the absence of an ethic of care appropriate to dangerous weapons.[201] There is a possibility that rule naivete can in part be responsible for nuclear proliferation and render 'meaningful enforcement' a charade.[202]

A mimetic charade that continues, as seen in the next chapter, with rhetorical invocation of discourses on 'exceptionalism' and 'human rights as a new standard of civilization in weapons control' in an effort to 'reconstellate' practices of weapons control.[203] In these efforts at reconstellating practices of weapons control one needs to exercise caution in two ways. One is in suggesting 'violence remains to be probably the only option for

[196] Walker, "Nuclear Enlightenment and counter-enlightenment," 436, 453.

[197] Walker, "Nuclear Enlightenment and counter-enlightenment," 453.

[198] Walker, "Nuclear Enlightenment and counter-enlightenment," 433, 431.

[199] Eric A. Posner, *The Twilight of Human Rights Law* (New York, Oxford: Oxford University Press, 2014), 7.

[200] Posner, *The Twilight of Human Rights Law*, 7.

[201] Posner, *The Twilight of Human Rights Law*, 110–111.

[202] Posner, *The Twilight of Human Rights Law*, 7.

[203] Mathur, "Human Rights as a New Standard of Civilization in Weapons Control?" 227–243.

people seeking either to defy abuses by sovereign authority or achieve admission into power.'[204] Second is exercising caution and acknowledging the 'catachrestic' power of mimesis that can destabilize identity-based discourses on exceptionalism by 'appropriating the metaphors of the oppressor and by "abusing" them through specific interventions that exceed the order of the oppressor.'[205] If mimetic excess with its sensuouness and immersion in the concrete be also understood as 'an excess creating reflexive awareness as to the mimetic faculty' then the subtle and yielding power of mimesis as an 'alternative science' can be wielded further.[206]

It can be wielded to question the 'myth of Enlightenment, with its universal, context free reason,' and to expose its relation to 'savagery.'[207] This is a possibility if one recollects that 'mimesis, once a dominant practice and component of knowing, becomes, in Western historical development, a repressed presence not so much erased by Enlightenment science and practice as distorted and used as hidden force.'[208] It can also be wielded to 'reconstellate' civilizational discourses on weapons control.[209] Whether this power to reconstellate is an ethical endeavor based on the 'constitutive,' intersubjective, fluid, power of mimesis to produce 'alterity in meaning' of 'justice' remains to be seen in the next chapter.[210] At present one can only note that the promise of an Enlightened nuclear order that could regulate and suppress practices of mimesis appears to be unravelling as destabilizing possibilities of mimesis surface with the emergence of other nuclear weapon states. Decades of humiliation experienced through stringent nonproliferation practices with their emphasis on compliance and export controls is now compounded with overt, vocal and emphatic insistence on American exceptionalism. The danger embedded in these civilizational discourses is that even as they unveil the secrecy associated with mimesis, they signal a vulnerability in an 'undefined time horizon.'[211]

[204] Polat, *Meaning and Mimesis*, 116.
[205] Polat, *Meaning and Mimesis*, 130, 140, 142–143.
[206] Taussig, *Mimesis and Alterity*, 254, 46.
[207] Taussig, *Mimesis and Alterity*, 2–3, 18.
[208] Taussig, *Mimesis and Alterity*, 45.
[209] Taussig, *Mimesis and Alterity*, 255.
[210] Polat, *Meaning and Mimesis*, 3, 15, 89.
[211] Stephen M. Meyer, *The Dynamics of Nuclear Proliferation* (Chicago: University of Press, 1984), 53, cited by Mario E. Caranza, "Rising Regional Powers," 16.

CHAPTER 6

New Standards of Civilization

Introduction

The urgency to reconstellate becomes apparent as the Doomsday Clock ticks one hundred seconds closer to midnight and civilizational time with its carefully crafted and curated practices of stereotyping, sly civility and mimesis deployed in the field of weapons control brings center stage the struggle for equality vis-à vis practices of exceptionalism. The aspiration of universal equality once shared by nationalists in developing countries is now gravely threatened by blatant practices of American exceptionalism and is therefore a subject of intense scrutiny. A postcolonial gaze is watchful of a growing tide of resurfacing, cyclical, discourses in the West extolling the virtues of colonialism, proclaiming civilizational differences, and giving electoral victories to candidates expounding American exceptionalism in explicit manifestos of 'America First.'[1] In this manifesto, there is an explicit argument that 'access to technology empowers and emboldens otherwise weak states'; partnership is to be maintained with 'like minded,' 'strong states'; and the mantle of power must remain with the US maintaining a 'forward military presence' to 'deter and defeat' as the mantra of 'always, always, always win' is to be upheld at any cost.[2]

[1] United States. *National Security Strategy of the United States of America*, December 2017, https://www.whitehouse.gov/wp-content/uploads/2017/12/NSS-Final-12-18-2017-0905.pdf

[2] *National Security Strategy of the United States of America*, 3, 39, 46, 25.

R. Mathur, *Civilizational Discourses in Weapons Control*,
https://doi.org/10.1007/978-3-030-44943-8_6

It is under these conditions that a postcolonial gaze ponders the question: How to reconstellate practices of arms control and disarmament? It is cognizant of the need for engagement with learning ethics as a social process often articulated in normative language and institutional embodiment in practices of arms control and disarmament. But it is carefully insistent on studying the tension between practices of exceptionalism and universalism as an urgent temporal problem and not simply a spatial problem. A postcolonial gaze now decries the illusions of universal science, law and technology that once attracted nationalists living in the colonies, as discussed in Chap. 3. It is no longer accepting of the idea that 'universality of human rights is to be derived from the most general features of humanity.'[3] On the contrary, it is interested in learning how the idea of universality is often qualified in 'historical struggles over inequality, domination and the refusal of appropriate recognition.'[4] This question encourages one to empathize with a postcolonial gaze, tired and wary of re-affirming faith in the idea of universal disarmament only to be qualified by temporal stabilizing discourses on arms control to maintain the status quo. A postcolonial gaze is no longer quiescent in accepting calls for 'human rights as a new standard of civilization' and naive assertions of faith in 'disarmament as humanitarian action.' On the contrary, it is insistent that we question the exceptional status of the West as a civilization and universalist aspirations enshrined in the idea of human rights as the 'last utopia' envisaged on the precipice of a nuclear holocaust.[5]

Contestation of Rights

Scholars inspired by the 'disarmament as humanitarian action' ethos are now seeking to invoke a human rights-based discourse on the problem of weapons control. They observe how the Nuclear Non-Proliferation Treaty (NPT) invokes a language of 'inalienable rights' and 'right to participate' borrowed from the human rights discourse.[6] They fail to register that the universalism associated with discourses on human rights is representative

[3] Richard J. Peterson, "Human Rights: Historical learning in the Shadow of Violence," *The American Journal of Economics and Sociology* 68, no. 1 (2009): 259.

[4] Peterson, "Human Rights," 259.

[5] Samuel Moyn, *The Last Utopia: Human Rights in History* (Harvard, Massachusetts: Belknap Press, 2012).

[6] Gabrielle Hecht, *Being Nuclear-Africans and the Global Uranium Trade* (Cambridge, Massachusetts: MIT, 2012), 32–33.

of a 'very precarious kind of cosmopolitanism that historically abetted the proliferation and competition of different states and nations more than it has helped imagine a world without moral borders.'[7] It is often difficult to 'sustain the very universalism with which rights were sometimes invoked' by states.[8] The implications of viewing the NPT as a human rights treaty can therefore be profound. Gabrielle Hecht observes,

> In an effort to accommodate postcolonial morality and palliate the ascendancy of the Cold War paradigm, the NPT essentially declared that nuclearity of the "peaceful" persuasion was a fundamental right. As far as I can tell, no other international treaty has ever referred to a scientific or technological activity as an "inalienable right" of special importance to "the developing areas of the world."[9]

This has encouraged countries like India and Iran to engage in a rights-based discourse pertaining to their nuclear programs. Iran in defense of its nuclear program asserts: 'Iran …is defending its right, its nation and its revolution; saying: I would like to use my right within the framework of the IAEA regulations and would like nothing more than that.'[10]

The significance of an emphasis on a rights-based discourse by the subaltern is that it has shifted the singular emphasis on a compliance-based discourse pursued by the West, as discussed in the previous chapter. Bowen and Moran observe,

> Iran's rights-based argument has proved difficult to oppose, primarily because Iran has succeeded in merging issues of treaty non-compliance with the more fundamental question of the right to access fuel cycle technology. Nothing in the Non-Proliferation Treaty prohibits a state from developing indigenous fuel cycle capabilities or stockpiling fissile materials. However, the NPT grants states the right of access to nuclear technology only "so long as their nuclear activities are exclusively peaceful", a condition that is fulfilled by adherence to IAEA safeguards.[11]

It can be argued that in advancing a 'nuclear rights'-based discourse Iran's leaders have taken recourse to appropriating a language of power

[7] Samuel Moyn, *The Last Utopia: Human Rights in History*, 13–14.
[8] Moyn, *The Last Utopia Human Rights in History*, 14.
[9] Hecht, *Being Nuclear*, 32–33.
[10] Bowen and Moran, "Iran's Nuclear Programme," 38.
[11] Bowen and Moran, "Iran's Nuclear Programme," 42.

traditionally used by the master. This has encouraged further 'politicization of the nuclear issue' and 'a brand of nuclear populism that would at once reduce the scope for eventual compromise and inflate the issue to a near-existential one.'[12] A rights-based discourse deployed in step with a victimization discourse has enabled representative subaltern states like Iran and India to make a strategic shift toward 'broader questions of rights and entitlements' under the NPT.[13] It has helped Iran to 'establish the principle of the right to enrichment and to demonstrate that this right is irreversible in that Iran has mastered the full fuel cycle and cannot unlearn it.'[14] A fierce contestation of rights in the nuclear realm has aroused racial anxieties about how 'Iran's technological gains pose challenge to the West.'[15]

In an effort to buy time an international agreement under the Joint Comprehensive Plan of Action (JCPOA) was negotiated between Iran and the West. This agreement extended the 'break-out time' for Iran to produce a nuclear bomb. It eliminated Iran's ability to produce weapons-usable plutonium, cut its stockpile of enriched uranium, limited the number of centrifuges for fifteen years, and subjected it to extensive inspections by the IAEA. Despite this agreement, the hawks in the US insist that they will 'deny the Iranian regime all paths to a nuclear weapon and neutralize Iranian malign influence' as it does not sit well with the US's 'interests or vision for a modern Middle East.'[16] This explicit articulation of the master's vision of strategic interests in the region compounded with its determination to impose harsh sanctions renders difficult any possibility of further negotiations with an 'Orientalized bad actor.'[17]

Shampa Biswas notes how these nuclear negotiations are always conducted in an atmosphere of suspicion and the constant threat of use of force.[18] Any attempt at further negotiation is susceptible to the willingness of the West to issue an invitation to the subaltern 'to breach a civilizational

[12] Bowen and Moran, "Iran's Nuclear Programme," 39.

[13] Bowen and Moran, "Iran's Nuclear Programme," 42.

[14] Bowen and Moran, "Iran's Nuclear Programme," 42.

[15] Shampa Biswas, "Iran v 'the international community': a postcolonial analysis of the negotiations on the Iranian nuclear program," *Asian Journal of Political Science* 26, no. 3 (2018): 336, see footnote 22; M. R Gordon & T. Erdbrink, "In nuclear talks, technological gains by Iran pose challenge to the West," *New York Times*, October 15, 2013, A11.

[16] *National Security Strategy of the United States of America*, December 2017, 48–49.

[17] Biswas, "Iran v. 'the international community,'" 343.

[18] Biswas, "Iran v. 'the international community,'" 340.

barrier…to enter civilization itself…to rehabilitate itself.'[19] As such, an assertion of a rights-based nuclear discourse provides 'room for manoeuvre and gives legitimacy to defiance' as it mobilizes nationalist sentiment, generates political consensus on nuclear advancement, but registers an ambivalence around intentions with regard to the nuclear bomb.[20] Biswas insists that it is no longer enough to seek inclusion for the subaltern in an unequal order but rather that it is necessary to investigate how subalterns are rendered 'exceptional' in the production of a statist global order. In other words, how are subaltern states such as Iran and North Korea stereotyped as the 'rogue' nuclear actors? This question of production of the subaltern as a 'rogue' or as 'exceptional' is pertinent and has received significant attention within the field.

Biswas further insists that any understanding of subaltern nuclear nationalism be tempered with the consideration that 'nuclearization as subaltern speech is a ruse,' a 'kind of colonial mimicry.'[21] She suggests that 'postcolonial nuclear mimicry-disguised as subaltern speech-consigns poorer states to forever remain disadvantaged.' This study seeks to temper such observations on the possibilities and limitations of the power of mimesis in nuclear politics by suggesting the need for widening the ambit of such queries with another key question: How did 'an internationalism based on rights come to the fore?'[22] An express concern with a discourse on rights and exceptionalism is pertinent if one recollects that 'the ideology of the civilizing mission resembles some of the thinking behind the modern human rights regime. The British were fond of saying that the conquered natives lacked a sense of rights…and thus could not govern themselves in an enlightened way.'[23]

The question that then arises is whether a subaltern's assertion of rights in the international order is an act of mimesis which will leave them disadvantaged or whether the absence of assertion of these rights is a path of constant condemnation for not being able to participate in practices of

[19] Biswas, "Iran v. 'the international community,'" 336.

[20] Bowen and Moran, "Iran's Nuclear Programme," 38–39.

[21] Biswas, *Nuclear Desire*, 184.

[22] Moyn, *The Last Utopia: Human Rights in History*, 118.

[23] Eric A. Posner, *The Twilight of Human Rights Law* (New York, Oxford: Oxford University Press, 2014), 66.

governance. A flashback into the history of human rights discloses how, among the competing narratives of origins of human rights, the subaltern's struggle for collective rights and the right to self-determination was swept aside by the West to exclusively emphasize a narrow understanding of human rights based on individualism.[24] This individualism was further crafted with practices of 'civilized violence' that used 'soft forms of repression' cultivated via 'loyalty tests and surveillance' to secure the subordination of the individual to the state.[25] These practices of civilized violence in modern state practices constrained public debate on nuclear politics, transforming it into a realm occupied by experts conscious of their vulnerability vis-à-vis a powerful military-industrial complex located in the West.

An internationalism based on rights is time and again threatened by an American exceptionalism insistent that 'American values are universal,' thus signaling that 'American interests and global interests are indivisible' and that these can best be secured if the US 'recreates the world in its own image.'[26] American exceptionalism seeks 'to justify preventive military action as being in conformity with new understandings of sovereignty that emphasize responsibilities as well as rights' and that 'decides when the sovereignty of others can be infringed.'[27] But the 'United States will not cede sovereignty to those that claim authority over American citizens and are in conflict with our constitutional framework.'[28] In this endeavor, 'if American power was going to be more constrained by circumstances beyond Washington's control, it made sense to apply constraints universally through, for example, arms control. This was partly about making a virtue out of perceived strategic necessity.'[29]

[24] Christopher N.J. Roberts, *The Contentious History of the International Bill of Human Rights* (Cambridge: Cambridge University Press, 2015), 19–52.

[25] Jessica Wang, "Scientists and the Problem of the Public in Cold War America, 1945–1960," Osiris 17, no. 2 (2002): 339–342.

[26] Condoleeza Rice, "Promoting the National Interest," *Foreign Affairs* 79, no. 1 (2000): 49; Nicholas J. Wheeler, "The Bush Doctrine: The Dangers of American Exceptionalism in a Revolutionary Age," *Asian Perspective* 27, no. 4 (2003): 207; United States. *National Security Strategy of the United States of America*, December 2017. https://www.whitehouse.gov/wp-content/uploads/2017/12/NSS-Final-12-18-2017-0905.pdf

[27] Wheeler, "The Bush Doctrine," 185.

[28] United States. *National Security Strategy of the United States of America*, 40.

[29] Andrew Butfoy, "American Exceptionalism and President Obama's Call for Abolition of Nuclear Weapons," *Contemporary Security Policy* 33, no. 3 (2012): 475.

Production of Exceptionalism

The practices of production of an exceptionalism in the context of rights can be traced further back in time. In the aftermath of the Second World War, 'the West succeeded in capturing the language of human rights' and constituted it as a tool for West European conservatives to signal their distinctive identity.[30] While the US did initially retreat 'from the language it had helped introduce,' it did not remain aloof for long, as 'the energy in the movement to defend and define human rights as the essence of European civilization' came from Christian conservatives on both sides of the Atlantic.'[31] Human rights discourses served as a new guise for practices of racial etiquette to re-establish the moral authority of the West, as mentioned in Chap. 4. These discourses constituted a performative act in an attempt to build on a disgraced legacy of exercising normative power rooted in 'Europe's attempt, after World War II, to imagine itself not only as against "cultural" others but specifically as against the temporal "other" of Europe's past.'[32] Nayak and Malone observe, 'While Europe historically imagined itself as against an Orient...it also imagined itself, particularly after World War II against its "own past which should not be allowed to become its future."'[33]

Hopgood notes, 'bourgeois Europeans responded to the erosion of religious authority by creating authority of their own from cultural resources that lay scattered around them. And then they globalized it via the infrastructure that the imperial civilizing project bequeathed to them.'[34] The rise of a human rights discourse 'did not mean the campaign for collective liberation against racial inequality or colonial legacies at home or abroad.'[35] On the contrary, the ascendance of human rights-based discourse signals a 'persisting national framework for rights' that does not conceal or alter the fact that the 'idiom of human rights' is used

[30] Moyn, *The Last Utopia*, 47.

[31] Moyn, *The Last Utopia*, 78.

[32] Meghana V. Nayak and Christopher Malone, "American Orientalism and American Exceptionalism: A Critical Rethinking of US Hegemony," *International Studies Review* 11, no. 2 (2009): 263.

[33] Nayak and Malone, "American Orientalism and American Exceptionalism," 263.

[34] Stephen Hopgood, *The Endtimes of Human Rights* (Ithaca & London: Cornell University Press, 2013), x.

[35] Moyn, *The Last Utopia*, 106.

to conceal strategic goals.[36] In the initial stages of the human rights discourse the US's 'international reputation' as a 'racial superpower' persisted as 'one of the last prominent countries where racial discrimination was still preached and practiced.'[37] It was understood that the US pursued a 'two-faced policy' officially denouncing racial apartheid to maintain prestige and exercise influence but never at the cost of undermining its 'military and economic interests.'[38]

This perception has persisted throughout the twentieth century onwards as the US's commitment to human rights is 'shaped by its image of exceptionalism.'[39] Mertus argues, 'human rights has become the "bait and switch" tool of choice of US foreign policy.'[40] She observes how 'the United States applies a double standard for human rights norms: one that applies to the United States and one that applies to the rest of the world.'[41] The US's commitment to human rights is always more 'rhetoric than reality.'[42] The US appears to be universalist but in practice applies double standards and 'as long as there is space for the interest in American exceptionalism to trump human rights, it will continue to do so.'[43] It is therefore not surprising that discourses on human rights have been called upon to serve 'brand new purposes' like arms control and disarmament within the US.[44] The very advocacy of human rights as a new standard of civilization to regulate and control weapons therefore deserves careful consideration.

[36] Moyn, *The Last Utopia*, 113; Eric A. Posner, *The Twilight of Human Rights Law* (New York, Oxford: Oxford University Press, 2014), 20.

[37] Ofra Friesel, "Race versus Religion in the Making of the International Convention Against Racial Discrimination, 1965," *Law and History Review* 32, no. 2 (2014): 363, 355.

[38] Friesel, "Race versus Religion," 358–360.

[39] Reza Afshari, "Relativity in Universality Jack Donnelly's Grand Theory in Need of Specific Illustration," *Human Rights Quarterly* 37, no. 4 (2015): 860.

[40] Julie A. Mertus, *Bait and Switch- Human Rights and US Foreign Policy,* 2nd edition (New York & London, Routledge, 2008), 227.

[41] Mertus, *Bait and Switch*, 227.

[42] Afshari, "Relativity in Universality," 860; David P. Forsythe, "United States Policy Toward Enemy Detainees in the 'War on Terrorism,'" *Human Rights Quarterly* 28, no. 2 (2006): 465–466.

[43] Mertus, *Bait and Switch*, 233.

[44] Moyn, *The Last Utopia*, 83.

The existence of a human rights regime has become an undeniable reality giving rise to consideration of 'disarmament as humanitarian action.'[45] Scholars and activists now argue that there is 'potential' to apply international human rights law to regulate testing, transfer and use of weapons.[46] They argue that 'the rights and protection of people should be at the forefront of any agreements…That is a fundamental change for how arms control and disarmament negotiations will be viewed in the future…Arms control and disarmament policy making may now encompass human rights.'[47] They justify these claims on the grounds that in the absence of armed conflict, international humanitarian law does not hold sway, and therefore 'human rights law must effectively control the behaviour of the State as it responds to unlawful violence' relying on the principles of necessity and proportionality.[48] But it is important to acknowledge that 'the rise of human rights in international law occurred not for reasons internal to international law as a profession, but due to the ideological changes' that took place in the context of the Cold War.[49] It is therefore observed that a new era of global Human Rights norms has 'colonized international humanitarian law,' undermining its authority.[50]

The rhetoric of human rights is now being championed as a new standard of civilization to regulate and prohibit weapons.[51] Jack Donnelly advocates human rights as a new standard of civilization by making a distinction between 'classic' and 'new' standards of civilization.[52] He argues that 'the classic standards of civilization (largely unintentionally) outlined a path for non-Western states to become recognized as sovereign equals and thus obtain the protections of (Western) international law.'[53] This

[45] John Borrie and Vanessa Martin Randin, *Disarmament as Humanitarian Action* (Geneva, Switzerland: United Nations Insitute for Disarmament Research, 2006).

[46] Stuart Casey Maslen, "The Use of Nuclear Weapons and Human Rights," *International Review of the Red Cross* 97, no. 889 (2015): 663.

[47] Matthew Bolton, Hector Guerra, Ray Acheson, Oliver Sprague, "The Road Forward for the Arms Trade treaty: A Civil Society Practitioner Commentary," *Global Policy* 5, no. 4 (2014): 475, retrieved from http://onlinelibrary.wiley.com/doi/10.1111/1758-5899.12172/full

[48] Maslen, "The Use of Nuclear Weapons," 664.

[49] Moyn, *The Last Utopia*, 210.

[50] Hopgood, *The Endtimes of Human Rights*, xiv.

[51] Jack Donnelly, "Human Rights a new standard of civilization," *International Affairs* 74, no. 1 (1998): 1–23.

[52] Donnelly, "Human Rights," 8.

[53] Donnelly, "Human Rights," 8.

premise of compliance to secure inclusion is presumptuously advanced further to suggest that the 'new' standard of civilization is 'beginning to be used in the context of overcoming, rather than institutionalizing differences.'[54] This is because unlike the exclusive and negative character of the classic standards of civilization that 'imposed minimal obligations primarily on barbarians' the new standards of civilization are positive and universal and tend to make 'more extensive (maximal) demands on states.'[55] The new standard of civilization is advocated as a 'purified form' of the morally appealing idea of 'adherence to shared standards of justice as a condition for full membership in international society.'[56]

These claims are touted with emphatic assertions that 'contemporary international human rights norms, no less than the classic standard of civilization, are European in origin' and that 'the rise of universal human rights ideas presents a story of moral progress.'[57] These narcissist claims are then buttressed with assertions that 'European human rights initiatives have been missionary in the best sense of that term, seeking to spread the benefits of (universal) values enjoyed at home.'[58] There is a facile attempt at acknowledgment that 'despite the fatal tainting of the language of "civilization" by abuses carried out under (and by exponents of) the classic standard of civilization, internationally recognized human rights share a similar legitimating logic.'[59] These very interesting proclamations by those advocating human rights as the new standard of civilization to be applied in the regulation and prohibition of weapons is critiqued by those that trace the development of this body of law as concurrent with the emergence of new states. Antony Anghie asserts that 'we might understand the monumental significance of international human rights law in these terms: it enabled international law and institutions to enter the interior, to address the unconscious and thereby to administer a "civilizing therapy" to the body politic of the sovereign state.'[60] It represented a quest for universal standards of civilization but also served to condition the character of non-European state sovereignty. This is undeniable 'to the extent that international human rights law and nationalism represent Western ideas of the

[54] Donnelly, "Human Rights," 10.
[55] Donnelly, "Human Rights," 11.
[56] Donnelly, "Human Rights," 14.
[57] Donnelly, "Human Rights," 20.
[58] Donnelly, "Human Rights," 15.
[59] Donnelly, "Human Rights a new standard of civilization," 16.
[60] Anghie, *Imperialism, Sovereignty and the Making of International Law*, 135.

individual, state and society they both create the paradox that Third World sovereignty through, and shaped by, Western structures.'[61] Ironically it was the smaller and non-Western states that had vested faith in human rights as universal and not a limited concept.[62]

An understanding of this complex historical legacy of human rights is imperative to question a simple narrative of 'West initiated human rights treaties, and the developing world either followed or resisted.'[63] A historical narrative of human rights being a 'form of Western imperialism' also 'holds less sway.'[64] This is because

> First, it implies that countries in Africa, Latin America, and Asia would be better off if they reverted to pre-colonial forms of rule. ... Second, commentators have pointed out that many non-Western countries have traditions that are compatible with modern human rights ...Third, the most prominent proponents of these arguments were dictators and their lackeys – and who wants to be associated with them?[65]

But it is difficult to deny 'the suspicion that modern human rights is an updated version of the civilizing mission of Western imperialists' and is 'a symptom of a weakness in humanitarian thinking that the civilizing impulse of the nineteenth century shared: a hubristic sense that we know better than people in foreign countries how to improve their lives, accompanied by sloppy mental habits that make it difficult to distinguish our interests from theirs.' It was the Western powers, especially colonial powers like Great Britain and the US, that sought to 'construct the human rights concept in the image of the empire' and resorted to legal positivism.[66]

This recourse to legal positivism by imperial powers is significant because a positivist approach to 'state sovereignty understood as the sole basis of the system seems to make inconceivable even the very notion of international law,' and 'international lawyers have never stopped questioning whether the order they describe, lacking a notion of obligation beyond

[61] Anghie, *Imperialism, Sovereignty and the Making of International Law*, 254.

[62] Christopher N.J. Roberts, *The Contentious History of the International Bill of Human Rights* (Cambridge: Cambridge University Press, 2015), 122.

[63] Eric A. Posner, *The Twilight of Human Rights Law* (New York, Oxford: Oxford University Press, 2014), 21–22.

[64] Posner, *The Twilight*, 67–68.

[65] Posner, *The Twilight*, 67–68.

[66] Roberts, *The Contentious History*, 128.

auto-limitation, is really "law."'[67] The idea of structural constraints or auto-limitation with its emphasis on state sovereignty 'may have robbed the law of a content to deal effectively and consistently with conflicts that arise within the system' such as the 'rights' of the subaltern.[68] It is also responsible for 'lasting ambivalence on the status of the normative scheme' based on human rights.[69] Polat goes so far as to argue, 'the discourse of universal human rights, introduced into the normative framework as an alleviating measure, is an oxymoron, given that it is formally a mere extension of sovereignty' and that 'the normative axis has been reduced to sovereignty.'[70]

Kinsella is skeptical of the 'self-consciously grafted' discourses of human rights on discourses of civilization.[71] She observes that 'discourses of humanity and human rights did not automatically displace those hierarchies of power and protection embedded in discourses of civilization.'[72] Kinsella agrees with Johnson's observation that

> The "principle of humanity" has become embedded in the international law of armed conflicts, and universally it is used to denote restraints on the use of force that are in principle accessible by moral reflection on the part of all segments of mankind, though at the same time (as.. .(the).. .preference of the term civilization reminds us) a higher moral goal that some cultures may better reflect than others in their conduct of hostilities.[73]

It is therefore possible to suggest a possibility that this Human Rights discourse with its heavy emphasis on legalization, cultural archetypes and performances of justice and retribution often creates a culture of alienation and abstract formality. The 'human rights law does not reduce the incentive to go to war by constraining how countries deploy weapons,' and is deemed to be 'on the verge of the imminent decay.'[74] Cognizance of this Janus-faced historical legacy of human rights in the field of arms

[67] Polat, *Meaning and Mimesis* (London & New York: Routledge, 2012), 105.

[68] Polat, *Meaning and Mimesis,* 105.

[69] Polat, *Meaning and Mimesis,* 112.

[70] Polat, *Meaning and Mimesis,* 114–116.

[71] Kinsella, *The Image Before the Weapon,* 138.

[72] Kinsella, *The Image Before the Weapon,* 138.

[73] Kinsella, *The Image Before the Weapon,* 138; James Turner Johnson, "Grotius' Use of History and Charity in the Modern Transformation of the Just War Idea," *Grotiana* 4, no. 1 (1983): 32; Hopgood, *The Endtimes of Human Rights* (Ithaca & London: Cornell University Press, 2013), ix.

[74] Hopgood, *The Endtimes of Human Rights,* viii.

control and disarmament is acutely necessary to generate an awareness in the subaltern of the constraints of resorting to a rights-based internationalism and is not aimed to detract attention from the necessity of international humanitarian discourses to combat violence, seek redress and demand "No more, stop, enough!"[75] Its aim is to draw attention to the caveat in discourses on rights-based internationalism where the lone superpower asserts its civilizational righteousness in policing the nuclear order.

Exceptional Exceptionalism

An understanding of internationalism based on rights is a matter of grave urgency as 'American exceptionalism has shaken the foundations of the humanist legacy.'[76] The US as 'successor to the great heritage of the Western enlightenment' has 'no commitment on principle to the idea of global norms, only a commitment to globalize *American norms*.'[77] The double jeopardy of a colonial legacy and a shaken humanist legacy with its aspirations for universalism is in a perpetual diabolical confrontation with explicit American 'attachment to sovereignty, self-determination, and national exceptionalism.'[78] Scholars argue that 'US presidents have increased their invocation of American exceptionalism since the Second World War,' are more 'likely to invoke American exceptionalism, particularly after the end of the Cold War' and 'that they have relied heavily on this concept in times of national crises.'[79] This problem is intensified with a constitutional tradition that for many Americans is superior to international law, and with a sense of their own 'manifest destiny.'[80] Mertus carefully scrutinizes how 'every American President since Carter has used human rights in an exceptionalist and unilateralist manner that serves to undermine the idea of human rights' to buttress national interests.[81]

[75] Hopgood, *The Endtimes of Human Rights*, viii.

[76] Hopgood, *The Endtimes of Human Rights*, 16.

[77] Moyn, *The Last Utopia*, 45; Hopgood, *The Endtimes of Human Rights*, 165, 176.

[78] Hopgood, *The Endtimes of Human Rights*, 4.

[79] Joseph Gilmore, Penelop Sheets and Charles Rowling, "Make no exception, save one: American exceptionalism, the American presidency, and the age of Obama," *Communication Monographs* 83, no. 4 (2016): 505–506.

[80] Hopgood, *The Endtimes of Human Rights*, 18.

[81] Julie A. Mertus, *Bait and Switch- Human Rights and US Foreign Policy*, 2nd edition (New York & London: Routledge, 2008), 86.

'US exceptionalism and ad hoc favoritism over true universalism' is now being conceptualized as 'exceptional exceptionalism.'[82] It is these practices of exceptional exceptionalism in the field of arms control and disarmament that encourage the US to promote 'short term instrumentalism over long-term ethical principles, double standards instead of fair dealing,' as seen in the previous chapter with regard to nuclear proliferation.[83] The idea of human rights now being advocated under practices of 'exceptional exceptionalism' by the US no longer incorporates fundamental principles of human dignity, moral worth and equality, but rather is being cast as 'something done "out there" and to "other people"' to help buttress 'a short list of American values, to be projected and applied to others in line with particular American national interests.'[84] These practices of sly civility give the appearance of 'ethical universalism' but are 'particularist in orientation.'[85]

These developments are taking place consonant with a growing discourse in the West insistent that the right to self-determination of postcolonial states is passé .[86] This is demonstrated by their growing willingness to wage interventionary wars for regime change on any given pretext, such as that they are 'potential conduits of WMD to the terrorists' and 'abusive of human rights and liberty.'[87] The political calculation and propaganda behind this concerted effort as seen in the case of Iraq undermines the right to self-determination of postcolonial states and is an imperial exercise that cannot be naively assumed to be a path to another 'utopia, the hope for a world of individual human rights.'[88] Hopgood cautions, 'Human Rights, capitalized' is highly legalized 'with aspirations to civilize the world.'[89] The transformation of 'human rights' to 'Human Rights' has seen a proliferation of a metanarrative, regardless of facts, of 'bourgeois cultural archetypes: victim, hero, good, evil' that helps mobilize resources

[82] Mertus, *Bait and Switch*, xi–xii.

[83] Mertus, *Bait and Switch*, 1.

[84] Mertus, *Bait and Switch*, 2.

[85] Mertus, *Bait and Switch*, 7.

[86] Moyn, *The Last Utopia*, 118–119; Vijay Prashad, "Third World Quarterlt row: Why some western intellectuals are trying to debrutalise colonialism," *Scroll.in*, September 21, 2017, retrieved from https://scroll.in/article/print/851305

[87] Nicholas J. Wheeler, "The Bush Doctrine: The Dangers of American Exceptionalism in a Revolutionary Age," *Asian Perspective* 27, no. 4 (2003): 186; Mertus, *Bait and Switch*, 129.

[88] Moyn, *The Last Utopia*, 119.

[89] Hopgood, *The Endtimes of Human Rights*, ix.

and resort to 'retribution.'[90] In this 'humanitarian marketplace' the emphasis is on 'professional global advocacy rather than to stimulate *transnational collective action.*'[91]

It is therefore not surprising that under the guise of waging a global 'War on Terror' the US has placed itself at the forefront of 'the nation-building business and secured its place as the central player in the democracy-promotion industry.'[92] In its quest to end 'terrible threats to the civilized world' the US has declared that 'nations are either with us or against us in the war on terror.'[93] The 'civilizing mission' has produced a sense of 'unprecedented urgency' in its continuous quest of 'transformation of "the other."'[94] This sense of urgency is 'powerfully linked to the idea of self-defence and survival, not only of the US but of civilization itself and a willingness for "endless war."'[95] American exceptionalism is 'predicated on the belief that eliminating dangerous weapons in the hands of "rogue states" requires nothing short of their removal from power,' as seen in the case of Iraq, Syria and Libya.[96] This encourages a potentially 'perverse consequence' of 'proliferation of WMD as potential targets of US intervention seek to acquire nuclear weapons as a deterrent against being attacked,' as seen in the case of North Korea.[97]

Biswas notes, 'Regime change was the refrain of the George W. Bush administration that had named Iran as part of the "Axis of Evil", and the possible exercise of the "military option" to prevent Iranian nuclearization remained the refrain of the Obama administration (and of Israel).'[98] This escalating rhetoric of regime change and threats of military intervention is often framed by the Western media in simple 'Huntingtonian terms—where the conflict appears civilizational and its roots priomordial.'[99] A trenchant sense of American exceptionalism has made it proclaim that it can no longer rely only on 'traditional strategies of deterrence and

[90] Hopgood, *The Endtime of Human Rights,* 45–46, 58.

[91] Hopgood, *The Endtimes of Human Rights,* 97.

[92] Mertus, *Bait and Switch,* 66.

[93] Mertus, *Bait and Switch,* 68, see footnote 322; The White House. "President Sworn-In to Second Term," January 20, 2005, http://www.whitehouse.gov/news/releases/2005/01/20050120-1.html

[94] Anghie, *Imperialism, Sovereignty and the Making of International Law*, 298.

[95] Anghie, *Imperialism, Sovereignty and the Making of International Law*, 298.

[96] Wheeler, "The Bush Doctrine," 207.

[97] Wheeler, "The Bush Doctrine," 210.

[98] Biswas, "Iran v. 'the international community.'" 334, 340.

[99] Biswas, "Iran v. 'the international community,'" 335.

containment' for its security post 9/11 and that the 'United States might have to strike before the danger materialized.'[100] The effect on decision-making time, in pursuing a strategic shift in strategy of 'preemption' based on imminent threat, to 'preventive' war based on anticipation of intent is significantly constraining and dangerous.[101] These declarations and time constraints have generated questions on whether these attempts to rewrite 'a new legal basis for the use of force' would be available to other states, and aroused racial anxieties about their attempts to emulate American exceptionalism.[102]

These developments strike at the very heart of the existing constitutional nuclear order as the US is increasingly reluctant to keep pace with the changing dynamics of weapons control and prohibition. As a result,

> the United States has found itself, if not totally at odds with the rest of the international community, then certainly a distinct minority. Washington has sometimes voted against UN arms control and nonproliferation resolutions that are supported by overwhelming majorities, occasionally casting the only opposing vote. It has not participated in meeting and activities that much of the rest of the world considers important, and its tendency to rely on standard practices and forums has been perceived as creating barriers to success.[103]

The US 'remains reluctant to engage in serious discussions if it cannot maintain leverage over when and how these issues will be discussed.'[104] Any effort to argue that the US should enjoy this leverage given its moral authority is refuted by scholars who argue that 'to claim that Americans live in a human rights culture is a gross overstatement. The level of awareness of human rights is extremely low.'[105]

Despite this brewing 'explosive cocktail of legal and moral exceptionalism,' claims regarding American providential mission are perpetuated in the field of arms control and disarmament.[106] It is assumed that the US has

[100] Wheeler, "The Bush Doctrine," 184, 186; "Remarks by the President at the 2002 Graduation Exercise of the United States Military Academy," West Point, June 1, 2002, online at www.whitehouse.gov/news/releases/2002.../20020601-3.htm

[101] Wheeler, "The Bush Doctrine," 188–194.

[102] Wheeler, "The Bush Doctrine," 184, 194, 199.

[103] Moodie and Moodie, "Alternative Narratives for Arms Control," 314.

[104] Moodie and Moodie, "Alternative Narratives for Arms Control," 317.

[105] Mertus, *Bait and Switch*, 229.

[106] Wheeler, "The Bush Doctrine" 205.

'honorable intentions' and more 'interest in peace than war.'[107] But as Butfoy observes,

> Washington carries too much historical baggage for American idealist rhetoric to be taken at face value by the wider world. This rhetoric has often been viewed as arrogant self-righteousness, even outrageous hypocrisy, and as cover for imposing a type of world order configured around American national interests. However, that much of the world does not accept American power as unconditionally and intrinsically virtuous is not always seen by Washington as cause for reflection, but as showing that some foreigners are on the wrong side of history.[108]

There is a sense of complacency in the assumption that the US is pursuing a policy of preemptive non-proliferation to prevent a nuclear 9/11 and that the US needs to 'uphold the gold standard for preventing uranium enrichment and reprocessing.'[109] These arguments are rhetorically circulated with an indignant self-righteousness, premised on the belief that the US pursues a 'prudent arms control agenda' based on deterrence vis-a vis rogue states, without which a nuclear war 'could mean the end of civilization as we know it.'[110]

It is further argued that American exceptionalism is capable of making a distinction among 'civilized' countries, particularly European countries, as well as asserting a sense of difference between the 'civilized' and 'non-civilized' countries.[111] American exceptionalism has an 'anxious desire to be both a beneficiary of centuries of Western civilization but to set a separate, unique course in the world.'[112] In this endeavor, 'American exceptionalism shows us, it is actually about a distinction being made as to who

[107] Ronald J. Bee, "Nuclear negotiations: back to the future?" Great Decisions, *Foreign Policy Association*, 2019, 44. A report by Donnelly shows how the standards on enrichment and processing were time and again modified by the US to meet its commercial and strategic interests vis-à-vis other states such as Pakistan; see Warren H. Donnelly, 'Evolution of U.S. Nuclear Export Controls,' Report No. 83-119S, June 1983, pp. 11–13, Congressional Research Service, Washington D.C.

[108] Andrew Butfoy, "American Exceptionalism and President Obama's Call for Abolition of Nuclear Weapons," *Contemporary Security Policy* 33, no. 3 (2012): 479.

[109] Bee, "Nuclear negotiations: back to the future?" 47, 49.

[110] Bee, "Nuclear negotiations: back to the future," 39.

[111] Nayak and Malone, "American Orientalism and American Exceptionalism," 255.

[112] Nayak and Malone, "American Orientalism and American Exceptionalism," 260–261.

will set the standards of civilization and normative power, and how.'[113] These observations are significant as they demonstrate that

> Orientalism and Exceptionalism share in common the discursive deployment of ontological difference and epistemological claims underlying the American providential mission to provide order to the world, the justifications for conquering and occupying territories, and the racial hierarchy that prioritizes Anglo-Saxons.[114]

The US has 'integrated the Orientalist apparatus and increasingly and aggressively aims to impose world order.'[115] In imposing this world order, it is helpful to recollect that 'Orientalism is a representational practice about the lurking figure that always threatens to destroy the US—read as not only the country but the world: Exceptionalism identifies the US as the only possible (Western) power to seek out and eliminate this threat.'[116] In this endeavor, the US has distinguished itself by 'strengthening the role of the military' and creating 'international institutions that would "civilize" international politics but that it would ignore at its whim.'[117]

The US is now actively pursuing a path of unraveling the constitutional nuclear order by withdrawing from bilateral agreements between the superpowers such as the Intermediate Nuclear Forces Treaty and the Strategic Arms Reduction Treaty. The US has refused to sign multilateral arms control agreements such as the Comprehensive Test Ban Treaty, the Ottawa Treaty banning landmines, the Cluster Munitions Treaty and the United Nations Nuclear Weapons Ban Treaty. It is unwilling to explicitly commit itself to not targeting non-nuclear weapons states by offering 'negative security assurances' and has 'preferred to use "calculated ambiguity" as a way of leveraging the usefulness of implicit nuclear threats against, for example, non-nuclear armed rogue states.'[118] Butfoy argues, 'the United States has superiority in conventional military power, and since the biggest threat to this superiority is nuclear proliferation, it makes strategic sense for Washington to de-emphasize nuclear weapons,' and the

[113] Nayak and Malone, "American Orientalism and American Exceptionalism," 263.

[114] Nayak and Malone, "American Orientalism and American Exceptionalism," 254.

[115] Nayak and Malone, "American Orientalism and American Exceptionalism," 263.

[116] Nayak and Malone, "American Orientalism and American Exceptionalism," 272.

[117] Nayak and Malone, "American Orientalism and American Exceptionalism," 268–269.

[118] Butfoy, "American Exceptionalism and President Obama's Call for Abolition of Nuclear Weapons," 471.

domestic 'constituency for arms control is even broader if it reinforces global non-proliferation efforts without requiring American disarmament in any tangible timeframe.'[119]

The US resists arms control and disarmament efforts by arguing that the 'time has not been "ripe"' to commit itself to such undertakings.[120] It is therefore pertinent for postcolonial states to question the idea of 'liberal progress' and the 'massive constellation of efforts' embodied in 'this or that treaty or organization' to address the problem of weapons.[121] The US continues to practice 'exceptionalism and ad hoc favoritism over true universalism.'[122] This is visible in the nuclear order where the US does not hesitate to castigate and condemn Iran as the bad regional actor that does not sit well with the US vision of promoting modernity in the Middle East. On the contrary, India is now seen as a strategic partner in its attempt to foster quadrilateral cooperation for security in the Indo-Pacific.[123] This binary vision of Iran as the 'bad actor' and India as the 'good actor' carefully produces a split, a time-lag, within which a subaltern state like India, long considered a nuclear outcast, 'an exception in the nuclear nonproliferation regime,' is now given 'access to nuclear material and technologies from the Nuclear Suppliers Group, despite being a non-signatory to the Nuclear Non Proliferation Treaty.'[124]

Chacko and Davis argue that the signing of the historic India—US nuclear deal signals how a subaltern can astutely gauge the need to 'resignify the Western discourse of nuclear responsibility' to potentially 'subvert' the existing nuclear order with its 'own civilizational mantra.'[125] It is argued that 'India's status as a responsible nuclear power is based, not on its compliance with international regimes or norms, but on its maneuvered mirroring of a discourse on "civilizational exceptionalism."'[126] This has led scholars to insist that in the field of arms control and disar-

[119] Butfoy, "American Exceptionalism and President Obama's Call for Abolition of Nuclear Weapons," 474.

[120] Butfoy, "American Exceptionalism and President Obama's Call for Abolition of Nuclear Weapons," 470.

[121] Biswas, *Nuclear Desire: Power and the Postcolonial Nuclear Order*, 24.

[122] Mertus, *Bait and Switch*, xii.

[123] *National Security Strategy of the United States of America*, December 2017, 46.

[124] Priya Chacko and Alexander E. Davis, "Resignifying 'responsibility': India, exceptionalism and nuclear nonproliferation," *Asian Journal of Political Science* 26, no. 3 (2018): 355.

[125] Chacko and Davis, "Resignifying 'responsibility,'" 355.

[126] Chacko and Davis, "Resignifying 'responsibility,'" 352.

mament, India is 'no longer framed within a Eurocentric "standard of civilization" but instead linked to a discourse on India's "civilizational exceptionalism."'[127] India's civilizational exceptionalism 'invokes its civilizational propensity for ethical behaviour' and 'exercise of power with restraint' based on its own particular history and cultural practices.[128]

For decades, India has harped on its civilizational legacy of non-violence and peace, championing the cause of disarmament, only to be marginalized by the West. In the post-Cold War era, the subaltern actor now sought to secure its advantage by opportunistically mirroring the deployment of civilizational discourses in the West with their emphasis on a culture of democracy, free market and nuclear deterrence. This mimetic assertion of shared modernity expressed in a language of desire to protect 'our way of life and values' exhibiting 'responsible' conduct by the subaltern found resonance in the West.[129] India is no longer to be readily mocked as a 'nuclear pariah,' 'emotional,' 'irresponsible' or 'dangerous.'[130] As a signatory to a nuclear deal with the US, India is temporally recognized as a strategic partner, and the US continues to issue exhortatory statements encouraging others to 'continue demonstrating' their responsibility in stewardship of 'nuclear assets.'[131]

This is not the first time that the principle of nuclear non-proliferation championed as being universal has been sabotaged by the master. Instead of repeating a ritual of mourning at such violations, it is imperative that we study the effects of colonial mirroring or mimesis in the nuclear order. In these encounters of colonial mirroring it is difficult to resign to Biswas' observation mentioned above that 'postcolonial nuclear mimicry-disguised as subaltern speech-consigns poorer states to forever remain disadvantaged.'[132] India with its mimetic practices has been able to access nuclear materials and technologies but it is at present difficult to ascertain

[127] Chacko and Davis, "Resignifying 'responsibility,'" 352.

[128] Chacko and Davis, "Resignifying 'responsibility'" 353, 357.

[129] President, Indian Prime Minister Singh Exchange Toasts. Retrieved from http://2001-2009.state.gov/p/sca/rls/rm/2005/49766.htm cited by Chacko and Davis, "Resignifying 'responsibility,'" 364; United States. *National Security Strategy of the United States of America*, December 2017, 50. https://www.whitehouse.gov/wp-content/uploads/2017/12/NSS-Final-12-18-2017-0905.pdf

[130] Vandana Bhatia, "The US-India Nuclear Agreement: Revisiting the Debate," *Strategic Analysis* 36, no. 4 (2012): 613; Chacko and Davis, "Resignifying 'responsibility,'" 362.

[131] United States. *National Security Strategy of the United States of America*, 50.

[132] Biswas, *Nuclear Desire*, 185.

'whether India will emerge as a supplier of nuclear technology and be drawn into the "proliferation" image entirely' or whether the US will accept the ethos of 'disarmament-development.'[133] The India—US nuclear agreement is a symbolic representation of an agreement between two states claiming to enjoy exceptional civilizational status in the world order. This temporal arrangement does not challenge the existing nuclear hierarchy but might give the temporal illusion of having moved the subaltern 'up the global nuclear hierarchy.'[134]

The India—US nuclear deal has given rise to much dissension and generated an impression that it bestows on 'an NPT nonparty more benefits than NPT parties.'[135] This nuclear deal appears to 'break the logic that states outside the system receive fewer advantages than compliant states inside the regime.'[136] The lack of rules for 'post-proliferation management of nuclear states' is decried as 'the NPT per se is exclusively focused on preventing the spread of nuclear weapons. There is no provision for dealing with states that cross the nuclear threshold.'[137] This problem of inclusion/exclusion in nonproliferation regimes and proliferating exceptionalism is compounded by Argentina and Brazil not signing the NPT Additional Protocol and claiming exceptions. It is argued that 'by not signing the IAEA's Additional Protocol, Brazil has left the door open to return to a nuclear weapon option program.'[138] This signals how practices of sly civility can undermine nuclear discourses based on equity but reaffirm mimetic assertions of civilizational exceptionalism.

In the face of civilizational exceptionalism, human rights-based discourses fail to address the 'ambivalence regarding the limits of sovereignty' that is often invoked in addressing the challenges of arms control.[139] Arguments on cultural relativism are easily manipulated in the service of national defense, political propaganda and war, and once 'each culture is

[133] Bhatia, "The US-India Nuclear Agreement," 620.

[134] Chacko and Davis, "Resignifying 'responsibility,'" 352.

[135] Sharon Squassoni, "The U.S. -Indian Deal and Its Impact," *Arms Control Today* 40, no. 6 (2010): 52, cited by Mario E. Caranza, "Rising Regional Powers."

[136] Irma Arguello, "The Position of an Emerging Global Power: Brazilian Responses to the 2010 US Nuclear Posture Review," *Nonproliferation Review* 18, no. 1 (2011): 193, cited by Mario E. Caranza, "Rising Regional Powers" 14.

[137] Bhatia, "The US-India Nuclear Agreement," 616.

[138] Mario E. Caranza, "Rising Regional Powers" 19.

[139] Roberts, *The Contentious History of the International Bill of Human Rights*, 78, 137–138.

perceived as living its time' it is possible to suggest that efforts be made to 'elevate the interstices between cultures.'[140] Anghie insists that 'International law can maintain its coherence and play its classic role of regulating state behaviour only by carefully defining the cultural sphere, the civilized world, in which it operates.'[141] This effort is imperative, as with a resurgence of mimesis and colonial mirroring in the acquisition of nuclear weapons, 'cultural relativism is clearly not an option here ("Let them believe what they want to, and we'll believe we want to"), because the different reactions are profoundly implicated in each other; they are "relative" to each other more than they are "relative" to what we used to call their "own cultural context."'[142]

Furthermore, in this type of 'second contact' of 'mimetic excess' and 'mimetic vertigo' the border logistics of 'us' and 'them' lose their polarity as 'Mastery is no longer possible.'[143] The 'First World and Other Worlds now mirror, interlock, and rupture each other's alterity' to such an extent that 'the West itself is no longer a stable identity against which mimetic alters can be confidently construed, so those alters too have a powerful capacity…to elude fixing.'[144] Mimetic 'runs the risk of self-annihilation.'[145] The emergence of a radically different border between the West and the Rest unleashed by a 'second contact' has generated a 'combination of fear and pleasure that mimetically capacious machines can create when inter-acted with mimetic reflections of the West as portrayed in the bodies, eyes, and handiwork of alters.'[146] This 'mimetic excess' rouses a 'mimetic self-awareness' compelling an interrogation, a self-inquiry, into the West and the Other 'in and partially constitutive of his many and conflicting selves, and as yet we have few ground rules for how such an interrogation should or might proceed.'[147]

It is questionable if a universal frame of reference based on human rights can address a problem of this magnitude as it is itself based on the 'episteme of natural history' that encourages a view of 'temporal relations

[140] Fabian, *Time and the Other*, 47.
[141] Anghie, *Imperialism, Sovereignty and the Making of International Law*, 314.
[142] Taussig, *Mimesis and Alterity*, 249.
[143] Taussig, *Mimesis and Alterity*, 246–249, 236–237.
[144] Taussig, *Mimesis and Alterity*, 236–237.
[145] Taussig, *Mimesis and Alterity*, 111.
[146] Taussig, *Mimesis and Alterity*, 252.
[147] Taussig, *Mimesis and Alterity*, 238.

as exclusive and expansive.'[148] In this naturalized, evolutionary, linear understanding of historical time, temporal relations are seen as 'exclusive and expansive. The pagan was already marked for salvation, the savage is not yet ready for civilization.'[149] The emphasis on legal positivism has problematized the concept of universality in human rights and arms control. Legal positivism with its emphasis on state sovereignty has fractured the concept of universality into three pillars trying to uphold its legitimacy. Thus the ideas of legal universality, overlapping consensus universality and functional universality are being mooted to articulate the concept of 'relative universality.'[150] But this idea of a qualified universality is resisted by Afshari to contend that

> Scholars, exploring the notion of "tempered" universality, should focus on the violating nation-states and posit their theories on the corpus of the available documentations and analyses. Hypothetical examples without references to specific human rights reports cannot be practically useful for monitoring and advocacy.[151]

Afshari emphasizes that the concept of human rights is a 'new invention without deep cultural roots' and 'a traditional culture must change for the culture of human rights to emerge.'[152] In other words, the emphasis must be on altering the traditional culture of arms control instead of succumbing to the 'grand theories' of human rights to address the problem of weapons control.[153] Posner has critiqued the 'hubris' vested in human rights agreements that 'does not require Western countries to change their behavior, while (in principle) it requires massive changes in the behavior of most non-Western countries.'[154] These problems are compounded by an embedded strategy of making new arms control rules through the strategy of consensus rather than consent as the basis of international legal obligations. The problem is political, not merely epistemological.

[148] Fabian, *Time and the Other*, 26.

[149] Fabian, *Time and the Other*, 26.

[150] Jack Donnelly, "The Relative Universality of Human Rights," *Human Rights Quarterly* 29, no. 2 (2007): 281.

[151] Afshari, "Relativity in Universality" 854.

[152] Afshari, "Relativity in Universality," 858, 879.

[153] Afshari, "Relativity in Universality," 855.

[154] Posner, *The Twilight of Human Rights Law*, 142–148.

Thus those that seek to address the state of abjection and humiliation experienced by postcolonial states in negotiating conditions of equality in weapons control might need to pause and reconsider a human rights-based approach to disarmament. Gandhi resisted a rights-based approach and considered it to possess little substantive meaning. Gandhi insisted that 'only by acting out the "duties" of a global citizen—and in doing so effacing the sovereign boundaries of an empire—that a sphere of human inviolability could first emerge.'[155] But 'could colonial inhabitants act out Gandhi's call to become global citizens and cross the structural barriers that currently held them as nonentities in international law?'[156] Christopher Robert poses this question but then claims, 'Gandhi was intensely ambivalent.'[157] The ambivalence of Gandhi is situated in his experiences as an astute lawyer representing the colonized and capable of configuring practices of lawfare in the international order. Despite this awareness of ambivalence the question persists.

Revolt to Reconstellate

How to reconstellate practices of arms control and disarmament? There is no easy civilizational mantra with which to address this significant question. This question persists even as we have tried to generate consciousness about civilizational time, made visible by the legacy of colonial practices in arms control and disarmament, and demonstrated above the subaltern's multi-pronged efforts at practices of hedging, assertion of rights-based internationalism and colonial mirroring of civilizational exceptionalism. An understanding of these liminal practices in weapons control has to be registered in writing within a growing postcolonial revolt to decolonize the field of security studies.

This postcolonial revolt decries an 'ethnocentric' bias in our understanding of practices of arms control and disarmament.[158] It is a revolt premised on an acknowledgment that 'Western security culture' has 'powerfully shaped the NACD policies and practices of states, and helped to

[155] Gandhi's view presented by Christopher N.J. Roberts, *The Contentious History of the International Bill of Human Rights*, 141.

[156] Roberts, *The Contentious History of the International Bill of Human Rights*, 141–142.

[157] Roberts, *The Contentious History of the International Bill of Human Rights*, 142.

[158] Barkawi and Laffey, "The Postcolonial Moment in Security Studies," 329–252; Gusterson, "Nuclear weapons and the Other in the Western Imagination," 111–143; Krause and Latham, "Constructing Non-Proliferation," 23–54.

define what it means for states to pursue their national interests.'[159] A revolt that is skeptical of the development of security studies in its 'modern form' post 1945 and its myriad attempts to represent itself as a 'seemingly neutral and timeless language of social science.'[160] It is now argued that 'conventional security studies as a field of knowledge is a product of Western power. The knowledge produced out of such a field is inadequate for its own clientele. It is even less adequate at addressing the security and strategic concerns of the weak.'[161]

This postcolonial revolt questions 'the assumption that it is the right of the West to bear arms to liberate the "natives"' and use force 'legitimated in terms of a civilizing mission of one kind or another.'[162] It is important to note that attempts to universalize the problem of arms is often premised on Eurocentric assumptions that 'agency, rationality, power and morality, as well as the fundamental dynamics of the world order…reside in the global North…these various others are assumed to be just like us, only weaker.'[163] These practices deny the historical experiences of the others. Barkawi and Laffy argue that,

> First, …security studies provides few categories for making sense of the historical experiences of the weak and the powerless who comprise most of the world's population. By default these experiences are conceived in categories derived from great power politics in the North…Second, and related, to the extent that it addresses them at all, a Eurocentric security studies, regards the weak and the powerless, as marginal and derivative elements of world politics, as at best the site of good liberal intentions or at worst a potential source of threats. Missed are the multiple and integral relations between the weak and the strong. Failing to study the weak and the strong together, as jointly responsible for making history, hamstrings IR and security studies ability to make sense of the world politics generally and North -South relations in particular.[164]

A postcolonial revolt is at present trying to bring visibility to the problem of Eurocentrism in security studies, and this book in particular is

[159] Krause and Latham, "Constructing Non-Proliferation," 23–24.

[160] Barkawi and Laffey, "The Postcolonial Moment," 334.

[161] Barkawi and Laffey, "The Postcolonial Moment," 334.

[162] Barkawi and Laffey, "The Postcolonial Moment," 351.

[163] Barkawi and Laffey, "The Postcolonial Moment," 346; N. Inayatullah and D. Blaney, *International Relations and the Politics of Difference* (New York: Routledge, 2004).

[164] Barkawi and Laffey, "The Postcolonial Moment in Security Studies," 332–333.

trying to bring visibility to the problem of arms control and disarmament in a civilizational context. This book is a contribution in this endeavor to trace the effects of colonial legacies circulating as civilizational discourses in weapons control. It is an endeavor to move practices of arms control and disarmament beyond 'the application of very general demands against specific practices and policies' to encourage 'a broader cultural rethinking that would inform an ethically informed politics.'[165]

Any effort to diagnose this revolt cannot be prescriptive or emotive only, but does suggest a possibility of further reflexions. In pursuing these reflexions it is important not to endorse the temptation espoused by some scholars that

> In such conditions and in the world of profound inequalities they produced, armed and other resistance is only to be expected. For us, the "natives" have the right to bear arms for purposes of their own liberatory projects, even those we profoundly disagree with. To advise the weak that they should not take up arms but instead await liberation in the hands of the West is wishful thinking given the historical record of the West in this regard.[166]

It is more helpful if awareness of a documented record of immense human suffering and violence produces a sense of pathos and induces one to issue a warning and the need for restraint against invocation of civilizational discourses stereotyping the West and the Rest. It is encouraging to invest faith in the argument that artificial polarized division maintained between the nuclear haves and have-nots is an 'unsustainable binary opposition' that cannot be maintained in the long run.[167] It cannot be maintained because in the construction and emphasis on differences under persistent conditions of hostility it is possible that neither party is 'the first to think that mimesis might be mined for political advantage, only to find themselves caught in its own dynamic.'[168] This mimetic struggle of violence and cunning develops a 'patho-logic of its own in which assimilation

[165] Richard J. Peterson, "Human Rights: Historical learning in the Shadow of Violence," *The American Journal of Economics and Sociology* 68, no. 1 (2009): 268.

[166] Barkawi and Laffey, "The Postcolonial Moment," 351.

[167] Gusterson, "Nuclear Weapons and the Other in the Western Imagination," 133.

[168] James Der Derian, "Imaging Terror: Logos, Pathos and Ethos," *Third World Quarterly* 26, no. 1 (2005): 32.

or extermination become plausible solutions for what appears to be an intractable problem.'[169]

To address this problem, Gusterson argues that we must be attentive to 'the way our conversations about policy choices on the nuclear issue may unthinkingly incorporate certain neocolonial hierarchies and assumptions that, when drawn to our attention, many of us would disown.'[170] It is imperative that we be critical of the racial undertones of these conversations, and he insists that in addressing these dangers, efforts should be made not to 'demean the peoples of the Third World. Nor should they be represented in ways that obscure both the dangers inherent in the continued maintenance of our own nuclear arsenals and the fact that our own actions are often a source of the instabilities we so fear in Third World nations.'[171] In this endeavor, Nandy suggests the need for 'authentic innocence.'[172] This authentic innocence cognizant of its own suffering and vulnerability has not 'lost the realism of its perception of evil or that of its own "complicity" with that evil.'[173] It encourages one to recognize the possibility of exercising some choices as one acknowledges that

> If there is the non-West which constantly invites one to be Western and to defeat the West on the strength of one's acquired Westernness—there is the non-West's construction of the West which invites one to be true to the West's other self and to the non-West which is in alliance with that other self. If beating the West at its own game is the preferred means of handling the feelings of self-hatred in the modernized non-West, there is also the West constructed by the savage outsider who is neither willing to be a player nor a counterplayer.[174]

It is unwilling to accept the politics of the 'undeveloped heart' that 'isolates cognition from affect' and triggers the 'banal violence' of imperialism. Nandy ruefully admits that his suggestions are a 'paean to the non-players.'[175]

[169] Der Derian, "Imaging Terror," 32, 774.
[170] Gusterson, "Nuclear Weapons and the Other in the Western Imagination," 133.
[171] Gusterson, "Nuclear Weapons and the Other in the Western Imagination," 133.
[172] Nandy, *The Intimate Enemy*, xiii.
[173] Nandy, *The Intimate Enemy*, xiii.
[174] Nandy, *The Intimate Enemy*, xiii.
[175] Nandy, *The Intimate Enemy*, 33–34.

For the postcolonial revolt to make further progress in the field of security studies scholars insist that we need to develop 'the conceptual apparatus to interrogate the fundamental characteristics of the colonial encounter' to investigate how 'colonial history insinuates itself into the discipline with enduring and far-reaching effect.'[176] This book has tried to articulate such a conceptual apparatus by distinguishing between civilizational time and postcolonial time, and has then tried to give meaning to the concepts of stereotyping, sly civility and mimesis by carefully mining particular practices within the history of arms control and disarmament. This book is an attempt at interrogating the colonial legacy of arms control and disarmament by careful 'immersion in the concrete' historical experiences of the subaltern in the field of arms control and disarmament. In the absence of a sustained interrogation it is possible that mimetic violence will succeed in overpowering virtuous intentions of arms control and disarmament, and the dynamic of difference will compel the 'West and the Rest' to remain embedded in a 'mimetic trap.'[177] There is an urgent need for reflexivity to grasp how the 'colonial origins of the discipline are re-enacted whenever the discipline attempts to renew itself, reform itself.'[178]

Gusterson suggests the need for a politics attentive to discursive strategies of 'exclusion,' 'participation' and 'renunciation' in practices of arms control and disarmament.[179] It is possible that these practices can help dissolve the binary of West and the Rest. The strategy of exclusion demands an honest rejection of 'easy racism' and 'phony moralism' with an acknowledgment that nuclear weapons 'are a prerogative of power, and the powerful have no intention of allowing the powerless to acquire them.'[180] The strategy of participation accepts that all countries pursue nuclear weapons 'in search of greater security vis-à-vis regional rivals and out of a desire to shift the balance of power in their client relationships with the superpowers.'[181] Then there is the more demanding strategy of renunciation that urges the need for greater reflexivity on Orientalist discourses that accompany weapons proliferation. This reflexivity will enable a confrontation with 'those parts of our own personality and culture which appear as the childish, irrational, lawless, or feminine aspects of the Other'

[176] Anghie, *Imperialism, Sovereignty and the Making of International Law*, 311–312.
[177] Der Derian, "Imaging Terror," 32.
[178] Anghie, *Imperialism, Sovereignty and the Making of International Law*, 313.
[179] Gusterson, "Nuclear Weapons and the Other in the Western Imagination," 133.
[180] Gusterson, "Nuclear Weapons and the Other in the Western Imagination," 133.
[181] Gusterson, "Nuclear Weapons and the Other in the Western Imagination," 133.

but which conceal 'our doubts about ourselves instead of harping continuously on our doubts about others.'[182] The existence of race thinking and its gross transformation into racism and neo-racism has destructive consequences for the comity of nations.

Victor Villanueva argues that the problem of racism persists because 'we're still unclear about what we're dealing with, so we must thereby be unclear about how to deal with it.'[183] Hannah Arendt suggests that race thinking exists by claiming lineage to a certain tradition, makes its appearance in the garb of national respectability, and becomes vitriolic in its imperialist ambitions as it exposes humanity to new and shocking experiences such as nuclear testing or the use of nuclear weapons in war. She urges us to be conscious of how race thinking is a 'source of convenient arguments for varying conflicts' and how race thinking sharpens and exploits 'existing political problems' such as the regulation and prohibition of weapons.[184] This might be feasible if we are willing to consider and question 'racism as a block to universalism' by paying particular attention not simply to the telos of disarmament but to the 'kind of learning' made possible by paying attention to everyday practices of stereotyping, sly civility and mimetic maneuvering in the nuclear order caught in contingent writings of history.[185]

This race thinking is embedded in an evolutionary or naturalized time conceptualized in this book as civilizational time fostering a sense of distance between the West and the Rest. In this naturalized time there is a persistent and systematic denial of coevalness. These practices of denial and distancing are to be carefully resisted by a postcolonial disposition toward time as it excavates dyadic relations on science, technology and culture among interacting civilizations. The polarizing dynamic of civilizational and postcolonial time demands confrontation with an 'entrenched vocabulary and obstinate literary conventions' that deny coevalness as demonstrated in this book.[186] A grasp of intersubjective time as an epistemological condition, a 'mode of temporal relations,' 'can only be inferred from results, i.e., from the different ways in which recognition or denial of

[182] Gusterson, "Nuclear Weapons and the Other in the Western Imagination," 133.

[183] Victor Villanueva, "On the Rhetoric and Precedents of Racism," *College, Composition and Communication* 50, no. 4 (1999): 648.

[184] Hannah Arendt, "Race-Thinking before Racism," *The Review of Politics* 6, no. 1 (1944): 72–73.

[185] Peterson, "Human Rights" 267.

[186] Fabian, *Time and the Other- How Anthropology Makes its Object*, 33.

coevalness inform…theory and writing.'[187] This book is a humble attempt at this endeavor as it insists on communication, coevalness or shared time and precludes distancing between the West and the Rest.

* * *

[187] Fabian, *Time and the Other*, 34.

Bibliography

Abraham, Itty. "'Who's Next?' Nuclear Ambivalence and the Contradictions of Non-Proliferation Policy," *Economic and Political Weekly* 49, no.43 (2010): 48–56.

Abraham, Itty. "From Bandung to NAM: Non-alignment and Indian Foreign Policy, 1947–65," *Commonwealth & Comparative Politics* 46, No.2 (2008): 195–219.

Abraham, Itty. "The Ambivalence of Nuclear Histories," *Osiris* 21, no.1 (2006a): 49–65.

Abraham, Itty. "The Contradictory Spaces of Postcolonial Techno-Science," *Economic and Political Weekly* 41, no.3 (2006b): 210–217.

Abraham, Itty. "What really makes a country nuclear? Insights from Non-Nuclear Southeast Asia," *Critical Studies on Security* 4, no.1 (2016): 24–41.

Abraham, Itty. *The Making of the Indian Atomic Bomb-Science, Secrecy and the Postcolonial State*. London & New York: Zed Books, 1998.

Adas, Michael. *Machines as the Measure of Men: Science, Technology, and Ideologies of Western Dominance*, Ithaca & London: Cornell University Press, 1989.

Afshari, Reza. "Relativity in Universality Jack Donnelly's Grand Theory in Need of Specific Illustration," *Human Rights Quarterly* 37, no.4 (2015): 854–912.

Aganthangelou, Anna M. and Kyle D. Killian, *Time, Temporality and Violence in International Relations*. New York: Routledge, 2016.

al-Azm, S. "Orientalism and Orientalism in reverse," in *Orientalism: A Reader*, ed. A.L. Macfie. Edinburgh: Edinburgh University Press, 2000.

Albright, David and Corey Hinderstein, "Unraveling the A.Q. Khan and Future Proliferation Networks," *The Washington Quarterly* 28, no.2 (2005): 109–128.

R. Mathur, *Civilizational Discourses in Weapons Control*,
https://doi.org/10.1007/978-3-030-44943-8

Alexandrowicz, C.H., "Grotius and India," *Indian Yearbook of International Affairs* 3, no.30 (1954).

Allman, Jean. "Rethinking Power and Politics in the African Diaspora: Nuclear Imperialism and the Pan-African Struggle for Peace and Freedom-Ghana 1959–1962," *Souls* 10, no.2 (2008): 83–102.

Anand, R.P. *New States and International Law*. Delhi: Vikas Publishing House Pvt Ltd, 1972.

Anderson, Benedict. *Imagined Communities: Reflections on the Origin and Spread of Nationalism*. London: Verso Books, 2016.

Anderson, Robert S. *Nucleus and Nation-Scientists, International Networks and Power in India*. Chicago & London: The University of Chicago Press, 2010.

Anghie, Antony. *Imperialism, Sovereignty and the Making of International Law*, Cambridge: Cambridge University Press, 2004.

Arendt, Hannah. "Race thinking before Racism," *The Review of Politics* 6, no.1 (1944): 36–73.

Arguello, Irma. "The Position of an Emerging Global Power: Brazilian Responses to the 2010 US Nuclear Posture Review," *Nonproliferation Review* 18, no.1 (2011): 183–200.

Arnett, Eric. "Iran is not Iraq," *Bulletin of the Atomic Scientists* 54, no.1 (1998): 12–14.

Ayson, Robert. "Arms Control in Asia: yesterday's concept for today's region?" *Australian Journal of International Affairs* 67, no.1 (2013): 1–17.

Baggini, Julian. "The Doomsday Clock: why there's no point worrying about Armageddon," *The Guardian*, January 26, 2015. https://www.theguardian.com/commentsfree/2015/jan/26/doomsday-clock-no-point-worrying-about-armageddon (downloaded on January 30, 2018).

Balibar, Etienne. "Is there a "Neo-Racism?" in *Race, Nation, Class: Ambiguous Identities*, ed. Etienne Balibar and Immanuel Wallerstein, translation of Etienne Balibar by Chris Turner, London, New York: Verso, 1991a.

Balibar, Etienne. "Race and Nationalism" in *Race, Nation, Class: Ambiguous Identities*, ed. Etienne Balibar and Immanuel Wallerstein, translation of Etienne Balibar by Chris Turner, London, New York: Verso, 1991b.

Balibar, Etienne. "Racism Revisited: Sources, Relevance, and Aporias of a Modern Concept," *PMLA* 123, no.5 (2008): 1630–1639.

Barkawi, Tarak and Mark Laffey, "The Postcolonial Moment in Security Studies," *Review of International Studies* 32, no.2, (2006): 329–352.

Beachy, R.W. "The Arms Trade in East Africa in the Late Nineteenth Century," *The Journal of African History* 3, no.3 (1962) 451–467.

Bee, Ronald J. "Nuclear negotiations: backs to the future?" in Great Decisions, *Foreign Policy Association*, 2019.

Benjamin, Walter. *The Arcades Project*. trans. By H. Eiland and K. McLaughlin. Cambridge: Belknap Press of Harvard University Press, 1982.

Bernstein, Barton J. "Understanding the Atomic Bomb and the Japanese Surrender: Missed Opportunities, Little-Known Near Disasters, and Modern Memory," *Diplomatic History* 19, no.2 (1995): 227–273.

Betts, Richard K. "Incentives for Nuclear Weapons: India, Pakistan, Iran," *Asian Survey* 19, no.11 (1979): 1053–1072.

Bhabha, Homi K. *The Location of Culture*. London & New York: Routledge, 1994.

Bhagat, Gawdat. "Nuclear Proliferation: The Islamic Republic of Iran," *International Studies Perspectives* 7, no.2 (2006): 124–136.

Bhatia, Vandana. "The US-India Nuclear Agreement: Revisiting the Debate," *Strategic Analysis* 36, no.4 (2012): 612–623.

Bidgood, Sarah. "The establishment of the London Club and nuclear export controls," *Adelphi Series* 56, (2016): 135–162.

Bilgin, Inar. "Temporalizing Security: Securing the citizen, insecuring the immigrant in the Mediterranean," in Anna M. Aganthangelou and Kyle D. Killian, *Time, Temporality and Violence in International Relations*. New York: Routledge, 2016.

Biswas, Shampa. "Iran v 'the international community': a postcolonial analysis of the negotiations on the Iranian nuclear program," *Asian Journal of Political Science* 26, no.3 (2018): 331–351.

Biswas, Shampa. "'Nuclear Apartheid' as Political Position; Race as a Postcolonial Discourse," *Alternatives: Global, Local, Political* 26, no.4, (2001): 485–552.

Biswas, Shampa. *Nuclear Desire: Power and the Postcolonial Nuclear Order*. University of Minnesota Press, 2014.

Blaut, J.M. *The Colonizer's Model of the World: Geographical Diffusionism and Eurocentric History*. New York: Guilford Press, 1993.

Bolton, M., Guerra, H., Acheson, R., and Sprague, O. "The Road Forward for the Arms Trade treaty: A Civil Society Practitioner Commentary," *Global Policy* 5, no.4 (2014): 469–473, http://onlinelibrary.wiley.com/doi/10.1111/1758-5899.12172/full

Bolton, Matthew. "The '-Pacific' part of 'Asia-Pacific': Oceanic diplomacy in the 2017 treaty for the prohibition of nuclear weapons," *Asian Journal of Political Science* 26, no.3 (2018): 371–389.

Borger, Julian. "'Doomsday Clock' ticked forward 30 seconds to 2 minutes to midnight," *The Guardian*, January 25, 2018, https://www.theguardian.com/world/2018/jan25/doomsday-clock-ticked-forward-trump-nuclear-weapons-climate-change (downloaded on January 30, 2018).

Borrie, John and Vanessa Martin Randin. *Disarmament as Humanitarian Action* (Geneva, Switzerland: United Nations Institute for Disarmament Research, 2006).

Bowden, Brett. *The Empire of Civilization: The Evolution of an Imperial Idea*. Chicago: University of Chicago Press, 2009.

Bowen, Wyn and Matthew Moran, "Iran's Nuclear Programme: A Case Study in Hedging?" *Contemporary Security Policy* 35, no.1 (2014): 26–52.

Brodie, Bernard. "On the Objectives of Arms Control," *International Security* 1, no.1 (1976): 17–36.

Bull, Hedley and Adam Watson. *The Expansion of the International Society*. Oxford [Oxfordshire]: Clarendon Press, 1984.

Bull, Hedley. "Arms control and World Order," *International Security* 1, no.1 (1976): 3–16.

Bull, Hedley. "Foreword" in Gerrit W. Gong's, *The Standard of 'Civilization' in International Society*. Oxford: Clarendon Press, 1984.

Bull, Hedley. *The Anarchical Society: A Study of Order in World Politics*. New York: Columbia University Press, 2002.

Bull, Hedley. *The Control of the Arms Race: Disarmament and arms control in the missile age*. New York: Praeger, 1965.

Bull, Hedley. "The Role of the Nuclear Powers in the Management of Nuclear Proliferation" in James Ed. Dougherty and J.F. Lehman Jr, ed., *Arms Control for the Late Sixties*. D. Van Nostrand Co, 1968.

Burrow, John. *Evolution and Society*. New York: Cambridge University Press, 1966.

Butfoy, Andrew. "American Exceptionalism and President Obama's Call for Abolition of Nuclear Weapons," *Contemporary Security Policy* 33, no.3 (2012): 462–486.

Butler, Declan. "Iranian nuclear scientists attacked: Murder and Cyber-Assault Target Nuclear Programme," *Nature* 468, (2010): 607.

Buzan, Barry. *An Introduction to Strategic Studies*, London: Macmillan for the International Institute for Strategic Studies, 1987.

Caranza, Mario E. "Rising Regional Powers and International Relations Theories: Comparing Brazil and India's Foreign Security Policies and their search for Great-Power Status," *Foreign Policy Analysis* 13, no.2 (2017): 255–277.

Carr, E. H. *What is History?* New York: Vintage, 1961.

Césaire, Aimé. *Discourses on Colonialism*, translated by Joan Pinkham, New York: Monthly Review Press, 2000.

Chacko, Priya and Alexander E. Davis, "Resignifying 'responsibility': India, exceptionalism and nuclear non-proliferation," *Asian Journal of Political Science* 26, no.3 (2018): 352–370.

Chakraborty, Dipesh and Kimberly Hutchings, "What is Orientation in Thinking? On the Question of Time and Timeliness in Cosmopolitical Thought," *Constellations* 18, no.2 (2011): 290–204.

Chakraborty, Dipesh. "Where is the Now?" *Critical Inquiry* 30, no.2 (2004): 458–462.

Chakraborty, Dipesh. *Provincializing Europe: Postcolonial Thought and Historical Difference*, Princeton & Oxford: Princeton University Press, 2000.

Chandhoke, Neera. "Equality for What? Or the Troublesome Relation between Egalitarianism and Respect," in Gopal Guru, ed., *Humiliation-Claims and Context*, (Oxford, New Delhi: Oxford University Press, 2009).

Chatterjee, Partha. "Nationalist Thought and the Colonial World," in *The Partha Chatterjee Omnibus*, (New Delhi: Oxford University, 1999a).

Chatterjee, Partha. "The Nation and its Fragments: Colonial and Postcolonial Histories," in *The Partha Chatterjee Omnibus*, (New Delhi: Oxford University, 1999b).

Checkland, Olive. *Humanitarianism and the Emperor's Japan 1877–1977*, New York: St. Martin's Press, 1994.

Chubin, Shahram and Robert Litwak, "Debating Iran's Nuclear Aspirations," *The Washington Quarterly* 26, no.4 (2003): 99–114.

Cipolla, Carlo M. *Guns, Sails and Empires: Technological Innovation and the Early Phases of European Expansion, 1400–1700*. New York: Pantheon Books, 1966.

Clary, Christopher Oren. "The A.Q Khan Network causes and implications" Thesis, Naval Postgraduate School, 2005.

Cohen, Avner. *Israel and the Bomb*. New York: Columbia University Press, 1999.

Cohen, Stephen P. *The Indian Army: Its Contribution to the Development of a Nation*. Los Angeles, London: University of California Press, 1971.

Cohn, Carol. "Sex and death in the rational world of defense intellectuals," *Signs: Journal of women in culture and society* 12, no.4 (1987): 687–718.

"Convention for the Control of the Trade in Arms and Ammunition," in *League of Nations Treaty Series* 7.

Cooper, Neil. "Race, Sovereignty, and Free Trade: Arms Trade Regulation and Humanitarian Arms Control in the Age of Empire," *Journal of Global Security Studies* 3, no.4 (2018): 444–462.

Cox, Robert. "Consciousness and civilization: The Inside Story," paper presented at York University, Toronto, October 29, 2012.

Croft, Stuart. *Strategies of Arms Control: A History and Typology*, Manchester & New York: Manchester University Press, 1996.

Cumings, Bruce. "On the Strategy and Morality of American Nuclear Policy in Korea – 1950 to the Present," *Social Science Japan Journal* 1, no.1 (1998): 57–70.

"Danger Area," paper by Air Vice-Marshal W. E. Oulton, 19 November 1956, No. GRA/TS.1008/1/Air.

De Kerckhove, Derrick. "On Nuclear Communication," *Diacritics* 14, no.2 (1984): 71–81.

de Queiroz Duarte, Sergio. "Brazil and the nonproliferation regime: a historical perspective," *The Nonproliferation Review* 23, no.5–6 (2016): 545–558.

Der Derian, James. "Imaging Terror: Logos, Pathos and Ethos," *Third World Quarterly* 26, no.1 (2005): 23–37.

Der Derian, James. "War/Virtual Theory," *International Affairs* 76, no.4 (2000): 771–788.

Deutsch, Karl W. "The Impact of Science and Technology on International Politics," *Daedalus* 88, no.4 (1959): 669–685.

Dibblin, Jane. *Day of Two Suns: US Nuclear Testing and the Pacific Islanders.* New York: New Amsterdam Books, 1988.

Dillon, M. and Andrew W. Neal. *Foucault on Politics, Security and War.* New York: Palgrave Macmillan, 2008.

Donnelly, Jack. "Human Rights a new standard of civilization," *International Affairs* 74, no.1 (1998): 1–23.

Donnelly, Jack. "The Relative Universality of Human Rights," *Human Rights Quarterly* 29, no.2 (2007): 281–306.

Donnelly, Warren H. "Evolution of U.S. Nuclear Export Controls," Report No.83-119S, Congressional Research Service, Washington, D.C. (1983): 11–13.

Dougherty, James Ed. and J.F. Lehman Jr, ed., *Arms Control for the Late Sixties.* D.Van Nostrand Co, 1968.

Dunn, Lewis A. "Nuclear 'Gray Marketeering'," *International Security* 1, no.3 (1977): 107–118.

Dupuy, Trevor N. and Gay H. Hammerman. *A Documentary History of Arms Control and Disarmament.* New York & London: T.T. Dupuy Associates in association with R.R. Bowker Company, 1973.

Duus, Peter. "Presidential Address: Weapons of the Weak, Weapons of the Strong-The Development of the Japanese Political Cartoon," *The Journal of Asian Studies* 60, no.4 (2001): 965–997.

Dyer, Henry. *Dai Nippon, the Britain of the East: A Study in National Evolution.* London: Blackie, 1904.

Edidin, Peter. "Pakistan's Hero: Dr. Khan Got What He Wanted, and He Explains How," *New York Times,* February 15, 2004.

Eglash, Ron. "Broken Metaphor: The Master-Slave Analogy in Technical Literature," *Technology and Culture* 48, no.2 (2007): 360–369.

Fabian, Johannes. *Time and the Other – How Anthropology Makes its Object.* New York: Columbia University Press, 2014.

Fanon, Franz. *Black Skin, White Masks,* translated by Charles Lam Markmann, New York: Grove Press, 1967.

Fatouros, A.A. "Participation of the 'New' States in the International Legal Order of the Future," in R.A. Falk and Cyril E. Black, *The Future of the International Legal Order*, vol. 1. Princeton: Princeton University Press, 1969.

Ferguson, James G. "Of Mimicry and Membership: Africans and the 'New World Society'" *Cultural Anthropology* 17, no.4 (2002): 551–569.

Firth, Stewart. *Nuclear Playground.* Honolulu: University of Hawaii Press, 1987.

Forsythe, David P. "United States Policy Toward Enemy Detainees in the 'War on Terrorism,'" *Human Rights Quarterly* 28, no.2 (2006): 465–491.

Foucault, Michel. *Discipline And Punish: the Birth of the Prison*. New York: Pantheon Books, 1977.

Friedman, W. "United States Policy and the Crisis of International Law: Some Reflections on the State of International Law in 'International Cooperation Year'," *American Journal of International Law* 59, no. (1965): 857–871.

Friedmann, W. "Half a Century of International Law," *Virginia Law Review* 50, no.8 (1964a): 1333–1358.

Friedmann, Wolfgang. *The Changing Structure of International Law*, New York: Columbia University Press; London: Steven & Sons, 1964b.

Friesel, Ofra. "Race versus Religion in the Making of the International Convention Against Racial Discrimination, 1965" *Law and History Review* 32, no.2 (2014): 351–338.

Fukuyama, Francis. *The End of History and the Last Man*, Oxford: Penguin, reissue 2012.

Furedi, Frank. *The Silent War – Imperialism and the Changing Perception of Race*, New Brunswick, New Jersey: Rutgers University Press, 1998.

Fu-sheng, Mu. *The Wilting of the Hundred Flowers: the Chinese Intelligentsia under Mao*. New York: Frederick A. Praeger, Inc., 1963.

Gallagher, Carole. *American Ground Zero: The Secret Nuclear War*, New York: Random House, 1993.

Gilmore, Joseph, Penelope Sheets and Charles Rowling, "Make no exception, save one: American exceptionalism, the American presidency, and the age of Obama," *Communication Monographs* 83, no.4 (2016): 505–520.

Goldschmidt, Bertrand. "A Historical Survey of Nonproliferation Policies," *International Security* 2, no.1 (1997): 69–87.

Gong, Gerrit W. *The Standard of 'Civilization' in International Society*, Oxford: Clarendon Press, 1984.

Gooday, Graeme J.N. and Morris F. Low, "Technology Transfer and Cultural Exchange: Western Scientists and Engineers Encounter Late Tokugawa and Meiji Japan," *Osiris* 13, (1998): 99–128.

Gordon, M.R. & T. Erdbrink, "In nuclear talks, technological gains by Iran pose challenge to the West," *New York Times*, October 15, 2013.

Grovogui, Siba N. "Time, technology and the imperial eye: Perdition on the road to redemption international relations theory," in *Time, Temporality and Violence in International Relations*, edited by Anna M. Aganthangelou and Kyle D. Killian, New York: Routledge, 2016.

Guru, Gopal. "Introduction – Theorizing Humiliation" in Gopal Guru, ed., *Humiliation-Claims and Context*, Oxford, New Delhi: Oxford University Press, 2009a.

Guru, Gopal. "Rejection of Rejection" in Gopal Guru, ed., *Humiliation-Claims and Context*, (Oxford, New Delhi: Oxford University Press, 2009b.

Gusterson, Hugh. 'Nuclear weapons and the Other in the Western Imagination, *Cultural Anthropology* 14, no.1 (1999): 111–143.

Gusterson, Hugh. *People of the Bomb: Portrait of America's Nuclear Complex*, Minneapolis, MN: Minnesota University Press, 2004.

Guy, Jeff. *Remembering the Rebellion – The Zulu Uprising of 1906*, Scottsville, South Africa: University of KwaZulu-Natal Press, 2006.

Harding, Sandra ed., *The 'Racial' Economy of Science: Toward a Democratic Future*, Bloomington: Indiana University Press, 1993.

Harding, Sandra. *Is Science Multicultural? Postcolonialisms, Feminisms, and Epistemologies*, Bloomington & Indianapolis: Indiana University Press, 1998.

Hardy, William McNeil. *The Age of Gunpowder Empires 1450–1800*, Washington, DC: American Historical Association, 1989.

Hassner, Pierre. "Who killed nuclear enlightenment?" *International Affairs* 83, no.3 (2007): 455–467.

Hecht, Gabrielle. *Being Nuclear: Africans and the Global Uranium Trade*, Cambridge: MIT Press, 2012.

Hecht, Gabrielle. edited., *Entangled Geographies: Empire and Technopolitics in the Global Cold War*, Cambridge: MIT Press, 2011.

Hecker, Siegfried S. and Abbas Milani, "Ending the assassination and oppression of Iranian nuclear scientists," *Bulletin of the Atomic Scientists* 71, no.1 (2015): 46–52.

Hellman, G., Herborth, B., Schlag, G., and Weber, C., "The West: a securitizing community?" *Journal of International Relations and Development* 17, no.3 (2013): 367–396.

Henry, Terrence. "The Covert Option: Can sabotage and assassination stop Iran from going nuclear?" *The Atlantic Monthly* 296, no.5 (2005): 54–55.

Hickel, W. *Who Owns America*? Englewood Cliffs, New Jersey: Prentice Hall, 1971.

Hindess, Barry. "Been there, done that..." *Postcolonial Studies* 11, no.2 (2008): 201–213.

Holland, T.E. *Lectures on International Law*, London: Sweet and Maxwell, 1933.

Hom, Andrew R. "Hegemonic metronome: the ascendancy of Western standard time," *Review of International Studies* 36, no.4 (2010): 1145–1170.

Hopgood, Stephen. *The Endtimes of Human Rights*, Ithaca & London: Cornell University Press, 2013.

Human Rights Council, Report of the Special Rapporteur on the Implications for Human Rights of the Environmentally Sound Management and Disposal of Hazardous Substances and Wastes, Calin Georgescu, Addendum, Mission to the Marshall islands (27–30 March 2012) and the United States of America (24–27 April 2012), UN Doc. A/HRC/21/48/Add.1, 3 September 2012, p. 4, para. 10, pp. 10–15.

Huntington, Samuel P. *The Clash of Civilizations and the Remaking of World Order*, New York: Simon & Schuster, 1997.

Huntington, Samuel. "Clash of Civilization," *Foreign Affairs* 72, no.3 (1993): 22–49.
Huntington, Samuel. "The West Unique, Not Universal," *Foreign Affairs* 75, no.6 (1996): 28–46.
Hutchings, Kimberly. "Happy Anniversary! Time and Critique in International Relations Theory," *Review of International Studies* 33, no.1 (2007): 71–89.
Hymans, Jacques E.C. "Of gauchos and gringos: Why Argentina never wanted the bomb, and why the United States thought it did," *Security Studies* 10, no.3 (2001): 153–185.
Ikenberry, G. John. *After Victory-Institutions, Strategic Restraint and the Rebuilding of Order after Major Wars,* Princeton & Oxford: Princeton University Press, 2001.
Ikuko, Nishimoto. "The Civilization of Time: Japan and the adoption of the wester time system," *Time & Society* 6, no.2/3 (1997): 237–259.
Inayatullah, N., Blaney, D. *International Relations and the Problem of Difference,* International Relations and the Problem of Difference. New York: Routledge, 2004.
Inden, R. "Orientalist Construction of India," *Modern Asian Studies* 20, no.3 (1986): 406–446.
Jackson, Patrick Thaddeus. *Civilizing the Enemy – German Reconstruction and the Invention of the West,* Ann Arbor: University of Michigan Press, 2009.
Jacobs, Robert. "Nuclear Conquistadors: Military Colonialism in Nuclear Test Site Selection during the Cold War," *Asian Journal of Peacebuilding* 1, no.2 (2013): 157–177.
Jamieson, Amber. "Doomsday Clock closer to midnight in wake of Trump presidency," *The Guardian*, January 26, 2017. https://www.theguardian.com/us-news/2017/jan/26/doomsday-clock-closer-to-midnight-in-wake of-donald-trump-election (downloaded on January 30, 2018).
Jehl, Doughlas. "CIA Says Pakistanis Gave Iran Nuclear aid," *New York Times,* November 24, 2004.
Johnson, James Turner. "Grotius' Use of History and Charity in the Modern Transformation of the Just War Idea," *Grotiana* 4, no.1 (1983): 21–34.
Johnston, Alastair Iain. "Thinking about Strategic Culture," *International Security* 19, no.4 (1995): 3264.
Katzenstein, Peter. ed. *Civilizations in World Politics-Plural and Pluralist Perspectives,* London & New York: Routledge, 2010.
Kelly, Robin D.G. "A Poetics of Anticolonialism," in Aimé Césaire, *Discourses on Colonialism,* translated by Joan Pinkham, New York: Monthly Review Press, 2000.
Khan, A.Q. "Uranium Enrichment at Kahuta," in Zahid Malik, *Dr. A.Q. Kan and the Islamic Bomb,* Islamabad: hurmat, 1992.

Kibaroglu, Mustafa. "Iran's Nuclear Ambitions from a Historical Perspective and the Attitude of the West," *Middle-Eastern Studies* 43, no.2 (2007): 223–245.

Kinsella, Helen M. *The Image Before the Weapon—A Critical History of the Distinction between Combatant and Civilian*, Ithaca & London: Cornell University Press, 2011.

Kissinger, Henry A. 'Nuclear Testing and the Problem of Peace,' *Foreign Affairs* 37, no.1 (1958): 1–18.

Kissinger, Henry. *A World Restored: Metternich, Castlereagh and the Problems of Peace, 1812–22.* Boston: Houghton Mifflin Company, 1957.

Klare, Michael. *Rogue States and Nuclear Outlaws: America's Search for a New Foreign Policy,* New York: Hill and Wang, 1995.

Krause, Joachim. "Enlightenment and nuclear order," *International Affairs* 83, no.3 (2007): 483–499.

Krause, Keith. "Conclusions: Security Culture and the non-proliferation, arms control and disarmament agenda," *Contemporary Security Policy* 19, no.1 (1998a): 221–222.

Krause, Keith and Andrew Latham, "Constructing non-proliferation and arms control: The norms of western practice," *Contemporary Security Policy,* 19, no.1 (1998): 23–54.

Krause, Keith. "Cross-cultural dimensions of multilateral non-proliferation and arms control dialogues: An overview," *Contemporary Security Policy* 19, no.1 (1998b): 1–22.

Krause, Keith. *Arms and the State: patterns of Military Production and Trade*, Cambridge: Cambridge University Press, 1992.

Krauthammer, Charles. "The Unipolar Moment," *Foreign Affairs* 70, no.1 (1991): 23–33.

Kroenig, Matthew. "Importing the Bomb: Sensitive Nuclear Assistance and Nuclear Proliferation," *The Journal of Conflict Resolution* 53, no.2 (2009): 161–180.

Krishna, Sankaran. "Race, Amnesia, and the Education of International Relations," in Branwen Gruffydd Jones, ed., *Decolonizing International Relations.* Plymouth: UK: Rowman & Littlefield Publishers, Inc, 2006.

Kumar, Deepak. *Science and the Raj – A Study in British India*, 2nd edition, Oxford: Oxford University Press, 2006.

Landes, David. "Clocks and the wealth of nations," *Daedalus* 132, no.2 (2003): 20–26.

Landes, David. "Clocks Revolution in Times," *History Today* 34, no.1 (1984): 26.

Landes, David. "Why Europe and the West? Why not China?" *Journal of Economic Perspectives* 20, no.2 (2006): 3–22.

Lapid, Yosef and Frederich Kratochwill, eds, *The return of culture and identity in IR theory*, Boulder, Colorado: Lynne Rienner, 1996.

Latham, Andrew. "Constructing national security: culture and identity in Indian arms control and disarmament," *Contemporary Security Policy* 19, no.1 (1998): 129–158.

Levite, Ariel. "Never Say never Again: Nuclear Reversal Revisited," *International Security* 27, no.3 (2002): 59–88.

Lewis, John and Xue Litai, *China Builds the Bomb*. Stanford: Stanford University Press, 1988.

Lissitzyn, O.J. "International Law in a Divided World," *International Conciliation*, no.542 (1963): 5758.

Lorcin, Patricia M.E. "Imperial Nostalgia; Colonial Nostalgia: Differences of Theory, Similarities of Practice?" *Historical Reflections/Reflexions Historiques* 39, no.3 (2013): 97–111.

Maclellan, N. and J. Chesneauix, *After Moruroa: France in the South Pacific*, Melbourne, Australia: Ocean Press, 1998.

Maclellan, N. "The Long Shadow of Bravo", *Inside Story*, February 24, 2014, http://insidestory.org.au/the-long-shadow-of-bravo.

Maclellan, N. "Grappling with the Bomb: Opposition to Pacific Nuclear Testing in the 1950s," in Philip Deery and Julie Kimber (eds), *Issues on War & Peace: Proceedings of the 14th Biennial Labour History Conference*. Melbourne: Australian Society for the Study of Labour History, 2015.

Mahbubani, Kishore. "The West and the Rest," *The National Interest*, no.28, (1992): 3–12.

Mallard, Gregoire and Catherine Paradeise, "Global Science and National Sovereignty: A New Terrain for the Historical Sociology of Science," in *Global Science and National Sovereignty: Studies in Historical Sociology of Science*, ed. Gregoire Mallard, Catherine Paradeise and Ashveen Peerbaye, New York & London: Routledge, 2009.

Mallard, Gregoire. *Fallout: Nuclear Diplomacy in an Age of Global Fracture*, Chicago: University of Chicago Press, 2014.

Maslen, Stuart Casey. "The Use of Nuclear Weapons and Human Rights," *International Review of the Red Cross* 97, no.889 (2015): 663–680.

Mateos, Gisela and Edna Suarez-Diaz, "'We are not a rich country to waste our resources on expensive toys': Mexico's version of Atoms for Peace," *History and Technology* 31, no.3 (2015): 243–258.

Mathur, Ritu. "Human Rights as a New Standard of Civilization in Weapons Control?" *Alternatives: Global, Local, Political* 2, no.42 (2018a): 227–243.

Mathur, Ritu. "Human Rights as a New Standard of Civilization in Arms Control & Disarmament," *Alternatives: Global, Local, Political* (2018b).

Mathur, Ritu. "Postcolonial Perspectives on Weapons Control," *Asian Journal of Political Science* 26, no.3 (2018c): 293–296.

Mathur, Ritu. "Sly Civility and the Paradox of Equality/Inequality in the Nuclear Order," *Critical Studies on Security* 4, no.1 (2016): 57–72.

Mathur, Ritu. Chapter on Chemical Weapons in *The International Committee of the Red Cross & Humanitarian practices of Arms Control & Disarmament*, Ph.D Dissertation, York University, 2011.

Mazrui, Ali. A. "Gandhi, Marx and the Warrior Tradition – Towards Androgynous Liberation," in *The Warrior Tradition in Modern Africa,* ed. Ali A. Mazrui, Leiden: E.J. Brill, 1977.

Mazrui, Ali A. ed., *The Warrior Tradition in Modern Africa*, Leiden: E.J. Brill, 1977.

McGlinchey, Stephen. "Lyndon B. Johnson and Arms Credit Sales to Iran 1964–1968," *The Middle East Journal* 67, no.2 (2013): 229–247.

Meisels, Tamar. "Assassination: Targeting Nuclear Scientists," *Law and Philosophy* 33, no.2, (2014): 204–234.

Memmi, Albert. *The Colonizer and the Colonized*, Boston" Beacon Press, 1967.

Mertus, Julie A. *Bait and Switch-Human Rights and US Foreign Policy,* 2nd edition, New York & London, Routledge, 2008.

Meyer, Stephen M. *The Dynamics of Nuclear Proliferation,* Chicago: University of Press, 1984.

Ministry of External Affairs India, *"Stand-still Agreement" Statement* in the Indian Lok Sabha, Nehru, Jawaharlal. April 2, 1954, retrieved from website: meaindia.nic.in.

Montgomery, Maureen. "Savage Civility: September 11 and the Rhetoric of 'Civilization'" *Australasian Journal of American Studies* 21, no.2 (2002): 56–65.

Moodie, Amanda and Michael Moodie, "Alternative Narratives for Arms Control," *The Nonproliferation Review* 17, no.2 (2010): 301–321.

Moyn, Samuel. *The Last Utopia: Human Rights in History*, Harvard, Massachusetts: Belknap Press, 2012.

Mu, Fu-sheng. *The Wilting of the Hundred Flowers: the Chinese Intelligentsia under Mao.* New York: Frederick A. Praeger, Inc., 1963.

Muller, Harald. "Non-Proliferation Policy in Western Europe: Structural Aspects," in *A European Non-Proliferation Policy, 1988–1992*, ed. Muller (European Interuniversity Press, 1993).

Mumford, Lewis. *Technics and Civilization,* New York, Harcourt: Brace & Company, 1934.

Muppidi, Himadeep. "Postcoloniality and the Production of Insecurity," in Jutta Weldes, Mark Laffey, Hugh Gusterson and Raymond Duvall, ed., *Cultures of Insecurity: States, Communities and the Production of Danger,* Minneapolis: University of Minnesota Press, 1999.

Mutimer, David. "Reimagining Security: The Metaphors of proliferation," *YCISS Occasional Paper*, no.25 (1994).

Mutimer, David. *The Weapons State-Proliferation and the Framing of Security,* London & Boulder: Lynnie Rienner Publishers, 2000.

Nandy, Ashish. "Humiliation-Politics and the Cultural psychology of the Limits of Human Degradation" in Gopal Guru, ed., *Humiliation-Claims and Context*, Oxford, New Delhi: Oxford University Press, 2009.
Nandy, Ashish. *Alternative Sciences – Creativity and Authenticity in Two Indian Scientists*, 2nd edition, Delhi: Oxford University Press, 1995.
Nandy, Ashish. *The Intimate Enemy – Loss and Recovery of Self under Colonialism*, 2nd Edition, New Delhi: Oxford University Press, 1983.
Narang, Vipin. "Strategies of Nuclear Proliferation: How States Pursue the Bomb," *International Security* 41, no.3, (2016/17).
Nayak, Meghana V. and Christopher Malone, "American Orientalism and American Exceptionalism: A Critical Rethinking of US Hegemony," *International Studies Review* 11, no.2 (2009): 253–276.
Neal, Andrew W. "Goodbye War on Terror? Foucault and Butler on Discourses of Law, War and Exceptionalism," in *Foucault on Politics, Security and War*, ed. Michael Dillon and Andrew W. Neal, New York: Palgrave Macmillan, 2008.
Nehru, Jawaharlal. The Discovery of India, New York: John Day, 1946.
Neidenthal, Jack. *For the Good of Mankind: A History of the People of Bikini and Their Islands*, Majuro: Bravo Publishers, 2001.
Nogee, Joseph L. "The Neutralist World and Disarmament Negotiations," *The Annals of the American Academy of Political and Social Science* 362, no. not available (1965): 75.
Northrop, F.S.C. *Taming of the Nations*, New York, 1952.
"Nuclear Non-Proliferation: Global Security In a Rapidly Changing World." IAEA. IAEA, June 20, 2004. https://ww.iaea.org/newscenter/statements/nuclear-non-proliferation-global-security-rapidly-changing-world.
Nye, Joseph S. "NPT: The Logic of Inequality," *Foreign Policy*, no.59 (1985): 123–131.
O'Connel, D.P. "Independence and Problems of State Succession" in William V.O'Brien, The New Nations in International Law and Diplomacy, New York, 1965.
O'Driscoll, Mervyn. "Diplomatic Triangles, the United Nations and the Problem of French Nuclear Testing, 1959–1960," *Journal of Cold War Studies* 11, no.1 (2009): 28–56. https://muse.jhu.edu/article/259184, downloaded on 1/29/2019.
Office of the Special Assistant for National Security Affairs, White House Office, *Memo*, June 23, 1954, NSC Series, DDE Library.
O' Hagan, Jacinta. *Conceptualizing the West in International Relations*, Hampshire & New York: Palgrave, 2002.
O'Neil, Robert and David N. Schwartz, *Hedley Bull on Arms Control*, New York: St. Martin's Press, 1987.
Palshikar, Sanjay. "Understanding Humiliation" in Gopal Guru, ed., *Humiliation-Claims and Context*, Oxford, New Delhi: Oxford University Press, 2009.

Pant, K.C. "Rajya Sabha Extensive Debate on India's Peaceful Nuclear Explosion," August 21, 1974, Indian Nuclear History collection, Wilson Center Digital Archive, pp. 251–253, http://digitalarchive.wilsoncenter.org/document/119760 cited by Vipin Narang, 'Strategies of Nuclear Proliferation: How States Pursue the Bomb,' *International Security* 41, no.3, (2016/17).

Perkovich, George. *Universal Compliance: A Strategy for Nuclear Strategy*, Washington: Carnegie Endowment for International Peace, 2005.

Persaud, Randolph B. and R.B.J. Walker, "Apertura: Race in International Relations," *Alternatives: Global, Local, Political* 26, no.4 (2001): 373–376.

Peterson, Richard J. "Human Rights: Historical Learning in the Shadow of Violence," *The American Journal of Economics and Sociology* 68, no.1 (2009): 253–272.

Petrova, Margarita H. "Rhetorical Entrapment and Normative Enticement: How the United Kingdom Turned from Spoiler into Champion of the Cluster Munition Ban," *International Studies Quarterly* 60, no.3 (2016): 387–399.

Polat, Necati. *International Relations, Meaning and Mimesis*, New York: Routledge, 2012.

Porter, Patrick. *Military Orientalism. Eastern war through western eyes*, New York: Oxford University Press, 2013.

Posner, Eric A. *The Twilight of Human Rights Law*, New York: Oxford University Press, 2014. Prashad, Vijay. "Third World Quarterly row: Why some western intellectuals are trying to debrutalise colonialism," *Scroll.in*, September 21, 2017, https://scroll.in/article/print/851305.

Price, Richard. *The Chemical Weapons Taboo*, Ithaca & London: Cornell University Press, 1997. Pusca, Anca. "Walter Benjamin, a Methodological Contribution," *International Political Sociology* 3, no.2 (2009): 238–259.

Rabinowitz, Or and Nicholas L. Miller, "Keeping the Bombs in the Basement: US Nonproliferation Policy toward Israel, South Africa, and Pakistan," *International Security* 40, no.1 (2015): 47–86.

Reid, Julian. "Life Struggles: War, Discipline and Biopolitics in the Thought of Michel Foucault," in *Foucault on Politics, Security and War*, ed. Michael Dillon and Andrew W. Neal, New York: Palgrave Macmillan, 2008.

Rice, Condoleezza. "Promoting the National Interest," *Foreign Affairs* 79, no.1 (2000): 45–62.

Roberts, Brad. "All the king's men? Refashioning global nuclear order", *International Affairs* 83, no.3 (2007): 549–574.

Roberts, Christopher N.J. *The Contentious History of the International Bill of Human Rights*, Cambridge: Cambridge University Press, 2015.

Roh, David S., Betsy Huang and Greta A. Niu, eds. *Techno-Orientalism. Imagining Asia in Speculative Fiction, History, and Media*, New Brunswick, New Jersey and London: Rutgers University Press, 2015.

Roling, B.V.A. *International Law in an Expanded World*, Amsterdam: Djambatan, 1960.
Rosenau, James. *Turbulence in World Politics,* Princeton: Princeton University Press, 1990.
Ruff, Tilman A. "The Humanitarian Impact and Implications of Nuclear Test Explosions in the Pacific Region," *International Review of the Red Cross* 97, no.889 (2015): 775–813.
Ruhle, Michael. "Enlightenment in the second nuclear age," *International Affairs* 83, no.3 (2007): 511–522.
Sagan, Scott Douglas, and Kenneth N. Waltz. *The spread of nuclear weapons: an enduring debate.* New York: W.W. Norton & Co. 2013.
Said, Edward. *Orientalism,* New York: Vintage Books, 1978.
Salter, Mark B. *Barbarians & Civilization in International Relations*, London: Pluto Press, 2002.
Sanders-Zakre, Alicia. "Marshall Islands Lose Nuclear Cases," *Arms Control Today* 46, no.9 (2016): 31–32.
Sanders, Mark. "Remembering Apartheid," *Diacritics* 32, no.3/4 (2002): 60–80.
Schell, Jonathan. "The Abolition I-defining the great predicament," *The New Yorker,* January 2, 1984.
Schulte, Paul. "Universal vision or bounded rationality?" *International Affairs* 83, no.3 (2007): 501–510.
Schwarzenberger, George. "The Standard of Civilization in International Law" *Current Legal Problems,* 1955.
Scott, J.C. *Domination and the Arts of Resistance: Hidden Transcripts*, New Haven, Connecticut: Yale University Press, 1990.
Scott, Richard. "A Ban on Nuclear Tests: The Course of Negotiations, 1958–1962," *International Affairs* 38, no.4 (1962): 501–510.
Seth, Suman. "Putting knowledge in its place: science, colonialism, and the post-colonial," *Postcolonial Studies* 12, no.4 (2009): 373–388.
Short, Nicola and Helen Kambouri. "Ambiguous universalism: theorising race/nation/class in international relations," *Journal of International Relations and Development* 13, no.3 (2010): 268–300.
Singh, Jaswant. "Against Nuclear Apartheid," *Foreign Affairs* 44, no.5 (1998): 41–52.
Slave Trade and Importation into Africa of Firearms, Ammunition, and Spiritual Liquors (General Act of Brussels), treat text of the Brussels Declaration (1890). July 2, 1890.
Smith-Norris, Martha. "'Only as Dust in the Face of the Wind': An Analysis of the BRAVO Nuclear Incident in the Pacific, 1954," *The Journal of American-East Asian Relations* 6, no.1 (1997): 134.
Snyder, Jack L. The Soviet Strategic Culture: Implications for Nuclear Options, R-2154-AF, Santa Monica, California: Rand Corporation, 1977.

Sotomayor, Arturo C. "Brazil and Mexico in the Nonproliferation Regime," *The Nonproliferation Review* 20, no.1 (2013): 81–105.

Southall, Aidan. "The Bankruptcy of the Warrior Tradition," in *The Warrior Tradition in Modern Africa* in ed. Ali A. Mazrui, Leiden: E.J. Brill, 1977.

Spektor, Matias. "The evolution of Brazil's nuclear intentions," *The Nonproliferation Review* 23, no.5–6 (2016): 635–652.

Spengler, Oswald. *Decline of the West,* New York: A. A. Knopf, 1928.

Squassoni, Sharon. "The U.S.-Indian Deal and Its Impact," *Arms Control Today* 40, no.6 (2010): 48–52.

State Department's Office of the Historian. "Memorandum by the Director of the Policy Planning Staff (Kennan) to the Secretary of State and Under Secretary of State (Lovett)," *Foreign Relations of the United States* 1 (24 February 1948).

Stone, David R. "'Imperialism and Sovereignty: The League of Nations' Drive to Control the Global Arms Trade," *Journal of Contemporary History* 35, no.2 (2000): 213–230.

Suzuki, Shogo. *Civilization and Empire: China and Japan's Encounter with European International Society*, London & New York: Routledge, 2009.

Tannenwald, Nina. "US Arms Control Policy in a Time Warp," *Ethics & International Affairs*, 15, no.1, (2001) 51–70.

Tannenwald, Nina. "Stigmatizing the Bomb: Origins of the Nuclear Taboo," *International Security*, 29, no.4, (2005): 5–49.

Tannenwald, Nina. "Justice and Fairness in the Nuclear Nonproliferation Regime," *Ethics & International Affairs*, 27, no.3 (2013): 299–317.

Tannenwald, Nina. "The Vanishing Nuclear Taboo," *Foreign Affairs*, 97, no, 6 (2018): 16–24.

Taussig, Michael. *Mimesis and Alterity: A Particular History of the Senses,* New York & London: Routledge, 1993.

Thapar, Romila. *Time as a Metaphor of History: Early India*, New Delhi: Oxford University Press, 1996.

Tinker, Hugh. *Race, Conflict and the International Order – From Empire to the United Nations,* London & Basingstoke: The Macmillan Press Ltd, 1977.

Tobey, William. "Nuclear Scientists as assassination targets," *Bulletin of the Atomic Scientists* 68, no.1 (2012): 61–69.

Todorov, Tzvetan. *Facing the Extreme: Moral Life in the Concentration Camps,* New York: Henry Holt, 1996.

Todorov, Tzetvan. *The Conquest of America: The Question of the Other*, Oklahoma: University of Oklahoma Press, 1999.

Toynbee, Arnold. *The World and the West,* New York & London: Oxford University Press, 1953. United States. *National Security Strategy of the United States of America,* December 2017. https://www.whitehouse.gov/wp-content/uploads/2017/12/NSS-Final-12-18-2017-0905.pdf.

Uzoigwe, G.N. "The Warrior and the State in Precolonial Africa: Comparative Perspectives" in Ali A. Mazrui, ed., *The Warrior Tradition in Modern Africa*, Leiden: E.J. Brill, 1977.

Valbjorn, Morten. "Before, during and after the cultural turn: a 'Baedeker' to IR's cultural journey," *International Review of Sociology* 18, no.1 (2008): 55–82.

van Bergen, Leo. "The poison gas debate in the inter-war years," *Medicine, Conflict and Survival* 24, no.3 (2008): 174–187.

Verzijl, J.H.W. "Western European Influence on the Foundations of International Law," in his *International Law in Historical Perspective*, Leyden, 1968.

Villanueva, Victor. "On the Rhetoric and Precedents of Racism," *College Composition and Communication* 50, no.4 (1999): 645–61.

Vincent, R.J. "Race in International Relations," *International Affairs* 58, no.4 (1982): 658–70.

Vine, David. *Islands of Shame: The History of the US Military Base on Diego Garcia*, Princeton: Princeton University Press, 2009.

Vitalis, "Birth of a Discipline," in David Long and Brian C. Schmidt, eds, *Imperialism and Internationalism in the Discipline of International Relations*, Albany: State University of New York Press, 2005.

Vitalis, Robert J. "The Graceful and Generous Liberal Gesture: Making Racism Invisible in American International Relations," *Millennium* 29, no.2 (2000): 331–356.

Vlverde, Mariana. "Law versus History – Foucault's Genealogy of Modern Sovereignty," in *Foucault on Politics, Security and War*, ed. Michael Dillon and Andrew W. Neal, New York: Palgrave Macmillan, 2008.

Walker, R.B.J. ed., *Culture, ideology and world order*, Boulder, Colorado: Westview, 1984.

Walker, William. "Nuclear Enlightenment and counter-enlightenment," *International Affairs* 83, no.3 (2007): 431–453.

Waltz, Kenneth. *Theory of International Politics*, Reading: Addison-Wesley, 1979.

Wang, Jessica. "Scientists and the Problem of the Public in Cold War America, 1945–1960," *Osiris* 17, no.2 (2002): 323–347.

Warner, Frederick and René J.C. Kirchmann (eds), Scientific Committee on Problems of the Environment (SCOPE) of the International Council for Science, *SCOPE 59. Nuclear Test Explosions: Environmental and Human Impacts*, John Wiley & Sons, New York, 1999.

Weltfish, Gene. "American Racism: Japan's Secret Weapon," *Far Eastern Survey* 14, no.17 (1945): 233–237.

Wheaton, *Elements of International Law*, Eighth Edition, London, 1866.

Wheeler, Nicholas J. "The Bush Doctrine: The Dangers of American Exceptionalism in a Revolutionary Age," *Asian Perspective* 27, no.4 (2003): 183–216.

The White House. "President Sworn-In to Second Term," January 20, 2005, http://www.whitehouse.gov/news/releases/2005/01/20050120-1.html.

Yost, David S. "Analysing international nuclear order," *International Affairs* 83, no.3 (2007): 549–574.

Young, Oran R. "Chinese Views on the Spread of Nuclear Weapons," *The China Quarterly*, no.26 (1966): 136–170.

Zoppo, Ciro. "Nuclear Technology, Weapons, and the Third World," *Annals of the American Academy of Political and Social Science*, no.386 (1969): 119.

Index[1]

[1] Note: Page numbers followed by 'n' refer to notes.

R. Mathur, *Civilizational Discourses in Weapons Control*,
https://doi.org/10.1007/978-3-030-44943-8

H

I

The manufacturer's authorised representative in the EU is Springer Nature Customer Service Centre GmbH, Europaplatz 3, 69115 Heidelberg, Germany. If you have any concerns regarding our products, please contact ProductSafety@springernature.com

Printed and bound by CPI Group (UK) Ltd, Croydon, CR0 4YY
25/09/2026
02222902-0004